ARCHITECTURAL
DRAFTING: STRUCTURE & ENVIRONMENT

ARCHITECTURAL DRAFTING:

Bobbs-Merrill Educational Publishing
Indianapolis

STRUCTURE & ENVIRONMENT

John D. Bies, Ph.D.

Copyright © 1983 by The Bobbs-Merrill Company, Inc.

Printed in the United States of America

The Bobbs-Merrill Company, Inc.
4300 West 62nd Street
Indianapolis, Indiana 46206

First Edition

First Printing

Design by Bob Reed

Cover design by Bob Reed

Editor: Dan Kirklin

Library of Congress Cataloging in Publication Data

Bies, John D., 1946–
    Architectural drafting.

    Includes index.
    1. Architectural drawing.   I. Title.
NA2700.B49   1983   720′.28′4   82-9719
ISBN 0-672-97855-5

CONTENTS

LIST OF FIGURES

LIST OF TABLES

ACKNOWLEDGMENTS

The author is grateful to the many individuals and firms that have gone out of their way to provide drawings and valuable information needed in the completion of this project:

Robert Long, Drafting Instructor, Northwest Mississippi Junior College

Roy P. Harrover, AIA, Roy P. Harrover and Associates, Architects

Charlie King, AIA, Roy P. Harrover and Associates, Architects

Robert Y. Fleming, AIA, Goforth/Fleming Associates, Architects

Alfredo De Vido, AIA, Alfredo De Vido Associates, Architects

Mitchell M. Hall, AIA, MMH/Hall, Architects, Planners

Benny Baggett, Architectural Drafter

George Johnson, Drafting Instructor, Madison County School District

Stanley T. Wooten, Assistant Director, Madison County Area Vocational School

Johnson Wax Company

Indiana Limestone Institute of America

Vaughan Walls, Inc.

Consolidated Aluminum Corporation of America

Keuffel & Esser Company

Memphis and Shelby County Office of Planning and Development

A special note of thanks is due to Deborah Moore Cunningham for her excellent typing (and retyping) and ability to produce a professional-looking manuscript.

Finally, the author would like to thank his family for their support and encouragement, without which this book would never have been completed.

PREFACE

This book was written to serve as both a textbook and a reference guide in architectural drafting. It was the author's objective to limit this book to the specific area of drafting and not deal with related topics, such as architectural design and construction. Although not exhaustive, this book includes the basic principles and practices of architectural drafting for both residential and commercial structures.

One of the major goals was to write a book in the most straightforward manner possible, eliminating any unnecessary textual explanations and descriptions. Numerous illustrations and examples were used to complement the written text in conveying the concepts of various methods and techniques. The reader will also notice that the techniques used in various examples are *not* always consistent (e.g., lettering and symbol styles). The purpose of this is to show the variety that is acceptable in the field.

This book is divided into several conceptual areas. The first, which some experienced drafters may question, is architectural occupations and the workplace. There is a wide variety of firms and individuals in the architectural field. No one description can fit all situations. Based upon a composite of experiences of numerous professionals, this presentation was written to give the reader a general idea of the various existing job descriptions and work-place conditions. Where there are regional differences, the reader is encouraged to seek out more information and find out the reasons for these differences.

The second conceptual area deals with drawings commonly associated with architectural plans, those normally presented in the first part of a set of working drawings. This includes such topics as site plans, foundation plans, floor plans, elevations, and detailed section drawings.

The third and last area picks up topics of a more specialized nature. This covers not only special types of drawings, e.g., electrical, HVAC, and alternate energy, but also deals with reproduction techniques currently used.

Following each chapter are Review Questions and Exercises. The Review Questions give the student a chance to review the content and apply the principles discussed in a simplified way. The Exercises, on the other hand, are structured to give the teacher the most flexibility possible. In most cases, additional specifications and problem parameters are required to complete the Exercise. Hence, the level of difficulty can be varied by the teacher for each class and even for each student.

John D. Bies

INTRODUCTION

Professions in the architectural field are wide open. The expectations and challenges in this field have certainly never been greater. Consider the problems being faced today in energy conservation, urban renewal, planning, renovations, remodeling, commercial developments, and many other areas. Not only is the field expanding and dynamic, but it involves many more jobs than just drawing plans, framing, wiring, and plumbing.

According to the U.S. Bureau of Labor Statistics, the construction industry employs over six million workers. These people are involved in residential and commercial planning, design, construction, and finishing. The construction industry is not only responsible for the building of our homes, offices, factories, churches, hospitals, and schools. It is also a vital element in the well-being of our economy, accounting for over four percent of our Gross National Product. If the number of new buildings being constructed is down, our economy is slow. On the other hand, if the number of new starts is up, this normally means the economy is healthy.

A look at the professions in the architectural field involves more than listing and describing various jobs. To make a decision about which profession to enter, one must consider several factors: the training involved, working conditions, instruments used by professionals, and the materials or media of the field. It is therefore the intent of the first part of this book to look at what architects, architectural technologists, and architectural technicians, as well as architectural drafters and people in specialized occupations, do. Then we will discuss the working conditions and practices of various types of architectural firms.

ARCHITECTS

GLOSSARY

Aesthetics factors relating to the artistic quality of a design and, in particular, those things that are considered to be beautiful or pleasing to the eye

Analogue a form of design in which the architect attempts to create a building that resembles (is *analogous* to) some natural form, such as a plant or geological formation

Compression test a test used to test the strength of materials or products under a load (weight), with compression strength normally measured in pounds per square inch (psi)

Contractor individual or firm responsible for the construction of a building

Dynamics science of forces, such as weight, and their relationship to motion

Environment surroundings that influence individual and community life

Formalization standardization of a particular design or procedure

Geometrical proportions relationships among various geometric shapes

Practicality usefulness of a particular design

Schematics plans or procedures presented in terms of units or portions of building parts

Spatial analysis examination of the relationship of objects and shapes in terms of distance and space

Specifications written information about building plans and directions that cannot be given by the drawings alone

Tensile test a test to measure the strength of materials or products under a "pulling" load. The tensile strength of a material is the psi it can take without tearing apart

One of the most important people in the design and organization of residential and commercial developments is the architect. Architects are usually hired to work in all phases of development, from the initial discussion of ideas and problems to the construction and sale of the building. Their responsibilities require them to have skills, knowledge, and good judgment in such areas as design, engineering, management, and supervision.

DUTIES AND RESPONSIBILITIES OF THE ARCHITECT

The architect, working alone or as part of a team, has the responsibility for the planning and design of attractive buildings and complex construction projects. These projects not only must be attractive to the eye, but should also improve the physical and social environment of the community. Besides concerning themselves with the physical appearance of buildings, architects must also be sure that their designs are both practical and functional. Whether for a single-family dwelling, apartment complex, service station, bank, office building, or shopping mall, if designs are not functional and do not meet the project objectives, the plans are unacceptable.

It is important that architects have the ability to work with people, for the first step in any project is to talk with potential clients about project goals, requirements, and costs. An architect who cannot communicate ideas and determine the clients' needs will be unlikely to receive the contract. Many contracts are awarded on the basis of bids and proposals. Before contracts are awarded, architects are usually required to prepare and submit sketches and drawings that communicate the physical design, structures, and relationships of building components. In the case of small architectural firms or self-employed architects, the sketches and drawings are all prepared by the architect. In larger firms, the architect prepares the sketches and works closely with the architectural technologist, drafter, or both in the preparation of finished drawings.

Once the sketches and finished drawings are prepared, the architect makes a formal presentation to the potential client, explaining all concepts, designs, and innovations used in the project. In other words, architects have to sell ideas to their clients. If the initial plans are favorable and a contract is awarded, the architect then develops designs for floor plans, structural details, and other physical systems of the project.

The job of the architect doesn't stop when all designs and plans are completed. Architects are responsible for exact dimensional specifications for buildings, plumbing, heating, air conditioning, and electrical systems, building materials, and sometimes interior designs and furnishings. When determining all job specifications, the architect must constantly check to make sure that the construction requirements are within the guidelines set by state and local codes, laws, and ordinances. Commercial and industrial projects must also meet the regulations of the Occupational Safety and Health Administration and the Environmental Protection Agency. In other situations, the architect is required to check and work with other agencies, such as the Army Corps of Engineers and regional utility companies.

During the design and specification process, architects are often required to change the original set of plans. Problems might arise from unforeseen regu-latory restrictions, structural problems, or even the client's change of mind. Unlike many other designers, the architect is at the mercy of the laws of nature, government, and the wants of the client. If the client doesn't like the design, regardless how good the architect may think it is, the design must be changed.

The architect and the contractor are seldom the same person. Once the client has accepted the plans, the architect either selects or helps select a contractor to build the project. When the terms of the contract are agreed upon, a legal document is drawn up by a lawyer and signed by all parties concerned.

While the project is under construction, it is the architect's responsibility to make on-site visits and inspections. This makes it possible to see that the designs, dimensional restrictions, and materials specified for the project are being used by the contractor. At times, when new designs or concepts are used, it may become necessary to explain certain structural methods to the contractor and tradesmen involved in the project. The architect remains active in the project until all construction is completed and inspected, all bills are paid, and guarantees are received.

The duties and responsibilities just described are typical. Depending upon the size of the project and the type of architectural firm, the architect may want to specialize in the design, administrative, or technological aspects of industry. Some architects' specialities are renovation, restoration, preservation, environmental controls, and systems building. Regardless of the area of specialization, the architect is expected and should be prepared to work in a variety of areas with a variety of people.

THE PRINCIPLES OF ARCHITECTURE

Generally speaking, the principles of design are simply what the architect looks for in a well designed project. Architects are designers who specialize in buildings. They are creative people; they must also function as decision makers, analysts, and supervisors. These building designers have skills in spatial analysis, structures, servicing, environmental control, cost analysis, and interior design. In effect, the architect is an artist as well as an engineer.

What does an architect look for when designing a building? In particular, how does the architect apply these principles? An architect must have the ability to visualize three-dimensional forms of buildings, interior spaces, and the spaces around buildings. Architects produce structural creations within a framework of five design principles: *practicality, formalization, geometry, conceptualization,* and *dynamics.*

PRACTICALITY

The first architect was some prehistoric person who first changed the environment by building a nest or shelter. The most important concept in this statement is that of *changing the environment.* Architecture as a science is defined as a designing process used to *improve the environment.* The distinction is worth noting.

Of necessity, the first architects were not concerned with the aesthetics of their structures. If the *designs* were practical, that is, if they stood up and kept out the weather, that was enough. Practical *building materials* were used—the materials used were readily available and served the purpose for which they were intended. The application of these two specifications was the beginning of the first principle of architecture: practicality.

Because there was no highly developed technology, primitive people were limited in what could be used and what materials could be used. The only reason for constructing a building was for protection. Human activities such as eating, sleeping, and socializing could then be carried out in comfort. All buildings designed today modify the human environment so that we can work and play in safety and comfort. Therefore they must be designed practically. Furthermore, buildings constructed today affect more than *physical* conditions; they influence the social, political, economic, moral, and aesthetic qualities of the living environment.

Practical design also uses testing procedures and test results. Because there was no other choice, early architects used trial and error. Today, architects apply the results of a variety of testing procedures to designs and construction materials. Examples of these procedures are experimentation, tensile and compression tests, chemical and physical analysis, and structural and geologic tests.

As an example of the importance of testing in architectural design, let us look at high- and low-gravity construction. As of now, there is virtually no practical theory of high- or low-gravity architecture. Therefore, we are in a position similar to the prehistoric architects who put up the first buildings. Someday, if we continue our exploration of space, it will be necessary to design and construct buildings on planets with different gravitational fields from ours. How can we test designs for structures in space? Experimentation and other related tests will have to be conducted to find optimum structural design and the most appropriate types of building materials. Clearly trial and error will be included. Architectural design for hostile environments will have to be, above all else, practical.

FORMALIZATION

Once a particular structure has been found to affect the environment in an efficient and effective manner, using the resources available, then there is good reason to copy it. For example, the American Indians needed to build shelters which could be easily constructed, then disassembled, and transported or left to deteriorate. There were many types of dwellings in early North America. The Plains people used the tepee, which could be folded up and moved easily. The people of the Great Lakes had the wigwam, which could be broken down and transported or abandoned. Even the large, permanent buildings of some tribes were practical in design and materials,

Fig. 1-1 *Monolithic Structure and Primitive Hut*

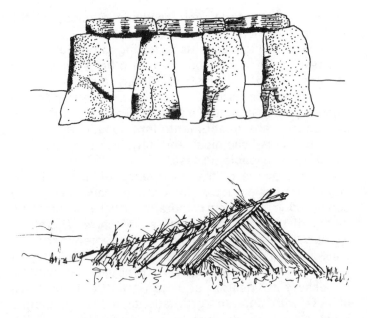

using what was available. Among the most striking examples of this is the Innuit igloo, a dome usually made of snow. Once a basic design of such a shelter was proven to be efficient and effective, it was duplicated by other people. That is, the design became *formalized*. See Fig. 1-1.

There is another reason designs are formalized. Familiar designs become what people expect and thereby are acceptable forms. People tend to feel comfortable with something that is familiar. The other side of the coin is that people are not quick to accept completely new designs or concepts. An example of this is the geodesic house, an efficient and effective design. But it "doesn't look like a house." Because it is an unfamiliar design and requires some adaptation, or getting used to, many people shy away from such architecture, in favor of more traditional dwellings.

GEOMETRY

The third principle of architectural design is *geometry*. The concepts of geometry make it possible to design buildings which conform to the laws of nature. Among the earliest structures in which the principle of geometry was consciously applied were the pyramids of Egypt. It is obvious that these structures, along with the temples of Greek and Roman culture, certainly had a system of proportions that showed the architects' understanding of geometry.

As defined by Plato, solid (three-dimensional) geometry, was based upon five major bodies: the tetrahedron (which has four sides, or faces), cube (six), octahedron (eight), dodecahedron (twelve), and icosahedron (twenty). Each of these sides is regular, i.e., each edge and each face is the same. For example, the cube has six faces, each a square, and twelve edges, all the same length. See Fig. 1-2. How are the other solids constructed? Variations on these and other solids make up almost all architectural forms. Though Plato's ideas of geometry were developed too late to influence early architectural design, his writ-

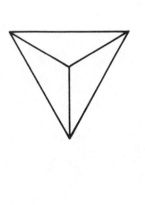
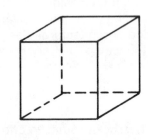
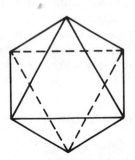
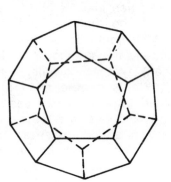
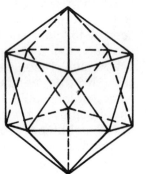

Fig. 1-2 *Tetrahedron, Cube, Octahedron, Dodecahedron, and Icosahedron*

ings were of great importance to the architects who designed the great cathedrals of the Middle Ages.

Geometric composition is found not only in the architecture of ancient civilization, but also in today's buildings. The Sears Tower in Chicago and the World Trade Center in New York City are both effective uses of geometry in architecture. Practicality, formalization, and geometry are the foundations for the fourth principle of architectural design.

CONCEPTUALIZATION

A *conceptual* design uses analogues to develop a structure that looks like or reminds one of something else. That is, the architect may imagine the building to be like a tree, mountain, or some other object in nature. Needless to say, if the architect expects the conceptualization to become reality, it will be necessary to develop sketches, drawings, and plans. This is the first architectural principle that requires plans to be prepared. The graphic presentation is the only method of translating the architect's ideas into physical reality.

The use of conceptual designs has proven to be the most effective way to bring out the creative talents of architects. Frank Lloyd Wright, for example, frequently used conceptualizations in his work. When designing the Johnson Wax Company's administrative building, he attempted to create a design analogous to water lilies or mushrooms. See Figs. 1-3A and 1-3B. Wright was also known to use analogy when criticizing other architectural designs, such as his comment "The building reminds me of a pig lying on its back and its feet pointed skyward."

DYNAMICS

The last principle of architectural design is *dynamics.* Dynamics has to do with change and adaptability in designs. If architectural designs cannot be changed to meet new structural and environmental conditions, they are of little realistic use to the construction industry. With the present increase in new products, materials, and construction techniques, architects must develop dynamic designs to meet the needs of their clients.

To make designs dynamic, architects must learn to apply new tools in the planning process. Systems analysis, operational research, computer modeling, and environmental processing are just a few procedures available to the architect. Architects are faced with many different design problems. They must use both established and new design procedures, for example, in situations where two structures must be built with different specifications, but must complement each other. The principles of architectural design are not only tools used by the architect, they are sources of information and education.

EDUCATION AND QUALIFICATIONS

To qualify as a licensed architect usually requires a combination of eight years of formal education and practical work experience beyond high school, plus a licensing examination. The architect not only must complete a five-year Bachelor of Architecture degree and have relevant work experience, but must also pass a two-day licensing examination. After receiving the degree, architects can qualify to take this examination after working for a licensed architect for at least three years. Those receiving a Master of Architecture degree need complete only two years of work experience under a licensed architect to qualify for the examination.

A person who does not have the formal training or degree requirements may wish to become a licensed architect. A number of states waive the degree requirements if the person has sufficient work experience—usually a minimum of twelve years.

At present, there are over a hundred schools of architecture in the United States. Of these, approximately eighty percent are fully accredited by the National Architectural Accrediting Board (NAAB). The

NAAB makes sure that schools of architecture come up to specified minimum standards. Those that do not are not accredited. For this reason, anyone interested in attending a school of architecture should check that it is meeting the minimum NAAB standards and is fully accredited.

As previously stated, most schools offer a five-year Bachelor of Architecture degree program, and some have a six-year Master of Architecture. Still other universities have special programs for those who have received their baccalaureate degree in related fields—this usually requires an additional three years of college work.

A typical five-year program in architecture takes 240–260 quarter hours or 160–174 semester hours of course work, mainly in architectural courses. An example of a typical program is shown in Table 1-1.

Fig. 1-3A *Exterior View of the Johnson Wax Company's Administration Building, Designed by Frank Lloyd Wright (Courtesy S.C. Johnson & Sons, Inc.)*

Fig. 1-3B *Lobby of the Administration Building at Johnson Wax's Frank Lloyd Wright-designed Administration and Research Center in Racine, Wisconsin. Visible are the various-shaped bricks necessary for unusual contours of the building. Also note the unusual columns, similar to mushrooms or golf tees, and the beautiful lobby planter, which is changed seasonally. (Courtesy S.C. Johnson & Sons, Inc.)*

Table 1-1 Typical Bachelor of Architecture Program

Course	Quarter Hours	Semester Hours
First Year		
Architecture	6–12	4–8
Art	12	8
Physics	8	5–6
English	8	5–6
Mathematics	12	8
Second Year		
Architecture	32–40	21–28
Physics	4	3
Mathematics	4	3
Social Sciences	8	5–6
Third Year		
Architecture	47	32
Humanities	12	8
Fourth Year		
Architecture	32	21
Electives	16	10
Fifth Year		
Architecture	30	20
Electives	18	12

The courses and electives are determined by the type of program and area of specialization the student selects. Some areas of specialization are as follows:

A. Design Concentration
   1. Architectural Design
   2. Architectural Design—Analysis
B. History-Humanities Concentration
   1. Architectural History
   2. Architectural Criticism
   3. Restoration/Preservation
C. Administration Concentration
   1. Managment
   2. Production
   3. Development
D. Technology Concentration
   1. Architectural Structures
   2. Environmental Controls
   3. Systems Building

If they seek employment in large firms, graduates of architectural programs usually start as junior drafters.

They prepare drawings, plans, and work on scale models. After a few years, they may be promoted to chief or senior drafter and supervise other drafters. Chief drafters are responsible for the development of major detailed drawings and the organization of various management procedures of a project. Once licensed, architects can work their way up to become project supervisors or partners in the firms, or they can start their own firm.

For further information about preparing for careers in architecture, write to:

The American Institute of Architects
1735 New York Avenue, N.W.
Washington, D.C. 20006

The Association of Collegiate Schools of Architecture, Inc.
1735 New York Avenue, N.W
Washington, D.C. 20006

The National Council of Architectural Registration Boards
1735 New York Avenue, N.W.
Washington, D.C. 20006

SUMMARY

Students interested in becoming architects should see their teachers and counselors about recommended course offerings and part-time employment. Other sources of information are college and university catalogs, school of architecture program descriptions, books about the profession, and personal contact with licensed architects. Visits to schools of architecture and to architectural firms will provide first-hand observation and contact with people responsible for the education and licensing of architects. Students must also look at themselves: do your abilities, aptitudes, and interests match the requirements of the profession?

Students who have concluded that their career goal is to become a professional architect must be prepared to go through five years of architecture school, plus another three years of work under a licensed architect, before the licensing examination. If they pass the examination, they can then work for an architectural or construction firm or go into business on their own. Once employed, the architect works with a variety of people in all aspects of a building project. Architects are responsible for all planning and building specifications, the selection and recommendation of building contracts, on-site inspections, final project guarantees, and various combinations of these.

When designing buildings, architects must always keep the objectives of the client in mind. At the same time, the architect must design buildings which are attractive and conducive to the physical and social environment of the community. This is accomplished by the use of the basic principles of architecture— *practicality, formalization, geometry, conceptualization,* and *dynamics.*

REVIEW QUESTIONS

1. What are the major responsibilities of the architect?
2. Why must the architect always keep his client's objectives in mind?
3. In relationship to good architectural design, what is the meaning of the following terms?

   a. practicality
   b. formalization
   c. geometry
   d. conceptualization
   e. dynamics

4. How does the term *environment* affect the designs of the architect?
5. What are the requirements for an individual who wishes to become a licensed architect?
6. What considerations should be given when selecting a school of architecture to attend?

ARCHITECTURAL TECHNICIANS, TECHNOLOGISTS, DRAFTERS, AND RELATED OCCUPATIONS

2

GLOSSARY

Drafters people who prepare working drawings and plans

Illustrators those who prepare special presentation drawings and graphics

Line weight the intensity of thickness and darkness of lines in a drawing

Model builders people who construct scale models of structures

Monotone a single unvaried drawing, with all lines or drawings the same

Technician people with a specific technical skill and competence within the architectural field, usually requiring two years of specialized formal education

Technologists individuals with a broader level of competence than that of technicians, usually with four years of specialized formal education

People who are interested in developing and using their skills in architectural drafting and communication should carefully consider the professions of architectural technician, technologist, drafter, and other specialized areas of architectural graphics. Architectural technicians and technologists work along with architects and designers, transforming their ideas into workable, understandable plans. The architectural drafter's primary responsibility, on the other hand, is to turn the architect's ideas into a graphical plan or procedure that can be understood by contractors, and building-trades specialists, as well as by the consumer.

Other specialized occupations, such as model builders, renderers, and commercial artists, provide attractive and meaningful presentations of architectural plans or projects. These may take the form of three-dimensional models, drawings and illustrations, and graphical presentations of internal and external details of the project.

Regardless of which profession you are interested in, they have one common element of preparation—a sound understanding of architectural drafting principles and practices.

DUTIES AND RESPONSIBILITIES OF ARCHITECTURAL TECHNICIANS AND TECHNOLOGISTS

Compared to many occupations in the field, architectural technicians and technologists are relatively new. Formal recognition of and specifications for these titles began to appear in the late 1950s and early 1960s, when a gap appeared between professional architects and the people in the construction trades. Though closely related in job, there are differences between the technician and technologist.

Architectural technicians apply *specific* technical skills and knowledge in the field of architecture, construction, or both, to their work. Technicians work closely with the architect and the architectural project staff, in their specific area of specialization. Areas in which technicians might specialize are architectural or structural drafting, illustration, cartography, construction estimation, and any phase of residential or commercial construction. Formal preparation for a technician frequently includes the completion of a two-year technical education program beyond the high school level. Normally this is an Associate degree.

Architectural technologists have a *broader* preparation and expertise in architecture, engineering, and construction. Technologists apply scientific and mathematical principles to architectural design and construction. The technologist works directly with the project architect and engineer on various aspects of design, planning, engineering, and construction.

The actual duties and responsibilities of architectural technicians and technologists vary according to the type and size of firm they work for. Normally, the smaller the operation, the more varied their job responsibilities. Large architectural and construction firms typically need a technician or technologist with a specific job skill, such as drafting, cartography, modeling, surveying, management, and supervision. Smaller firms require competence in several technical areas. In large organizations, technicians and technologists are assigned to specific departments, e.g., research and development, design, marketing, or construction; those in smaller concerns participate in both field and office activities.

Regardless of the working environment, architectural technicians and technologists must have a sound foundation in science and mathematics as they apply to architectural design and construction. Technicians and technologists are not to be looked at as nonprofessionals, because of their emphasis on the practical or applied side of architecture rather than on the theoretical. On the contrary, though they do not have the breadth or depth of preparation of architects, they must be able to put the theories and ideas of architects into a practical framework that can be understood and carried out by construction contractors.

Architectural technicians' and technologists' specialized skills help turn architectural and development dreams into concrete projects. During the planning stages, they are assigned to any number of jobs. These may include estimating project costs, preparing specifications for construction materials, supervising site surveys, preparing plans and drawings, and even designing specific components for the project. The bottom line in planning, however, is for the technician and technologist to translate the architect's ideas into workable solutions.

Once construction begins, the technician and technologist assist the contractor in scheduling and arranging specific building activities. In some cases, they help order materials and make sure that the written specifications are being followed. Finally, they may have the responsibility for inspecting all construction sites to make sure that all drawings and plans are being followed and that tolerances are kept within project specifications.

DUTIES AND RESPONSIBILITIES OF ARCHITECTURAL DRAFTERS

The success of the day-to-day operation of an architectural and design firm may well depend upon the quality of the drafting staff. The architectural drafter is a specialist in the architectural field, the specialty being drafting. It is the drafter's responsibility to translate the ideas, calculations, specifications, and sketches of the architect into a complete set of working drawings.

Regardless of the training and educational experiences of newly graduated drafters, they are normally required to pass through the ranks in the drafting department of an architectural firm. These levels are typically tracer, checker, detailer, and senior drafter. Some firms may use different titles and more levels of drafters, e.g., tracers, junior drafter, drafter, detailer and layout drafter, and designer. However the concepts and responsibilities attached to each rank remain much the same.

The tracer, or first-level drafter, normally has been hired with little or no work experience or is not familiar with the standard operating procedures used in the firm. In order to let the novice drafter get a feel for the work expected and to develop skills and speed, the tracer is made responsible for preparing plans for reproduction by tracing them on some drafting medium, such as paper, cloth, or plastic film. Once tracers build their skills up to an acceptable level, they are expected to make minor corrections in architectural plans, such as room and utility system relocations. The length of time drafters spend at this or any other level, depends on their ability to master the skills of the job and on the type and size of firm they work for. However, as new methods of reproducing drawings are developed, the tracer's job will change considerably.

Checkers, the second level of drafters, examine all drawings produced in the drafting department to be sure that there are no errors in dimensions, calculations, specifications, or interpretation of project designs. Checkers not only must be able to produce and interpret working drawings, but must be able to interpret the ideas and concepts in any architectural design.

The next level within the drafting department is either the detail or layout drafters. They are respon-sible for preparing detailed architectural plans, based upon the design and layouts. Specifically, the detail and layout drafters draw floor plans, sections and details, elevations, and, in some cases, special presentation drawings. Detailers, therefore, are responsible for producing all working drawings the contractor and construction engineer need to build the architectural project.

The highest-level drafter is the senior or design drafter. They consistently work closely with the architect and project engineers. It is their responsibility to prepare designs and layouts of architectural projects, based upon the architect's sketches and the conversations they have had. In exceptionally large or specialized firms, senior drafters may become highly competent in one particular type or area of architectural design. Typical areas of specialization are engineering design, special presentation drawing, or computer-assisted design.

As we said, whether or not drafters are required to pass through the various ranks of the drafting department depends upon two major factors—individual technical competence and the size of the firm. Drafters with extensive drafting experience who have demonstrated their technical competence may not start at the bottom of the ladder, but somewhere higher. Drafters without this high level of technical competence most definitely start at the bottom and work their way up. The speed of their rise depends upon their talents, ability to adjust to the job, and productivity.

The second major factor is the size of the firm. The smaller the drafting department, the fewer the ranks to pass through. However, since the staff will not be large enough to take up slack caused by the new drafter's lack of experience, it is very important that drafters are technically competent and able to adjust to the job soon. Larger drafting departments tend to be more structured than small ones. The advantages of large over small firms, and vice versa, depend upon the type of firm, the projects that are handled, and the desires and goals of the employees.

DUTIES AND RESPONSIBILITIES OF RELATED OCCUPATIONS

There are many specialty jobs in the firm, but two major occupational areas rely especially heavily upon the principles and practices of architectural drafting. They are the professional model builder and the architectural or commercial illustrator. Larger firms have these specialists, whose sole responsibility is to produce architectural models or special illustrations; smaller firms give these staff members other duties as well.

Most architectural and construction firms rely upon layouts, plans, details, sections, and elevations to express their designs. At times, however, these standard drawings are not enough to sell an idea to prospective buyers and financial backers. Thus some special type of presentation is needed. This is usually the three-dimensional model. The three-dimensional model gives the untrained person a better idea of what the project will look like when completed than a standard drawing does. Because of this advantage, many architectural firms are becoming increasingly dependent upon three-dimensional models. In fact, a few firms have full-time employees whose only job is to produce architectural models.

MODEL BUILDER

Most architectural model builders have backgrounds in one or more of the other architectural occupations discussed so far. Some architects themselves specialize as model builders. Traditionally, however, model builders have been architectural drafters first. It has been only recently that builders have had backgrounds as architectural technicians or technologists.

ILLUSTRATOR

Another specialist is the illustrator. More of an artist than a technician, the illustrator is responsible for producing special presentation drawings. Like three-dimensional models, these communicate special features and characteristics of designs. Media used in the preparation of special presentation drawings range from pastels to paints to photographs.

Traditionally, specialty presentation drawings have been prepared by the architectural staff or the drafting department. Only recently have architectural firms turned to specialists for such presentations. Like model builders, illustrators come from other architectural occupations, most commonly that of architect or drafter. In a few cases, however, they have had specialized training in art, media, and presentation techniques as applied to architectural illustration. See Fig. 2-1.

EDUCATIONAL QUALIFICATIONS OF ARCHITECTURAL TECHNICIANS AND TECHNOLOGISTS

There are presently no state licensing requirements for either architectural technicians or technologists. Individuals interested in either area should complete either a two-year Associate or a four-year Bachelor degree program, with major concentrations in architectural technology. Without a college education, it may be possible to qualify as a technician or technologist with a combination of related work experience, e.g., as a drafter or construction tradesman, and with some form of continuing education, such as adult education, apprenticeship courses, or evening college courses. Just as there are differences between the jobs of the architectural technician and the technologist, there are also differences in their educational preparation.

REQUIREMENTS FOR ARCHITECTURAL TECHNICIANS

Many educational institutions have specialized educational programs to prepare students as architectural technicians. Though the typical program is the Asso-

Fig. 2-1 *Architectural Illustration of the Johnson Wax Administration and Research Center (Courtesy S.C. Johnson & Sons, Inc.)*

ciate degree in architectural technology, other programs are offered in vocational-technical high schools, area vocational schools, and in some colleges and universities. In a few cases, a student who has completed two or three years of a Bachelor degree in engineering, architecture, or related science areas may also qualify as an architectural technician. Employers, however, usually employ graduates from community-college or two-year technical-institute programs.

Other, less formal forms of training may also qualify a person as a technician. Typical examples are on-the-job training with architectural or construction companies, apprenticeship programs in the building trades, or related experiences in the Armed Forces. As the profession becomes more established and formalized, it will probably be more difficult for a person to be employed as a technician without an Associate degree in architectural technology.

Most two-year architectural technology programs are intended to help students understand the ar-

chitectural design process, the nature of building materials, and the working relationship between the technician and the architectural staff. A typical two-year program includes 95–115 quarter hours or 62–72 semester hours of course work. Most of the courses are in technology and related areas, such as construction materials and methods, mechanical and electrical equipment, construction costs and estimates, specifications, and contracts.

An example of a typical program is shown in Table 2-1.

REQUIREMENTS FOR ARCHITECTURAL TECHNOLOGISTS

The architectural technologist today is a lot like the architect of twenty years ago. The technical knowledge in the field has expanded and jobs have become so specialized that a gap has developed between the highly trained architect and the various construction personnel involved in architectural projects.

Table 2-1 Architectural Technician Program

Course	Quarter Hours	Semester Hours
First Year		
Architectural Technology	10–14	7–9
Graphics and Architectural Drafting	8–12	5–8
Physics	4–6	3–4
Mathematics	8–12	5–8
English	4	3
Social Sciences	4	3
Second Year		
Architectural Technology	18–22	12–15
Architectural Drafting	4–8	3–5
Physics	4–6	3–4
Mathematics	4	3
English	4	3
Social Sciences	8	5

Technologists have graduated with a four-year Bachelor degree in architectural technology or architectural engineering technology. Most such college or university programs teach the various phases of architectural and engineering design, as related to the construction industry.

Sometimes less training with an extensive amount of job-related experience can be a substitute for the Bachelor degree. Architectural technologists who do not have a four-year degree normally have an Associate degree in a related field and also have a wide variety of experience and expertise in the architectural and construction industry.

The four-year architectural technology program is designed to teach students architectural, construction, and management procedures, as well as the design and drafting techniques required in architectural and construction engineering companies. The typical Bachelor degree in architectural technology involves approximately 186 quarter hours or 126 semester hours of course work. The emphasis is on the scientific and mathematical principles and theories of architecture and construction. Naturally, a majority of courses are in architectural and related technologies. Some examples of these are strength of materials, mechanical and electrical equipment, architectural models, building codes and regulations, construction methods and equipment, architectural specifications and contracts, surveying techniques, and presentation drawings. An example of a typical four-year program is as follows:

Table 2-2 Architectural Technologist Program

Course	Quarter Hours	Semester Hours
First Year		
Architectural Technology	18–21	12–14
Graphics and Architectural Drafting	9–12	6–8
Mathematics	9–12	6–8
English	9	6
Humanities	9	6
Second Year		
Architectural Technology	12–16	8–14
Design and Architectural Drafting	3–6	2–4
Physics	6–12	4–8
Chemistry	6–12	4–8
Speech	3	2
English	9	6
Third Year		
Architectural Technology	32–45	21–30
Architectural Design and Drafting	3–6	2–4
Social Sciences	9	6
Fourth Year		
Architectural Technology	12–16	8–11
Architectural Design and Drafting	16–21	11–14
Electives	9–12	6–8

EDUCATIONAL QUALIFICATIONS OF ARCHITECTURAL DRAFTERS

Architectural drafters have a better chance of securing a position with an architectural or construction firm if they have completed a two-year postsecondary program in architectural drafting. Well-qualified high school graduates may be able to secure employment if they have received a sound foundation in the principles and practices of architectural drafting. Because of the large number of complex designs and drawings used in the architectural and construction industry, more and more employers seek drafters who have completed a well-rounded training program, such as the Associate degree. An Associate degree in architectural drafting may be earned at a community college or technical institute.

Like the technician, the drafter may receive training in various educational programs. Besides the Associate degree, formal programs are offered in vocational and technical high schools, postsecondary vocational-technical schools, and college and university evening schools. Less formal education programs are also available through on-the-job training, apprenticeship programs, and in the Armed Forces. Note that the less formal and less specialized the training program, the smaller the chance that the graduate will be employed in a high-level drafting position. For example, high school graduates would probably start as tracers, but Associate degree graduates would be more likely to start as junior drafters or detailers.

Associate-degree programs provide a concentration in drafting, illustration, and the design principles used in the field. The two-year program usually averages 110 quarter hours or 74 semester hours of course work, with the major emphasis on drafting. Typical drafting courses include basic graphics, architectural graphics and design, illustration techniques, structure design, plot design and drawings, site design, architectural working drawings, and presentation drawings. An example of a typical two-year program in architectural drafting is as follows:

Table 2-3 Architectural Drafter Program

Course	Quarter Hours	Semester Hours
First Year		
Graphics and Architectural Drafting	10–14	7–9
Architectural Technology	8–12	5–8
Physics	6–9	4–6
Mathematics	6–9	4–6
English	4	3
Second Year		
Architectural Drafting	12–18	8–12
Architectural Technology	6–9	4–6
English	4	3
Social Sciences	6	4
Art	3–9	2–6

EDUCATIONAL QUALIFICATIONS OF RELATED OCCUPATIONS

There is an extremely limited number of formal programs specifically designed for architectural model builders. They can best be trained in one of three different types of educational programs: architecture, two-year architectural technology, and four-year architectural technology. Elective courses in related shop and art courses help develop competence in the use of the tools and materials of the profession.

Less formal training may also be obtained in vocational schools, vocational-technical centers, adult vocational evening courses, and in college and university extension programs. Within a number of manufacturing industries, there are related apprenticeship programs in model and pattern making. Though these apprenticeship programs do not prepare architectural model builders as such, they do provide the principles of constructing three-dimensional models.

Perhaps the most direct method is to first get a position as a technician, technologist, or drafter, and then receive on-the-job training as a model builder. A person would have an excellent opportunity to specialize in three-dimensional model building.

Those interested in architectural illustration may find it somewhat easier to secure training, for a number of educational programs are designed to prepare technical and commercial illustrators. With a sound foundation in architectural drafting and design, an illustrator could be employed within the drafting or design department as a specialist in presentation drawings. There are few structured programs specifically designed to prepare architectural illustrators. Therefore, students enrolled in technical or commercial illustration programs should take elective courses in architectural drafting and design. Students in an architectural technology or drafting program should select elective courses in commercial and technical illustration and related art courses.

Less formal training is also available in vocational schools, vocational technical centers, adult vocational evening courses, and in college and university extension programs. A person interested in a career as an architectural illustrator should also acquire on-the-job training.

SOURCES OF ADDITIONAL EDUCATIONAL INFORMATION

For additional information about the types of educational programs in architectural technology, drafting, and other specialized occupations, contact one or more of the following agencies:

The Association of Collegiate Schools of Architecture, Inc.
1735 New York Avenue, N.W.
Washington, D.C. 20006

American Association of Community and Junior Colleges
Suite 410, 1 Dupont Circle
Washington, D.C. 20036

National Association of Trade and Technical Schools
Accrediting Commission
2021 L Street, N.W.
Washington, D.C. 20036

SUMMARY

The field of architectural technology is relatively new. Technicians and technologists who complete two- and four-year degrees may plan to concentrate on drafting, cartography, modeling, surveying, or management and supervision. As part of the architectural team, the technician and technologist translate the ideas and concepts of the architect into workable solutions and designs. Architectural drafters, on the other hand, translate project designs and specifications into complete sets of working drawings. In most firms, drafters are required to work their way up in the drafting department, starting as tracers or junior drafters and advancing to become designers or senior drafters.

Two specialty areas are model building and illustrating. Three-dimensional models are used for presentation of designs to prospective clients and financial backers. Special drawings and illustrations also help in selling the project to nonspecialists. The model builder and illustrator are usually architects, technologists, technicians, or drafters who have become involved in these specialty fields full-time.

Educational preparation for the architectural technologist includes completion of a four-year architectural technology program. Architectural technicians and architectural drafters usually have completed two-year programs in community colleges or technical institutes. In some cases, well-prepared high school graduates may be employed as drafters. Since there are few programs specifically in architectural model building or illustration, the most direct method of training is to complete an architectural technology or drafting program and then get on-the-job training. Less formal means of training include evening courses, college and university extension programs, and the Armed Forces.

REVIEW QUESTIONS

1. What are the major educational and occupational differences between architectural technicians and architectural technologists?
2. How do the technician and technologist differ from the architect in job responsibility?
3. How does the architectural technician function as a member of the architectural project staff?
4. What is the major responsibility of architectural drafters?
5. Briefly explain the responsibilities of the following levels of architectural drafters:

   a. tracer
   b. detailer
   c. checker
   d. senior drafter

6. What are the responsibilities of an architectural model builder?
7. What are the responsibilities of an architectural illustrator?
8. Identify the preferred method of receiving training as an architectural technologist, technician, and drafter.
9. What is the general nature of training for architectural technologists, technicians, and drafters?
10. Briefly explain the various training procedures for architectural model builders and illustrators.

CHAPTER 3

INSTRUMENTS, MATERIALS, AND TECHNIQUES OF ARCHITECTURAL DRAFTERS

The quality and often the success of architectural plans depends on the type and quality of instruments and materials used in their preparation. Furthermore, the techniques and special effects used can enhance or detract from the plan. It is therefore essential that students of architectural drafting secure quality instruments and materials and develop acceptable techniques in using them. High-quality drawings result from proper use of good materials and good tools.

Beginning students and drafters are often confused by the variety of drafting instruments and materials to choose from. There are so many drafting supply stores and equipment manufacturing companies that the uninformed often buy more than necessary. Architectural drafters really need rather few—but carefully chosen—drafting instruments. Thus, the rule of thumb in buying any drafting instrument or materials is to buy the best quality that you can afford, rather than the greatest quantity.

The beginner should consider only reputable companies when making a purchase. Those who have no idea which companies can be trusted should ask their teachers or other drafters. Students who follow this simple advice will make the best decisions in buying equipment and supplies.

Finally, even the most expensive and highest quality instruments are only as good as their owner lets them be. Drafting instruments are not made to be abused. They are precise instruments, to be handled in a careful and professional manner. In most cases, the qual-

GLOSSARY

Hypotenuse the side of a right triangle opposite the 90° angle

Line expressions a variety of lines, drawn differently from one another, used to communicate certain ideas in drawings

Natural paper paper that is not coated with any chemical, in contrast to "prepared" paper, which is coated with chemicals such as sizing and light-sensitive materials

Scaled drawings drawings that are prepared at a certain ratio (scale) to the actual size of the architectural structure

SI dimensions dimensions based upon the metric system, or *le Système International d'Unités*

Sizing a starch used on cloth and some papers

Tracing paper drawing paper with high translucency and partial transparency, sometimes used to mean the same as *vellum paper*

Vellum paper the paper usually used in preparing architectural drawings; typically not as translucent as tracing paper

ity of one's work reflects the quality of care and use of the equipment. To make a good impression on future employers, be sure to treat the tools of the trade with care.

DRAFTING EQUIPMENT AND INSTRUMENTS

There is a wide variety of equipment and instruments available. Some are used in all fields of drafting; others are specially designed for specific areas of the profession. This section discusses drafting equipment and instruments commonly used in architectural drafting.

DRAWING BOARDS

Drawing boards and tables are available in many sizes. Choose one on the basis of the size of drawings you require. Students and beginning drafters typically start on drawings of smaller size (24″ × 36″), but they eventually will have to produce larger-sized drawings, e.g., 36″ × 48″. The size depends upon the type of firm the drafter works for and the requirements of local codes and legal specifications. Thus, the drawing board or table should be big enough to accommodate the largest drawing frequently required. Exceptionally large and specialized drawings are not drawn on ordinary drawing boards and tables, but rather on boards and tables specifically designed for them. These range in size up to 42″ × 84″.

Drawing boards are made of basswood or white pine, laminated and constructed to avoid any warping or distortion on the drawing surface. See Fig. 3-1. Drawing boards are recommended for smaller drawings and should be considered portable, in that they can be moved from location to location without much difficulty. This characteristic makes the drawing board a convenient drawing surface for plans 24″ × 36″ or smaller. Larger drawings should be made on drawing tables.

Fig. 3-1 *Drawing Board with Cut-Away Section (Courtesy of Keuffel & Esser Company, Morristown, NJ)*

TABLES

Drawing or drafting tables should be considered drafting room furniture. They are not as portable as drawing boards, but they do offer a number of advantages. First, the drawing surface itself holds up to a variety of drawing conditions and operations. Second, the drawing surface can easily be adjusted to various heights and angles to suit the requirements of individual drafters. Finally, the drafting table has a more comfortable and stable drawing surface.

Drafting tables are available in a variety of designs, from an economical wood construction (Fig. 3-2) to a more elaborate combination table and desk (Fig. 3-3). Tables come in different drawing surface sizes, from 32″ × 42″ to 43½″ × 84″. Again, the size and type of table required depends on the type, size, and number of drawings required.

T-SQUARES, PARALLELS, AND DRAFTING MACHINES

T-Squares are almost symbolic of drafting. The T-square was one of the first standardized tools used for drawing horizontal lines. Still preferred by some drafters, T-squares (Fig. 3-4) are typically used in drawing plans 24″ × 36″ or smaller. They are somewhat cumbersome to use for larger drawings. T-squares have a tendency to loosen where the head and blade join. Therefore, they should be securely fastened to eliminate as much play as possible. If not, the movement can throw the drawing out of square—the lines drawn would not be parallel. If there is movement, tighten the head with a screwdriver. If the movement persists, do not use the T-square.

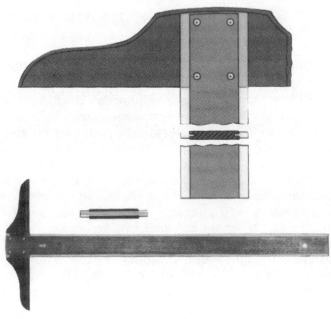

Fig. 3-4 *T-Square (Courtesy of Keuffel & Esser Company, Morristown, NJ)*

Parallels are excellent guides for drawing horizontal lines. Parallels (Fig. 3-5) come in standard lengths of 42″, 48″, 54″, 60″, 72″, 84″, and 96″. They are made of hardwood or metal, with clear plastic edges. Parallels move up and down on the drawing surface; they are always kept horizontal by the wires they ride on, which pass over pulleys to the corners of the drawing board. Unlike T-squares, parallels can be fitted with rollers to keep the contact with the drawing surface minimal. This reduces the chance of getting dirt on the drawing or damaging the plan. Of the three guides for drawing horizontal lines, the parallel is perhaps the most popular among architectural drafters.

Drafting Machines can be used to draw horizontal, vertical, and angular lines. There are two types of drafting machines—standard and track-type. The standard drafting machine is the most common (Fig. 3-6) and is particularly applicable for drawings 24″ × 36″. The track-type drafting machine (Fig. 3-7) was developed for larger drawings, but is also quite adaptable for any size. The straightedges on drafting machines are made of transparent plastic, boxwood, or aluminum. They come in a variety of scales and in standard lengths of 12″, 18″, 24″, and 36″. Drafting machines

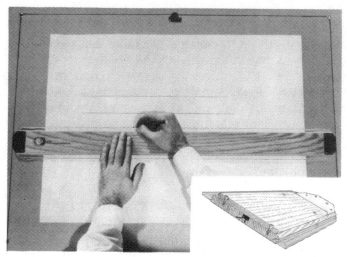

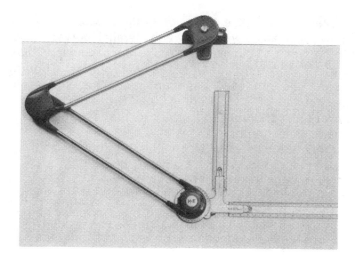

Fig. 3-5 *Parallels (Courtesy of Keuffel & Esser Company, Morristown, NJ)*

Fig. 3-6 *Drafting Machine (Courtesy of Keuffel & Esser Company, Morristown, NJ)*

are equipped with rotating heads (Fig. 3-8) and protractors. The head is capable of locking in automatically at 15° increments or manually within ½° increments.

TRIANGLES, CURVES, AND TEMPLATES

Triangles are used by drafters to draw vertical and standard (30°, 45°, and 60°) angular lines. In combination, they can also be used to draw lines at 15° increments. The two basic types of triangles are the 30°-60° and 45° triangles (Fig. 3-9). Both triangles come in different heights, ranging from 4″ to 18″, in 2″ increments. Since the triangles are normally used in combination, it is good practice to have the 30°-60° triangle 2″ longer than the 45° triangle, so that their hypotenuses are approximately equal.

Another common triangle is the adjustable triangle (Fig. 3-10). This has an attached protractor that makes it possible to adjust the hypotenuse to various angles, within about 1½°. The adjustable triangle is usually found in two sizes—8″ and 10″.

Drafting triangles are usually made of heavy transparent acrylic plastic, chemically treated to maintain clearness and dimensional stability. Some manufac-

Fig. 3-7 *Track-Type Drafting Machine (Courtesy of Keuffel & Esser Company, Morristown NJ)*

Fig. 3-8 *Detail of Rotating Head of Drafting Machine (Courtesy of Keuffel & Esser Company, Morristown, NJ)*

turers make fluorescent colored triangles for drafters who want to eliminate any shadows cast by the triangle itself. Others produce nonfluorescent blue or green tinted triangles to eliminate the glare caused by the fluorescent coloring.

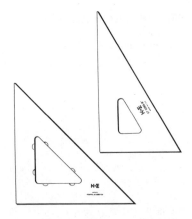

Fig. 3-9 *30°-60° and 45° Triangles (Courtesy of Keuffel & Esser Company, Morristown, NJ)*

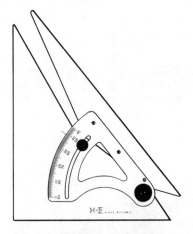

Fig. 3-10 *Adjustable Triangle (Courtesy of Keuffel & Esser Company, Morristown, NJ)*

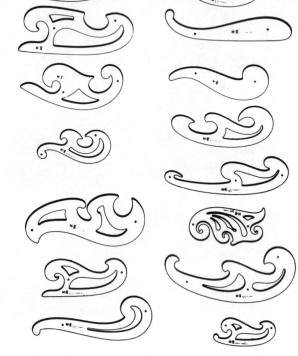

Fig. 3-11 *French Curves (Courtesy of Keuffel & Esser Company, Morristown, NJ)*

Curves are valuable tools for drafters who frequently draw mechanically curved and parallel curved lines. Three types of curves are used: *French* curves, *radius* curves, and *adjustable* or *flexible* curves. Though curves are not used as often in architectural as in mechanical or civil drafting, they are excellent time savers in drawing topographic maps, plot plans, charts, and graphs.

French curves may be purchased either as a set or individually (Fig. 3-11). The radius curve (Fig. 3-12) is of particular value in drawing the parallel edges of highways, roads, paths, or sidewalks. Adjustable curves (Fig. 3-13) are becoming more popular among drafters, for they can be shaped to any curved plotting or layout. They are available in lengths of 12″, 18″, 24″, and 30″.

Templates enable architectural drafters to draw standard symbols fast and efficiently. There are literally hundreds of templates available on the market, but only a few are really useful to the architectural drafter. Fig. 3-14 illustrates several templates for the architectural field. Templates are designed for drawing plans of residential, office, and store layouts, house furnishings, landscaping symbols, and civil and structural symbols. Templates common to all areas of drafting are the circle, ellipse, square, triangle, and lettering templates.

SCALES

Scales are one of the most important tools of architectural drafters. Students must become familiar with the types and uses of scales and become proficient in using them. Three types of scales are used in the architectural field—*architect's* scales, *engineering* scales, *metric* scales.

Architect's Scales are available in four standard shapes (Fig. 3-15)—*two-bevel, opposite-bevel, four-bevel,* and *triangular*. The two-bevel scale has a wide, flat base, with the scale face always visible to the drafter. It is the preferred shaped scale of many experienced architectural drafters. The opposite-bevel scale is typically used on slanted drawing surfaces; its unique shape makes it easy to lift and move. The four-bevel scale is preferred as a pocket scale—convenient and easy to use when checking or transferring measurements from one drawing to another. The most common scale found in schools is the triangular scale. It has one major advantage over all others: it has eleven scales on it. The triangular scale is also available with either flat or concave surfaces. See Table 3-1.

Civil Engineering Scales may be used when drawing plot plans, laying out acreage measurements, developing utility plans, and doing various types of structural plans, e.g., bridges and dikes. The civil engineering scale is unlike other scales; it has ten divisions per inch, rather than eight, sixteen, thirty-two, etc. The reason for this is that many civil drafting and design procedures are calculated and laid out on a decimal system, using tenths, hundredths, and thousandths of inches, rather than halves, quarters, eighths, etc. See Table 3-2.

Metric Scales, unlike other scales, are not often found in architectural drafting departments. However, it appears that an increasing proportion of drawings will be drawn to metric scale in the 1980s and 1990s. Eventually, all designing and plans may be drawn in the SI measurements, as is the case in Canada and non-English speaking countries.

Since the United States is legally committed to changing over to the metric system, a large number of drawings are now being scaled. This is necessary for plans for the international market. Unlike the other two scales, the metric scale is not based upon divi-

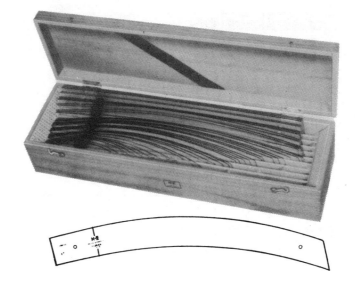

Fig. 3-12 *Radius Curves (Courtesy of Keuffel & Esser Company, Morristown, NJ)*

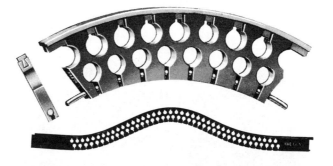

Fig. 3-13 *Adjustable Curve (Courtesy of Keuffel & Esser Company, Morristown, NJ)*

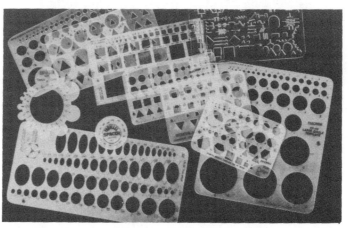

Fig. 3-14 *Templates (Courtesy of Keuffel & Esser Company, Morristown, NJ)*

Table 3-1 Architect's Scales

Shape	Lengths Available	Graduations Available (to the Foot)
Two-bevel	6″, 12″	1/8″, 1/4″, 1/2″, 1″
Opposite-bevel	6″, 12″	1/8″, 1/4″, 1/2″, 1″
Four-bevel	6″	1/8″, 1/4″, 3/8″, 1/2″, 3/4″, 1″, 1 1/2″, 3″
Triangular Scales	6″, 12″	3/32″, 1/8″, 3/16″, 1/4″, 3/8″, 1/2″, 3/4″, 1″, 1 1/2″, 3″

Table 3-2 Civil Engineer's Scales

Shape	Lengths Available	Graduations per Inch Available
Two-bevel	6″, 12″	10, 20, 40, 50
Opposite-bevel	6″, 12″	10, 20, 40, 50
Four-bevel	6″	10, 20, 30, 40, 50
Triangular	6″, 12″	10, 20, 30, 40, 50, 60

Fig. 3-15 *Architect's Scale Shapes*

sions of the inch (Table 3-3). Instead, scales are specified according to ratios. That is, a 1:1 ratio is a full-sized drawing, a 1:50 ratio is one-fiftieth of full size, and so on.

Table 3-3 Metric Scales

Shape	Lengths Available	Ratios Available
Two-bevel	150 mm, 300 mm	1:10, 1:5, 1:2, 1:1
Opposite-bevel	150 mm, 300 mm	1:10, 1:5, 1:2, 1:1
Four-bevel	150 mm	1:10, 1:5, 1:2, 1:1
Triangular	150 mm, 300 mm	1:1000, 1:5000, 1:2000, 1:100, 1:50, 1:80, 1:50, 1:33$\frac{1}{3}$, 1:20, 1:10, 1:5, 1:2, 1:1, 2:1

DRAWING INSTRUMENTS

Select your drawing instruments according to what type of work you will use them for. Case instruments, that is, sets of drawing tools, come in a variety of combinations. Fig. 3-16 shows a basic set with three instruments. Fig. 3-17 is a more comprehensive set. Some drafters prefer to purchase their instruments individually. This lets you choose exactly the right drawing instruments for your own particular needs. Regardless of whether you buy a set or individual instruments, get what you *need*. There is no point in paying for a set containing a lot of tools you will never use. On the other hand, it is false economy to do without a tool you need frequently.

Look for high-quality design, good materials, and proper fit when choosing drafting instruments. Good workmanship and materials can be determined by the precision of fit among the various working parts of each instrument. The best materials used in drafting instruments are nickel-silver, stainless steel, and chrome-plated hard brass.

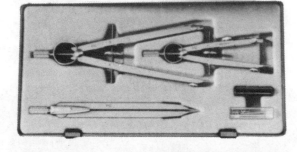

Fig. 3-16 *Simple Set of Case Instruments (Courtesy of Keuffel & Esser Company, Morristown, NJ)*

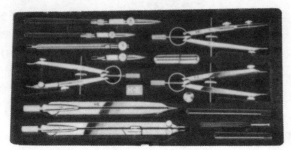

Fig. 3-17 *Set of Case Instruments with Wide Variety of Instruments (Courtesy of Keuffel & Esser Company, Morristown, NJ)*

DRAFTING MATERIALS

A wide variety of drafting materials and media are available to the architectural drafter. Some are essential; some are not but can make architectural plans look more professional. The correct selection and use of materials and media can both save time and give the plans the added quality that helps sell the project. Supplies discussed in this section are drawing paper, film, and cloth; lead-substitute pencils and holders; and specialized transfer overlays.

DRAWING PAPER, FILM, AND CLOTH

The paper, film, and cloth used in drafting come in standard sizes, in both sheets and rolls. Preprinted standard architectural and construction forms may be ordered by the sheet on a variety of drawing media. These forms eliminate drawing borders, title blocks, logos, etc., used on many architectural drawings. Drafting paper, film, and cloth can be bought in rolls of either 20 or 50 yards, in 24″, 30″, 34″, 36″, 42″, and 54″ widths. The standard sheet sizes are listed in Table 3-4. Though all sizes are used, four are especially common in architectural drawings. They are 8½″ × 11″, 12″ × 18″, 18″ × 24″, 24″ × 36″.

Paper is used for a majority of architectural plans and renderings. Papers are available as vellum and tracing vellum and as tracing paper. The most important factor is their ability to reproduce well. There is little difference between many vellums and tracing papers. In fact, the terms are often used interchangeably. When there is a difference, the tracing paper is more translucent.

Before the development of high-quality papers, master drawings were prepared in pencil on heavy, non-translucent paper, usually yellow-buff or light green in color, then traced in ink on translucent or opaque papers. Today, the heavy, non-translucent papers have given way to high quality vellums and tracing papers. The master plan is prepared in pencil on vellum. Copies are reproduced from this drawing, thus saving time and effort.

Translucent drawing papers are available as either *natural* (untreated) or *prepared* papers. Prepared papers tend to be thicker and stronger, with little or no loss of transparency. If frequent changes are required in the drawings, it is best to use prepared paper, though it is usually slightly more expensive than natural paper.

Film is the most recent medium to appear. Because of its dimensional stability, strength, high transparency,

Table 3-4 Standard Sheet Sizes

Size (in Inches)	Designation	Quantities Available (in Sheets)
8½ × 11	A	50, 100, 250
11 × 17	B	50, 100, 250
12 × 18	none	50, 100, 250
17 × 22	C	50, 100
18 × 24	none	50, 100
22 × 34	D	50, 100
24 × 36	none	50, 100
34 × 44	E	50, 100

resistance to age and heat, non-solubility, and water-proofness, polyester film is an excellent medium for architectural drawings. Films are used especially when many high-quality copies are required.

Pencil lines appear as high-quality dark lines on polyester film. Since leads and pencils tend to wear faster on film than on paper, the pencil used should be two or three degrees harder than the leads used on paper. (See the next section.) Inks and other specialized drawing supplies are also effective on films. One of the problems with the use of films is cost. It is generally not cost-effective to change over all drawings to polyester film.

Cloth was perhaps the first drawing medium ever used. Ancient drawings and writings were produced on surfaces made of cellulose fibers and containing sizing (glue or starch) for smoothness and hardness. Because of the excellent papers and films available today, there is little need to draw architectural plans on cloth. However, cloth is still used occasionally to meet contractural or code requirements.

Drawing cloth is made of linen or cotton, sized with starch and, in some instances, with moisture-resistant sizing. It resists aging and reproduces well. Drawing cloth accepts lead and pencil; ink is better. For this last reason and because of its cost, cloth has been replaced by papers and film.

LEADS AND LEAD-SUBSTITUTE PENCILS AND HOLDERS

Leads and Substitutes should be carefully selected. The leads are made of a combination of clay and graphite and may be purchased in fourteen degrees of hardness: 6H, 5H, 4H, 3H, 2H, H, F, HB, B, 2B, 3B, 4B, 5B, and 6B.

The two softest leads, 6B and 5B, are too soft for architectural work. Lead with hardness ratings between 4B and HB are used for architectural renderings and sketches; those with ratings between F and 4H are used for drawings and plans. Leads rated as Very Hard are of little use to architectural drafters, except for initial layouts.

The darkness of lines drawn with different leads is determined by two factors: the amount of pressure applied and the manufacturer. The more pressure, or *heavy-handedness*, applied, the darker the lines. Drafters with a rather light hand should use an F or H lead to acquire the same darkness an average drafter would get with a 2H. On the other hand, a heavy-handed drafter might use a 3H or 4H lead to achieve that darkness. Lead ratings vary between manufacturers; drafters should stay with one brand of lead rather than mixing brands. That is, a lead rated 2H by one manufacturer may be harder or softer than a 2H lead made by another company.

Leads and pencils are used on drawing papers, films, and cloth. When drawings are prepared on film, a *special lead substitute* may be used. The lead substitute is made of a plastic-base material that tends to wear longer than pencil does on polyester film. Leads also tend to smear on polyester films; the lead substitute almost eliminates this problem.

Pencils and Holders are relatively new in drafting supplies. The traditional container for leads was the pencil. It was so essential that elaborate systems of sharpening have been developed, to provide drafters with the best lead points to draw with. There are special sharpeners that remove only the wood, to expose a shaft of lead approximately ½'' long. A point

is then put on the lead by using either a sandpaper card or a pointer. See Fig. 3-18. Several years ago, mechanical holders came on the market. These made it possible for the drafter to expose as much lead as desired, without the need for a special wood-removing sharpener. Lead in a mechanical holder is also sharpened with a pointer or sandpaper card.

This system of pencil and lead sharpening is giving way to stick lead in mechanical holders. See Fig. 3-19. Stick-lead holders are available in a variety of body designs, grips, and weights. The most important aspect of these holders is their ability to hold very small stick leads. The most common size is 0.5 mm, a medium-thickness line. Stick-lead holders are also available in 0.3 mm for thin lines and 0.9 mm for thick ones.

To operate a stick-lead holder, place a stick of lead into the barrel and feed it out by pushing down or rotating the eraser end of the holder. The small size of the lead eliminates the need for sharpening. Like pencils and the older mechanical holders, lead sticks come in all hardnesses.

SPECIALIZED TRANSFER OVERLAYS

Specialized transfer overlays, Fig. 3-20, are a practical and economical method of applying symbols, title blocks, letters, and numbers to drawings. There are transfer overlays for individual symbols and letters. You can get overlays on printed transparent film for title blocks, legends, and other common figures. Individual letters are normally transferred to drawings by placing the letter on its location and rubbing down on its backing; the letter then transfers to the paper. Transfer overlays provide a black line that is excellent for reproduction.

More complex figures, such as title blocks, legends, logos, and other frequently used illustrations are printed on polyester film. The back of the film has a clear adhesive that can be stuck to any part of the drawing surface. They are available in standard forms or can be custom made to meet specific requirements.

Fig. 3-18 *Pencil Sharpener and Mechanical Lead Holder (Courtesy of Keuffel & Esser Company, Morristown, NJ)*

Fig. 3-19 *Stick Lead and Holder (Courtesy of Keuffel & Esser Company, Morristown, NJ)*

METHODOLOGIES IN THE ARCHITECTURAL FIELD

Many drafting procedures and methodologies are consistent in all areas. However, there are also some practices unique to each area. Those in the architectural field that are slightly different from those in other areas are lettering, line weights and expressions, and abbreviations and symbols.

LETTERING

Lettering presents information that is not available in the drawings alone. Dimensions, materials, specifications, and special notations are examples where lettering is used. Therefore, the architectural drafter's lettering must be clear and legible.

Unlike the lettering in other disciplines, architectural lettering usually takes on much of the style of the drafter. Architectural lettering therefore tends to be more artistic in presentation than in other fields. Lettering styles vary from individual to individual; drafters should use a lettering style that is not fancy and difficult to read. Remember that your lettering *reflects* your style; do not make letters different just so they will be different. Good lettering style develops through practice and experience. To deliberately make letter forms in an eccentric way will not produce a good style, and this may result in illegible letterings. An example of several good lettering styles is presented in Fig. 3-21. Note that, though the styles are different from one another, each letter and number can easily be read.

Except for a few instances, lettering on architectural drawings should be uppercase (capital) letters. The firm may have a house style. Lowercase letters should be used only for special notations or dimensional considerations. These may identify specific materials and equipment to be installed or construction techniques to be applied (e.g., stone coping, composition roof, scrupper, etc.). Special dimensional considerations are usually limited to SI notations, such as mm, cm, cd, and lx.

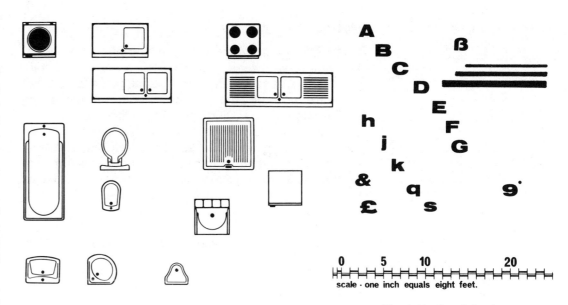

Fig. 3-20 *Specialized Architectural Transfer Overlays*

ABCDEFGHIJKLMNOPQ
RSTUVWXYZ 1234567890

ABCDEFGHIJKLMNOP
QRSTUVWXYZ 1234567890

ABCDEFGHIJKLMNOPQ
RSTUVWXYZ 1234567890

ABCDEFGHIJKLMNOP
QRSTUVWXYZ 1234567890

Fig. 3-21 *Good Lettering Styles*

General dimensions and notations are commonly ⅛″ high. Common titles and subtitles, such as sections, details, elevations, and floor plans are ¼″ high. Special titles and labels used to identify the name of the project, developer, or financing agent should be lettered ½″ high.

METRIC CONVERSION

The conversion process is a two-phase program. The first is *soft* conversion, that is, the actual dimensions and quantities in architectural plans and specifications will not change, but will only be expressed in the appropriate SI terms. For example, nominal-sized 2″ × 4″ lumber is actually $1^9/_{16}″ × 3^9/_{16}″$. The actual size in SI terms is 39.7 mm × 90.5 mm. At first, in converting architectural plans to SI, a straight conversion of all dimensions, such as set-back distances, floor area, and elevation heights, is used.

The *hard* conversion process, except in a very few instances, will actually involve changes in the dimensions and quantities in architectural plans and specifications. Hard conversion will involve the use of SI even in the design stage. Thus, instead of keeping the traditional nominal-sized 2″ × 4″ lumber that is actually 39.7 mm × 90.5 mm, the physical piece of lumber will be different. It might be 40 mm × 93 mm, for example. With these changes in architectural designs and construction procedures, it is clear that hard conversion will be difficult, costly, and take a long time to complete. Even so, in the long run, the difficulties may well be worth the effort. Conversion to SI will put the United States on an equal footing with the rest of the international market.

RULES OF SI DIMENSIONING NOTATIONS

Dimensions in most architectural plans are given with foot (′) and inch (″) notations. In most situations, SI dimensioning will eliminate the need for identifying unit notations. The reason for this is that all measurements will be based upon one unit, identified through scale indications, notations, or both. For example, a scale indication might read "Scale 1:50" with the notation "NOTE: All dimensions are given in millimeters." The notation eliminates the need to follow each dimension with "mm." However, if such a note were not included, then the "mm" notation would be needed after each dimension.

There are several differences between our conventional system and SI dimensions. Unlike the English system, SI terms express fractional dimensions with the decimal system. Since most SI drawings are dimensioned in millimeters, the drafter frequently has to give numbers of four or more places. When long numbers are required, such as 43,264.89734, the comma is eliminated and a space is used to separate groups of three integers on *both* sides of the decimal point. Thus, the above number would be expressed "43 264.897 34." When there is a four-integer number, such as 2,364, the space is optional: it may be written either "2364" or "2 364." Whether the space is used is up to the individual drafter or company standards, but usage must be consistent throughout the drawing and set of plans.

LINE WEIGHTS AND EXPRESSIONS

Technicians, construction workers, and consumers must be able to interpret drawings correctly. To assure that the information conveyed in the drawings is understood, drafters must prepare simple, clear drawings that conform to basic architectural standards. To do so, architectural drafters depend upon a special system of line weights and expressions.

Lines of various types make up plans, elevations, and other drawings. The drawings drafters prepare are the heart of all architectural presentations. Every line drawn has significance and is important in explaining the plan. Furthermore, each line has a relationship with the other lines in the drawing. If plans are drawn correctly, important lines can be immediately recognized. The more important lines are drawn in heavier line weights; the heavier a particular type of line, e.g., object line, hidden line, etc., is drawn, the more prominent it is. For example, lines of major significance, such as the outline of a building, will be drawn more heavily than lines of little significance, such as those showing the location of hidden edges of the buildings. Line *weight* refers to the *darkness* of the line.

Thickness of a line is also part of the line weight; heavy, medium, and light correspond to thick, medium, and thin lines.

Each line weight is used for specific purposes. Examples of lines drawn heavily are outlines of new buildings and site boundaries, primary features in section drawings, primary components in assemblies, profiles, and any other features requiring emphasis. Examples of lines drawn with medium weights are outlines of existing buildings, general building components and landscaping, mechanical assemblies, profiles, components, and assemblies in elevations. Lines drawn lightly include reference and dimension lines, hatchings, and reference grids.

The relationship of each line to the total drawing should be evaluated. Fig. 3-22 gives examples of lines that are used inappropriately and compares them to those in an acceptable elevation drawing. Elevation *A* presents the basic outline or start of a drawing of a structure and its roof layout, all lines have the same weight. Elevation *B* demonstrates what can happen when there is no variation in line weight; the drawing is monotone and difficult to interpret. Elevation *C* is an example of good variation in line weight. Elevations *D* and *E* are other examples of line weights used for presenting shadows and depth.

Expressions, that is, a number of technically defined lines and symbols, are used in architectural drafting. Eleven basic line expressions should be mastered. Students should be able to determine when and where to use each. See Fig. 3-23.

Break lines show breaks, removals, or terminations of edges or parts of the structure in the drawing. Break lines are of two varieties—those drawn freehand and those drawn mechanically. Short breaks are usually drawn freehand, with thick lines. Long breaks are drawn mechanically as thin lines, with intermittent *Z* symbols.

Center lines locate the centers of holes and of cylindrical and concentric objects; they also show the centers of doors and windows. They are drawn as al-

ternating long lines and short dashes. Center lines are extended beyond the object or hole referenced.

Cut or section lines illustrate the location of a cutting plane and refer to a detailed sectional view of the object. Cut lines are drawn as thick broken lines, alternating with two short dashes. At the ends, lines with arrowheads are drawn at a right angle to show the direction of the cutting-plane view and the number or letter reference of the sectional view.

Dimension lines indicate length, height, and width. These lines are drawn thin and usually have arrowheads at either end, although slashes or dots may be used instead. Numerical dimensions are drawn either on top or centered along the lines.

Extension lines are used with dimension lines. They are thin lines that show which distances the dimension lines refer to. Extension lines are drawn beyond the last (longest) dimension line and do not quite come in contact with the object lines being dimensioned.

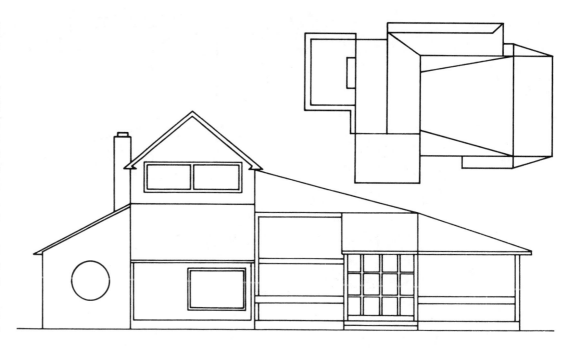

Fig. 3-22A *Elevation. All lines in this elevation are the same weight, with no presentation of texture of surface, depth perception, or significance of individual lines. This is acceptable only as the initial layout of the building's elevation and roof plan.*

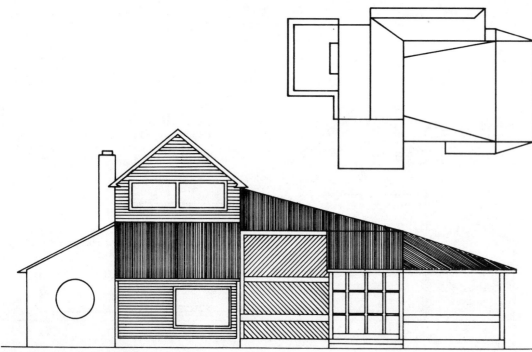

Hidden lines are drawn as medium-weight lines made up of dashes about $1/8''$ long and spaces between $1/32''$ and $1/16''$. Hidden lines show edges, surfaces, and intersections that are hidden from view. They are also used to show the existing construction that is either to remain or to be removed in renovation and remodeling.

Leader lines are thin lines, with an arrowhead or dot at the end, used for special notations, specifications, or dimensions of a specific part of a building or detail. Leader lines never cross each other. They may be drawn freehand or mechanically.

Object lines are drawn as thick lines. Sometimes referred to as *visible lines*, object lines show the outline and walls of a building. Any important shapes, profiles, or surfaces that should be emphasized in the plans should be drawn with object lines.

Outlines are a form of object lines. They should be the heaviest lines in the drawing; they bring out the basic shape of the building or emphasize a particular

Fig. 3-22B *Elevation. All lines in this elevation are the same weight, including all detailing and texture lines. Using the same weight of line throughout makes the drawing bland and monotonous in appearance. Such a technique does little to sell a design to potential buyers.*

Fig. 3-22C *Elevation. This elevation is perhaps the best example of appropriate use of various line weights. Note that the thick object lines stand out, defining the shape of the building, while the medium and thin lines illustrate less significant aspects of the structure.*

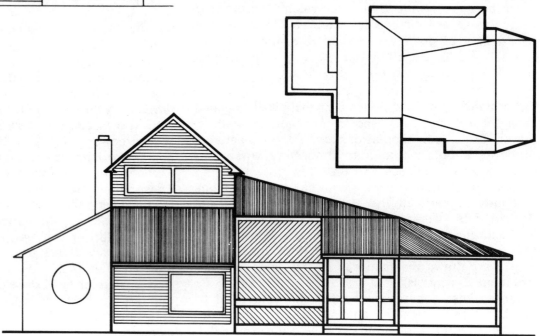

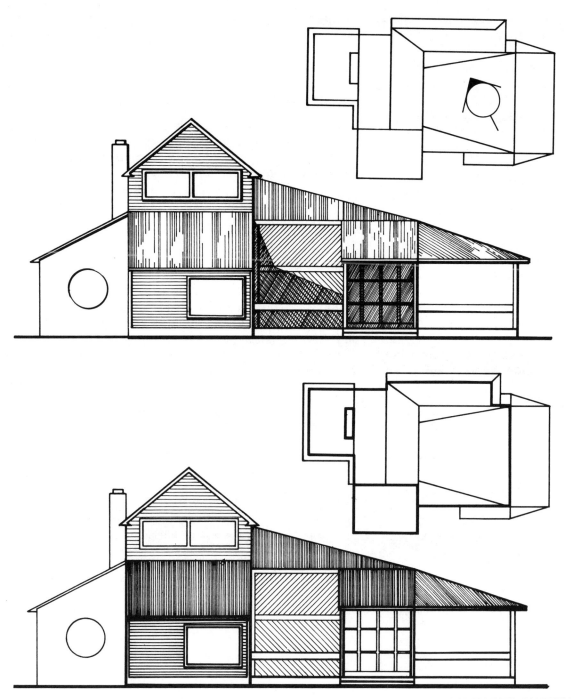

Fig. 3-22D *Elevation. This elevation uses various line weights to show certain features of the building, for instance, how shadows will fall on the structure during afternoon hours.*

Fig. 3-22E *Elevation. This elevation illustrates use of line weight to show depth. The walls closer to the viewer are drawn in thick lines. The more distant the walls are, the thinner the lines used to show them. Note that, in the roof plan, emphasis is placed on the shape of the house rather than on the roof itself.*

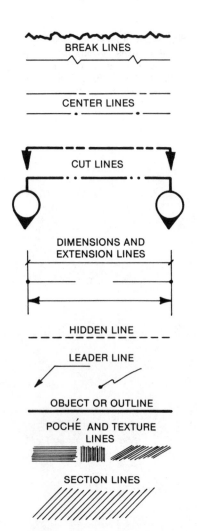

BREAK LINES

CENTER LINES

CUT LINES

DIMENSIONS AND
EXTENSION LINES

HIDDEN LINE

LEADER LINE

OBJECT OR OUTLINE

POCHÉ AND TEXTURE
LINES

SECTION LINES

Fig. 3-23 *Common Lines Used in Architectural Drafting*

Fig. 3-24 *Architectural Symbols Used for Materials*

part or section of the structure. Sometimes outlines are drawn even thicker than the object lines used in the drawing.

Poché or *texture lines* are drawn as thin vertical, horizontal, or diagonal lines. They give the surface something of the appearance of a photograph. Poché lines are used to show shadows, to give a feeling of depth, and to denote certain types of building materials.

Section lines are thin lines that show a surface or part of a surface drawn in a section view. The characteristics of the section lines depend upon the materials the sectioned object is made of.

ARCHITECTURAL ABBREVIATIONS AND SYMBOLS

Architectural drawings and plans convey certain ideas and concepts *in the simplest manner possible.* Two ways of simplifying architectural drawings are abbreviations and symbols. To assure conformity and consistency in architectural plans, abbreviations and

symbols have been standardized by the American Institute of Architects (AIA) Task Force for National Adoption.

ABBREVIATIONS

Architectural plans usually contain notes and references to materials used and the location of building components. Instead of writing complete descriptions of materials and locations, a system of AIA abbreviations is used. Table 3-5 is a listing of common construction-material abbreviations used in architectural drawings.

SYMBOLS

Like abbreviations, AIA architectural symbols simplify the task of the drafter. Symbols indicate types of materials, directions on drawings, parts of buildings, and equipment to be installed in the building. Figs. 3-24 through 3-28 present basic symbols architectural drafters commonly work with.

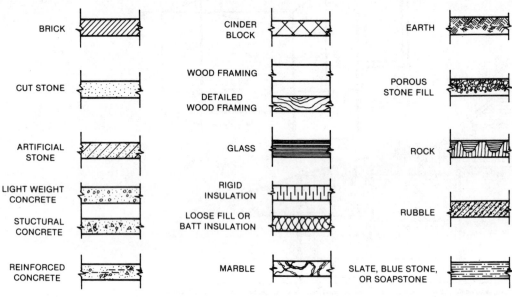

Table 3-5 Material Abbreviations

ACPL	acoustical plaster	DS	downspout	GKT	gasket(ed)	LVR	louver
ACT	acoustical tile	D	drain	GA	gauge	MB	machine bolt
ACR	acrylic plastic	DT	drain tile	GLB	glass block	MI	malleable iron
ADH	adhesive	DRB	drainboard	GLF	glass fiber	MRB	marble
AGG	aggregate	DWR	drawer	GL	glass, glazing	MAS	masonary
A/C	air conditioning	DWG	drawing	GCMU	glazed concrete masonry	MO	masonary opening
AL	aluminum	DF	drinking fountain		units	MC	medicine cabinet
AB	anchor bolt	DW	dumbwaiter	GST	glazed structural tile	MMB	membrane
ANC	anchor; anchorage	ELEC	electric(al)	GB	grab bar	MET	metal
ANOD	anodized	EP	electrical panelboard	GD	grade	MFD	metal floor decking
ASB	asbestos	EWC	electrical water cooler	GRN	granite	MTFR	metal furring
ASPH	asphalt	ELEV	elevator	GVL	gravel	MRD	metal roof decking
AT	asphalt tile	ESC	escalator	GF	ground face	MTHR	metal threshold
BP	back plaster(ed)	EXCA	excavate	GT	grout	MWK	millwork
BRG	bearing	EXH	exhaust	GPDW	gypsum dry wall	MIR	mirror
BPL	bearing plate	EXG	existing	GPL	gypsum lath	MOD	modular
BJT	bed joint	EB	expansion bolt	GPPL	gypsum plaster	MLD	molding
BIT	bituminous	EXT	exterior	GPT	gypsum tile	MR	mop receptor
BLK	block	FB	face brick	HBD	hardboard	NAT	natural
BLKG	blocking	FOC	face of concrete	HDW	hardware	NI	nickel
BD	board	FOF	face of finish	HWD	hardwood	NMT	nonmetallic
BRK	brick	FOM	face of masonary	HJT	head joint	NTS	not to scale
BRZ	bronze	FOS	face of studs	HDR	header	OC	on center
CAB	cabinet	FAS	fasten, fastener	HTG	heating	OJ	open-web joist
CAD	cadmium	FN	fence	HVAC	heating/ventilating/air	OPG	opening
CPT	carpet(ed)	FBD	fiberboard		conditioning	OD	outside diameter
CSMT	casement	FGL	fiberglass	HES	high-early-strength cement	OHMS	ovalhead machine screw
CB	cast basic	FFE	finished floor elevation	HC	hollow core	OHWS	ovalhead wood screw
CST	cast stone	FFL	finished floor line	HM	hollow metal	OA	overall
CIPC	cast-in-place concrete	FA	fire alarm	HK	hook(s)	OH	overhead
CI	cast-iron	FBRK	fire brick	HB	hose bibb	PNT	paint(ed)
CEM	cement	FE	fire extinguisher	HWH	hot water heater	PNL	panel
CER	ceramic	FEC	fire extinguisher cabinet	INCIN	incinerator	PB	panic bar
CMT	ceramic mosaic (tile)	FHS	fire-hose station	INS	insulate(d); insulation	PTD	paper towel dispenser
CT	ceramic tile	FRC	fire-resistant coating	INSC	insulating concrete	PTR	paper towel receptor
CHBD	chalkboard	FRT	fire-retardant	INSF	insulating fill	PBD	particle board
CR	chromium-plated	FPL	fireplace	INT	interior	PTN	partition
CIR	circle	FP	fireproof	JT	joint	PV	pave(d); paving
CIRC	circumference	FLG	flashing	JF	joint filler	PED	pedestal
COL	column	FHMS	flathead machine screw	J	joist	PLAS	plaster
COMPO	composition; composite	FHWS	flathead wood screw	KCPL	Keene's cement plaster	PLAM	plastic laminate
CONC	concrete	FD	floor drain	KPL	kickplate	PL	plate
CMU	concrete masonry unit	FPL	floor plate	KIT	kitchen	PG	plate glass
CPR	copper	FLR	floor(ing)	LAB	laboratory	PWD	plywood
CORR	corrugated	FJT	flush joint	LAD	ladder	PVC	polyvinyl chloride
CTR	counter	FTG	footing	LB	lag bolt	PE	porcelain enamel
CTSK	countersunk screw	FND	foundation	LAV	lavatory	PCPL	portland-cement plaster
CRG	cross grain	FS	full size	LT	light	PTC	post-tensioned concrete
DP	damproofing	FUR	furred; furring	LC	light control	PCC	precast concrete
DTL	detail	FUT	future	LP	lightproof	PSC	prestressed concrete
DIAM	diameter	GV	galvanized	LW	lightweight	QT	quarry tile
DR	door	GI	galvanized iron	LWC	lightweight concrete	REFR	refrigerator
DTA	dovetail anchor	GP	galvanized pipe	LMS	limestone	REG	register
DTS	dovetail anchor slot	GSS	galvanized steel sheet	LTL	lintel	RCP	reinforced-concrete pipe

Table 3-5 Material Abbreviations (cont.)

RVT	rivet	SKL	skylight	TC	terra cotta	VF	vinyl fabric
RD	roof drain	SL	sleeve	TZ	terrazzo	VT	vinyl tile
RFH	roof hatch	SC	solid curve	TPD	toilet paper dispenser	VAT	vinyl-asbestos tile
RFG	roofing	SP	soundproof	TPTN	toilet partition	WSCT	wainscot
RB	rubber base	SPC	spacer	T & G	tongue and groove	WC	water closet
RBT	rubber tile	SPK	speaker	TB	towel bar	WWF	welded-wire fabric
RBL	rubble stone	SST	stainless steel	TR	transom	WHB	wheel bumper
SFGL	safety glass	ST	steel	UR	urinal	WIN	window
SCN	screen	SD	storm drain	VB	vapor barrier	WM	wire mesh
SNT	sealant	SCT	structural clay tile	VAR	varnish	WG	wired glass
SSK	service sink	TKBD	tackboard	VNR	veneer	WD	wood
SHTH	sheathing	TKS	tackstrip	VRM	vermiculite	WB	wood base
SG	sheet glass	TEL	telephone	VIN	vinyl	WI	wrought iron
SH	shelf, shelving	TV	television	VB	vinyl base		

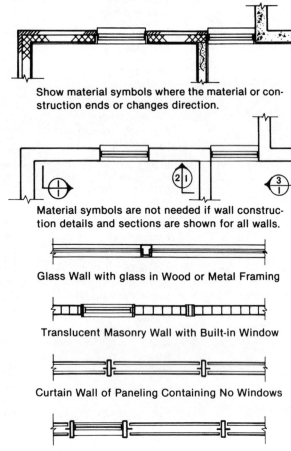

Show material symbols where the material or construction ends or changes direction.

Material symbols are not needed if wall construction details and sections are shown for all walls.

Glass Wall with glass in Wood or Metal Framing

Translucent Masonry Wall with Built-in Window

Curtain Wall of Paneling Containing No Windows

Curtain Wall of Paneling, Containing One Window

Fig. 3-25 *Wall Representations*

METRICATION

The Metric Conversion Act of 1975 committed the United States to a conversion to the metric system, or SI. This means that our country will gradually change from the traditional English system used in the U.S. to the system almost all the rest of the world uses. The abbreviation *SI* stands for *le Système International d'Unités*. This abbreviation is used worldwide, regardless of language, to indicate the International System of Units.

Spacing between a number and the unit of measurement is required for most measurements. A dimension "534mm" is incorrect, since there is no space; the correct dimension is "534 mm." The only exception to this rule is the symbol for "degrees" in angle and temperature measurements. For example, a 30-degree angle is denoted with "30°," and not "30 °." Correct labeling of temperature measurements is "15°C" and "3 to 15°C" or "3°C to 15°C." Such temperature designations as "15° C" and "3° to 15°C" are incorrect. A last rule to remember is to place a zero before the decimal point in all numbers less than 1 and greater than -1. The reason is to prevent missing a faint decimal point. Examples are "0.98," "0.32," "-0.01," and "0.75."

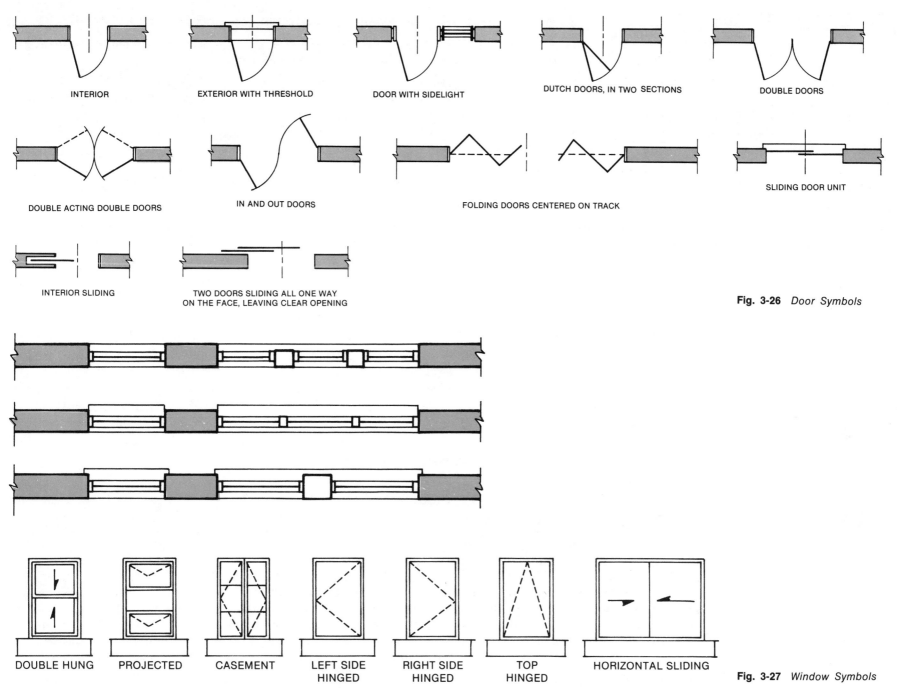

INTERIOR

EXTERIOR WITH THRESHOLD

DOOR WITH SIDELIGHT

DUTCH DOORS, IN TWO SECTIONS

DOUBLE DOORS

DOUBLE ACTING DOUBLE DOORS

IN AND OUT DOORS

FOLDING DOORS CENTERED ON TRACK

SLIDING DOOR UNIT

INTERIOR SLIDING

TWO DOORS SLIDING ALL ONE WAY
ON THE FACE, LEAVING CLEAR OPENING

Fig. 3-26 *Door Symbols*

DOUBLE HUNG   PROJECTED   CASEMENT   LEFT SIDE HINGED   RIGHT SIDE HINGED   TOP HINGED   HORIZONTAL SLIDING

Fig. 3-27 *Window Symbols*

INSTRUMENTS, MATERIALS, AND TECHNIQUES OF ARCHITECTURAL DRAFTERS   **35**

Fig. 3-28 *Other Commonly Used Architectural Symbols*

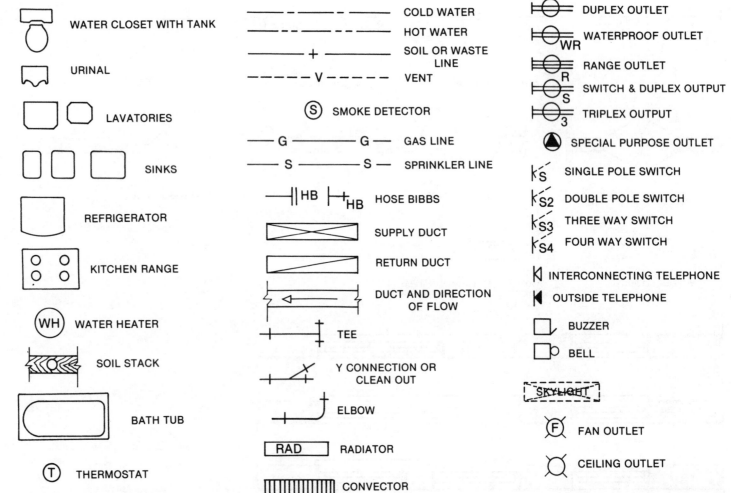

WATER CLOSET WITH TANK	
URINAL	
LAVATORIES	
SINKS	
REFRIGERATOR	
KITCHEN RANGE	
WATER HEATER	
SOIL STACK	
BATH TUB	
THERMOSTAT	

COLD WATER
HOT WATER
SOIL OR WASTE LINE
VENT
SMOKE DETECTOR
GAS LINE
SPRINKLER LINE
HOSE BIBBS
SUPPLY DUCT
RETURN DUCT
DUCT AND DIRECTION OF FLOW
TEE
Y CONNECTION OR CLEAN OUT
ELBOW
RADIATOR
CONVECTOR

DUPLEX OUTLET
WATERPROOF OUTLET
RANGE OUTLET
SWITCH & DUPLEX OUTPUT
TRIPLEX OUTPUT
SPECIAL PURPOSE OUTLET
SINGLE POLE SWITCH
DOUBLE POLE SWITCH
THREE WAY SWITCH
FOUR WAY SWITCH
INTERCONNECTING TELEPHONE
OUTSIDE TELEPHONE
BUZZER
BELL
SKYLIGHT
FAN OUTLET
CEILING OUTLET

PREFERRED UNITS OF DIMENSIONS

In the English system, there are 12 inches in a foot, 3 feet in a yard, 5280 feet in mile. These multiples can be awkward. (How many inches are there in a mile, for example?) SI terms are base units and their multiples and submultiples of 10. That is, prefixes tell how many times to multiply the base unit by 10. The SI units used in architectural drafting are given in Table 3-6. Note that the *meter* is the base unit of length.

Length in architectural plans should be specified in meters (m) or millimeters (mm). Millimeters are preferred. In site and block plans where exceptionally long distances must be expressed, the kilometer (km) may be used. It is recommended that drafters *not* use the centimeter (cm), hectometer (hm), decimeter (dm), or dekameter (dam). SI has adopted these preferred units of dimensioning for three major reasons. It is easier to work with multiples and submultiples that are related to the meter by a factor of 1000. Using

Table 3-6 SI Units of Length and Distance Used in Architectural Drafting

Unit		Symbol
Millimeter	(= 0.001 meter)	mm
Meter	(= 1000 millimeters)	m
Kilometer	(= 1000 meters)	km

only the meter and millimeter, the drafter need not place the symbol after all dimensions. The use of dimensional units other than meter and millimeter can cause many problems in interpreting and checking the drawing. Until all drawings are completely converted to SI, the following note should be included on all drawings: "All dimensions are in millimeters."

Expressing area or volume, especially for an entire building or structure, involves very large numbers. A house with overall dimensions of 11 500 mm × 7200 mm, for instance, has an area of 82 800 000 mm². To eliminate difficulties with such large numbers, use scientific notation. The above area can be expressed as 8.28×10^7 mm². For individual rooms and smaller spaces, it is acceptable to give areas to the nearest tenth of a square meter (0.1 m²). Table 3-7 presents the preferred multiples and submultiples recommended for scientific notation.

DRAFTING PRACTICES

Two concerns in SI drafting practice are the size of the drawing surface and the scales used. Other than the rules and practices specially discussed in this section, most SI procedures are the same as those traditionally used.

Paper sizes in SI are based upon a hard and not a soft conversion. That is, metric paper sizes are not the standard sizes traditionally used in the drafting field. The SI paper-size system is based upon an "A" series. The largest size is AO, which has an area of 1 m² (841 mm × 1189 mm). The next smaller size has half that area, about 0.5 m² (594 mm × 841 mm), the

next size has an area of 0.25 m², and so on. Table 3-8 lists SI paper sizes.

Scaling is indicated in metric drawings with a *ratio* system rather than the *equal* system traditionally used (e.g., Scale ¼" = 1'-0"). Common metric scales used range from 1:1 (full size) to 1:2000 (one two-thousandths of actual size). Scale selection depends upon the type of drawing. Table 3-9 summarizes common architectural scales.

Table 3-7 Scientific Notation

Conventional	Scientific Notation
Multiples	
1 000 000 000 000 000 000 000	10^{21}
1 000 000 000 000 000 000	10^{18}
1 000 000 000 000 000	10^{15}
1 000 000 000 000	10^{12}
1 000 000 000	10^{9}
1 000 000	10^{6}
1 000	10^{3}
1	1
Submultiples	
0.001	10^{-3}
0.000 001	10^{-6}
0.000 000 001	10^{-9}
0.000 000 000 001	10^{-12}
0.000 000 000 000 001	10^{-15}
0.000 000 000 000 000 001	10^{-18}
0.000 000 000 000 000 000 001	10^{-21}

Table 3-8 SI Paper Sizes

Size Designation	Dimensions in Millimeters
AO	841 × 1189
A1	594 × 841
A2	420 × 594
A3	297 × 420
A4	210 × 297
A5	148 × 210
A6	105 × 148
A7	74 × 105
A8	52 × 74
A9	37 × 52
A10	26 × 37

Table 3-9 SI Architectural Drawing Scales

Recommended SI Scale	Type of Drawing	Traditional Scale (with Ratios)
1:2000	Block Plans	1″ = 200′-0″ (1:2400)
1:1000		1″ = 100′-0″ (1:1200)
1:500		1″ = 40′-0″ (1:480)
1:500	Site Plans	1″ = 40′-0″ (1:480)
1:200		1/16″ = 1′-0″ (1:192)
1:200	General Plans and	1/16″ = 1′-0″ (1:192)
1:100	Location Drawings	1/8″ = 1′-0″ (1:96)
1:50		1/4″ = 1′-0″ (1:48)
1:50	Location and	1/4″ = 1′-0″ (1:48)
1:20	Assembly Drawings	1/2″ = 1′-0″ (1:24)
1:20	Detail Drawings	1/2″ = 1′-0″ (1:24)
1:10		1″ = 1′-0″ (1:12)
1:5		3″ = 1′-0″ (1:4)
1:1		Full size (1:1)

When the appropriate scale is selected, the information should be noted either on the drawing panel or on the drawing surface itself. Where two or more scales are used on the same sheet, each should be clearly noted under the drawing it is used for. If a drawing is not drawn to scale, it should be noted as "Scale: Not to scale" or "NTS." In some cases, it is helpful to graphically present the scale being used, as shown in Figure 3-29, along with a standard scale statement.

scale 1:500.

SUMMARY

Much of the success of architectural drafters depends upon their instruments, materials, and techniques. A wide variety of drafting equipment and instruments is available to drafters, and care should be taken to select the right tools for the right job. Ar-

chitectural drafters must make sure that they buy the appropriate drafting instruments and equipment for their type of work. Among the most important equipment and instruments are drawing boards and tables; T-squares, parallels, and drafting machines; triangles and curves; a variety of templates; architectural, civil engineering, and metric scales; and individual or case instruments.

Drafters must also take care in selecting materials for drawing architectural plans and presentations. Drawings are usually prepared on vellum or tracing paper, but they can also be produced on polyester films and cloth—all are available in individual sheets and in rolls. Traditionally, drafters drew with pencils and mechanical lead holders. Within recent years, however, stick-lead holders have become more popular. Their primary advantage is the elimination of sharpening, since leads come in standard diameters of 0.3 mm, 0.5 mm, and 0.7 mm. Transfer overlays are also available for complex figures, diagrams, or illustrations, so that these need not be drawn over and over again.

Architectural lettering usually takes on the character of the individual drafter. All good lettering has the qualities of clarity and legibility. Line weights are important, since each line conveys a certain message; students and beginning drafters must become competent at drawing the appropriate weights for given lines. Typical lines are break, center, cut or section, dimension, extension, hidden, leader, object, poché or texture, and section lines, as well as outlines.

The AIA has a system of abbreviations and symbols. Abbreviations are used where it would be cumbersome to write out a word many times; symbols indicate the types of materials and hardware used.

The use of the SI system is becoming increasingly important to architecture. The United States is committed to convert its traditional system of weights and measures to metrics. This is happening through a two-stage process—soft then hard conversion. The notation of metric dimensions and the presentation of exceptionally large and small numbers have all been

Fig. 3-29 *Graphical Scale*

standardized in the SI system. Metric drawings should have ratio scales with dimensions given in millimeters (mm), meters (m), or in a few cases kilometers (km).

REVIEW QUESTIONS

1. When is it better to use a drawing board? A drafting board?
2. Which of the following are used most often?

   a. T-squares
   b. Parallels
   c. Drafting machines
   d. They are equally used.

3. What are the three most common types of triangles?
4. What type of templates are most used?
5. Name the three types of scales used.
6. What is the advantage of individual instruments over sets of instruments?
7. What drawing medium is most frequently used?
8. Give the advantages of stick-lead holders over pencils and mechanical holders.
9. When should transfer overlays be used?
10. What are the characteristics of good architectural lettering?
11. What line weights are typically used for the following line expressions?

Center lines	Hidden lines
Broken lines	Outlines
Cut lines	Leader lines
Poché lines	Dimension lines

12. What does *AIA* stand for?
13. What does *SI* stand for?

14. Place an *X* by the metric notations that are incorrect.

1,233 m	.73 m
22.22mm	$9.7 \times 10^4 m^2$
15° C	0.7 mm

15. In the metric paper-size series, what is the area of the largest size?

EXERCISES

1. Using one of the styles of archtectural lettering shown, letter the alphabet in uppercase letters, including the numbering from 1 to 10, at standard heights of ⅛'', ¼'' and ½''. Repeat the exercise at least five times, until you feel comfortable using this lettering style.
2. Based on the examples in this chapter, make at least twenty samples of AIA symbols for commonly used building materials.
3. Using appropriate line weights, make samples of each of the following lines:

Center lines	Leader lines
Break lines	Poché lines
Cut lines	Section lines
Hidden lines	Object lines
Dimension and Extension lines	

4. Convert the following measurements to millimeters:

   ³/₁₆'', ⅛'', ¼'', ½'', 1'', 2'', 4'-3'', 26'-7½'', and 46'-11''.

5. Identify which metric ratio scale should be used to convert the following traditional scales:

¼'' = 1'-0''	½'' = 1'-0''	1'' = 40'-0''
⅛'' = 1'-0''	1'' = 1'-0''	1'' = 100'-0''
¹/₁₆'' = 1'-0''	Full size	1'' = 200'-0''

4

THE WORK PLACE AND ARCHITECTURAL DRAFTERS

GLOSSARY

Contract drafter a drafter who works on a sub-contract basis for various firms
Employee hierarchy the set of levels or jobs through which employees advance in a firm
Sub-contract a job conducted outside the firm responsible for an entire project

Architectural drafters will most likely be hired by a small architectural firm. It has been found that almost eighty percent of all architectural firms employ fewer than ten staff workers, (e.g., drafters, secretaries, bookkeepers, architects) and ninety-five percent have fewer than twenty-five.

It may appear that there is a shortage of positions, but this is not the case. True, there are few large firms, but the number of small ones continues to grow. The ratio of support personnel, including drafters, to registered architects is more than two to one.

Employee hierarchies and responsibilities, working conditions and equipment, and standard operating procedures and policies depend not only on the size of the firm, but also on the personality and philosophy of the head architects. Self-employed architectural drafters have a completely different work environment from those in a firm. Because of the differences in these situations, we will discuss each separately.

LARGE FIRMS

It is difficult to say exactly what number of employees makes a firm "large." For our purposes, a large firm is considered to be one that employs ten or more support personnel—junior architects, drafters, secretaries, etc. Of these support personnel, the majority will be drafters or have drafting responsibilities.

EMPLOYEE HIERARCHY AND RESPONSIBILITIES

Large firms typically require beginning drafters to start at the bottom. Movement up can be as fast as the drafter can acquire experience and demonstrate his or her technical competence.

Beginning drafters first work as assistants to the head drafter or designer, until they become comfortable with and competent at their responsibilities. By working under an experienced drafter, the novice learns about new procedures, detailing, and sources of information. Drafters hired with experience and demonstrated ability are required to handle a full load after a brief orientation period.

Architectural drafters with two or more years of relevant work experience can expect to be given full drafting responsibilities soon, including design interpretation and preparation of working drawings. They are expected to work closely with the head architect, project supervisor, other technical personnel, research staff, and the client.

WORKING CONDITIONS

Architectural offices should always be well lighted, and the environment should be conducive to productivity. When selecting an office, architects try to keep in mind the major functions performed by their staff. Briefly, these functions are

Administrative functions: interoffice communications, project discussions, contract review and formulation, proposal presentations and clerical procedures—performed in reception and waiting areas, individual and small group offices, conference rooms, and secretarial areas

Production functions: preparation of working drawings and renderings, model making, copying and print making, developing specifications, and listing hardware and components—conducted in drafting rooms, model-making areas, libraries and reference rooms, special viewing areas, and reproduction areas.

Storage functions: contract copies, bookkeeping records, drawings, microfilm of drawings, models, and other elements of completed projects—filed away in vaults or cabinets

Staff-servicing functions, in rooms such as lounges, lavatories, and snack areas

AIA guidelines recommend that offices have about 150 square feet of space per employee to adequately handle the major architectural functions. Using this formula, a firm employing 10 staff members, plus the head architect, requires approximately 1650 square feet of office space. It is not uncommon, however, to find architectural offices above or below this guideline.

The type of equipment in a large firm depends on the type of work (renovations, structural, commercial, industrial, etc.) frequently contracted. Examples of this equipment are print machines, drafting tools and equipment, photographic and duplication equipment, charts, calculators and minicomputers, airbrushes, workbench and tools for model building, lettering devices, drawing desks, and reference files. This list is not exhaustive.

STANDARD OPERATING PROCEDURES AND POLICIES

The new drafter's first job is to learn the overall and specific practices of the firm. Major procedures are covered in the standards manual, which varies from firm to firm. In larger firms, as policies change, memos are distributed to each employee. In smaller, less formal settings, drafters must ask experienced workers specific questions about procedures as they get their on-the-job experience.

When a job comes into the office, the architect prepares the preliminary sketches. These are then turned over to the head drafter, who together with the staff determines construction specifications. Technical data are then collected and tabulated on checklists. The preliminary specification list is normally developed closely with the client.

Drafters begin work on the complete set of working drawings. The head drafter frequently checks them for design and construction specifications, making comments and changes as needed. Other information vital to the project is passed along to the drafters via memos or staff and team conferences.

In a large firm the architectural drafters usually work in specialized areas of the office. These might include sections where schematics are prepared, designs are developed, working drawings are finalized, or architectural models are constructed. Other specialized areas might be for electrical, mechanical, and structural aspects of projects.

SMALL FIRMS

Small firms have from one to ten support personnel, besides the architect. The architect may hire newly graduated architects as drafters; this gives them the experience required for their licensing exam. Whether a new architect or a drafter is hired depends upon the philosophy of the firm and the technical expertise required of the position.

EMPLOYEE HIERARCHY AND RESPONSIBILITIES

The hierarchy of the small firm is basically the same as that in larger firms, though there are probably fewer ranks. Again, the degree and type of responsibilities of the drafter depend upon training and experience. Newly employed drafters, however, receive assistance and information from the head drafter or even directly from the architect.

Drafters with less than two years of experience often have a wide range of duties, from running prints and filing to drawing simple details and making plan revisions. Generally, drafters in smaller firms spend less time learning office routines and practices and are required to carry a full load sooner. Drafters in small firms are more generalists than specialists, since they are required to complete a wider variety of jobs and are not usually assigned to any particular area of operation. Small-firm drafters can expect to have more opportunities in drawing, model making, client contact, and job supervision than those in large firms.

WORKING CONDITIONS

The type of work environment varies more in a small firm. Drafters are not only expected to draw, they are also expected to help the architect in the field. Field work includes such functions as land surveying, site inspection and layout, construction-site inspection, specification checks, and client interviews.

The type of equipment in small firms is more limited in scope. It is suited to the specific type of work the firm does. These firms tend to subcontract specialty items (e.g., model making, special renderings, structural plans) to other specialized firms. Thus, drafters need to know how to work with common drafting tools and equipment and also with electronic calculators, lettering devices, print machines, and various drafting aids.

STANDARD OPERATING PROCEDURES AND POLICIES

Small firms are less formal about office practices than large ones. Company standards manuals are the exception rather than the rule. A policy or procedure change is usually passed along by word of mouth rather than by a written memo. If drafters have questions or problems, it is normally easier to go directly to the head architect, because of the shorter chain of command and the proximity of all staff members. Drafters should expect to start producing drawings earlier. They are also expected to function within the firm's guidelines much sooner.

When the small firm accepts a contract, the architect prepares the schematic and preliminary sketches and holds a conference with support personnel. Together, they work out the construction specifications and develop a preliminary data checklist. The drafter may or may not be involved with the client in determining final construction specifications.

When the preparation of drawings begins, the drafter may be given complete responsibility for developing the first set of working drawings. On the other hand, the architect may do this, depending on the organizational philosophy of the firm and the number of contracts then under way. If the firm is quite busy, the architect usually assigns a larger proportion of the job to the drafter.

When the first set of drawings is completed, the architect, in conjunction with the support staff, reviews, comments on, and recommends changes in the drawings. When the architect is satisfied, the client reviews the project. If further changes are needed, the architect assigns this duty to the drafter. When construction starts, the drafter may go alone or with the architect to make sure that all architectural and structural specifications are being followed.

SELF-EMPLOYED ARCHITECTURAL DRAFTERS

Self-employed or contract architectural drafters are in a much different situation. These people are not beginning drafters but experienced technicians with specialized skills. Most of these drafters have a wide range of experience in architectural drawing and designing with licensed architects. It should be kept in mind that self-employed drafters are not licensed architects. On the contrary, these drafters offer their special talents to architectural firms on a contract basis.

SECURING CONTRACTS

Drafters who decide to go it alone are in a less secure position than drafters who work for a firm. They are not guaranteed a paycheck. They must go out and secure contracts and negotiate fees with architectural and construction firms. Independent contract drafters are frequently those with special talent for rendering techniques and producing high-quality drawings efficiently. They must have demonstrable drafting skills, or a firm will not offer them a contract.

Independent drafters find it necessary to specialize in certain types of drawings and preparations, because standard drawings are prepared within the firm itself. For example some drafters contract only for special-purpose pictoral drawings, interior drawings, or technical illustrations and renderings. Others take a slightly different path, specializing in model building or field surveying.

Drafters use several methods of securing contracts. These vary from advertisement to word of mouth, but the most effective is personal association with architects and contractors. For this reason, experience and knowledge of the market place are essential for survival.

In a few instances, drafters contract with customers to design and prepare working drawings for a structure. The drafter, however, is frequently limited by law to designing and preparing drawings for residential structures no larger than three-family dwellings. Even then, sometimes these designs and drawings must be reviewed and approved by a licensed architect. This practice is dictated by the laws set up in each state to assure that minimum building standards are met.

PROCEDURES AND POLICIES UNDER CONTRACT

The contract drafter assumes more responsibility than any other architectural drafter. He or she is required to work with the client, make various design and material decisions, and be responsible for all quality control. In some situations, the contract may require the drafter to make site visitations and even supervise certain aspects of construction.

Contract drafters typically meet with prospective clients, secure notes and make sketches of the client's designs, work with architects in land surveying and interpreting design schematics, prepare working drawings and details, write specifications, prepare material take-offs for the proposed project, inspect construction and act as liason between the client and contractor. The procedures, such as how drawings are prepared, noted, dimensioned, and presented, vary from contract to contract, for they must meet the requirements of the client and the local building codes.

WORKING CONDITIONS

Contract drafters work out of either small offices, with secretarial help, or their home. In both cases, the primary concern is an environment where they can be as productive and efficient as possible. Since they are paid by the job rather than by the hour, the faster they can produce a high-quality product, the more profit they will make.

Most equipment is their own. Both the proper use of the equipment and its proper care and maintenance are important. Typical tools and materials owned by self-employed drafters, besides the basics, are reference manuals, local building and housing codes, zoning requirements, plumbing and electrical charts, and print machines.

starting position in the hierarchy depends on the drafter's education and experience. Drafters hired in a new position must learn the standard operating procedures and policies of the company and then be able to implement them. Drafters with more experience will be expected to learn company policies and practices faster than beginners. They also must produce work and assume a responsible position more quickly.

The working conditions of architectural drafters may include areas set aside for client contact, production activities, administrative duties, drawing storage, and staff servicing. Self-employed drafters, on the other hand, work out of their homes or small offices.

SUMMARY

Beginning drafters should expect to work for a small firm, since only five percent of the architectural firms in the United States have more than twenty-five support personnel. Self-employed drafters should have several years of experience with a firm. After several years of developing skills and building a positive reputation, they may then begin on their own.

Both large and small firms usually require drafters to start at the bottom and work their way up. The

REVIEW QUESTIONS

1. Compare the working situations of drafters in large and small architectural firms.
2. What is meant by an *employee hierarchy?*
3. Describe the career path of a person who begins as a tracer in an architectural firm and works up to the position of chief drafter. Do the same for a person who becomes a model builder.
4. Explain what is meant by *standard operating procedures and policies.*
5. Describe some of the procedures the self-employed drafter might use to secure drawing contracts.

GLOSSARY

Alluvium clay, silt, gravel, or similar material deposited by running water

Aquifer a stratum of permeable rock or gravel holding water

Canopy the uppermost part of a forest

Commercial structure any building intended for the purpose of carrying out a business or service

Compaction the degree to which material, such as earth, is packed together firmly

Contours lines showing the topographical outlines of hills, valleys, and other physical characteristics of land

Hydrology the study of the properties and characteristics of water on the land, in soils, and in rocks

Glacial till clay, silt, gravel, or similar material deposited by glacial movement

Migration movement from one location to another

pH measurement of the degree of acidity or alkalinity of materials

Physiography the study of the physical characteristics of land

Promontory a high point of land or rock

Residential structure any building used for living purposes

Setback the minimum legal distance from a property line or street a building can be built

Silt sedimentary material less than 0.05 mm in size; soil containing eighty percent silt and twelve percent or less clay

Site plans drawings that show the relationship between the project and the natural features of the property on which it is to be located

Spatial determinants factors, such as distances, location, and shape, that affect the design of a project

Topography the graphical illustration of land contours on maps, charts, and topographic drawings

PLANNING FOR BUILDING STRUCTURE AND ROOMS

A variety of basic structures can meet the residential or commercial needs of a client. Room specifications, on the other hand, are determined by type of usage (e.g., recreation, work, sleep) and the expected type of traffic, but they are not governed by specific design parameters. For these reasons, planning for building structures and room specifications varies from one residence to another and from one commercial building to another. No single design is applicable to all situations, for just as people are individuals, so are the uses and applications of buildings.

Residential buildings provide living space for a person, a family unit, or a group of family units. Residential structures are built to accommodate three major activities: cooking and eating; sleeping, resting, and personal hygiene; and recreation and work. See Fig. 5-1. The number and size of the rooms for these activities depend upon cost, available floor space, and the requirements of the client. Examples of typical rooms for each activity in residential structures are given in Table 5-1.

Commercial buildings are used to conduct business activities; this does not preclude their conversion to other uses. Typical activities are production and service of goods and products, sales and marketing, and providing health and counseling services to people. There are almost as many types of commercial structures as there are industrial and business concerns. These buildings range from large, heavy commercial structures used in the manufacture of durable goods to smaller and lighter structures housing small banks

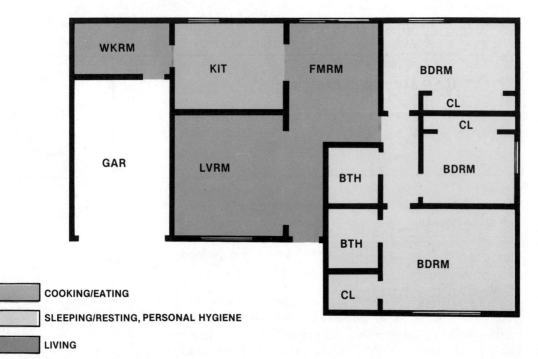

COOKING/EATING

SLEEPING/RESTING, PERSONAL HYGIENE

LIVING

Fig. 5-1 *Major Activity Areas for a Simple Residential Structure*

Table 5-1   Rooms Identified for Residential Activities

Activities	Rooms
Cooking and Eating	Kitchen Breakfast Room Dining Room
Sleeping, Cleaning, and Personal Relief	Bedroom Guest Room Bathroom Powder Room
Living	Living Room Family/Recreation Room Study/Library Utility Room Workshop/Sewing Room

Table 5-2   Rooms and Areas Identified for Commercial Activities

Activities	Room or Area
Work	Customer Service Area Production Area Diagnostic Room Clinical Area Sales Area Design/Construction/Assembly Area
Material Handling and Storage	Stock Room Tool Room Raw and Finished Goods Storage Area Conveyor and Material Movement Area
Rest and Comfort	Restrooms/Lavatories Locker Room Wash and Shower Room Cafeteria Lounge Area Safety Area

and retail outlets. There is no simple, clear-cut distinction, however. As with residential buildings, commercial structures are designed around three major activity areas. See Fig. 5-2. These are based upon the functions of a concern: work; material handling and storage; and rest and comfort areas. Table 5-2 gives examples of rooms or areas that accommodate commercial activities.

BASIC STRUCTURES

The vast array of designs for residential and commercial buildings are all based on a few basic structures. With combinations of these structures and use of various roof lines and exterior and interior arrangements, the possibilities in the design, appearance, and functions of buildings are almost unlimited.

RESIDENTIAL STRUCTURES

There is great variety in residential structures. Five basic structures are used in planning for residential buildings. These are *one-story, one-and-a-half story, two-story, split-level,* and *multiple-story.*

One-Story Structures are popular. See Fig. 5-3. The one-story or single-floor-plan structure is especially good for families whose members have difficulty climbing stairs (e.g., the handicapped and the aged) and for those with young children, who might fall down stairs or off ledges, balconies, or porches.

A single-floor plan can be built on a concrete slab, over a crawl space or piers, or with partial or full basements. This design requires more square feet of foundation material per unit of living space than a multiple-story structure. The result is higher cost per square unit. Further, single-floor plans also require more land than multiple-story plans, since the floor space is spread out.

One-and-One-Half-Story Structures provide two levels of activity area, with most of the living space on the first level. See Fig. 5-4. The second level is often built as a recreational room, a bonus room, or an unfinished room. The major advantages of this floor plan over the single-floor plan are the reduced cost per unit of living space and the smaller amount of land needed. Note that the addition of more living space per foundation area is not a one-to-one saving. Some living space is lost to the stairway area.

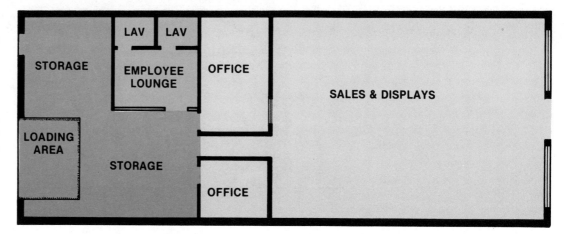

	WORK
	MATERIALS HANDLING AND STORAGE
	REST/COMFORT

Fig. 5-2 *Major Activity Areas for a Small Commercial Building*

Two-Story Structures provide two full levels of living space. See Fig. 5-5. The second floor usually has the same area as the first. This is generally considered the most economical design for a single-family residence. Furthermore, this structure requires less land than most others.

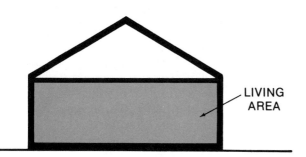

LIVING AREA

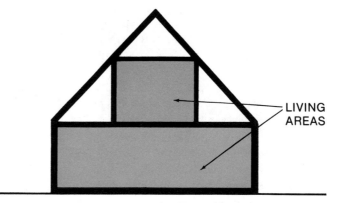

LIVING AREAS

Fig. 5-3 *One-Story Residential Structure*

Fig. 5-4 *One-and-One-Half Story Residential Structure*

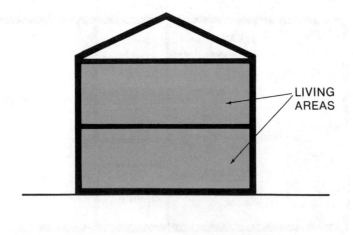

Fig. 5-5 *Two-Story Residential Structure*

LIVING AREAS

In two-story and other multiple-story structures, the traffic flow from one level to another must be considered. Stairs must be carefully planned and properly placed. The width and type of construction is often determined by building codes. Their location plays an important part in the use of rooms.

Split-Level Structures have one advantage over the previously mentioned buildings. They provide three levels of living area in a two-story structure. Most split-level houses have a staggered floor plan, with the second *level* between the first and second *floors*, but off to the side. Since this design requires more foundation area per living space, it is usually the most expensive design in residential planning. See Fig. 5-6. The main advantage is that each level is separate from the others, distinctly defining the activity areas of the house.

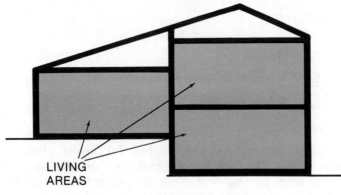

Fig. 5-6 *Split-Level Residential Structure*

LIVING AREAS

Multiple-Story Structures (those with three or more stories) are normally used for multiple residences. In dense population areas, however, these buildings may provide living space for a single family, with about the same total square footage as other single-resident structures. Multiple-story buildings are good where the amount of land to build on is limited or where a high concentration of families is desirable. As the number of floors increases, the cost of foundation construction and materials also goes up because of the greater support needed. These structures provide many residential units on a small area. Where land is limited and therefore expensive, these structures may be most economical, because the high cost of construction is offset by the saving in the cost of the lot.

COMMERCIAL STRUCTURES

Like residential structures, commercial buildings are constructed of various materials and designed with various concepts in mind. Three basic structures form the basis for most commercial building considerations: *one-story, two-story,* and *multiple-story build-*

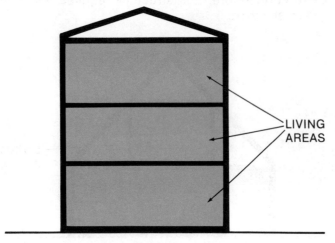

Fig. 5-7 *Multiple-Story Residential Structure*

LIVING AREAS

ings. Table 5-3 gives examples of commercial concerns typically associated with each basic type.

Table 5-3 Basic Commercial Structures

Basic Structure	Examples of Use
One-Story	Grocery stores Service stations Small retail stores Banks Insurance offices Manufacturing companies
Two-Story	Medical clinics Clothing stores Small business offices
Multiple-Story	Corporate headquarters Office buildings Hotels Department stores

One-Story Structures are used for businesses concerned with the movement of large quantities of goods, the use of heavy equipment and materials, or the even flow of materials or people. The size of the business can also dictate the basic structure to be used—the smaller the commercial venture, the smaller the commercial structure. See Fig. 5-8.

It is possible for companies with heavy equipment and materials to locate all their operations in two- or multiple-story buildings. In most cases, however, this is not only too cumbersome, but also too expensive. The additional supports and heavier construction needed to hold the weight of equipment and materials on the upper levels of the building means extra expense. Single-floor-plan buildings are also more economical in situations that require considerable movement of material and personnel, since product movement is usually faster and cheaper on a horizontal system without elevators or conveyors than on a vertical system.

Fig. 5-8 *Single-Story Commercial Structure*

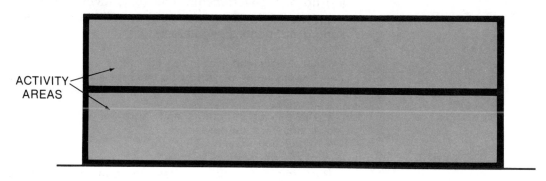

Fig. 5-9 *Two-Story Commercial Structure*

Two-Story Structures are used where activities do not involve heavy equipment and goods. See Fig. 5-9. Like residential buildings, two-story commercial structures are less expensive per square foot, because of the relatively small amount of foundation required. The two-story structure is typically used in office and retail concerns where activity is stationary or so light that it is not inhibited by two levels. The second floor is often used for office functions, stock storage, and lounge or rest areas.

Multiple-Story Structures are most appropriate for complex office and light retailing activities. See Fig. 5-10. Multiple-story buildings are used where work activities are departmentalized, or independent of one another. This is most often true of large department stores.

Fig. 5-10 *Multiple-Story Commercial Structure*

PLANNING FOR BUILDING SITES

Most incorporated municipalities have legal specifications that bind architects to site selections that are appropriate for a particular type of structure. These specifications, called *zoning regulations* or *ordinances,* are used to control the growth and pattern of community development.

Zoning may be described as the division or breaking up of a governmental unit (city, town, county, village, etc.) into areas or districts. Within each area, zoning ordinances regulate:

1. the height and area of all structures
2. the minimum lot size to be used for a particular structure, with the amount of open, unused spaces to be provided
3. the use of structures and lands for residential and commercial purposes
4. population density

Planning for building sites not only must include reviewing and meeting legal requirements, but should also account for the characteristics of the proposed site. To determine whether a particular site is acceptable, a site inventory and resource analysis are often conducted. Nine factors must be accounted for when conducting an inventory and analysis:

1. soils
2. vegetation
3. hydrology
4. climate
5. topography
6. aesthetics
7. historical significance
8. existing land use
9. physiographic obstructions

Without this information, architects and planners cannot accurately and appropriately identify optimum building-site locations. See Table 5-4 for examples of each of the nine factors.

Most of the information collected on the location of community resources is presented on data maps. See

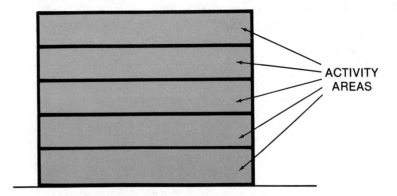

Fig. 5-11. Data maps are drawn to various scales; the most common is 1:24 000. Separate maps are drawn to show the location of specific resources and are then superimposed on one another for final analysis. In combination, the complete data map helps the architectural team decide on the site location.

SITE CONSIDERATIONS

Once the legal requirements have been reviewed, the site inventory conducted, and the natural-resources analysis made, the architectural team is ready to compare the advantages and disadvantages of each site. The optimum site—where the building can best become a complementary integral part of its surroundings—is chosen with three conditions in mind, in relationship to the inventory and analysis. These conditions are *lot size and contour, excavation,* and *external environment.*

Lot Size and Contour The lot must be large enough for the building to be constructed. Some lots may be better for a single-floor plan than others. Others may be too small or have a greater setback requirement, which would all but eliminate a one-story building. If the lot is too small, the building will look crowded and oversized. On the other hand, if the lot is too large, the building may appear to be lost and overpowered by its surroundings.

Table 5-4 Site Inventory and Resource Analysis Examples and Considerations

Factors	Examples	Considerations	Factors	Examples	Considerations
Soils	Glacial till (shallow water table; deep, well-drained; deep but pan; shallow bedrock, shallow water) Stratified drift (deep, well-drained; shallow water table) Flood-plain alluvium Muck Peat Rock outcroppings	Depth of horizon Depth to seasonal high water Depth to bedrock Drainage characteristics Suitability for septic tanks, excavation, grading, and various foundation designs Susceptibility to compaction Susceptibility to erosion pH rating (alkaline or acidic) Soil fertility	Hydrology	First-, second-, or third-order streams River Pond Lake Reservoir Drainage basin and watershed Springs Pumping wells Artesian wells	Runoff rates Siltation Oxygen content Subsurface water characteristics
Climate	Monthly and annual average temperature ranges and extremes Monthly and annual average precipitation Intensity and duration of winds Season and frequency of damaging storms Monthly and annual average snowfalls Killing frost dates Growing season Sun angles	Temperature Precipitation Wind Snowfall National Weather Service	Topography	Elevation above sea level Topographic orientation (flat, east to west, north to northeast, west to east) Topographic slope (indicated in terms of percentage of slope)	On-site inspections U.S. Geological Survey U.S. Corps of Engineers
			Aesthetics	Spatial determinants Promontory Scenic vista Tree and vegetation cover Water images	Three-dimensional land forms Landmarks and points of reference Visual panorama Open expanse view Surface water areas
Vegetation	No vegetation Scrub growth Streamside vegetation Pondside vegetation Wetlands vegetation growth (brush, tree, bog) White pine Oaks and other mixed hardwoods Spruce and fir	Density of canopy Understory heights Overstory heights	Physiographic	Major and minor fault zones 10-, 50-, and 100-year flood plains Migration routes Tornado and hurricane paths Quicksand Peat bogs Poisonous snakes Mosquito breeding areas Poison ivy and oak	Fault zones Flood plains Critical wildlife habitat areas Aquifer recharge Storm damage zones Topography Wildlife and wild lands

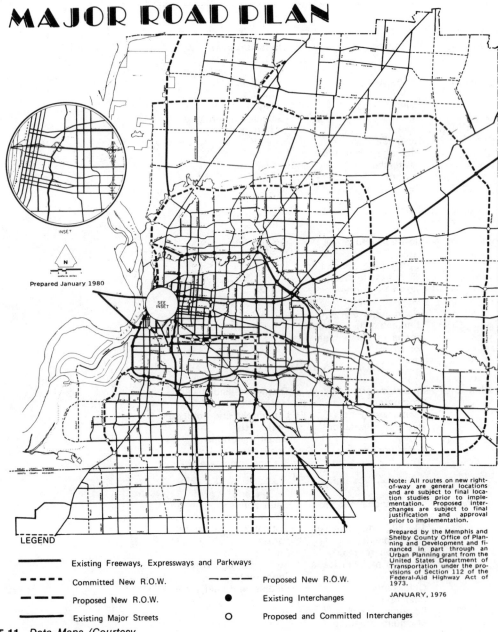

MAJOR ROAD PLAN

INSET

N

Prepared January 1980

Note: All routes on new right-of-way are general locations and are subject to final location studies prior to implementation. Proposed interchanges are subject to final justification and approval prior to implementation.

Prepared by the Memphis and Shelby County Office of Planning and Development and financed in part through an Urban Planning grant from the United States Department of Transportation under the provisions of Section 112 of the Federal-Aid Highway Act of 1973.

JANUARY, 1976

LEGEND

—————— Existing Freeways, Expressways and Parkways

– – – – – Committed New R.O.W.   — — — Proposed New R.O.W.

– – – – Proposed New R.O.W.   ● Existing Interchanges

—————— Existing Major Streets   ○ Proposed and Committed Interchanges

Fig. 5-11 *Data Maps (Courtesy of Memphis and Shelby County Office of Planning and Development)*

Along with lot size, designers must consider the contours of the lot and surrounding area. See Fig.

5-12. If the slope is too great, the building design may require change or not be acceptable at all for the location. The same may be true if the contour is very flat. In either case, excavation is then considered. Other considerations include utility easements, property lines, roads and right-of-ways, and screening requirements.

Excavation Excessive excavation should be avoided whenever possible, for two major reasons—cost and protection of the natural environment. The process of leveling, filling, and grading development sites is extremely expensive. It can double or triple the cost of a project. Furthermore, good design always tries to use the environment to enhance the design of buildings and the quality of life for its residents. The natural setting should not be destroyed for the convenience of the developer or contractor. In nearly all cases, excessive excavation can be avoided if the proper type structure is built on the site. See Fig. 5-13.

External Environment The direction the building faces and its location on a lot can dramatically affect its occupants' comfort. The direction a building faces determines how much useable sunlight it receives. This affects the amount of insulation and other protection needed. It is obvious that, in the northern hemisphere, windows on the south side of the building will allow more sunlight to enter than windows on the north side. See Fig. 5-14.

The southern exposure of a house should include the living and high-activity areas. In a commercial building, the south side should be where the majority of business is conducted. The southern exposure permits efficient use of solar energy for heat and light, an important practical and pleasing esthetic consideration.

Buildings in the southern hemisphere, on the other hand, should be built with windows on the northern exposure.

Seasonal prevailing winds can be used to control interior temperatures of buildings. In moderate cli-

NON-ATTAINMENT AREA

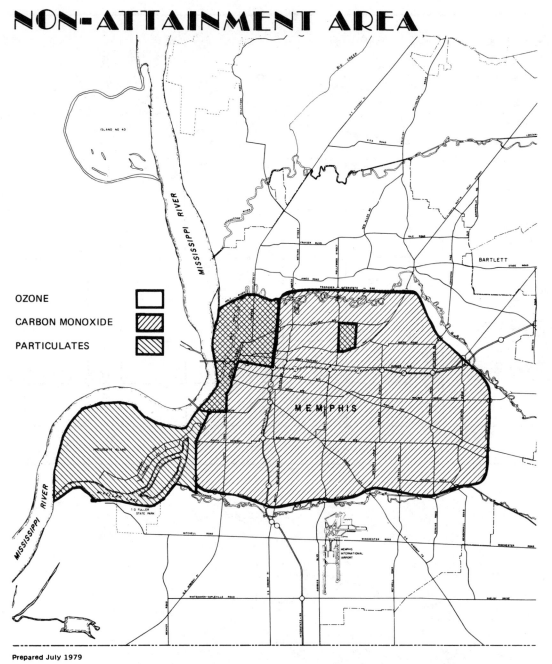

OZONE

CARBON MONOXIDE

PARTICULATES

Prepared July 1979

NOTE: "NON-ATTAINMENT AREAS" ARE THOSE GEOGRAPHIC LOCATIONS
THAT DO NOT MEET MINIMUM EPA AIR QUALITY STANDARDS.

Fig. 5-11 *(cont.)*

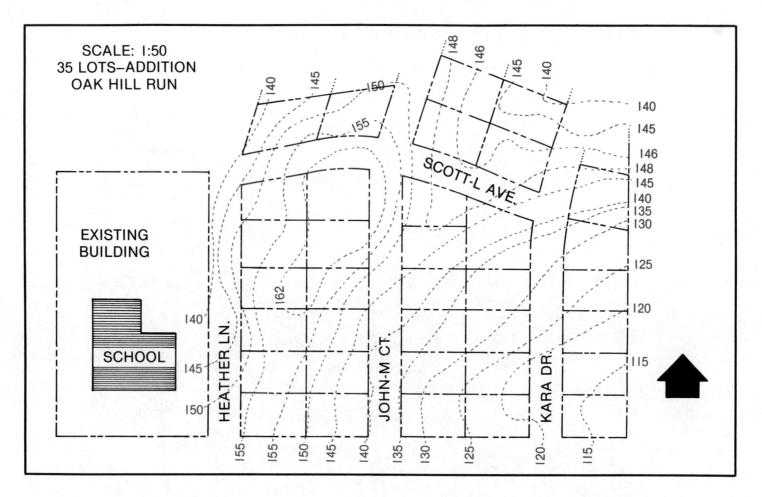

Fig. 5-12 *Contour Map for Part of a Subdivision*

SCALE: 1:50
35 LOTS–ADDITION
OAK HILL RUN

EXISTING BUILDING

SCHOOL

HEATHER LN.

JOHN-M CT.

SCOTT-L AVE.

KARA DR.

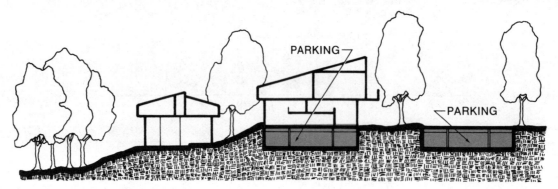

PARKING

PARKING

Fig. 5-13 *Appropriate Use of Land Contours. Appropriate design keeps excavation to a minimum.*

PLANNING FOR ROOM LOCATIONS

Most buildings are designed with some rooms for general and some for specific activities. To a great extent, the location of rooms in relationship to one another depends on the type of activities to take place in them. For example, in a house, the kitchen and dining room are near each other, and bathrooms and bedrooms are close together. Commercial plans locate rooms and activity areas so that the business functions economically. The same principles are used in both situations. Although the location of rooms is part of building design, which is beyond the scope of this book, we will review briefly the basic concepts involved in planning room locations, to familiarize the drafter with what is involved.

LOW-USAGE AREAS

Examples of areas used for remote, individual, and light-traffic functions in a residential building are bedrooms, bathrooms, studies, and libraries. In a commercial building, low-traffic areas are for individual work, counseling and personnel work, and examination and testing, normally performed in individual offices, testing centers, examination rooms, and conference rooms.

Quiet areas are usually designed to be located farthest from high-usage areas. See Fig. 5-15. This gives people a feeling of relaxation and security. The location of these rooms lets people work without unnecessary interruptions.

MEDIUM-USAGE AREAS

Areas of a house with average traffic flow and activity are used periodically rather than continuously, but they open on high-activity areas. Examples are dining rooms, breakfast rooms, and, in some cases, living rooms. Medium-activity areas in a commercial building are lounges, safety areas, and stock or material rooms. Good design usually places medium-

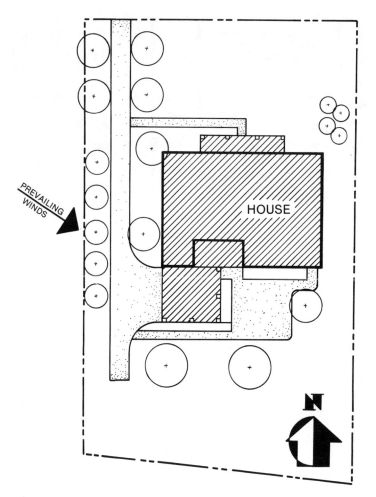

Fig. 5-14 *House Location on Lot. Notice the trees to protect the house from prevailing winds during the winter months and the large trees on the southern exposure to protect the house from the summer sun.*

mates, the wind is funneled into structures; the building is shielded from them in harsher climates. During the summer months, trees, bushes, and other large vegetation can effectively lower interior temperatures by as much as 10°F; in winter, they can also protect the building from the winds. The use of natural vegetation on a lot can be an economical method of cooling a building, it can also add to the beauty of the structure and its setting.

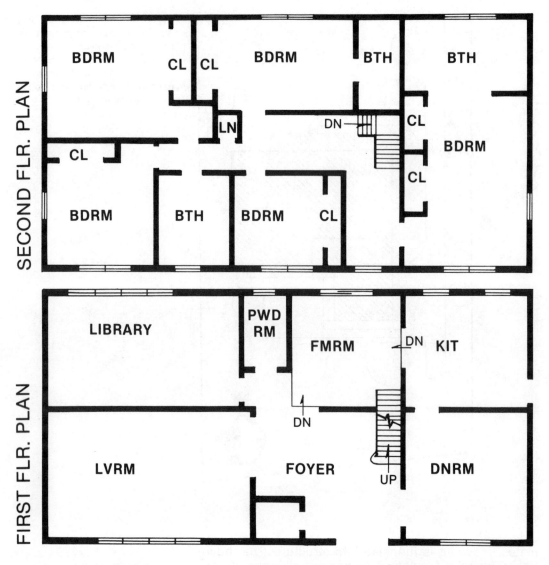

SECOND FLR. PLAN

BDRM · CL · CL · BDRM · BTH · BTH · LN · DN · CL · BDRM · CL · CL · BDRM · BTH · BDRM · CL

FIRST FLR. PLAN

LIBRARY · PWD RM · FMRM · DN · KIT · DN · LVRM · FOYER · UP · DNRM

Fig. 5-15 *Appropriate Room Location. In this two-floor plan, the quiet, secure areas are located on the second floor, away from major activity areas. The library on the first floor is away from other areas on the floor, and all major activity areas are grouped together.*

ens, family rooms, workshops, and recreational rooms. In commercial buildings, the high-usage areas include, for example, customer service, production, sales, and assembly areas. High-activity areas are usually located at or near the front of the building, to provide easy access for workers and clientele.

SITE PLANS

The site plan shows the relationship between the proposed project and the natural features of the property. In order to produce an effective and appropriate plan, a series of steps is followed. These steps generally conform to the local government's regulations on project proposals and site-plan specifications. Regardless of the requirements of planning and design-review commissions, the following sequence or one like it should be used in producing site plans.

STEP ONE: SKETCH SITE PLANS

The sketch site plan is more than just a freehand sketch. It is called a sketch because the plan lacks detail. It is used to determine whether the general character of the project is consistent with local regulations and good design. Sketch site plans normally contain the following information:

1. Title of the project, name of the owner, name of the architectural firm
2. Date, north point and acreage; location of project property lines; location and width of all existing streets and alleys; the location of all existing structures on the property
3. Names (optional) of owners of property contiguous to the project property; the adjoining property lines of contiguous subdivisions and properties
4. Proposed location and dimensions of all streets, lots, buildings, parks, and open spaces

STEP TWO: DESIGN SITE PLANS

The design site plan is normally presented to the local planning commission for review. It is checked

activity areas as buffer zones between low- and high-activity areas.

HIGH-USAGE AREAS

Areas for day-to-day activities and functions are high-activity areas. Examples in the home are kitch-

against local regulations, codes, and guidelines. The design site plan contains the same information as the sketch site plan, plus:

1. Proposed name, location, and width of all streets, alleys, and lots; zoning districts in which the land to be divided is located
2. Contours at a standard vertical interval, which depends upon the severity of land contours
3. Preliminary location of water mains, storm sewerage, and sanitary sewerage
4. Location map showing the relationship of project property to other properties
5. Aerial photograph of the project property

STEP THREE: DRAW FINAL SITE PLANS

The final site plan is drawn up after the design site plans have been approved. Frequently, decisions of the local planning commission and other government agencies, e.g., city engineering and health departments, dictate changes. These are drawn into the final site plans. The final site plans are usually drawn to a scale of 1:10 or 1:20. They contain the same information as the design site plan plus the following:

1. Boundaries of the property, all proposed streets and alleys, with their widths and names and intended dedications to public use
2. Lines of all adjoining properties, streets and alleys, with their widths and names
3. All lot lines and numbers; building lines; and utility easements
4. All linear and angular dimensions necessary for locating the boundaries of the project property
5. Radii, arcs, and chords; points of tangency, central angles for curvilinear streets, and radii for all rounded corners

Figs. 5-16, 5-17, and 5-18 are examples of final site plans. Note that not all information presented on these plans corresponds exactly with those outlined in the three-step process. The reason is that local requirements for these projects differ slightly from the specifications given here. These final site plans reflect the local government's regulations, codes, and guidelines.

SUMMARY

Buildings can be put in two categories—residential and commercial. Each category has a series of identifiable basic forms. For residential buildings, these are one-story, one-and-one-half-story, two-story, split-level, and multiple-story buildings. The basic forms of commercial buildings are one-story, two-story, and multiple-story plans. In either case, interior and exterior designs, materials, and finishes provide a great variety of architectural structures.

Planning for building sites entails many considerations for architects and planners. Zoning regulations must be checked to make sure building specifications and site locations meet minimum community standards. After this, site inventories and resource analyses are conducted. Other considerations are lot size and contour, excavation, and external environment.

Residential and commercial buildings are designed to house three basic types of rooms or areas. These are quiet and low-usage areas; medium-activity areas, and high-activity areas.

Fig. 5-16 *Site Plan for Park Area. This is a site plan for a fairly large area of land, with contours marked for every ten feet of elevation. Also note that the contour lines are drawn beyond the project area, thus giving a good idea of how the site is related to bordering properties. (Courtesy of MMH/Hall, Architects, Planners)*

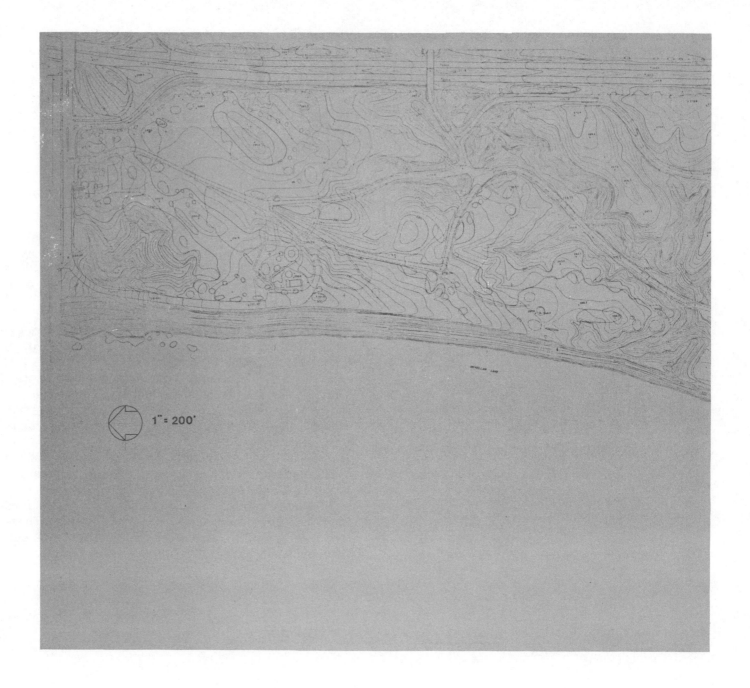

1" = 200'

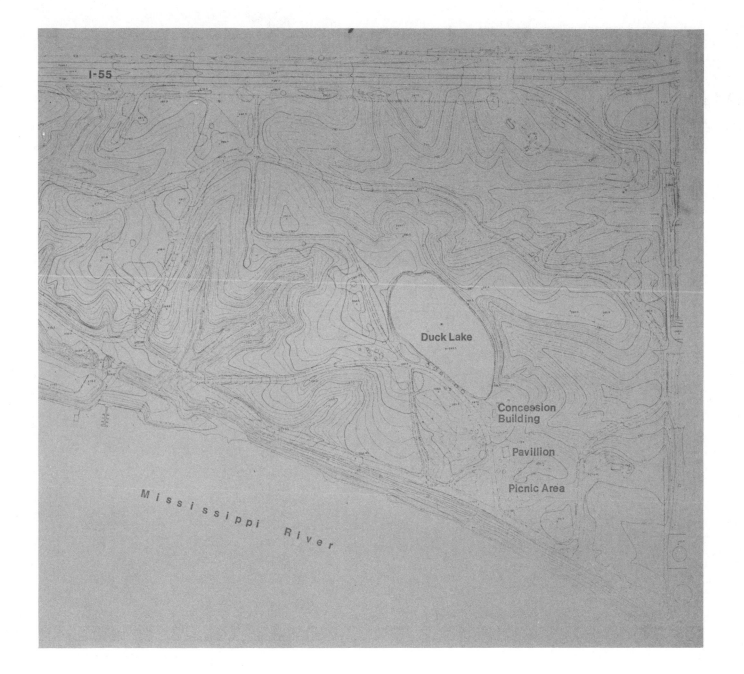

Fig. 5-16 (cont.)

I-55

Duck Lake

Concession Building

Pavillion

Picnic Area

Mississippi River

Pages 60–61
Fig. 5-17 *Site Plan for Bank. This site is for a smaller project than Fig. 5-16. Point elevations are used rather than contour lines, because the site for the building is fairly flat. If contours were shown for every ten or five feet, only one line would be drawn. (Courtesy of Roy P. Harrover and Associates, Architects)*

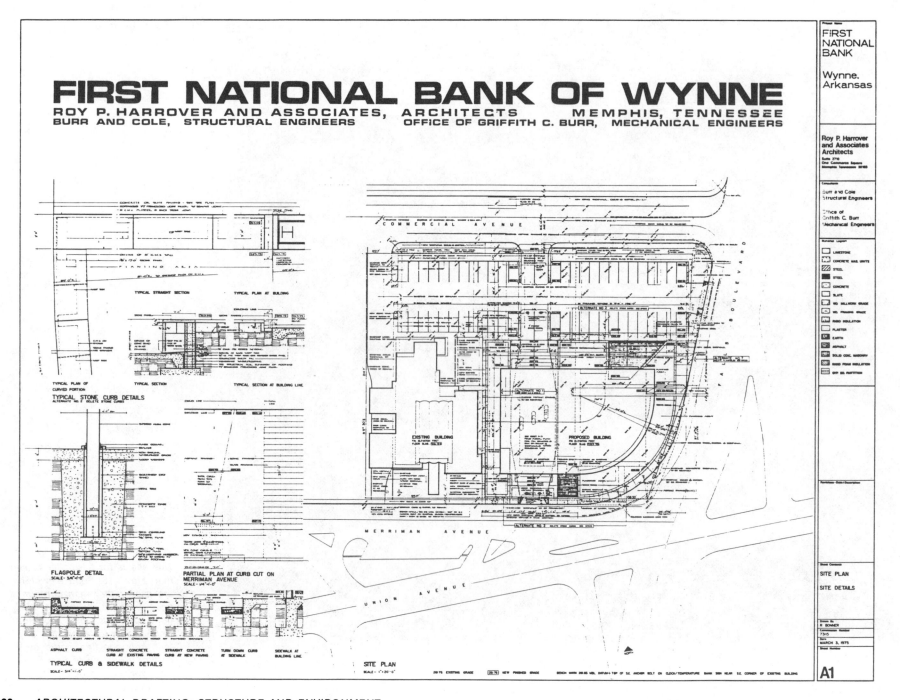

FIRST NATIONAL BANK OF WYNNE

ROY P. HARROVER AND ASSOCIATES, ARCHITECTS   **MEMPHIS, TENNESSEE**
BURR AND COLE, STRUCTURAL ENGINEERS   **OFFICE OF GRIFFITH C. BURR, MECHANICAL ENGINEERS**

TYPICAL STRAIGHT SECTION   TYPICAL PLAN AT BUILDING

TYPICAL PLAN OF CURVED PORTION   TYPICAL SECTION   TYPICAL SECTION AT BUILDING LINE

TYPICAL STONE CURB DETAILS
ALTERNATE NO. 2 DELETE STONE CURBS

FLAGPOLE DETAIL
SCALE - 3/4"=1'-0"

PARTIAL PLAN AT CURB CUT ON MERRIMAN AVENUE
SCALE - 1/4"=1'-0"

ASPHALT CURB   STRAIGHT CONCRETE CURB AT EXISTING PAVING   STRAIGHT CONCRETE CURB AT NEW PAVING   TURN DOWN CURB AT SIDEWALK   SIDEWALK AT BUILDING LINE

TYPICAL CURB & SIDEWALK DETAILS
SCALE - 3/4"=1'-0"

COMMERCIAL AVENUE

EXISTING BUILDING

PROPOSED BUILDING

MERRIMAN AVENUE

UNION AVENUE

SITE PLAN
SCALE - 1"=20'-0"

Panel (right side):

FiRST NATIONAL BANK

Wynne. Arkansas

Roy P. Harrover and Associates Architects
Suite 2710
One Commerce Square
Memphis Tennessee 38103

Burr and Cole
Structural Engineers

Office of Griffith C. Burr
Mechanical Engineers

LIMESTONE
CONCRETE MAIL UNITS
STEEL
CONCRETE
SLATE
WD. MILLWORK GRADE
WD. FRAMING GRADE
RIGID INSULATION
PLASTER
EARTH
ASPHALT
SOLID CONC. MASONRY
RIGID FOAM INSULATION
GYP. BD. PARTITION

SITE PLAN
SITE DETAILS

Drawn By
R BONNER
Commission Number
73H5
Date
MARCH 3, 1975

A1

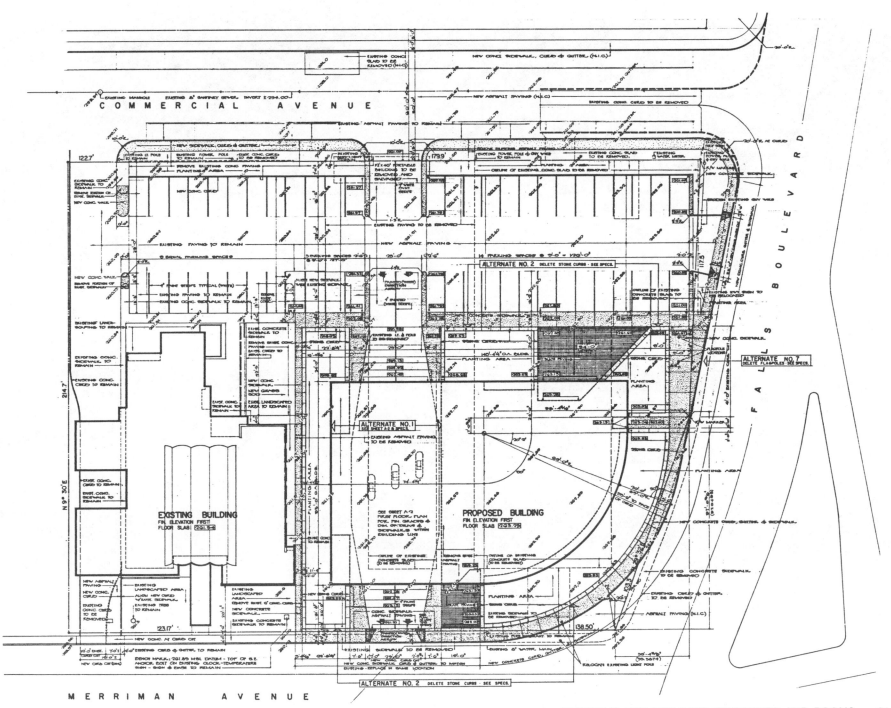

COMMERCIAL AVENUE

FALLS BOULEVARD

EXISTING BUILDING
FIN. ELEVATION FIRST
FLOOR SLAB 291.84

PROPOSED BUILDING
FIN. ELEVATION FIRST
FLOOR SLAB 293.79

ALTERNATE NO. 1
SEE SHEET A-2 & SPECS.

ALTERNATE NO. 2 DELETE STONE CURBS - SEE SPECS.

ALTERNATE NO. 7
DELETE FLAGPOLES - SEE SPECS.

ALTERNATE NO. 2 DELETE STONE CURBS - SEE SPECS.

MERRIMAN   AVENUE

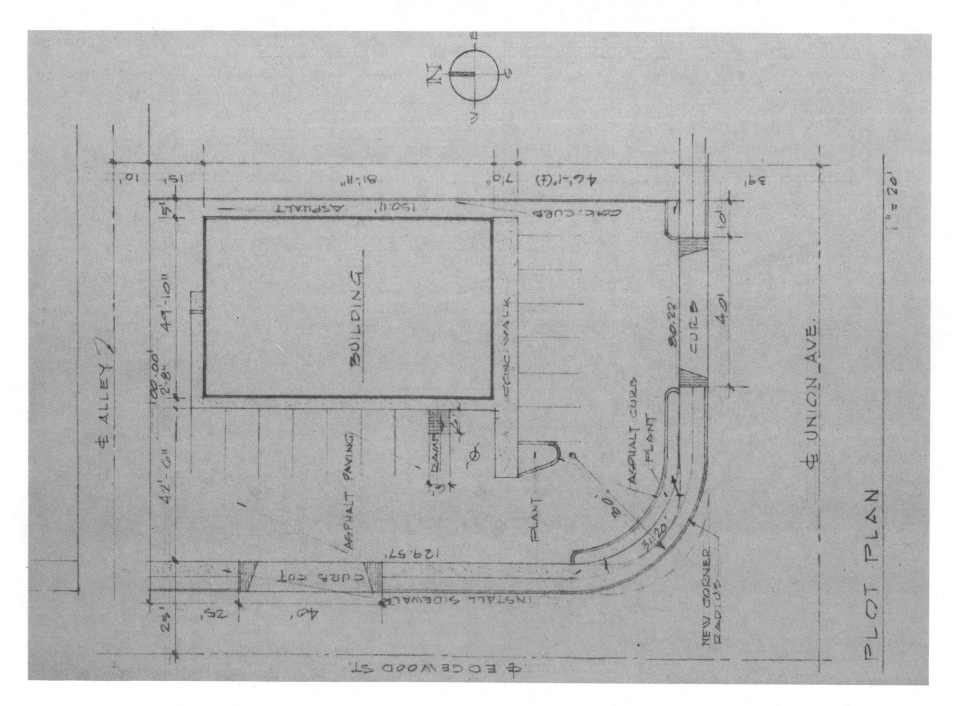

PLOT PLAN

REVIEW QUESTIONS

1. What is the difference between residential and commercial buildings?
2. Explain the advantages of the following *residential* structures:

   a. One-story building
   b. One-and-one-half-story building
   c. Two-story building
   d. Split-level building
   e. Multiple-story building

3. What four things do zoning ordinances regulate?
4. Identify those factors that should be accounted for in conducting a site inventory.
5. Explain how resource-analysis information is presented.
6. Explain the importance of the following in proper site selection:

   a. Lot size
   b. Lot contour
   c. Excavation

7. Identify problems that might arise when a building is improperly located on a lot.
8. Explain the appropriate functions for the following types of rooms in residential and commercial buildings:

   a. Low-usage areas
   b. Medium-usage areas
   c. High-usage areas

9. Discuss the principles of proper room location for both residential and commercial buildings.
10. Explain the purpose of site plans, and discuss why the information on them may vary from community to community
11. Explain the differences among the following types of site plans:

    a. Sketch site plans
    b. Design site plans
    c. Final site plans

EXERCISES

1. Develop a room-location plan for a single-story residential structure of approximately 1400 square feet.
2. Develop a room location plan for a two-story or split-level residential structure of approximately 2200 square feet.
3. Develop a room plan for a retail store with an area of over 21,000 square feet. About 4500 square feet will be needed for office space, 10,000 square feet for sales display and advertising areas, and at least 6000 square feet for storage and material handling.
4. Draw a site plan for the retail store in Exercise 3. Observe minimum frontage and site sizes according to your community's zoning regulations.

Page 62
Fig. 5-18 *Site Plan for Small Commercial Building. Again, in small site plans such as this one, contours are not shown, because of the flatness of the land. (Contours would be drawn for this piece of property if the elevations were more variable.) Also note the specifications for the exact location of the building, size of the building, curbs and curb cuts, radii, sidewalks, and other features included in the plans. (Courtesy of Goforth/Fleming, Architects)*

6 FOUNDATION PLANS

GLOSSARY

Beam a structural member subjected to loads

Caisson a drilled shaft that is filled with concrete and used to support a load or provide a foundation for other structural members

Dead weight sometimes referred to as *static weight*: weight that is applied and has no movement, i.e., stationary weight

Internal pier a pier located within a structure

Live weight sometimes called *dynamic weight:* applied weight, that is, weight that has movement

Piers masses of structural material used for supporting bridges or girders; also, short foundation columns

Piles members made of wood, steel, or concrete driven into the ground to support a load

Architectural foundation plans appear at first to be simple and uncomplicated and to contain very little information. After careful examination of the design principles of foundation planning and the resulting drawings, we see that foundation plans are intricate and essential features of the total plan. They are literally the foundation for the architectural project, the system upon which the entire building will be stand.

It is essential that the foundation system be properly designed and constructed. It affects the overall design of the building: any movement or settling can easily cause structural damage which renders the building unsafe. Foundations therefore have two major functions in the architectural plan: they show how the static (dead) weight of the building is be effectively distributed, and they show how the dynamic (live) weight of the building is supported. If the architectural firm does not employ an engineering specialist, foundation design is subcontracted to outside civil or structural engineering firms.

FOUNDATION CONSIDERATIONS

Foundation systems are complex substructures made up of various components. These are the major considerations for all foundation plans, designs, and drawings. Most foundation systems consist of three major parts: earth or soil, footings resting on the soil, and walls built upon the footings. See Fig. 6-1. Each depends upon the others for proper support and load distribution.

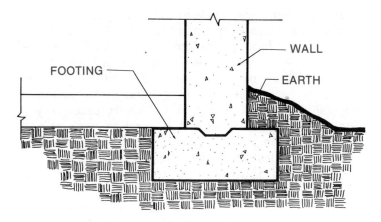

Fig. 6-1 *Basic Parts of All Foundation Systems*

TYPE OF SOIL	SYMBOL	ABBREV.	COLOR
WELL GRADED GRAVEL		GW	RED
POORLY GRADED GRAVEL		GP	RED
SILTY GRAVELS		GM	YELLOW
CLAYEY GRAVELS		GC	YELLOW
WELL GRADED SANDS OR GRAVELY SANDS		SW	RED
POORLY GRADED SANDS		SP	RED
SILTY SANDS		SM	YELLOW
CLAYEY SANDS		SC	YELLOW
INORGANIC SILTS AND FINE SAND		ML	GREEN
INORGANIC SILTS OF LOW TO MEDIUM PLASTICITY		CL	GREEN
ORGANIC SILT CLAYS OF LOW PLASTICITY		OL	GREEN
INORGANIC SILTS, MICACEOUS OR DIAMACEOUS FINE SANDY OR SILTY SOILS		MH	BLUE
INORGANIC CLAYS OF HIGH PLASTICITY		CH	BLUE
ORGANIC CLAYS OF MEDIUM TO HIGH PLASTICITY		OH	BLUE
PEAT AND HIGHLY ORGANIC SOILS		Pt	ORANGE

Fig. 6-2 *Types of Soils and Their Graphic Representations*

EARTH

Foundation engineering and design professionals are interested in the type of earth an architectural structure is to be built on. See Fig. 6-2. *Earth* is composed of rock, soil, or both, mixed with varying proportions of air and water. *Rock* is technically defined as any material found in nature that is composed of various minerals held together so firmly that only great force can separate them. *Soil* is naturally found minerals and organic materials that can easily be separated into small pieces.

Structurally, soils are divided into two categories: residual and transported. *Residual* soils have been formed at their location and have not been moved by any external forces. *Transported* soils, on the other hand, are those that have been formed at one place and moved by natural forces (wind, water, ice, and gravity) to their present site.

FOOTINGS

Footings tranfer the load (weight) of columns and walls to the earth. Large, heavy buildings frequently require deep foundations; footings transfer the loads through piles, caissons, or piers. Under these circumstances, footings are often called *pile caps,* since they sit on top of the added supports.

One of the first considerations is the necessary depth of the footing. This is determined by a detailed soil and weather analysis. For proper design and

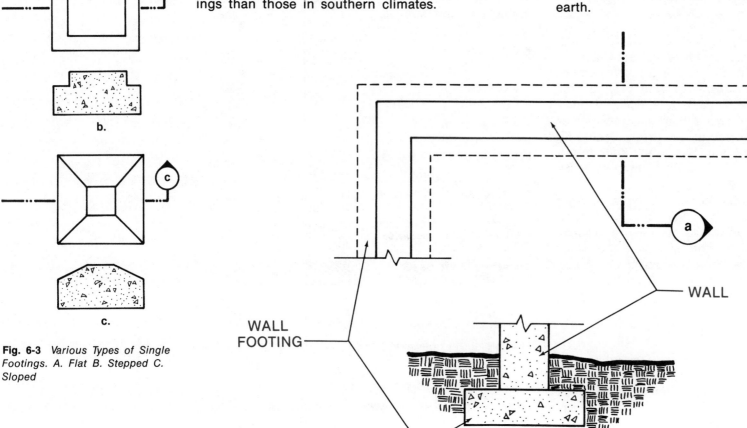

construction, footings should be built on compacted earth below:

1. the frost line
2. topsoil and organic materials
3. peat and muck
4. areas of high moisture change
5. garbage dumps and loosely filled sites

The poorer the soil grade and compaction rating and the colder the climate, the deeper the footings must be. Footings must be constructed on properly compacted earth to be unaffected by frost. Structures built in northern climates therefore have deeper footings than those in southern climates.

Though there are many footing designs and applications, there are only three classifications. The first is the *single footing,* designed to support a single column. See Fig. 6-3. These are also referred to as *spread* footings, because they spread the weight from the column to the earth. The second classification is the *wall footing.* See Fig. 6-4. This is essentially a single footing, but longer. It is used to support and transfer the weight of a wall to the earth. The last footing classification is the *pedestal footing.* See Fig. 6-5. Pedestal footings are used where there is significant distance between the structure floor and the footing itself. The weight of the structure is transmitted through the pedestal and footing to the earth.

Fig. 6-3 *Various Types of Single Footings. A. Flat B. Stepped C. Sloped*

Fig. 6-4 *Example of Wall Footing*

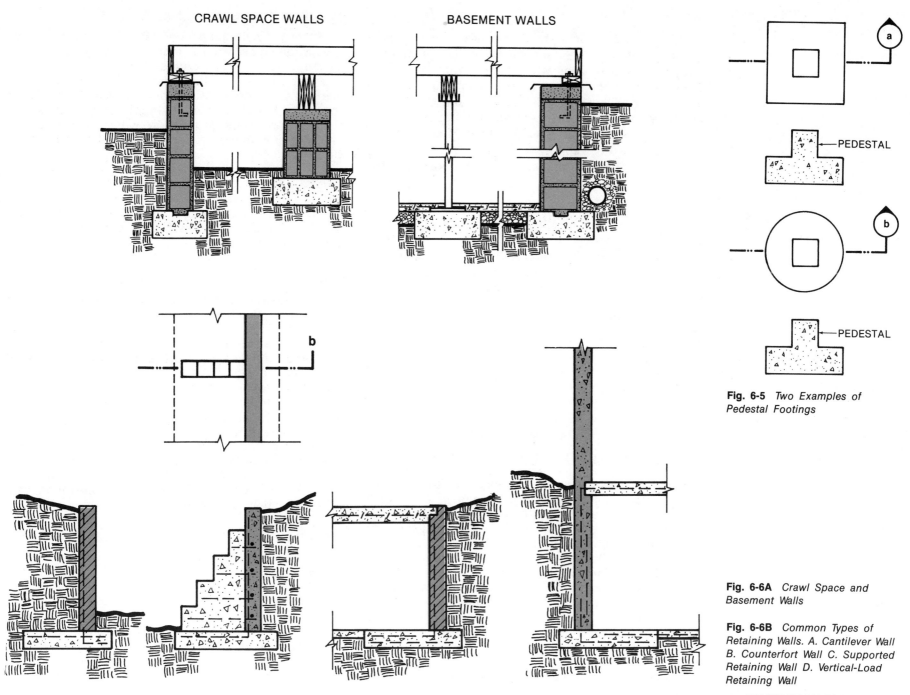

CRAWL SPACE WALLS

BASEMENT WALLS

PEDESTAL

PEDESTAL

Fig. 6-5 *Two Examples of Pedestal Footings*

Fig. 6-6A *Crawl Space and Basement Walls*

Fig. 6-6B *Common Types of Retaining Walls. A. Cantilever Wall B. Counterfort Wall C. Supported Retaining Wall D. Vertical-Load Retaining Wall*

WALLS

Walls in the foundation system are of two general types: basement and support walls. *Basement walls* house the cavity over which the structure is built. Crawl spaces are similar to basements, in that they create a cavity for the building to sit on, but they do not provide space for an activity area. *Support walls* are also referred to as *retaining* walls. These typically hold back earth. Support walls are usually found in areas with erosion problems. Fig. 6-6 shows the two types of foundation walls.

FOUNDATION SYSTEMS

Before drafters can prepare foundation plans, they must develop a clear understanding of the various foundation systems used in residential and commercial structures. Five basic types of foundations have been identified. These are

1. continuous
2. floating
3. grade beam
4. pier and piling
5. spread foundations

CONTINUOUS-FOUNDATION SYSTEMS

These foundations use a solid wall instead of a system of columns and pedestals. See Fig. 6-7. They are commonly used in residential buildings and in some light commercial structures. Footings in continuous foundations are at least 18 inches (457 mm) wide and at least 12 inches (305 mm) thick or deep. Walls usually have a width of 12 inches (305 mm). This design permits the building load to be transmitted through the walls and footings to the earth.

Where the foundation system is built on a slope, stepped footings are used. Stepped footings are a form of wall footings. See Fig. 6-8. Stepped foundation construction is typical of hilly terrain, especially buildings specifically designed to take advantage of a slope. Use of this technique is dictated by local building codes and architectural requirements.

FLOATING-FOUNDATION SYSTEMS

Where the soil compaction is poor and spread footings would cover more than half the foundation, it usually proves more economical to use a floating foundation. This system uses reinforced concrete slabs, also called *mats* and *rafts,* laid under the building. The building load is then transmitted evenly through the unified foundation, which "floats" on the site. Fig. 6-9 shows an example of a floating foundation.

Where there are added stresses, unstable soil conditions, or a sloping site, which might cause excessive or uneven structural settling, individual footings are constructed to support the columns. Without this additional support, cracks could cause both structural and cosmetic problems.

GRADE-BEAM-FOUNDATION SYSTEMS

Grade-beam foundations are normally used in commercial structures having either no basement or very limited construction under the building. See Fig. 6-10. The grade-beam-foundation system consists of reinforced concrete beams placed on footings or piles. The word *grade* is used because the beams are placed at ground (grade) level.

Grade beams supporting exceptionally heavy weight are placed in parallel and supported by a series of piers. Where grade beams are used to support the perimeter of the building, slab or floating-foundation floors are used. In either case, this foundation system would not prove feasible for residential structures, since the live load is normally insufficient to warrant such a relatiely expensive substructure.

PIER-AND-PILING-FOUNDATION SYSTEMS

Pier-and-piling foundation systems are used where proper earth compaction is not found until some distance below grade level. At first, pier-and-piling foundations appear alike, but there are distinct differences in their use, design, and construction. *Pilings* are an old method of supporting heavy structures on soft earth, such as peat and muck. There are two types of piling: *end-bearing* and *friction* piles. See Fig. 6-11. End-bearing piles support the weight placed upon the end or point of the pile; the piles are supported on the firm, compacted earth below the surface. Friction piles support weight by the friction between the pile surfaces and the earth into which the piles are forced. In both cases, piles are driven to a depth that properly supports the weight of the structure. Many different piles are available. Piling materials vary, depending on soil and structure requirements. Commonly used materials are timber, steel, and concrete. The decision to use them is usually left to structural engineers rather than architects. See Fig. 6-12.

Piers and columns are similar in construction but different in use. Columns support part of a structure above the foundation system; they are concealed by finishing materials or soil. Piers are either external or internal. *External* piers are a part of the foundation, exposed to the elements. They not only support the weight of the structure, they must also resist the forces of nature. *Internal* piers are used almost exclusively to support such structures as bridges and industrial apparatus. See Fig. 6-13 for a typical detailed section drawing of a pier.

SPREAD-FOUNDATION SYSTEMS

Spread-foundation systems distribute the weight of the building walls to the earth. See Fig. 6-14. Spread foundations are used almost always for industrial and commercial structures which require the support of heavy loads. Walls for spread foundations are frequently thick in areas requiring added strength. This gives the effect of a buttress. Because the foundation spreads the load of the building, steel or concrete columns can be used as the building's skeletal system.

DRAWING FOUNDATION PLANS

Two types of foundation plans have been developed, each for specific purposes. The first is the *structural foundation plan* used to detail all structural components of the foundation system. The second and perhaps most familiar is the *architectural foundation plan,* drawn to present the entire foundation sys-

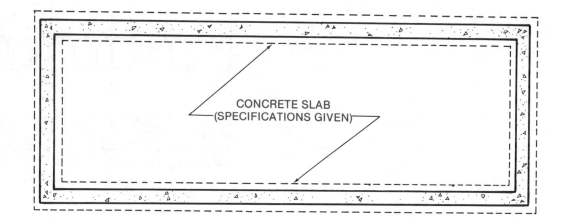

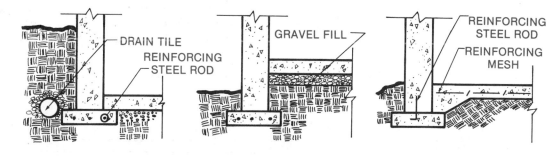

Fig. 6-7 *Continuous Foundations. These are examples of common construction techniques used in continuous-foundation systems.*

tem as an integral part of the structure. Foundation plans are drawn as if seen at grade level or slightly higher, so that they do not include basement construction. Basement plans are considered separate from the foundation plan. In some cases, however, especially for residential structures, the basement plan is drawn as an integral part of the foundation plan. Therefore, basement plans will be discussed in this section, both as separate and as integral parts of the foundation plan.

The foundation plan is the only architectural plan specifically designed to include vertical measurements. These are needed to construct foundation footings and wall components at the appropriate depths. Thus, foundation plans are best drawn separately from all other architectural drawings.

Fig. 6-8 *Example of Stepped Footing Used on Slope*

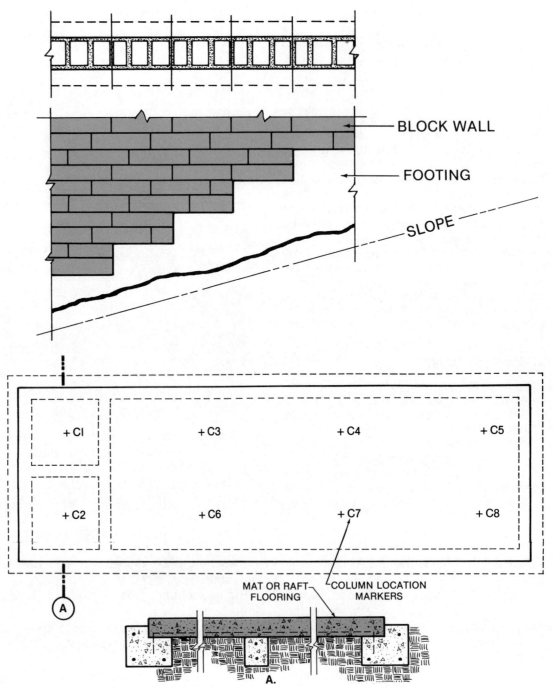

BLOCK WALL

FOOTING

SLOPE

+ C1

+ C3

+ C4

+ C5

+ C2

+ C6

+ C7

+ C8

A

MAT OR RAFT FLOORING

COLUMN LOCATION MARKERS

A.

Fig. 6-9 *Example of Floating Foundation System. In this example, two additional features can be observed: the column location markers, identified as a number prefaced with "C," and the supplementary footings to support "C1" and "C2." Such additional footings are common.*

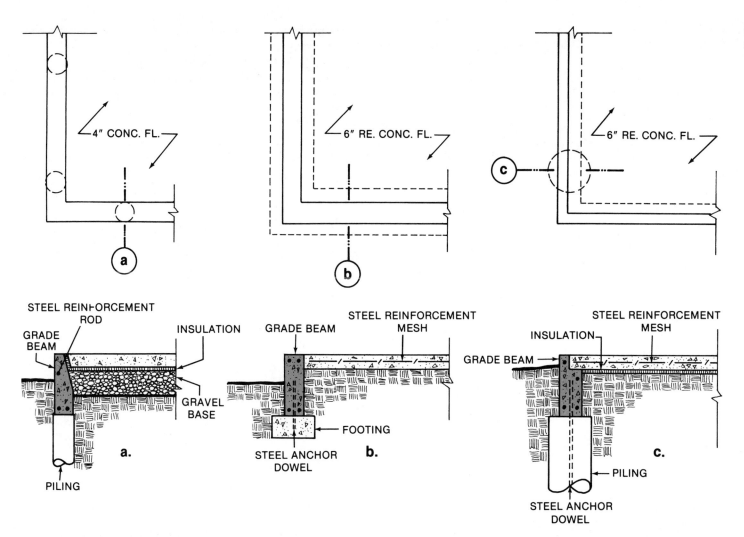

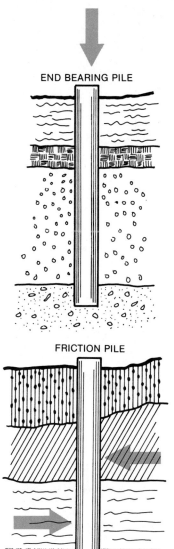

4″ CONC. FL.

6″ RE. CONC. FL.

6″ RE. CONC. FL.

a

b

c

STEEL REINFORCEMENT ROD

GRADE BEAM

INSULATION

GRAVEL BASE

PILING

a.

STEEL REINFORCEMENT MESH

GRADE BEAM

FOOTING

STEEL ANCHOR DOWEL

b.

STEEL REINFORCEMENT MESH

INSULATION

GRADE BEAM

PILING

STEEL ANCHOR DOWEL

c.

Fig. 6-10 *Three Examples of Grade-Beam Foundation Systems*

END BEARING PILE

FRICTION PILE

Fig. 6-11 *Two Categories of Piles. A. End-Bearing B. Friction*

STRUCTURAL FOUNDATION PLANS

Structural foundation plans are used almost exclusively for commercial and industrial buildings. Their purpose is to illustrate in detail the integration of the structural components of medium and heavy foundation systems. Because structural design and drawing are so specialized, many architectural firms contract outside structural engineers to provide these plans. In smaller architectural firms, the drafter may prepare the plans for less complicated foundation systems. Plans must include all layouts and details of the structural design and construction of the foundation. The plans show the position and specifications for the parts of the foundation system. Specifications for footings, columns, walls, and other foundation components are found in *schedules* on the plan itself. A well designed structural foundation includes such elements as caisson and pier details, steel-column and member connections, expansion joints, rein-

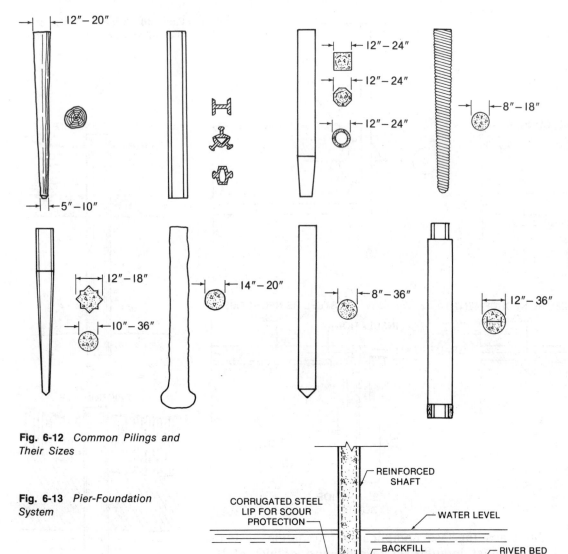

Fig. 6-12 *Common Pilings and Their Sizes*

Fig. 6-13 *Pier-Foundation System*

Fig. 6-14 *Types of Spread-Foundation Systems*

Page 73
Fig. 6-15 *Structural Foundation Plans for Small Commercial Bank. (Courtesy of Roy P. Harrover and Associates, Architects)*

REINFORCED SHAFT

CORRUGATED STEEL LIP FOR SCOUR PROTECTION

WATER LEVEL

BACKFILL

STEEL SEAT

RIVER BED

REINFORCEMENT STEEL BEAMS

BOTTOM SHELL

TREATED WOOD PILES

forcement rods and beams, weld joints, mechanical-fastening systems, and anchoring devices.

Fig. 6-15 presents structural foundation plans for a commercial bank. Several parts of these drawings should be noted: dimensioning techniques; footing, wall, and column marks; footing, wall, and column schedules; and details.

Dimension Techniques Dimensions for this system include overall foundation wall sizes, wall locations, and column locations. Note that dimensions are not given for the footings, which are not visible at grade level and appear as hidden lines. See Fig. 6-15A. Footing sizes and depths can be determined by reviewing individual footing details.

Footing, Wall, and Column Marks In the foundation plan in Fig. 6-15A, there is a series of numbers inside

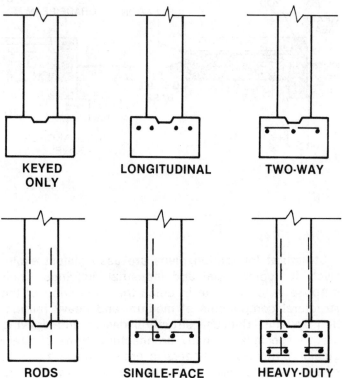

KEYED ONLY

LONGITUDINAL

TWO-WAY

RODS

SINGLE-FACE

HEAVY-DUTY

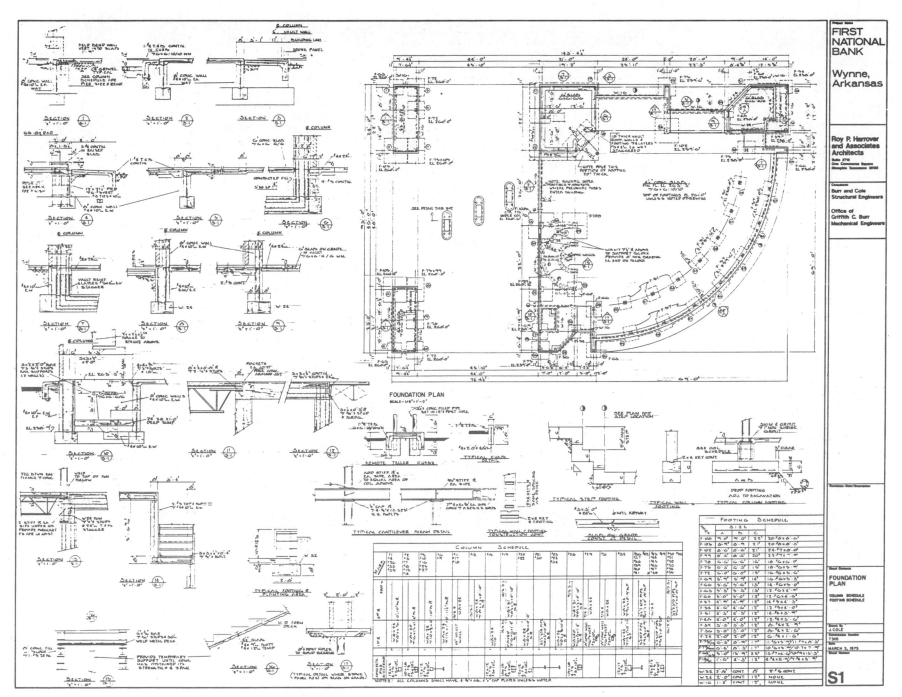

FOUNDATION PLAN

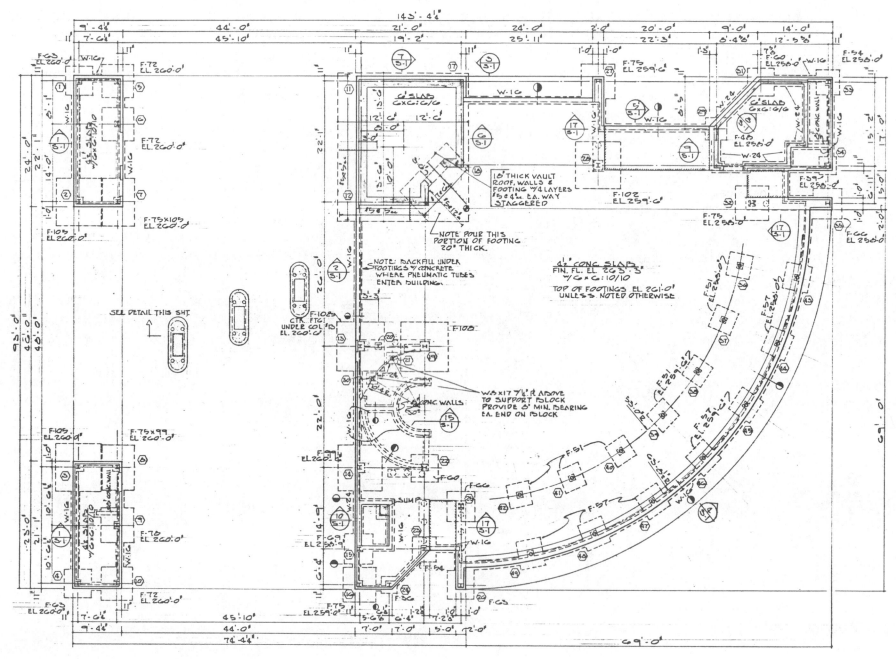

Fig. 6-15A *Foundation-Plan Layout*

FOUNDATION PLAN
SCALE—1/8" = 1'-0"

hexagons, following the *F* and *W* designations. These numbers refer to the location of specific columns. For example, the number *49* inside a hexagon refers to column number 49. Numbers preceded by an *F* refer to the type of footing at that location. *F-108*, therefore, refers to footing number 108. Finally, the *W* refers to a type of wall at that location. Both footing and wall columns are delineated in the drawing schedule.

Footings, Walls, and Columns The schedules in Fig. 6-15B cover the specifications for constructing each footing, wall, and column. The information pertains to size and construction. Note that the column schedule graphically indicates whether the column is to be located on concrete piers, the first floor, or the second floor.

Details The details show the structural make-up of each component of the foundation system. The term *Typical* in the drawings means that all foundation components are to be constructed in this manner unless otherwise indicated in other details. See Fig. 6-15C.

ARCHITECTURAL FOUNDATION PLANS

Architectural foundation plans show the size and locations of foundation system components. Unlike structural foundation plans, these normally do not show detailed structural parts of the foundation, such as reinforcing rods and beams, welded joints, and detailed mechanical fasteners. The plans do show, however, the size and location of the various parts of the foundation system, e.g., footings and walls. When drawing architectural foundation plans for commercial and industrial buildings, do not include the basement plan, since it is a different type of drawing.

Fig. 6-16 is an architectural foundation plan for a simple commercial building. Note that the plan contains all the information needed for construction. Dimensions for the foundation walls and columns are

Fig. 6-15B *Footing, Wall, and Column Schedules*

Footing Schedule

MARK	SIZE			
	A	B	C	
F-108	9'-0"	9'-0"	22"	20-#8x8'-6"
F-105	8'-9"	8'-9	21"	20-#8x8'-3"
F-102	8'-6"	8'-6"	21"	24-#7x8'-0"
F-99	8'-3"	8'-3"	20"	22-#7x7'-9"
F-78	6'-6"	6'-6"	16"	18-#6x6'-0"
F-75	6'-3"	6'-3"	15"	18-#6x5'-9"
F-72	6'-0"	6'-0"	15"	16-#6x5'-6"
F-69	5'-9"	5'-9"	14"	16-#6x5'-3"
F-66	5'-6"	5'-6"	13"	14-#6x5'-0"
F-63	5'-3"	5'-3"	13"	12-#6x4'-9"
F-60	5'-0"	5'-0"	12"	12-#6x4'-6"
F-57	4'-9"	4'-9"	12"	14-#5x4'-3"
F-54	4'-6"	4'-6"	12"	12-#5x4'-0"
F-51	4'-3"	4'-3"	12"	14-#4x3'-9"
F-48	4'-0"	4'-0"	12"	12-#4x3'-6"
F-39	3'-3"	3'-3"	12"	8-#4x2'-9"
F-36	3'-0"	3'-0"	12"	8-#4x2'-6"
F-24	2'-0"	2'-0"	12"	6-#4x1'-6"
F-77⅒₄	6'-3"	8'-9"	17"	11-#6x5'-9"/11-#7x8'-3"
F-77⅒₃	6'-3"	8'-3"	17"	10-#6x5'-9"/10-7x7'-9"
F-69⅒₃	5'-0"	13'-9"	25"	13-#7x4'-6"/10-9x13'-3"
F-18⅒₁	1'-6"	4'-3"	12"	4-#4x3'-9"/7-#4x3'-9"
W-32	2'-8"	CONT.	8"	2-#5 CONT.
W-24	2'-0"	CONT.	12"	NONE
W-16	1'-4"	CONT.	12"	NONE

NOTES: ALL COLUMNS SHALL HAVE 4-¾"Ø A.B. & ½" CAP PLATES UNLESS NOTED.

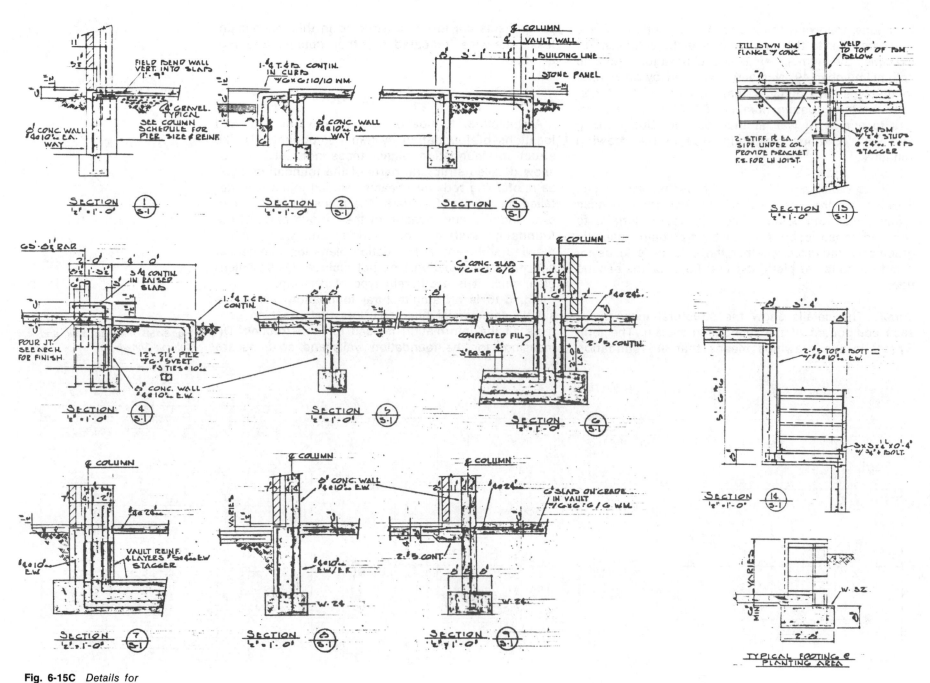

Fig. 6-15C *Details for Foundation Plans*

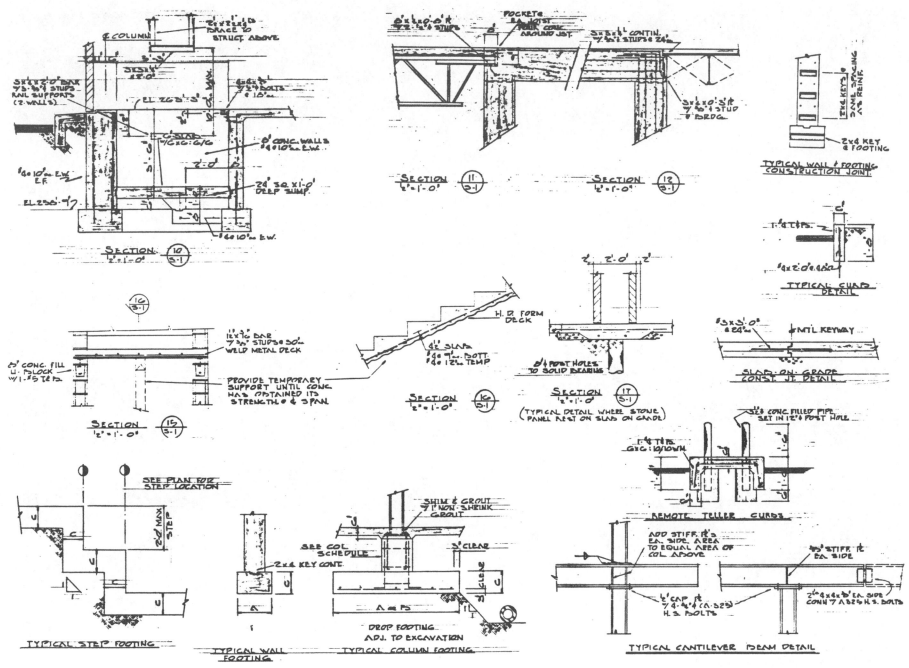

Fig. 6-15C (cont.)

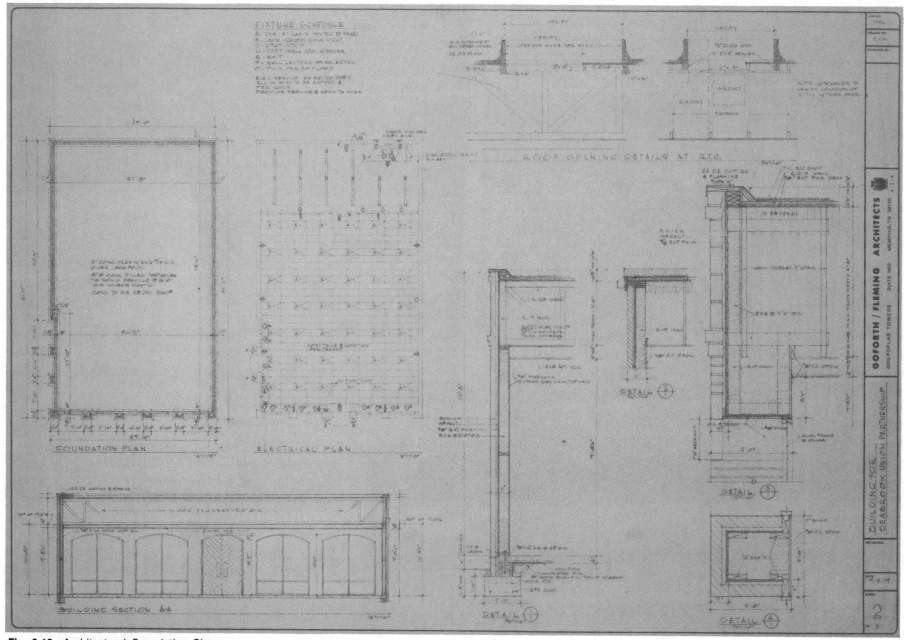

Fig. 6-16 *Architectural Foundation Plans
for Small Commercial Building. (Courtesy
of Goforth/Fleming, Architects)*

shown in Fig. 6-16A. Vertical dimensions are shown in the detail drawing in Fig. 6-16B.

BASEMENT PLANS

There are times when basement plans *are* drawn as part of the foundation plan, usually for residential structures. Fig. 6-17 is an example of a combined foundation and basement plan. Note the identification and location of footings around the basement walls and column or post supports. These are shown as hidden lines and are not dimensioned. Fig. 6-18, on the other hand, is an example of a basement plan for a small commercial structure. Notice that the *type* of information in the basement plan is almost the same as that in the combined plan. By eliminating the foundation, the basement plan presents only what is needed in the basement.

SUMMARY

Foundation plans are an essential part of architectural design. Because the foundation supports and transfers not only the dead load of the building, but the live load as well, these plans must show all the essential aspects of the foundation system.

Though all foundations consist of earth, footings, and walls, a few basic types must be understood. The first is the continuous-foundation system, used primarily in residential and light commercial buildings. The others are used almost entirely for nonresidential structures. They are *floating, grade-beam, pier-and-piling,* and *spread* foundations.

Drafters should be aware of three types of drawings when preparing foundation plans. The first is the *structural* foundation plan, normally prepared by engineers to show detailed drawings of all components. The second is the *architectural* foundation plans, showing the general integration of the foundation system. Last is the *basement* plan, technically not part of the foundation system.

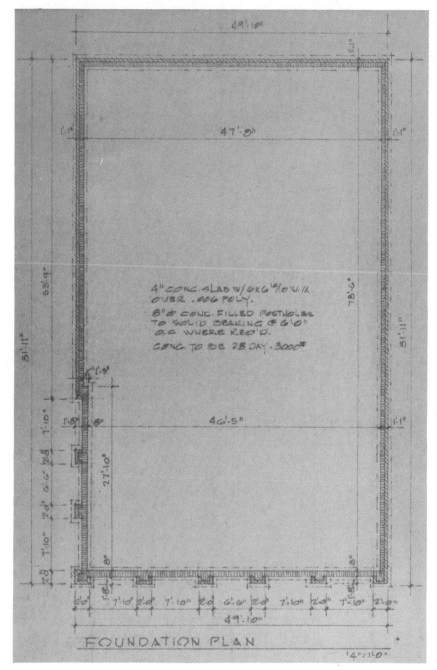

Fig. 6-16A *Foundation Plan*

Fig. 6-16B *Foundation Detail*

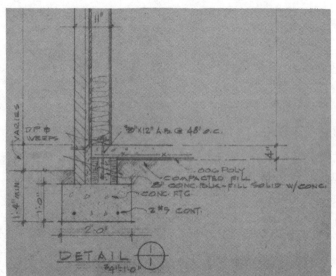

REVIEW QUESTIONS

1. What three component parts of all foundation systems are identified in the text?
2. What is the purpose of footings?
3. What are the three types of footings?
4. Explain the differences between the two types of foundation walls.
5. Explain the characteristics of the following foundation systems:

   a. Continuous
   b. Floating
   c. Grade beam
   d. Pier and piling
   e. Spread

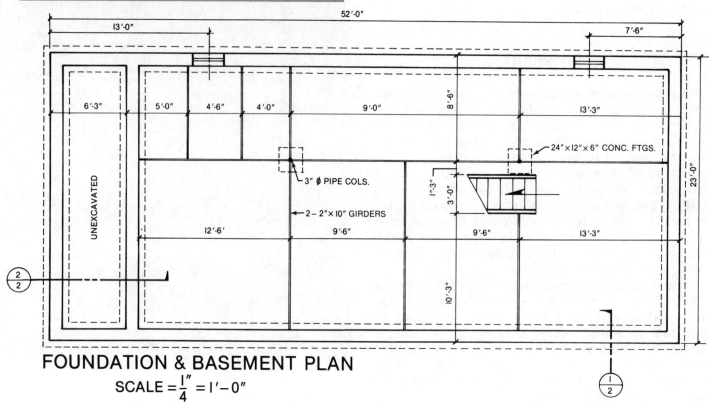

# FOUNDATION & BASEMENT PLAN
SCALE = $\frac{1''}{4}$ = 1'−0"

Fig. 6-17 *Foundation and Basement Plan for Small Residential Building*

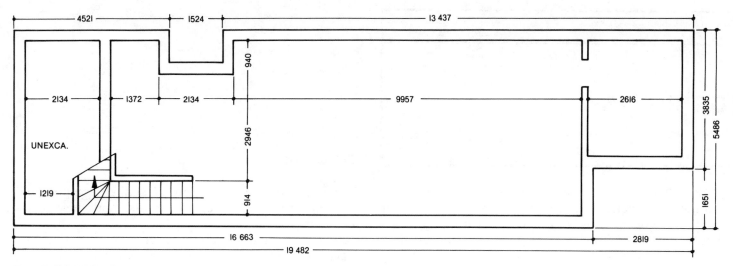

Fig. 6-18 *Basement Plan for Small Commercial Structure*

BASEMENT PLAN

SCALE: 1:50

NOTE: ALL DIMENSIONS
GIVEN IN MILLIMETERS

EXERCISES

1. Develop foundation plans for a one-story residential structure with approximately 1500 square feet of living space. Provide for a crawl space and no basement.

2. Draw foundation plans for a light commercial structure with an area of about 12,000 square feet. There are no unusually heavy weight considerations, but ground compaction is poor at the site.

3. Draw foundation plans for a commercial or industrial structure requiring considerable load conditions.

7

FLOOR PLANS

GLOSSARY

Drawing schedule a listing of similar components, e.g., windows, columns, and doors, and their specifications
Hardware fittings, equipment, or their components
Material symbols markings that indicate a building material, such as brick or wood

No other part of the architectural plan is more important and central to good design than the floor plan. The floor plan is an architectural drawing in the horizontal plane. That is to say, it shows the building as viewed from above or below. Of all the different types of plans and drawings, perhaps no other is given as much time, consideration, and effort as the floor plan. Theoretically, floor plans show how a building would look if it were sectioned or cut off at a height of about 4'-0'' to 4'-6'' (1219–1372 mm) above floor level. This height is used because it includes a majority of the openings, equipment, and other details contained in the walls.

These drawings are so essential that almost all city building codes require that floor plans be submitted and reviewed before a building license is issued. In some communities, specialized drawings, such as foundation, electrical, and mechanical plans, may be waived for some residential structures if a detailed floor plan is submitted. Floor plans contain more information and are used by more people than any other type of drawing. The nonprofessional consumer can easily recognize the use of and understand the basic concepts in the plans. Tradesmen refer more frequently to the floor plan than to other plans, because of its central importance.

DRAWING FLOOR PLANS

There are many ways to approach drawing a floor plan. A five-step process can be followed in drawing either residential or commercial floor plans. After they are completed, the drafter should update and revise the drawing as new information is gathered and design considerations are reevaluated. It is common for drafters to revise residential plans three or four times; complex commercial plans can be revised ten or more times. However, if floor plans are properly prepared, less effort will be required in revisions.

STEP 1: SCALING AND LAYOUT

The first step is to select the proper scale. The scale used for most drawings is $1/2'' = 1'-0''$ for the traditional U.S. system of measurement, or 1:50 for a metric drawing. For exceptionally large buildings, scales of $1/8'' = 1'-0''$ and 1:100 are used. In either case, be sure that the scale selected is the best for the size and type of building being drawn. See Table 3-9.

Lay out the overall floor plan with a fairly hard lead (3H or 4H). The initial layout is not a finished drawing, so don't worry if the lines extend beyond their limits. What is important is accurately drawing all dimensional limitations for the floor plan. Once the outside dimensions are drawn, it is necessary to determine appropriate interior and exterior wall placement and thickness. Again, these should be drawn lightly but accurately. See Table 7-1 for examples of common thicknesses.

After wall thickness has been determined and drawn, locate the *centers* of all windows and doors. The centers should be identified with centerlines. Make sure that these centers are properly located for the specified doors and windows indicated on the building specifications. See Fig. 7-1, Step 1.

STEP 2: DRAWING IN DETAILS

The second step in drawing floor plans is to locate and lay out all building details, such as stairs, cabinets, bath fixtures, and fireplaces. The term *detail*, as used here, is not the same as the detailed drawings discussed in Chapter 8. Details on floor plans

Table 7-1 Common Wall Thicknesses

Types of Walls	Wall Thickness	
	Inches	Millimeters
Wood Frame Walls		
Exterior	6	152
Interior	5	127
Brick Veneer Walls	10 (4 brick and 6 wood)	254 (102 brick and 152 wood)
Concrete and Concrete Block Walls	4, 8, and 12	102, 203, and 305
Solid Brick Walls	8 and 12	203 and 305
Brick Cavity Walls	10 (with 2 air cavity)	254 (with 51 air cavity)

pertain to all equipment, components, and hardware that must be placed in the building other than the walls themselves.

Now draw the windows and doors in the spaces indicated by their centerlines. Make sure that the correct sizes and symbols are used for each. Standard residential depths are 24'' (610 mm) for base cabinets and 12'' (305 mm) for wall cabinets. Standard commercial depths range from 12'' (305 mm) to 36'' (914 mm) for base cabinets and from 10'' (254 mm) to 24'' (610 mm) for wall cabinets. It is common practice to draw all cabinets and hardware as hidden lines, since they normally are above the theoretical height of the cutting plane.

Bathroom and lavatory fixtures are all standard and can be drawn easily with the aid of templates or transfer overlays. If fixtures are specially designed and so have no standard dimensions, special care should be given to drawing them and giving their specifications accurately. See steps 3 and 4. Built-in hardware must also be drawn in the appropriate locations so that it can be installed without difficulty. Be certain that all components and hardware are properly located and drawn according to specifications. See Step 2 in Fig. 7-1.

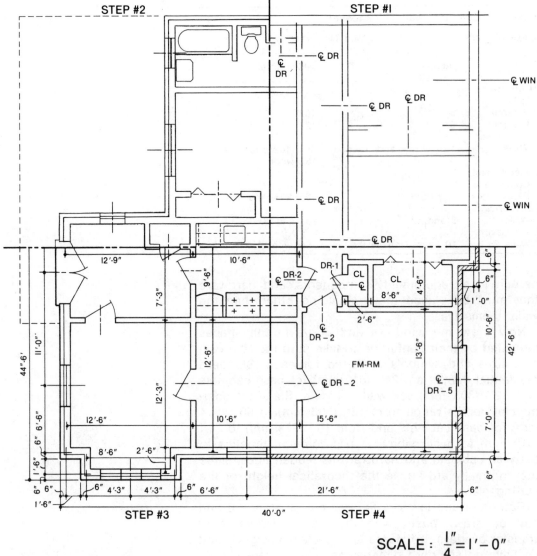

SCALE : $\frac{1''}{4} = 1' - 0''$

NOTE: DOOR AND WINDOW
SCHEDULES GIVEN ON S – 4.

Fig. 7-1 *Steps in Preparing Floor Plans. Step 1–Scale and lightly lay out major structural components. Step 2–Draw in floor-plan details. Step 3–Dimension floor plan. Step 4–Draw in symbols and hatchings, and give all necessary notations.*

STEP 3: DIMENSIONING

Several techniques can be used when dimensioning floor plans. Figs. 7-2 and 7-3 show techniques for dimensioning different construction materials. Whether these techniques are used is determined by the drafting practices of the firm and by building and zoning codes. In either case, printed materials, e.g., drawing standards manuals, previously drawn plans, building codes, and zoning regulations, should be made available for the beginning drafter to review and become accustomed to.

Be sure that all dimensions are clearly and accurately given on the floor plans. Do not overcrowd, repeat, or give unnecessary dimensions. Give *only* the dimensions needed for construction. Check to be sure that cumulative dimensions add up to overall dimensions. Provide dimensions or references for all wall surfaces, so that the construction crew can easily follow the plans. See Step 3 in Fig. 7-1.

STEP 4: LETTERING TITLES AND NOTES AND DRAWING MATERIAL SYMBOLS

Each room or other area of the building is identified with a title name. Place the title as close to the center of the room or area as possible. Doors, windows, columns, floorings, and other materials that are not specified on the floor plan itself should be given in the drawing schedule. Drawing schedules are used to identify the location (usually coded) of each item, the item name, the material(s) the item is made of, the size, the type of finish, and any other pertinent information. Other notations may be placed on the drawing itself.

Material symbols and hatchings should be drawn where appropriate. Symbols and hatchings must be explained in a table on the drawing itself. This is especially important if many types of symbols and hatchings are used. It is not required to draw material symbols for walls if a detailed section view is presented. See Chapter 8. Some drafters and architectural firms prefer to show material symbols and hatchings even if there are detailed section drawings. It is common practice to provide a legend for infrequently used symbols. There should be no hatching over dimension lines, dimensions, or notations in the hatched areas. See Step 4 in Fig. 7-1.

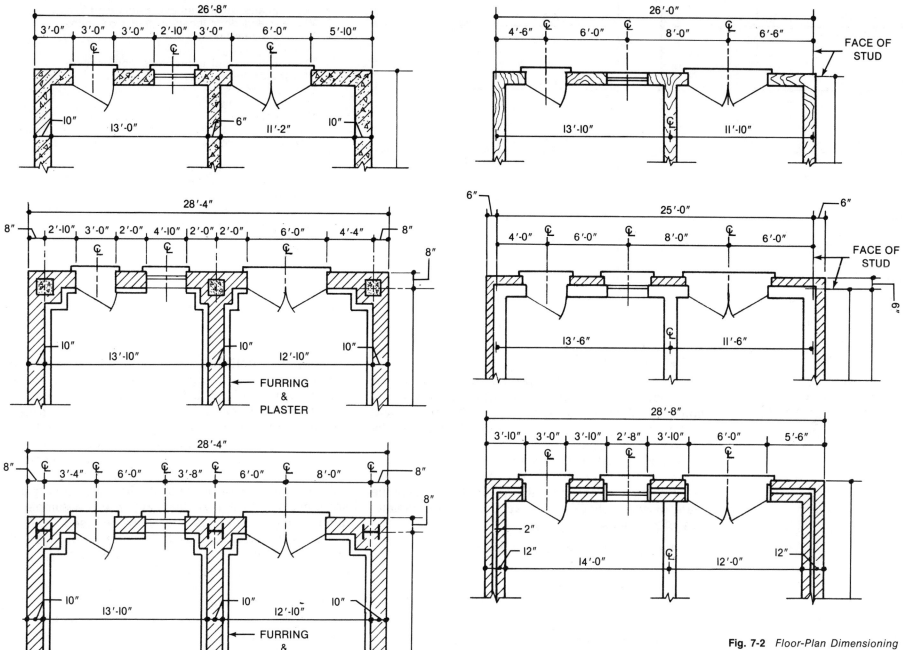

Fig. 7-2 *Floor-Plan Dimensioning Techniques for Various Types of Construction*

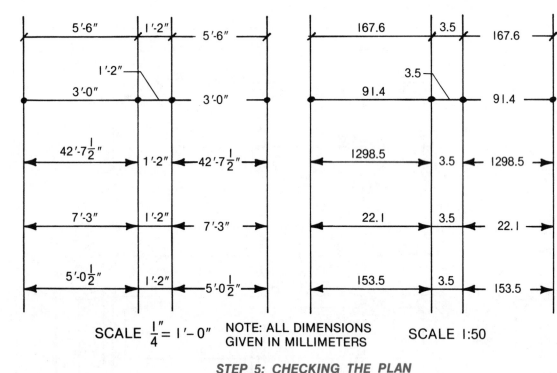

SCALE $\frac{1''}{4} = 1'-0''$ NOTE: ALL DIMENSIONS GIVEN IN MILLIMETERS   SCALE 1:50

Fig. 7-3 *Various Types of Dimensioning Systems Acceptable in Architectural Drafting*

2. Window and door symbols, with swing
3. Window and door location marks or codes
4. Window centerlines
5. Types of passageways
6. Stair symbols and appropriate notations
7. Thresholds for exterior doors
8. Fixture symbols
9. Material symbols
10. Built-in items
11. Changes in levels in various portions of the building
12. Mechanical hardware and equipment symbols
13. Mill work
14. Cutting-plane lines for section details
15. Titles and identification of building rooms or areas
16. Fireplace symbols
17. Special beams or overhead structural members (shown as hidden lines)
18. Floor slopes
19. Columns
20. Surface finishes
21. Schedules
22. Floor plan titles and scale

STEP 5: CHECKING THE PLAN

When the floor plan is drawn and dimensioned and all the appropriate notations and symbols are given, it should be checked for accuracy by the drafter and another trained person. Plans are usually reviewed by the checker or senior drafter.

It is good practice to use the firm's checking procedure as the drawing is being prepared. Here is a list of the more common things drafters should be aware of when checking the accuracy and completeness of drawings.

1. Are all necessary dimensions given?

   a. Outside walls
   b. Interior walls and partitions
   c. Edges and thicknesses of all building materials
   d. Window and door openings
   e. Hardware, with locations
   f. Special and nonstandard construction items
   g. Sizes and locations of walks, drives, and terraces
   h. Distances to all reference points

SAMPLE FLOOR PLANS

It may be surprising that floor plans, the most important type of drawing, take up a relatively small amount of the printed text of this book. The reason is that it is impossible to put into words every aspect and item of information that can appear in these drawings. The best method to communicate this is through actual floor plans developed by architectural drafters.

Four examples of various architectural floor plans are presented in this section. Fig. 7-4 is a sample of dimensional techniques that may be used in floor plans, in this case, a residential floor plan. Figs. 7-5 and 7-6 are floor plans for two different types of commercial structures. Fig. 7-7 is a unique set of drawings: the floor plans for a steamboat to be built as part of a museum. This illustrates the versatility drafters must demonstrate. Though the techniques used in each plan are slightly different, they are all acceptable practices and are not limited to the types of structure they are used for here.

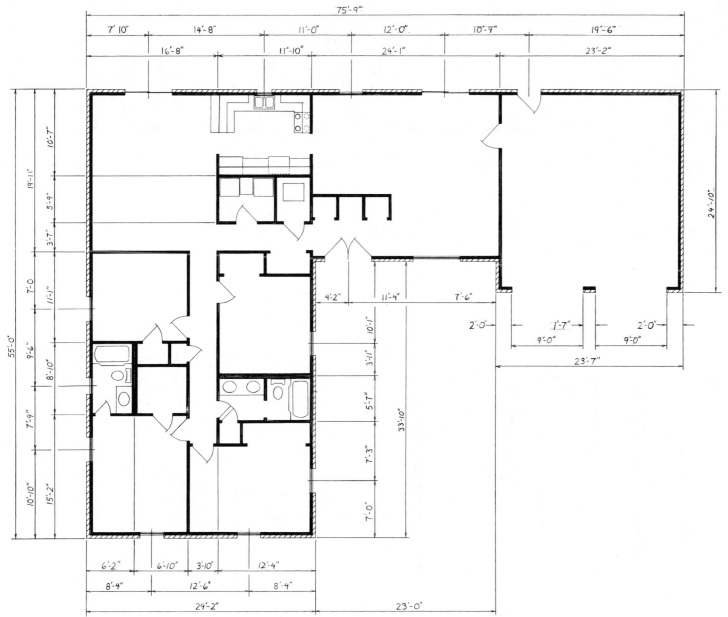

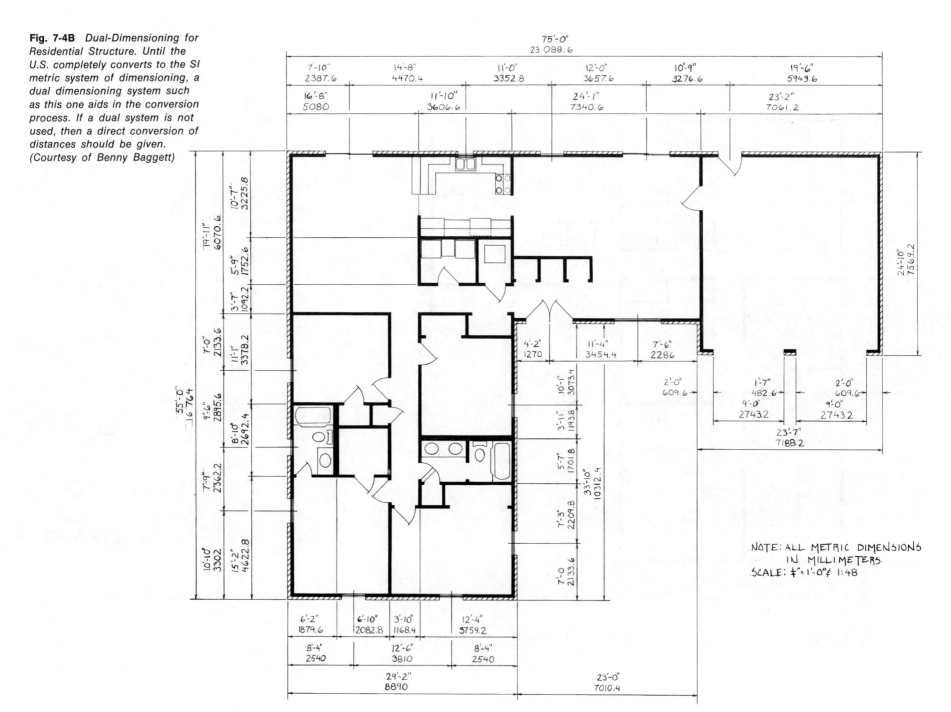

Fig. 7-4B *Dual-Dimensioning for Residential Structure. Until the U.S. completely converts to the SI metric system of dimensioning, a dual dimensioning system such as this one aids in the conversion process. If a dual system is not used, then a direct conversion of distances should be given. (Courtesy of Benny Baggett)*

NOTE: ALL METRIC DIMENSIONS IN MILLIMETERS.
SCALE: ¼"=1'-0" & 1:48

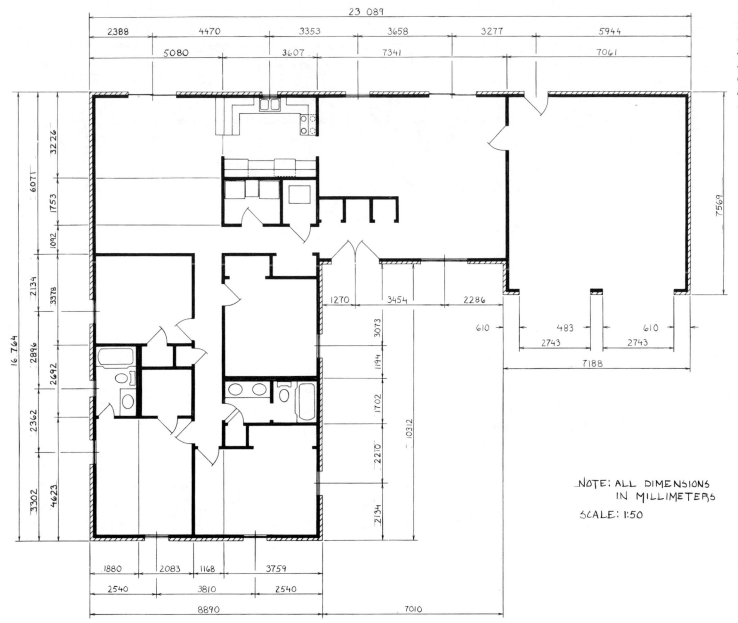

Fig. 7-4C *SI Metric Dimensioning for Residential Structure. This residential structure, though otherwise similar to 7-4A & B, has been dimensionally designed in metrics. (Courtesy of Benny Baggett)*

NOTE: ALL DIMENSIONS IN MILLIMETERS

SCALE: 1:50

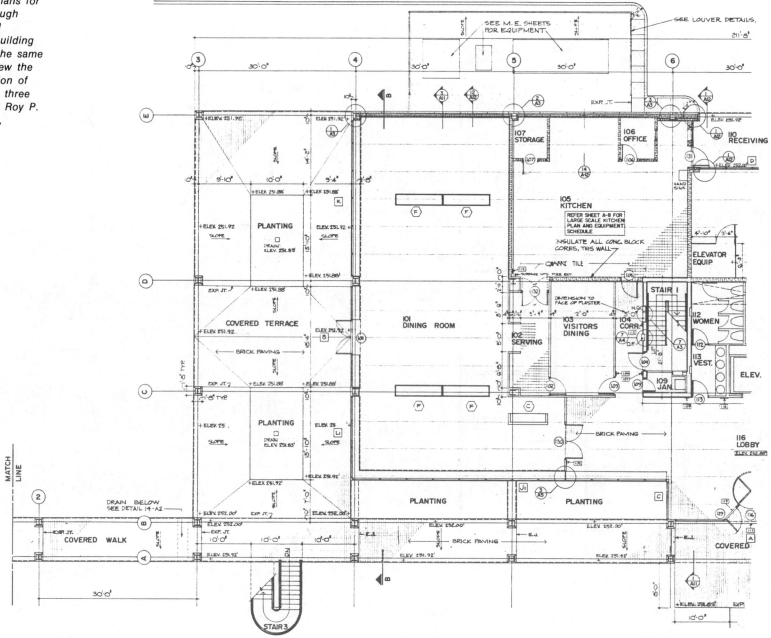

Fig. 7-5A, B, C *Floor Plans for Industrial Structure. Though different from residential structures, commercial-building floor plans incorporate the same principles. Carefully review the treatment and presentation of building design in these three floor plans. (Courtesy of Roy P. Harrover and Associates, Architects)*

Fig. 7-5A

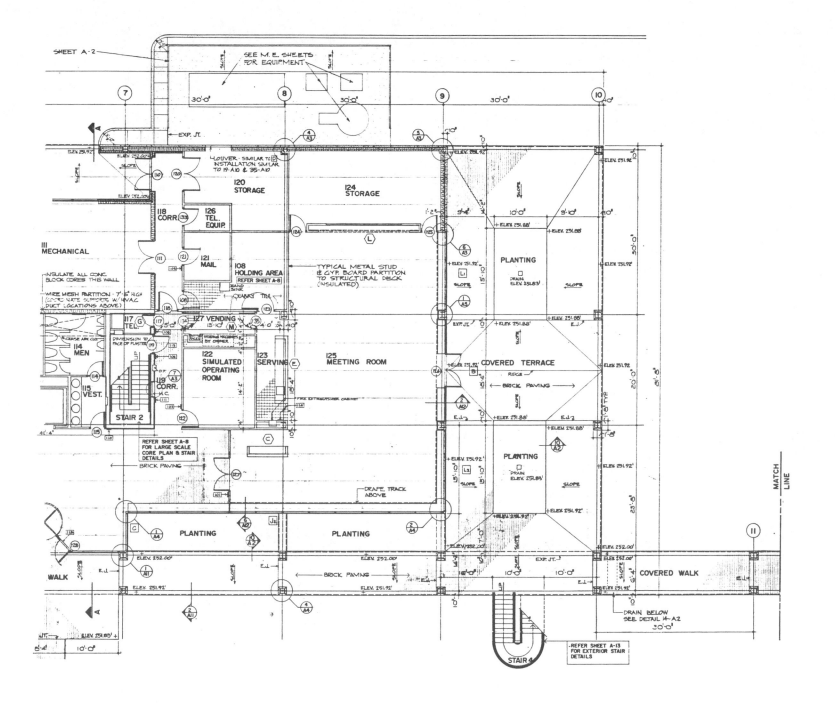

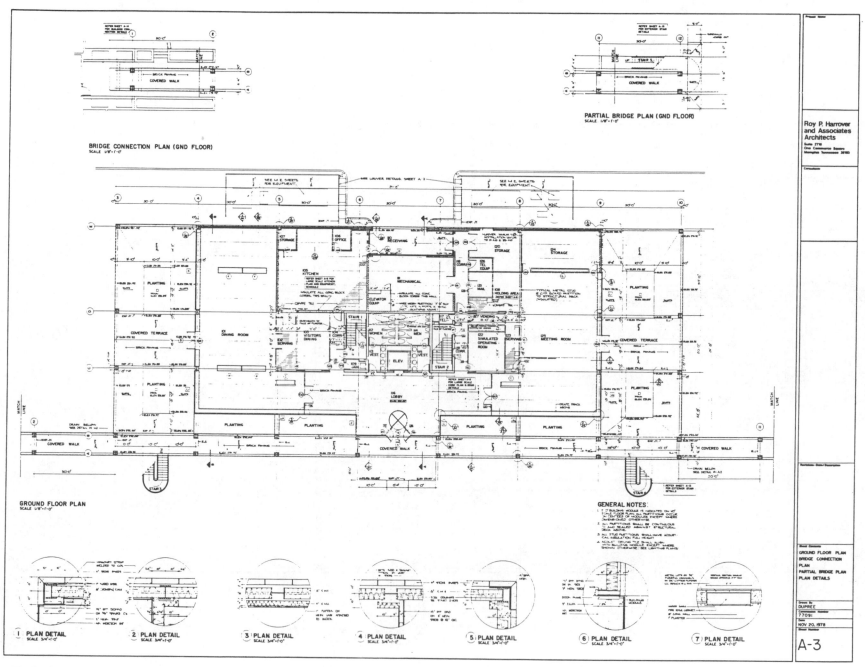

BRIDGE CONNECTION PLAN (GND FLOOR)
SCALE 1/8"=1'-0"

PARTIAL BRIDGE PLAN (GND FLOOR)
SCALE 1/8"=1'-0"

GROUND FLOOR PLAN
SCALE 1/8"=1'-0"

GENERAL NOTES:

PLAN DETAIL
SCALE 3/4"=1'-0"

PLAN DETAIL
SCALE 3/4"=1'-0"

PLAN DETAIL
SCALE 3/4"=1'-0"

PLAN DETAIL
SCALE 3/4"=1'-0"

PLAN DETAIL
SCALE 3/4"=1'-0"

PLAN DETAIL
SCALE 3/4"=1'-0"

PLAN DETAIL
SCALE 3/4"=1'-0"

Roy P. Harrover
and Associates
Architects

GROUND FLOOR PLAN
BRIDGE CONNECTION
PLAN
PARTIAL BRIDGE PLAN
PLAN DETAILS

Drawn By
DUPREE
77091
NOV 20, 1978

A-3

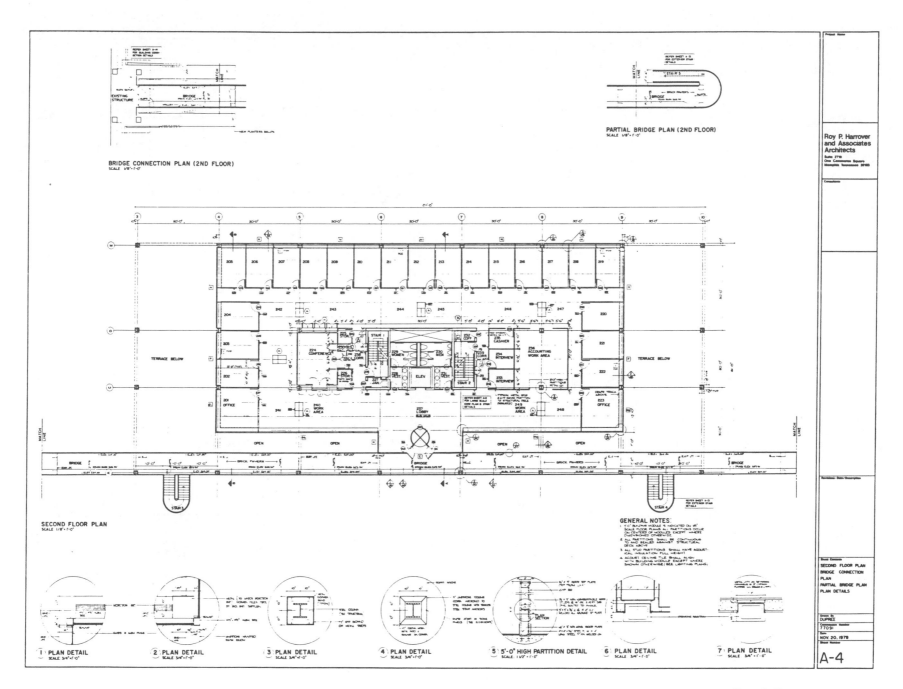

BRIDGE CONNECTION PLAN (2ND FLOOR)
SCALE 1/8"=1'-0"

PARTIAL BRIDGE PLAN (2ND FLOOR)
SCALE 1/8"=1'-0"

SECOND FLOOR PLAN
SCALE 1/8"=1'-0"

GENERAL NOTES:

1 PLAN DETAIL
SCALE 3/4"=1'-0"

2 PLAN DETAIL
SCALE 3/4"=1'-0"

3 PLAN DETAIL
SCALE 3/4"=1'-0"

4 PLAN DETAIL
SCALE 3/4"=1'-0"

5 5'-0" HIGH PARTITION DETAIL
SCALE 1 1/2"=1'-0"

6 PLAN DETAIL
SCALE 3/4"=1'-0"

7 PLAN DETAIL
SCALE 3/4"=1'-0"

Roy P. Harrover
and Associates
Architects

SECOND FLOOR PLAN
BRIDGE CONNECTION
PLAN
PARTIAL BRIDGE PLAN
PLAN DETAILS

A-4

Fig. 7-5B

FLOOR PLANS 93

Fig. 7-5B *(cont.)*

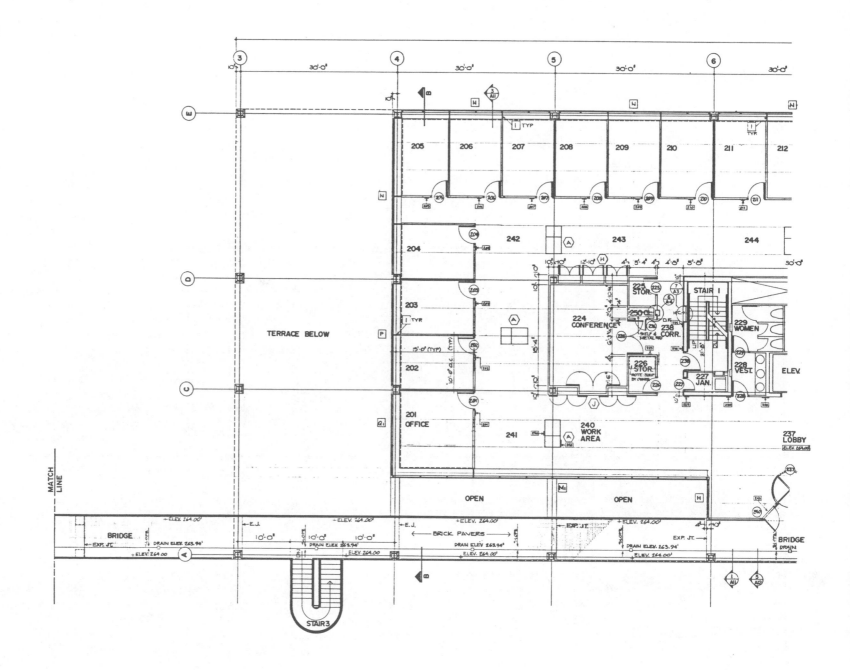

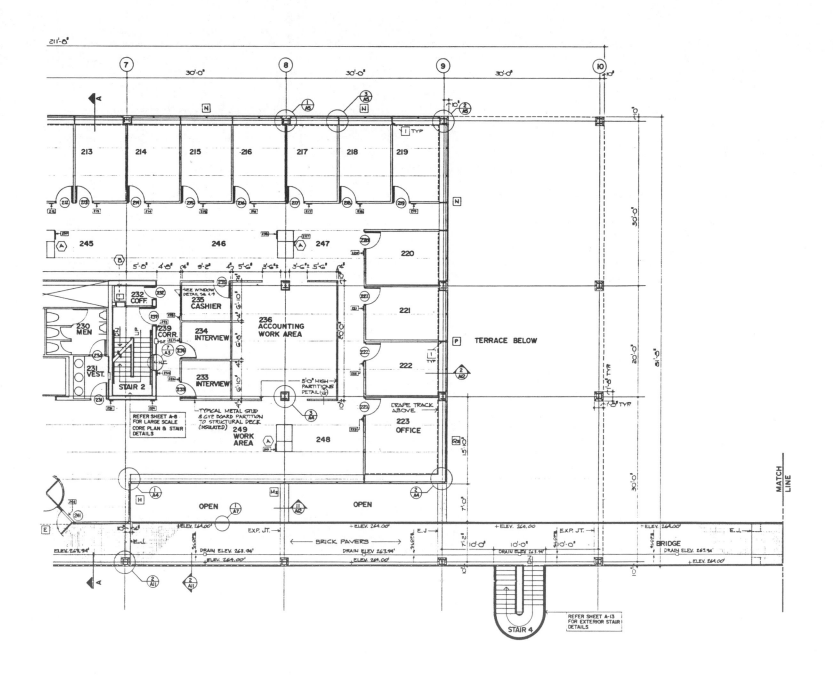

Fig. 7-5C

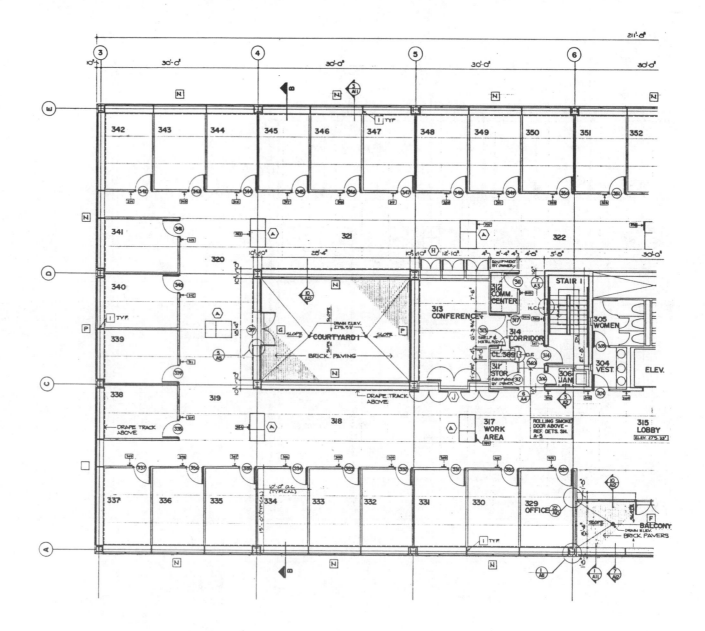

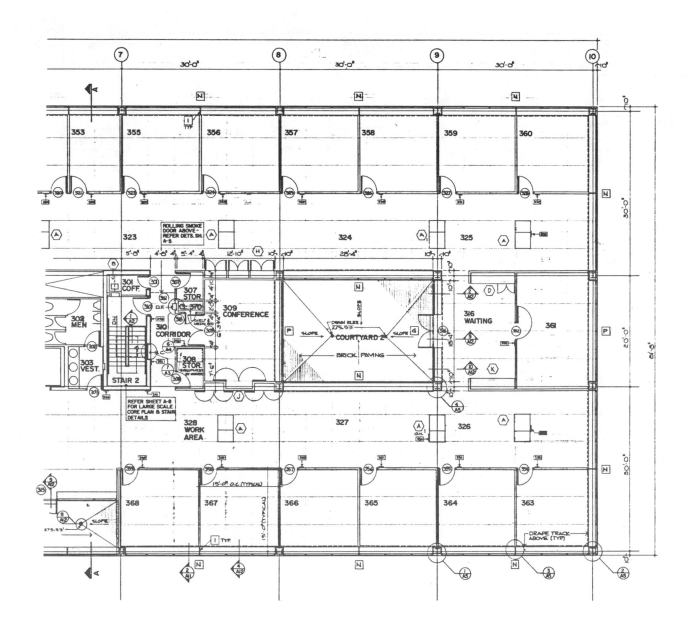

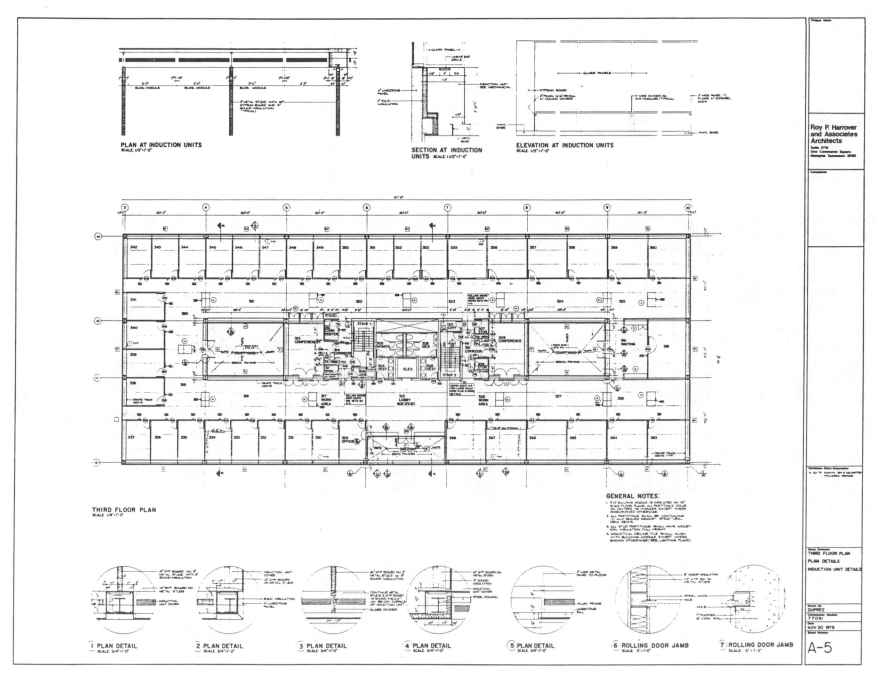

PLAN AT INDUCTION UNITS
SCALE 1/2"=1'-0"

SECTION AT INDUCTION UNITS SCALE 1 1/2"=1'-0"

ELEVATION AT INDUCTION UNITS
SCALE 1/2"=1'-0"

THIRD FLOOR PLAN
SCALE 1/8"=1'-0"

GENERAL NOTES:

Roy P. Harrover
and Associates
Architects

Suite 2710
One Commerce Square
Memphis Tennessee 38103

THIRD FLOOR PLAN
PLAN DETAILS
INDUCTION UNIT DETAILS

Drawn By
DUPREE

77091

Date
NOV 20 1978

A-5

① **PLAN DETAIL** SCALE 3/4"=1'-0"

② **PLAN DETAIL** SCALE 3/4"=1'-0"

③ **PLAN DETAIL** SCALE 3/4"=1'-0"

④ **PLAN DETAIL** SCALE 3/4"=1'-0"

⑤ **PLAN DETAIL** SCALE 3/4"=1'-0"

⑥ **ROLLING DOOR JAMB** SCALE 3"=1'-0"

⑦ **ROLLING DOOR JAMB** SCALE 3"=1'-0"

Fig. 7-5C *(cont.)*

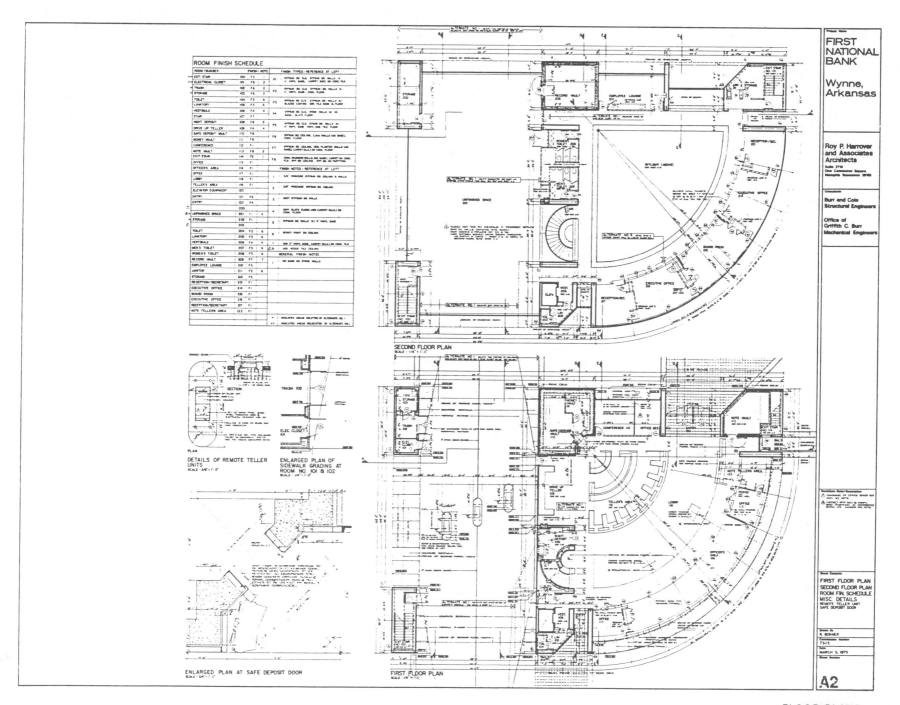

ROOM FINISH SCHEDULE

DETAILS OF REMOTE TELLER UNITS
SCALE: 3/4" = 1'-0"

ENLARGED PLAN OF SIDEWALK GRADING AT ROOM NO. 101 & 102
SCALE: 1/4" = 1'-0"

ENLARGED PLAN AT SAFE DEPOSIT DOOR
SCALE: 1/4" = 1'-0"

SECOND FLOOR PLAN
SCALE: 1/8" = 1'-0"

FIRST FLOOR PLAN
SCALE: 1/8" = 1'-0"

FIRST NATIONAL BANK

Wynne, Arkansas

Roy P. Harrover and Associates Architects
Suite 2770
One Commerce Square
Memphis Tennessee 38103

Burr and Cole Structural Engineers

Office of Griffith C. Burr Mechanical Engineers

FIRST FLOOR PLAN
SECOND FLOOR PLAN
ROOM FIN. SCHEDULE
MISC. DETAILS
REMOTE TELLER UNIT
SAFE DEPOSIT DOOR

Drawn By
R. BONNER

Commission Number
73-115

Date
MARCH 5, 1973

A2

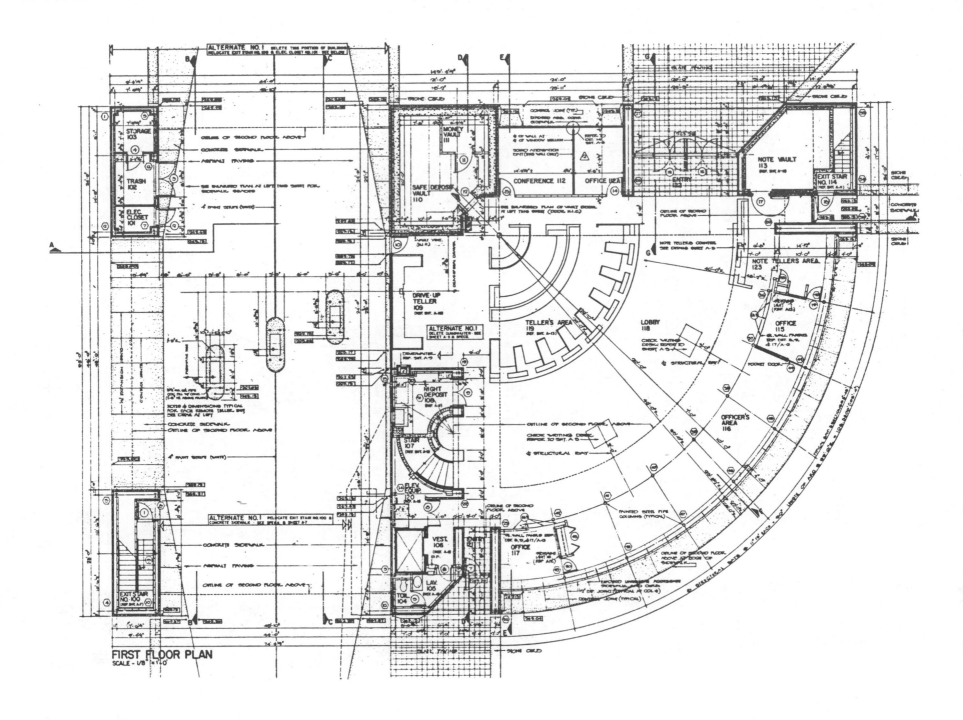

FIRST FLOOR PLAN
SCALE - 1/8" = 1'-0"

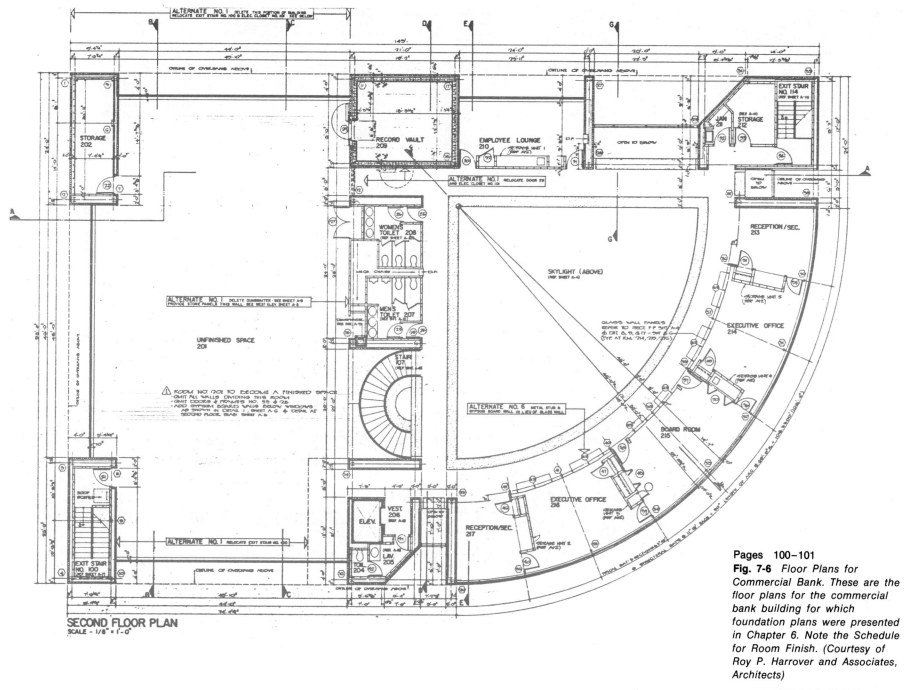

SECOND FLOOR PLAN
SCALE - 1/8" = 1'-0"

Pages 100–101

Fig. 7-6 *Floor Plans for Commercial Bank. These are the floor plans for the commercial bank building for which foundation plans were presented in Chapter 6. Note the Schedule for Room Finish. (Courtesy of Roy P. Harrover and Associates, Architects)*

FLOOR PLANS **101**

Fig. 7-7 *Floor Plans for a Steamboat to Be Included in a Museum. (Courtesy of Roy P. Harrover and Associates, Architects)*

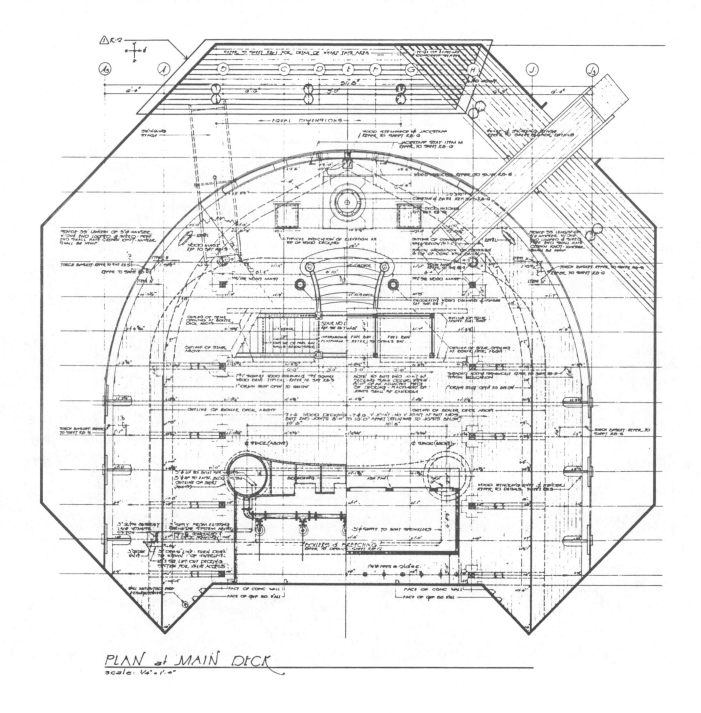

PLAN at MAIN DECK
scale: 1/4" = 1'-0"

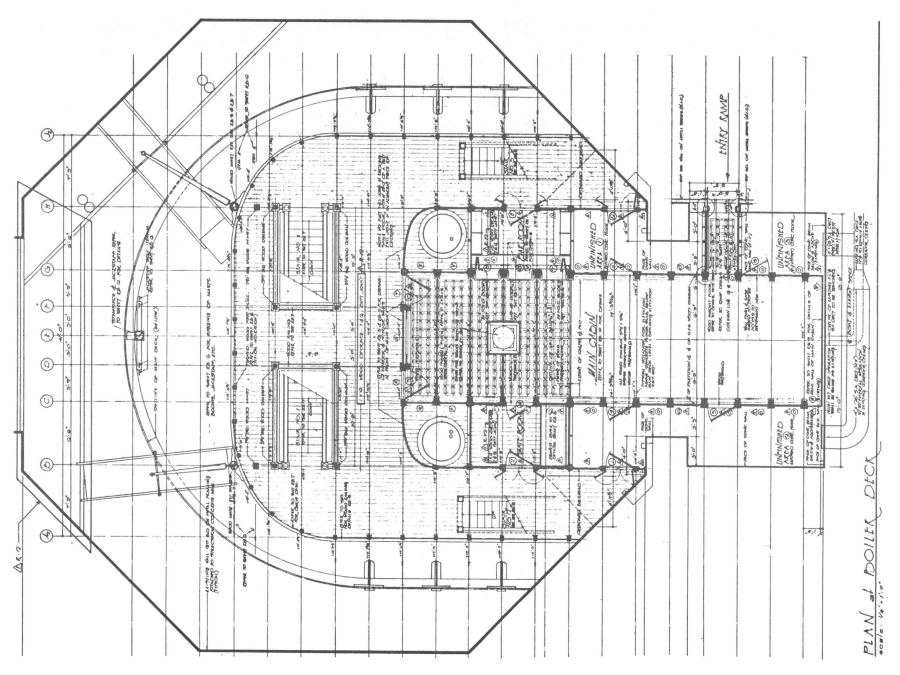

PLAN at BOILER DECK

scale: 1/4" = 1'-0"

Fig. 7-7 (cont.)

FLOOR PLANS **103**

SUMMARY

Perhaps the most important set of drawings an architectural drafter prepares is the floor plan. Floor plans show the building as it would look if the walls were sectioned or cut off at a theoretical height.

When drawing the floor plans, a five-step process may be followed. The five steps are scale and layout; drawing in details; dimensioning; lettering titles and notes and drawing material symbols; and checking the plan.

REVIEW QUESTIONS

1. What are floor plans?
2. Why are floor plans the most important type of architectural drawings?
3. What are the two most common metric and standard scales used for floor plans?
4. What dimensions should be given on floor plans?
5. What are drawing schedules?
6. When are material symbols and hatchings required in floor plans?
7. What are some of the major points that should be checked when reviewing floor plans?

EXERCISES

1. Draw the floor plans for the building you developed foundation plans for in the previous chapter.
2. Dimension your plans in the metric system.
3. Draw the floor plans for a two-story residential structure with approximately 1800 square feet of living area.
4. Draw the floor plan for a two-story multi-purpose commercial building with about 8000 square feet of activity area. Define the purpose and nature of the commercial building.

GLOSSARY

Baluster an upright support for a rail, often in the shape of a vase

Balustrade a series of balusters supporting a rail

Demountable wall an interior wall that can be taken apart and reassembled elsewhere

Details architectural drawings that show special features and characteristics of construction

Fixed walls stationary walls, not temporary or constructed to be moved

Movable walls walls that can be moved without disassembling

Roof pitch the slope of a roof

Specialized construction construction not commonly used, of such complexity that it requires special explanation; construction for which specially trained tradesmen may be needed.

A lot of time, energy, and resources are devoted to specifying and preparing architectural detail drawings. Detail drawings—or *details*—are large drawings that illustrate specifications for the construction of buildings. Details define structural members of the building and show contractors and tradesmen how the work is to be done.

Several factors determine how many and what kind of details are needed. The first, *complexity of the structure,* is the number and types of engineering and structural problems associated with the building. If the building uses many construction techniques and design concepts, then there is a need for many details. In less complex buildings, such as most residential structures, common details are used to show how all construction is to be handled. *Common* details show techniques used throughout the entire building. The second factor taken into consideration is the *amount of specialized construction* required. Special construction techniques, hardware, materials, or designs usually require one detail drawing each. The more specialized the structure, the more details are required. The third factor is *the amount of time and supervision* that the architectural team can give the project. Normally, if only a few details are prepared for a large or complex project, then more time and cost must be built into the project for construction supervision. Most firms provide details for any construction that deviates from the norm.

An exact formula for the number of details needed for a given project is impossible. Detail drawing re-

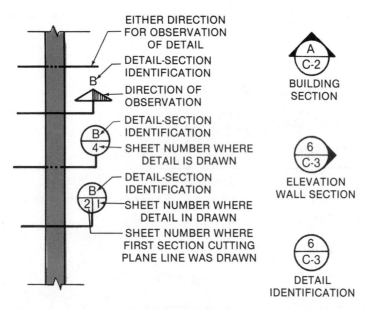

EITHER DIRECTION
FOR OBSERVATION
OF DETAIL

DETAIL-SECTION
IDENTIFICATION

DIRECTION OF
OBSERVATION

DETAIL-SECTION
IDENTIFICATION

SHEET NUMBER WHERE
DETAIL IS DRAWN

DETAIL-SECTION
IDENTIFICATION

SHEET NUMBER WHERE
DETAIL IN DRAWN

SHEET NUMBER WHERE
FIRST SECTION CUTTING
PLANE LINE WAS DRAWN

BUILDING
SECTION

ELEVATION
WALL SECTION

DETAIL
IDENTIFICATION

quirements vary from one job to another. It is important to realize that no factor is considered in isolation. When determining how many drawings are to be prepared, the architectural team looks at each of the three factors in relationship to the other.

DETAILING CONSIDERATIONS

Before drafters begin to draw the details, the architect and members of the project team review the building specifications, schedules, and designs. When they determine exactly which details are needed, they list those details by name. Once the drafter receives the list, the appropriate *scaling, notation system,* and *drawing location* must be decided on.

SCALING

The scales selected for architectural details depend upon the size of the construction material and hardware to be drawn, the amount and types of details to be shown, and where the details are to be located on

the sheet. Details are drawn in scales ranging from $1/2'' = 1'-0''$ (1:20 in SI) to full size (1:1). In a few instances, details are drawn as small as $1/4'' = 1'-0''$ (1:50) and as large as double size (2:1).

The larger the physical area the detail represents, the smaller the scale used. Details of large construction members or assemblies are frequently drawn to a scale of $1/2'' = 1'-0''$ (1:20). Small construction members and assemblies, such as molding and mechanical fasteners, should be drawn full size (1:1).

NOTATION SYSTEM

The notation system to identify and locate detail drawings can vary from one project to another, but it must be constant throughout a set of drawings for the project. Examples of notation systems commonly used in the architectural field are shown in Fig. 8-1.

Material symbols in detail drawing should conform to AIA standards. In some cases, coloring or shading may be used to highlight a particular section of the detail. Such practices vary from one architectural firm to another. Use of color can cause problems when the drawings are reproduced. Note that, where two colors are used in this book, the purpose is to clarify a point being discussed. Most of these drawings would be in a single color in actual practice.

DRAWING LOCATION

Whenever possible, it is best to draw the detail on the same page as the corresponding cutting-plane line and notation. When they are on the same page details are easier to find and match with appropriate notations and easier for untrained personnel to understand. Details are usually drawn off to the side of or next to the cutting-plan line. See Fig. 8-2. If there is not enough room or there are many details, they should be placed to one side. See Fig. 8-3.

When working drawings are being prepared for a large and complex structure, the architectural drafter may be required to prepare a detail manual or book.

All the architectural detail drawings are prepared on standard-size sheets of paper, such as $8\frac{1}{2}'' \times 11''$, bound in book form. This ensures that all details required for construction are kept together.

WALL DETAILS

If the building uses one type of construction for all exterior walls and roofs, the number of wall details is greatly reduced. Use of the same construction techniques throughout means that only one wall detail is required. Buildings with many different construction techniques and materials need a wall detail for each type. Most buildings come somewhere between these extremes. Properly drawn wall details include cross-sections of the footings, sills, and cornices. See Fig. 8-4. Wall details show how the entire wall is to be constructed.

DRAWING WALL DETAILS

To draw wall details properly, the drafter first decides on the right type of details to express the construction requirements. There are basically two types of wall detail presentations: vertical wall cross-sections (Fig. 8-5) and cross-sectional elevations (Fig. 8-6). Regardless of the type, of course, the drafter follows all design and construction specifications.

When drawing these details, a number of items should be checked. Some of these are listed below:

1. Depth of footing
2. Size and material specification of footing
3. Construction of footing
4. Type of foundation
5. Arrangement of framing members in sill
6. Height construction and finish of the floor
7. Mechanical fasteners
8. Interior and exterior stairways
9. Type of wall and construction (wood framing, brick veneer, solid masonry, stone, etc.)
10. Type of insulation and wall finishing materials
11. Wall and roof intersection

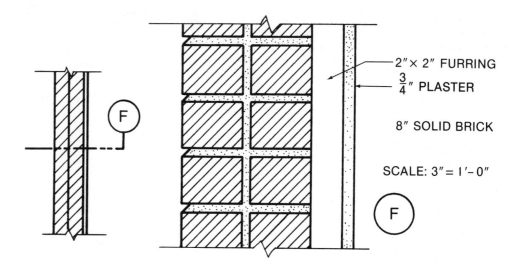

2" × 2" FURRING

$\frac{3}{4}''$ PLASTER

8" SOLID BRICK

SCALE: 3" = 1'-0"

Fig. 8-2 *Detail Drawing Placed Next to Cutting Plane*

12. Rafters and ceiling joist locations
13. Wall plates
14. Roof construction and materials
15. Highlighting requirements, i.e., portions of the drawing that should be emphasized with heavier line weights

STEPS IN DRAWING DETAILS

Details can be drawn easily with a three-step process. These can be used regardless of the type of detailing. The step-by-step progression of detail drawings is shown in Figs. 8-7A, B, C and 8-8A, B, C.

Step 1: Lay Out Basic Forms and Shapes. In this first stage, the basic shapes of the construction components are drawn in lightly, so that any overlapping lines can be easily removed.

Step 2: Include Details. All component parts are illustrated in detail. Note how each part of the construction is drawn in clearly.

Step 3: Add Symbols and Specifications. In the last step, the material symbols and part identifications are

Pages 108–112
Fig. 8-3 *Details Drawn on the Same Page As the Referenced Cutting-Plane Lines. The detail notation system used in this drawing indicates that all details are drawn on page A10. (Courtesy of Roy P. Harrover and Associates, Architects)*

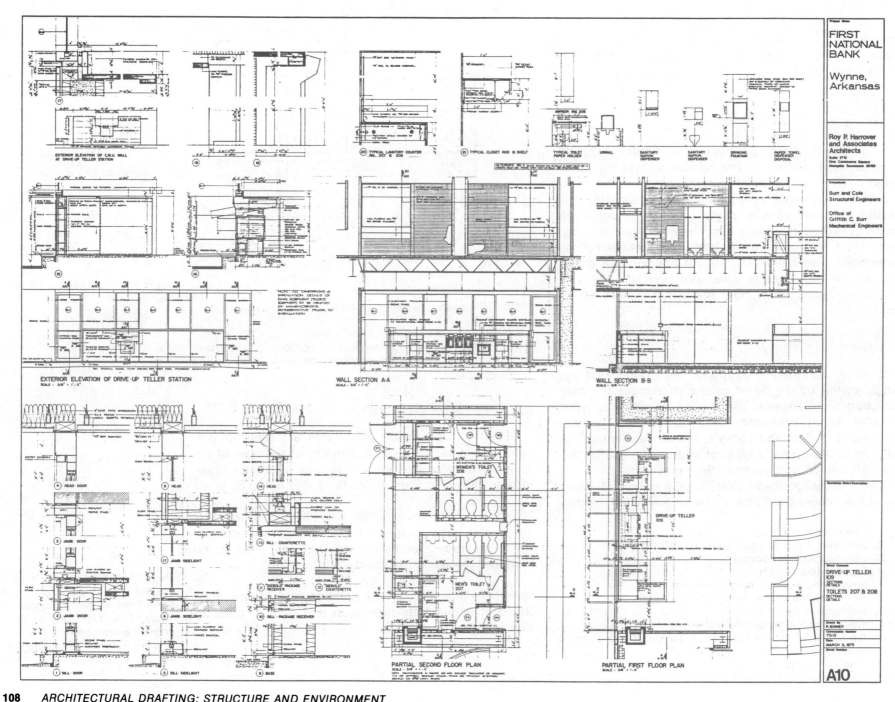

PARTIAL SECOND FLOOR PLAN

PARTIAL FIRST FLOOR PLAN

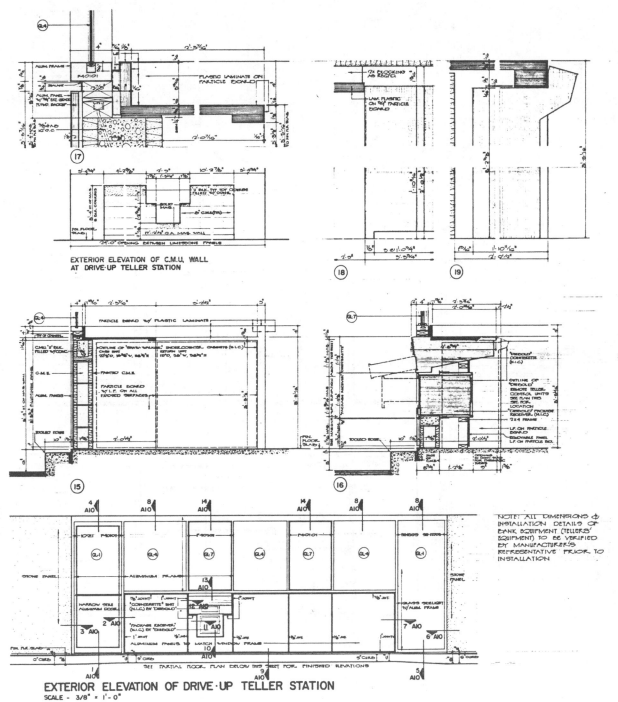

Fig. 8-3 *(cont.)*

EXTERIOR ELEVATION OF C.M.U. WALL
AT DRIVE-UP TELLER STATION

NOTE: ALL DIMENSIONS &
INSTALLATION DETAILS OF
BANK EQUIPMENT (TELLERS'
EQUIPMENT) TO BE VERIFIED
BY MANUFACTURER'S
REPRESENTATIVE PRIOR TO
INSTALLATION

EXTERIOR ELEVATION OF DRIVE-UP TELLER STATION
SCALE - 3/8" = 1'-0"

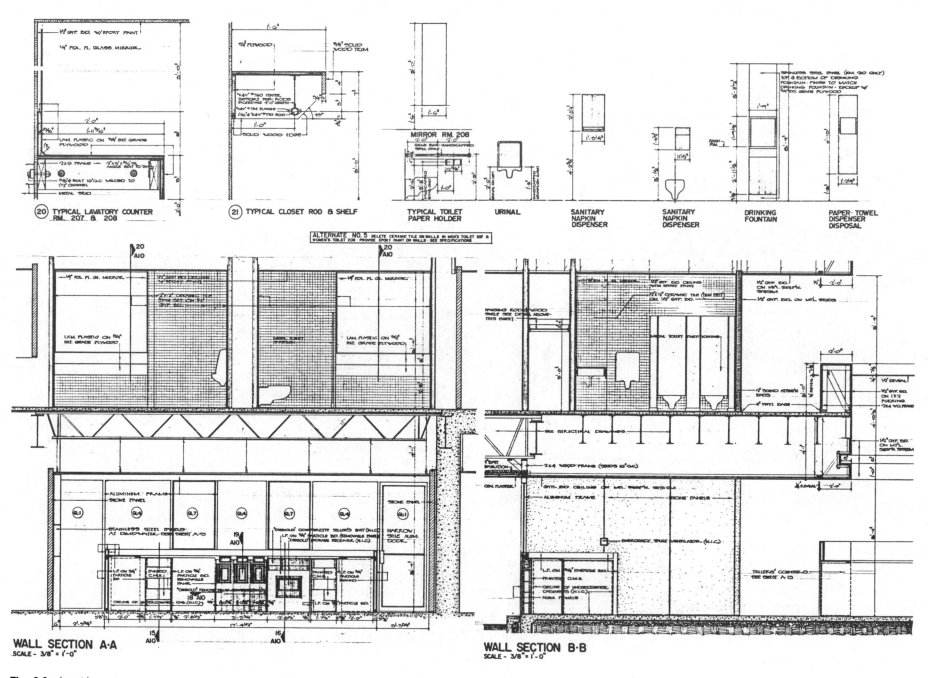

20 TYPICAL LAVATORY COUNTER RM. 207 & 208

21 TYPICAL CLOSET ROD & SHELF

TYPICAL TOILET PAPER HOLDER

URINAL

SANITARY NAPKIN DISPENSER

SANITARY NAPKIN DISPENSER

DRINKING FOUNTAIN

PAPER TOWEL DISPENSER DISPOSAL

MIRROR RM. 208

ALTERNATE NO. 5 DELETE CERAMIC TILE ON WALLS IN MEN'S TOILET 207 & WOMEN'S TOILET 208 PROVIDE EPOXY PAINT ON WALLS. SEE SPECIFICATIONS

WALL SECTION A·A
SCALE - 3/8" = 1'-0"

WALL SECTION B·B
SCALE - 3/8" = 1'-0"

Fig. 8-3 *(cont.)*

Fig. 8-3 (cont.)

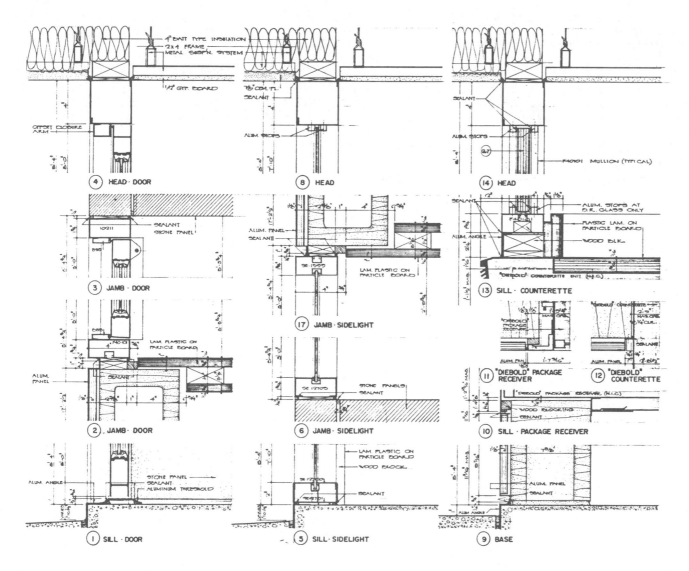

COMMON DETAIL DRAWINGS

added. Needed dimensions and other similar specifications can be added. In the examples, however, component identification was used.

Unlike wall details, which are typical examples for general areas, other architectural detail drawings illustrate particular areas of construction. They show how building components and hardware are constructed, fit into place, or both. The amount of information in these drawings depends upon the types of control over the construction process the architect has.

The more details drawn and the more information given, the more experience and technical knowledge

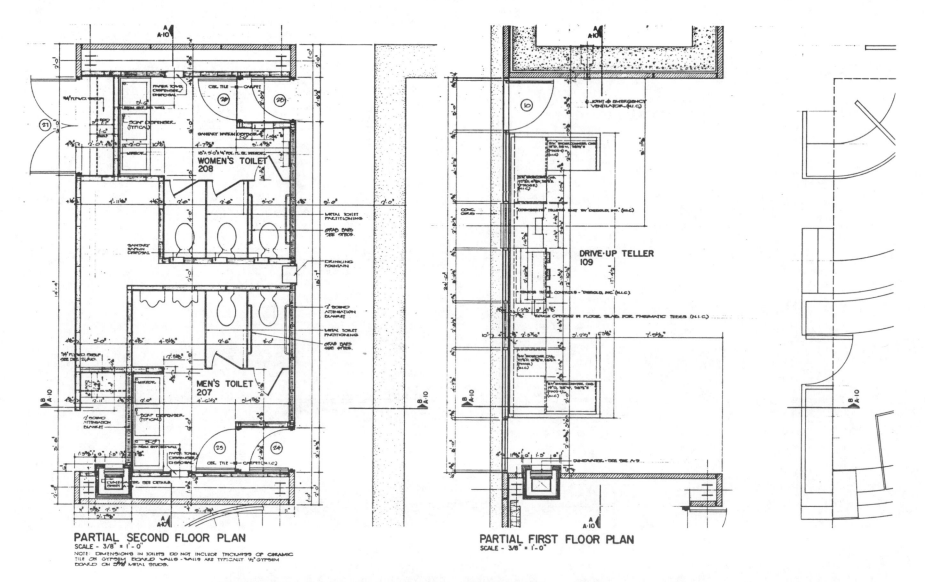

PARTIAL SECOND FLOOR PLAN
SCALE - 3/8" = 1'-0"
NOTE: DIMENSIONS IN TOILETS DO NOT INCLUDE THICKNESS OF CERAMIC
TILE ON GYPSUM BOARD WALLS - WALLS ARE TYPICALLY 1/2" GYPSUM
BOARD ON 3 5/8" METAL STUDS.

PARTIAL FIRST FLOOR PLAN
SCALE - 3/8" = 1'-0"

Fig. 8-3 *(cont.)*

are required of the drafter. A common mistake of beginning drafters is to draw too many details. It is neither practical nor useful to draw details for every component and piece of hardware in the building. For example, it is a waste of time to prepare detail drawings for the installation of all doors in the building, since most door installations follow constant construction practices. Only door installations that deviate from common construction practice require special detail drawings.

As a rule of thumb, details are not needed for standard hardware or for common construction and installation procedures. The hardware is ordered directly from the building-supply company, and the contractor and the construction crew know the procedures for installation. Remember that detail drawings are used almost only for *special* construction designs, procedures, hardware and materials, and specifications.

Various types of detail drawings show the specific elements of construction. Examples of common types are doors, windows, walls, and roof and ceiling elements. Though these details are in most sets of architectural working drawings, the illustrations themselves vary considerably.

WINDOW AND DOOR DETAILS

Many types of windows and doors are available. The most efficient way of specifying which doors and windows are to be installed in which openings is to use symbols and notations. These are then listed in the window and door schedules. Frequently, it is also up to the drafter to show *how* the windows and doors are to be installed.

To illustrate how windows and doors fit into their assigned openings, draw details, showing cutting-plane lines in the openings. It is important to show how the doors and windows are to be installed in relationship to the head, jamb, and sill. This is illustrated in Figs. 8-9 and 8-10. Other window and door details used in actual building projects are shown in Figs. 8-11 through 8-16.

WALL SYSTEM DETAILS

All exterior wall construction should be illustrated with one or more wall details. If there are special interior systems, draw details to show how these systems are to be constructed and fitted into the interior spaces of the building. In all, there are three major categories of wall systems: *stationary* or *fixed, demountable,* and *relocatable* or *movable* wall systems.

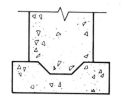
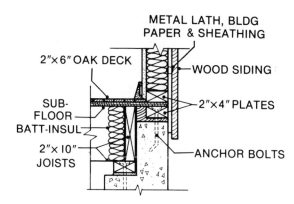

Fig. 8-4 *Three Basic Components of Wall Details*

METAL LATH, BLDG PAPER & SHEATHING

2"×6" OAK DECK

WOOD SIDING

SUB-FLOOR

2"×4" PLATES

BATT-INSUL

2"×10" JOISTS

ANCHOR BOLTS

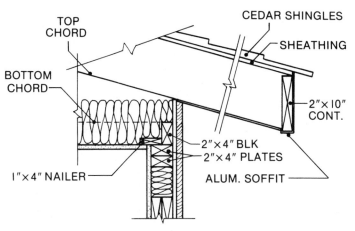

CEDAR SHINGLES

TOP CHORD

SHEATHING

BOTTOM CHORD

2"×10" CONT.

2"×4" BLK

2"×4" PLATES

1"×4" NAILER

ALUM. SOFFIT

Stationary wall systems (Fig. 8-17) are permanently installed in the building, until any future redesign and renovation. Demountable wall systems are those that can be installed and later taken down with little effort (Fig. 8-18). Movable wall systems are just that: systems that can be constructed, taken down, and moved to another location, making the interior design very flexible.

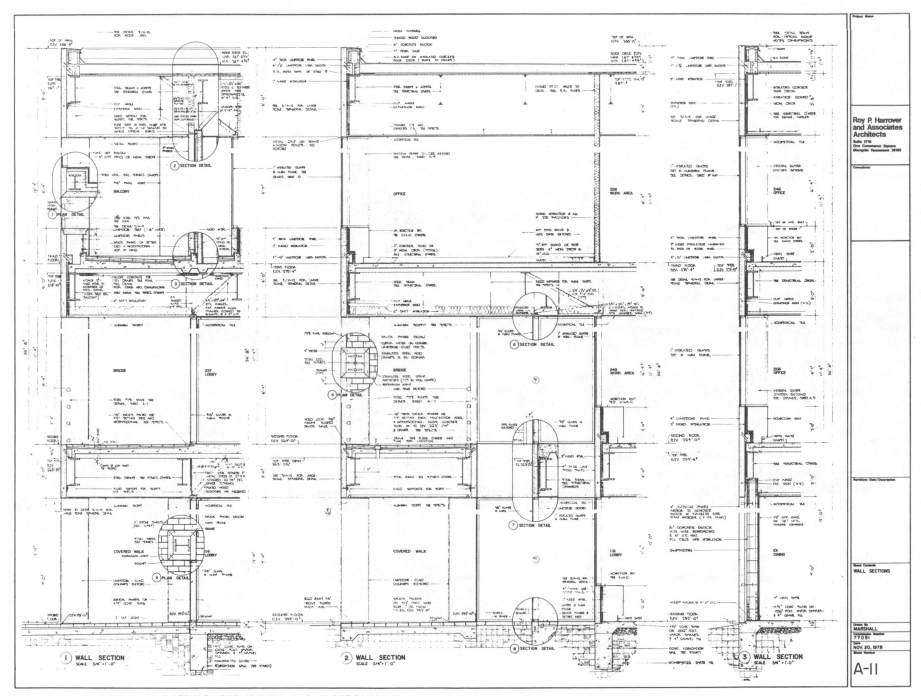

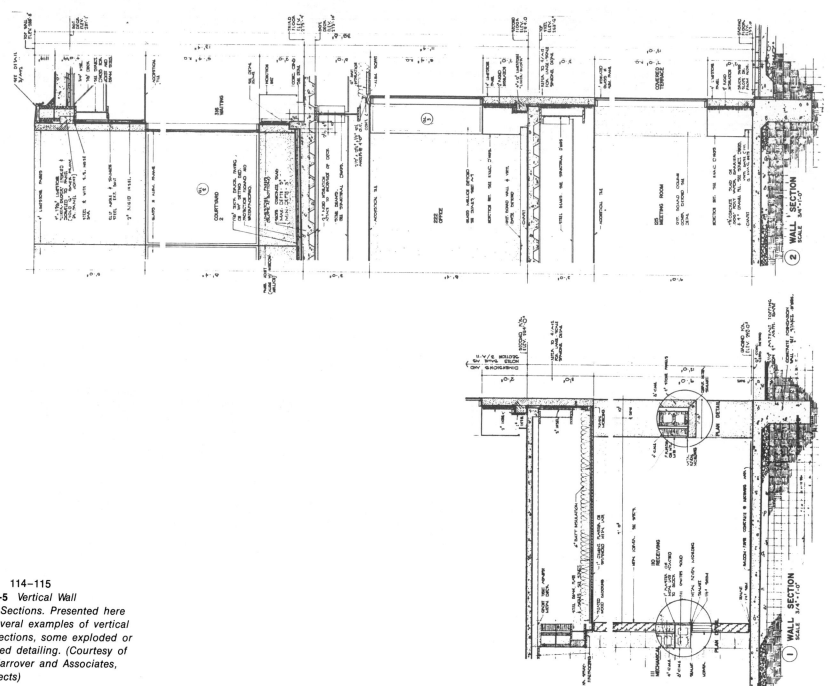

Pages 114–115

Fig. 8-5 *Vertical Wall Cross-Sections. Presented here are several examples of vertical wall sections, some exploded or enlarged detailing. (Courtesy of Roy Harrover and Associates, Architects)*

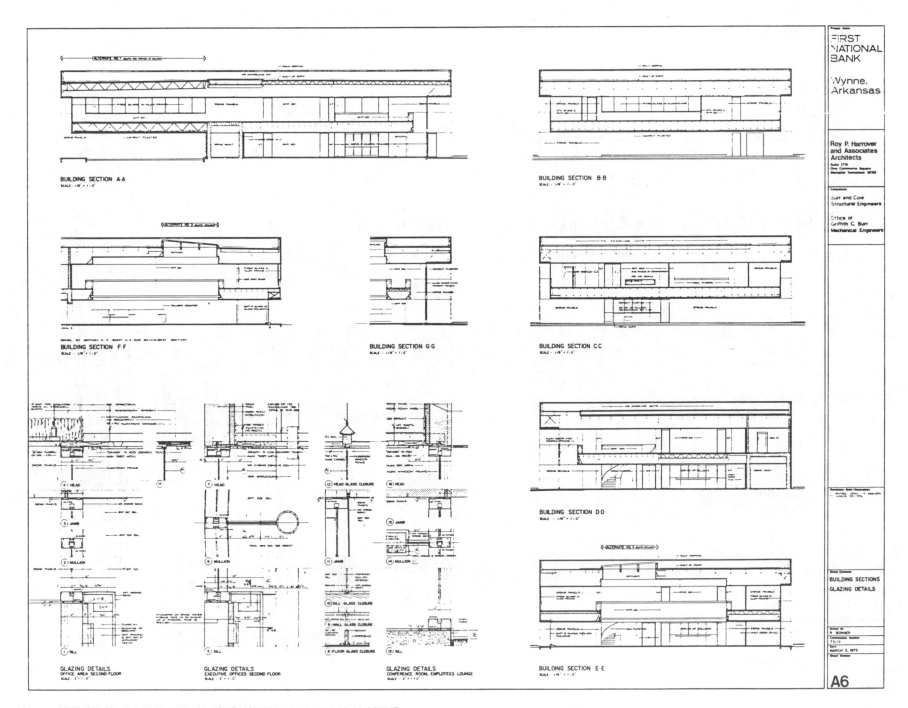

BUILDING SECTION A-A
SCALE : 1/8" = 1'-0"

BUILDING SECTION B-B
SCALE : 1/8" = 1'-0"

BUILDING SECTION F-F
SCALE : 1/8" = 1'-0"

BUILDING SECTION G-G
SCALE : 1/8" = 1'-0"

BUILDING SECTION C-C
SCALE : 1/8" = 1'-0"

BUILDING SECTION D-D
SCALE : 1/8" = 1'-0"

BUILDING SECTION E-E
SCALE : 1/8" = 1'-0"

GLAZING DETAILS
OFFICE AREA SECOND FLOOR
SCALE : 3" = 1'-0"

GLAZING DETAILS
EXECUTIVE OFFICES SECOND FLOOR
SCALE : 3" = 1'-0"

GLAZING DETAILS
CONFERENCE ROOM, EMPLOYEES LOUNGE
SCALE : 3" = 1'-0"

FIRST NATIONAL BANK

Wynne, Arkansas

Roy P. Harrover and Associates Architects
Suite 2710
One Commerce Square
Memphis Tennessee 38103

Consultants

Burr and Cole Structural Engineers

Office of Griffith C. Burr Mechanical Engineers

Building Sections Glazing Details

Date
MARCH 3, 1975

A6

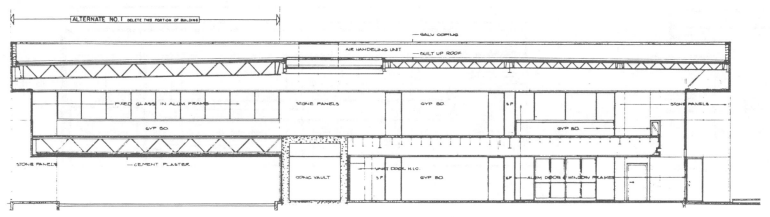

BUILDING SECTION A·A
SCALE - 1/8" = 1'-0"

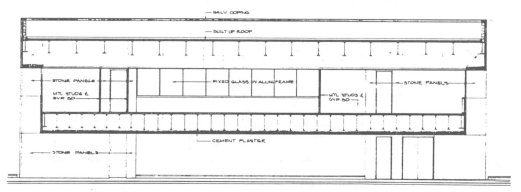

BUILDING SECTION B·B
SCALE - 1/8" = 1'-0"

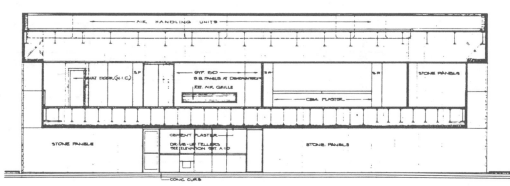

BUILDING SECTION C·C
SCALE - 1/8" = 1'-0"

Pages 116–118

Fig. 8-6 *Examples of Elevation Cross-Sections. (Courtesy of Roy P. Harrover and Associates, Architects)*

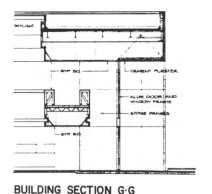

BUILDING SECTION G·G
SCALE - 1/8" = 1'-0"

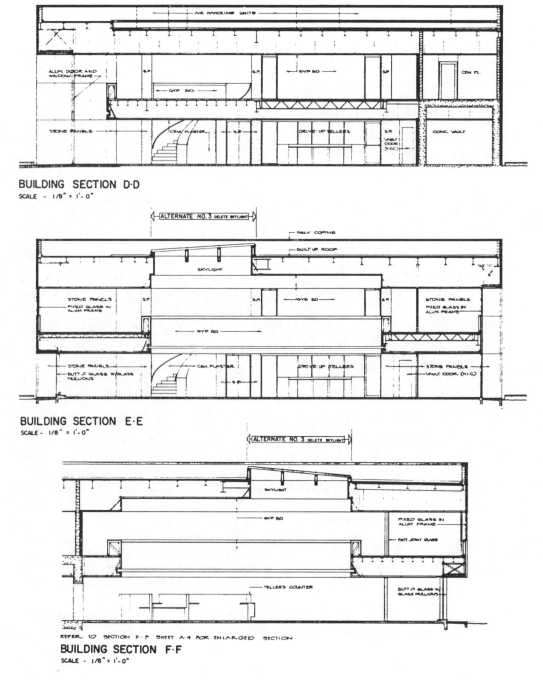

BUILDING SECTION D·D
SCALE - 1/8" = 1'-0"

BUILDING SECTION E·E
SCALE - 1/8" = 1'-0"

BUILDING SECTION F·F
SCALE - 1/8" = 1'-0"

Fig. 8-6 *(cont.)*

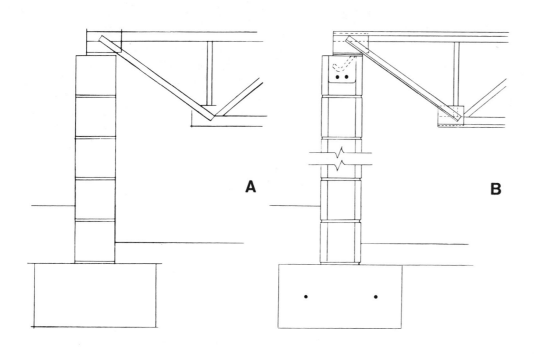

A

B

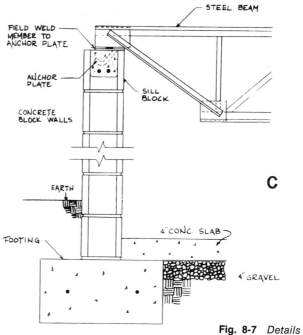

STEEL BEAM

FIELD WELD
MEMBER TO
ANCHOR PLATE

ANCHOR
PLATE

SILL
BLOCK

CONCRETE
BLOCK WALLS

EARTH

FOOTING

4" CONC. SLAB

4" GRAVEL

C

Fig. 8-7 *Details*

Fig. 8-8 *Details*

A

B

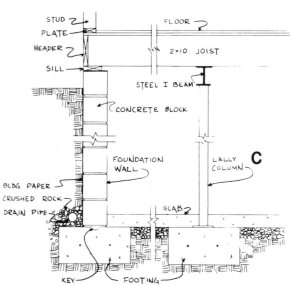

STUD

PLATE

HEADER

SILL

FLOOR

2×10 JOIST

STEEL I BEAM

CONCRETE BLOCK

FOUNDATION
WALL

LALLY
COLUMN

BLDG. PAPER

CRUSHED ROCK

DRAIN PIPE

SLAB

KEY

FOOTING

C

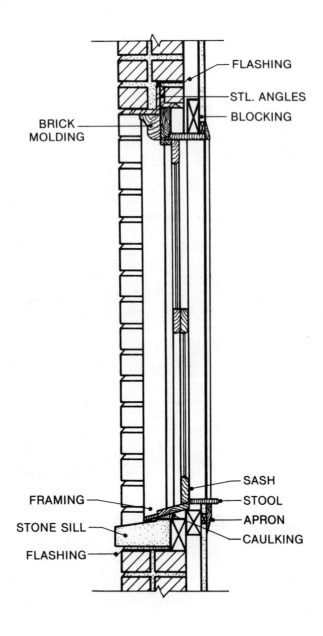

FLASHING

STL. ANGLES

BLOCKING

BRICK MOLDING

SASH

FRAMING

STOOL

STONE SILL

APRON

FLASHING

CAULKING

Fig. 8-9 *Window Detail. This drawing shows the relationship between the window and the opening it is to be installed in. Special construction features are also identified.*

ROOF AND CEILING DETAILS

Roof and ceiling details are becoming more common. The reason is the application of new design principles and the use of new construction technology and materials. *Roof details* show how the roof is constructed; they are not to be confused with roof pitch notations. With the increased popularity of skylighting and environmental-control principles, exact detailing of roof construction is more necessary than ever. See Fig. 8-19. *Ceiling details*, on the other hand, show how interior construction of the roof-ceiling system is to be handled. These details show special fire-protection designs—e.g., sprinklers, nonflammable materials, air supply and air-flow allowances, and lighting considerations. Figs. 8-20 and 8-21 are sample ceiling details.

OTHER DETAILS

In addition to the window and door, wall, and roof and ceiling details, many other architectural details are prepared. Just a few examples are stairway details, curtain-wall systems, cornices, balustrades and balusters, and mechanical assemblies. Figs. 8-22 through 8-27 give some examples of such details.

SUMMARY

Architectural detail drawings show tradesmen how a building is constructed and how the hardware is fitted in place. Details show how *special* construction and materials relate to other members of the building; they should not be used to illustrate common construction practices. The number and type of details drawn are determined by the complexity of the structure, the amount of special construction, and the amount of supervision time the architectural team can spend on the construction site.

To prepare architectural details, the drafter decides the scaling, notation system, and the location of the details in relationship to the cutting-plane lines. Wall details illustrate the type of construction for exterior walls and roofs. The cross-sectional wall detail shows specifications and construction of the footing, sill, and cornice. Other commonly drawn details include window and door, wall system, roof and ceiling, stairway, and mechanical assemblies.

REVIEW QUESTIONS

1. What is an architectural detail drawing?
2. When should detail drawings be drawn and when should they not be drawn?
3. What is the most common range of scales for detail drawings?
4. What is meant by a *detail manual*?
5. What are wall details and what should be included in them?
6. What are some factors that should be considered when preparing wall details?
7. What is the purpose of window and door details?
8. Name three types of wall systems.
9. What is the difference between roof pitch notations and roof details?
10. Why are ceiling-detail drawings needed? What features might be included in a ceiling detail drawing?

EXERCISES

1. Identify and draw the details required for the floor plan developed in Chapter 7.
2. Develop details showing how windows and doors are to be installed in the following types of construction:

    a. Wood framing
    b. Brick veneer
    c. Solid brick
    d. Brick-masonry

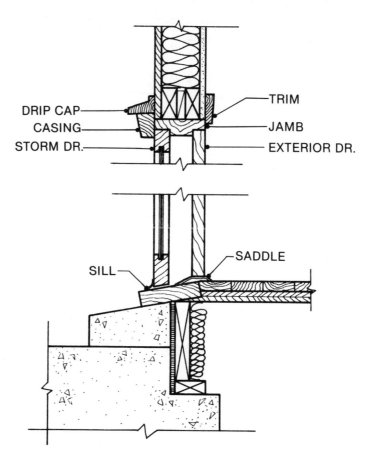

Fig. 8-10 *Door Detail. This shows an exterior door with a storm door.*

DRIP CAP — TRIM
CASING — JAMB
STORM DR. — EXTERIOR DR.

SADDLE
SILL

3. Identify a special stairway design and prepare the appropriate stair details.
4. Plan, organize, and make a detail manual for the floor plan developed in Chapter 7.

Fig. 8-11 *Door Details (Courtesy of Indiana Limestone Institute of America)*

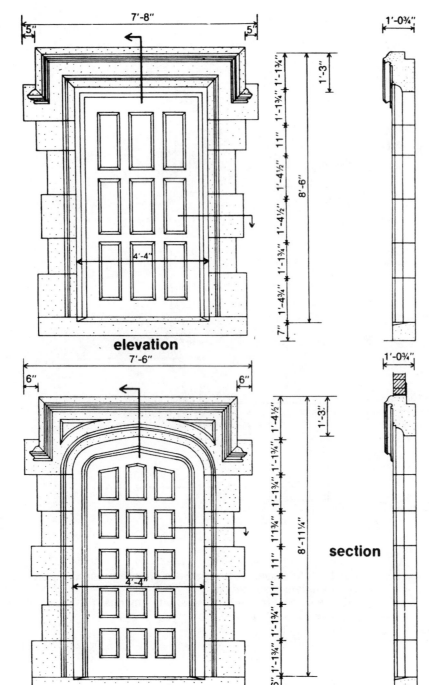

elevation

section

header section

jamb plan

section

Page 123
Fig. 8-12 *Window and Door Details (Courtesy of Indiana Limestone Institute of America)*

Page 124
Fig. 8-13A *Rose Window Detail. This shows a Gothic tracery window, both exterior and interior. (Courtesy of Indiana Limestone Institute of America)*

Page 125
Fig. 8-13B *Tracery Window Detail. This shows a tracery window, both exterior and interior. (Courtesy of Indiana Limestone Institute of America)*

Shown are but two of the many designs available using limestone to accent doorways.

Dimensions and design are custom co-ordinated to each individual architectural desire.

Limestone can be used as interior trim as well as exterior or can be cut in one piece to satisfy both conditions, thereby eliminating unnecessary joints.

Consult with the fabricator concerning intricate moldings and carvings. Slight changes in design can reduce fabrication cost.

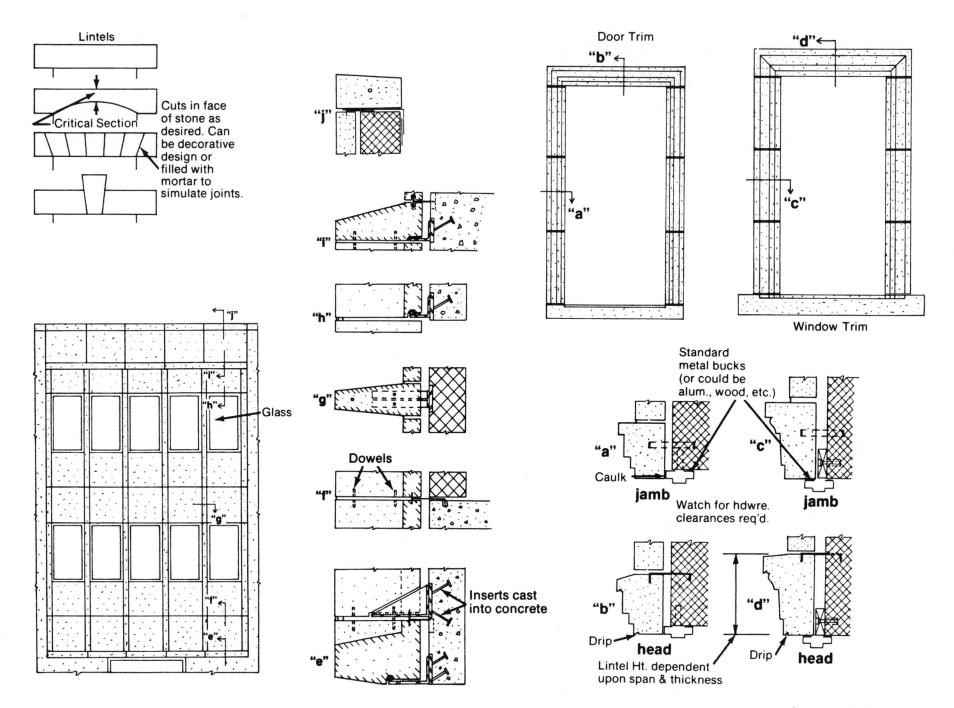

Lintels

Critical Section

Cuts in face of stone as desired. Can be decorative design or filled with mortar to simulate joints.

Glass

"j"

"i"

"h"

"g"

Dowels

"f"

Inserts cast into concrete

"e"

Door Trim

"b"

"a"

"d"

"c"

Window Trim

Standard metal bucks (or could be alum., wood, etc.)

"a"

Caulk

jamb

"c"

jamb

Watch for hdwre. clearances req'd.

"b"

Drip

head

"d"

Drip

head

Lintel Ht. dependent upon span & thickness

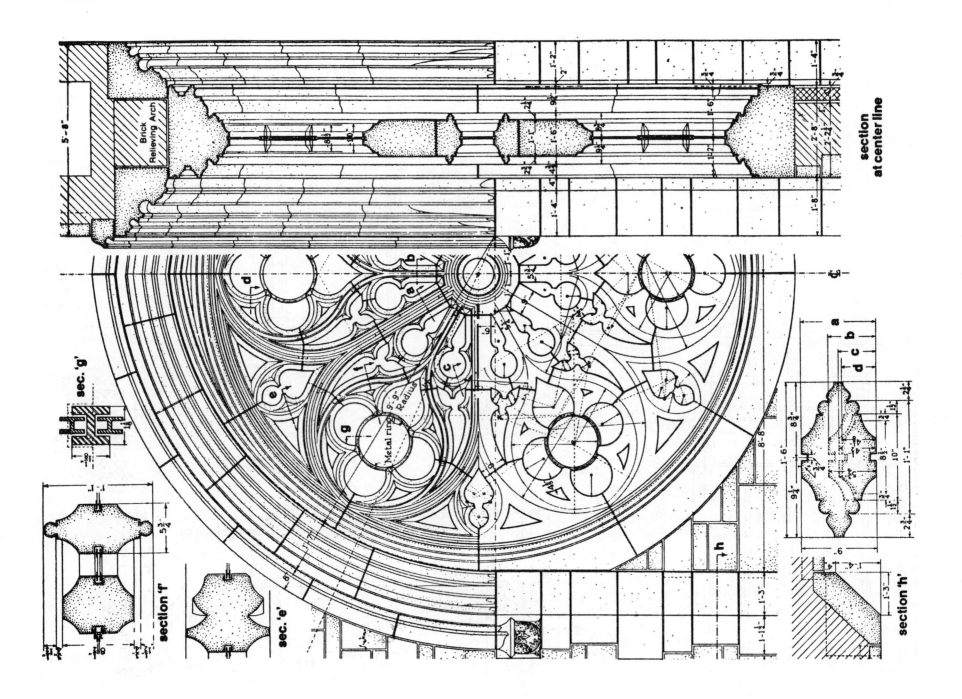

section at center line

Brick Relieving Arch

sec. 'g'

section 'f'

sec. 'e'

Metal ring 9'-9" Radius

section 'h'

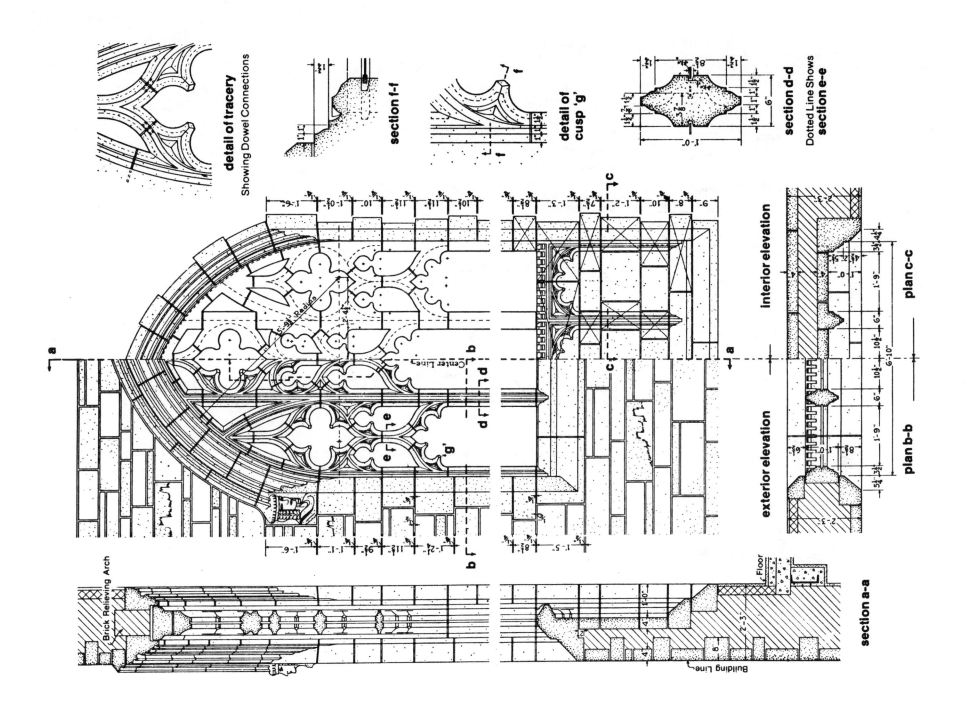

detail of tracery
Showing Dowel Connections

section f-f

detail of cusp 'g'

section d-d
Dotted Line Shows
section e-e

interior elevation

plan c-c

plan b-b

exterior elevation

section a-a

Brick Relieving Arch

Center Line

Building Line

Floor

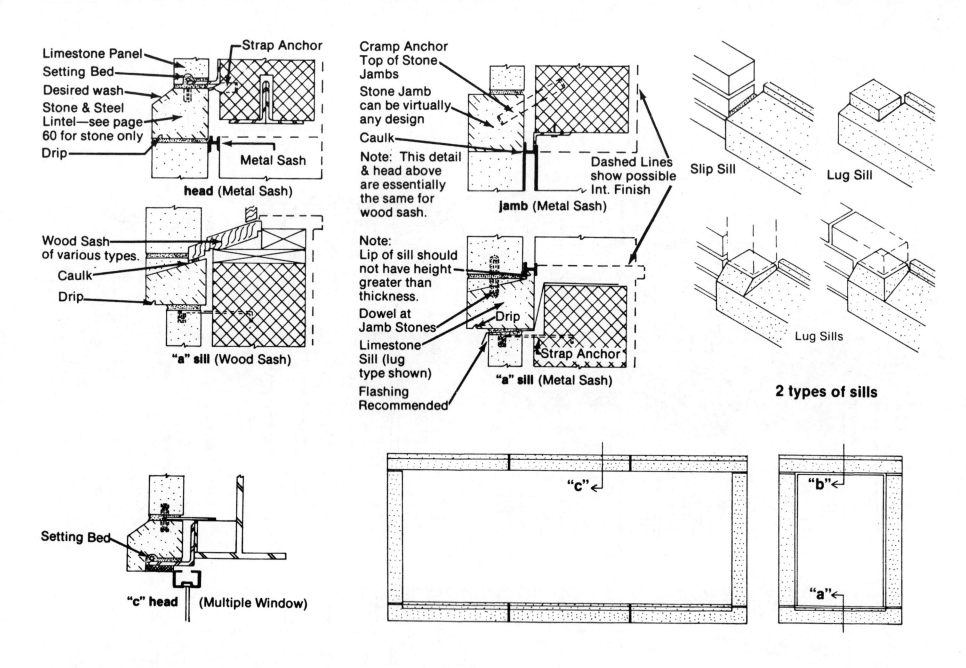

head (Metal Sash)

Limestone Panel
Setting Bed
Desired wash
Stone & Steel Lintel—see page 60 for stone only
Drip
Strap Anchor
Metal Sash

Wood Sash of various types.
Caulk
Drip

"a" sill (Wood Sash)

Cramp Anchor Top of Stone Jambs
Stone Jamb can be virtually any design
Caulk

Note: This detail & head above are essentially the same for wood sash.

jamb (Metal Sash)

Dashed Lines show possible Int. Finish

Note: Lip of sill should not have height greater than thickness.
Dowel at Jamb Stones
Limestone Sill (lug type shown)
Flashing Recommended
Drip
Strap Anchor

"a" sill (Metal Sash)

Slip Sill
Lug Sill
Lug Sills

2 types of sills

Setting Bed

"c" head (Multiple Window)

"c"

"b"

"a"

Fig. 8-14 *Window Element Details (Courtesy of Indiana Limestone Institute of America)*

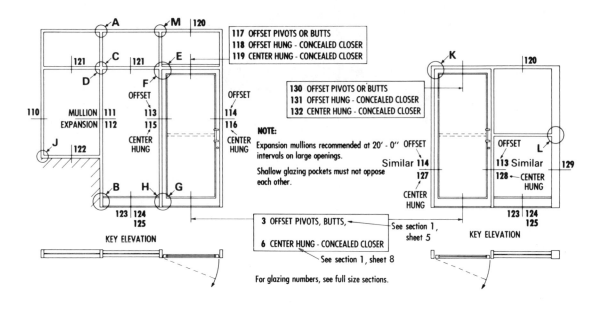

117 OFFSET PIVOTS OR BUTTS
118 OFFSET HUNG - CONCEALED CLOSER
119 CENTER HUNG - CONCEALED CLOSER

130 OFFSET PIVOTS OR BUTTS
131 OFFSET HUNG - CONCEALED CLOSER
132 CENTER HUNG - CONCEALED CLOSER

NOTE:

Expansion mullions recommended at 20' - 0'' intervals on large openings.

Shallow glazing pockets must not oppose each other.

3 OFFSET PIVOTS, BUTTS,
See section 1, sheet 5

6 CENTER HUNG - CONCEALED CLOSER
See section 1, sheet 8

For glazing numbers, see full size sections.

KEY ELEVATION

KEY ELEVATION

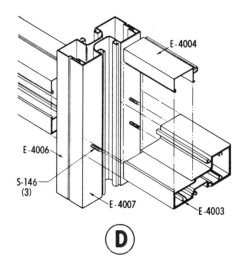

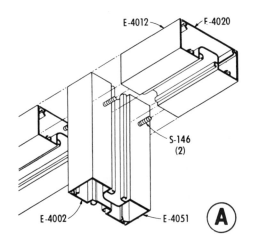

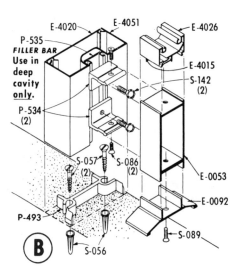

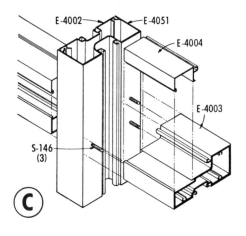

Fig. 8-15 *Window-Door Isometric Detail Drawings. This is an example of how isometric techniques can effectively show architectural detail drawings. (Courtesy of Consolidated Aluminum Corporation)*

ARCHITECTURAL DETAIL DRAWINGS   127

Fig. 8-15 *(cont.)*

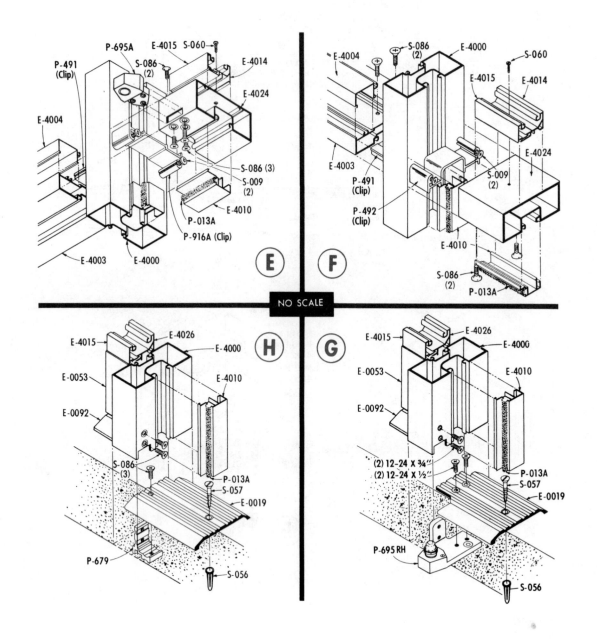

NO SCALE

E

F

H

G

Panel E labels: P-491 (Clip), E-4004, P-695A, S-086 (2), E-4015, S-060, E-4014, E-4024, S-086 (3), S-009 (2), E-4010, P-013A, P-916A (Clip), E-4003, E-4000

Panel F labels: E-4004, S-086 (2), E-4000, S-060, E-4015, E-4014, E-4003, E-4024, P-491 (Clip), S-009 (2), P-492 (Clip), E-4010, S-086 (2), P-013A

Panel H labels: E-4015, E-4026, E-4000, E-0053, E-4010, E-0092, S-086 (3), P-013A, S-057, E-0019, P-679, S-056

Panel G labels: E-4015, E-4026, E-4000, E-0053, E-4010, E-0092, (2) 12-24 X ¾", (2) 12-24 X ½", P-013A, S-057, E-0019, P-695 RH, S-056

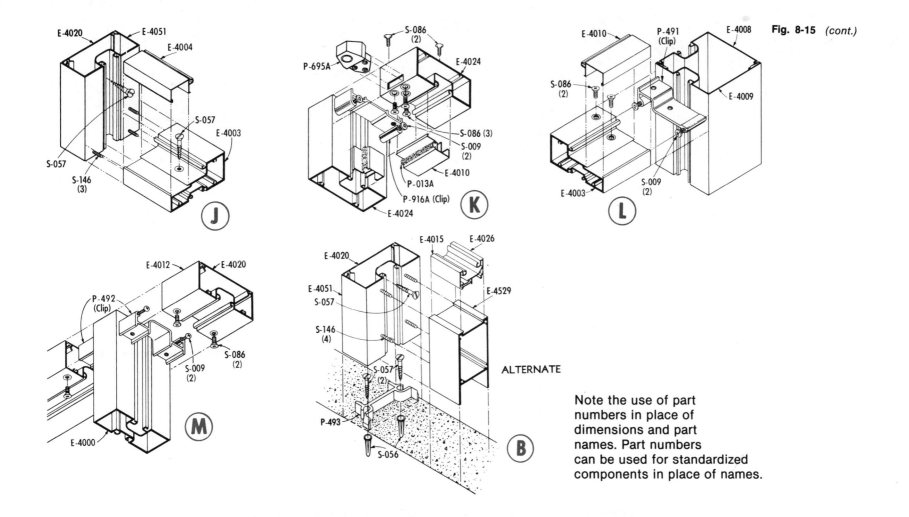

ALTERNATE

Note the use of part numbers in place of dimensions and part names. Part numbers can be used for standardized components in place of names.

Fig. 8-15 *(cont.)*

Fig. 8-16 *Examples of Complete Door Details (Courtesy of Consolidated Aluminum Corporation)*

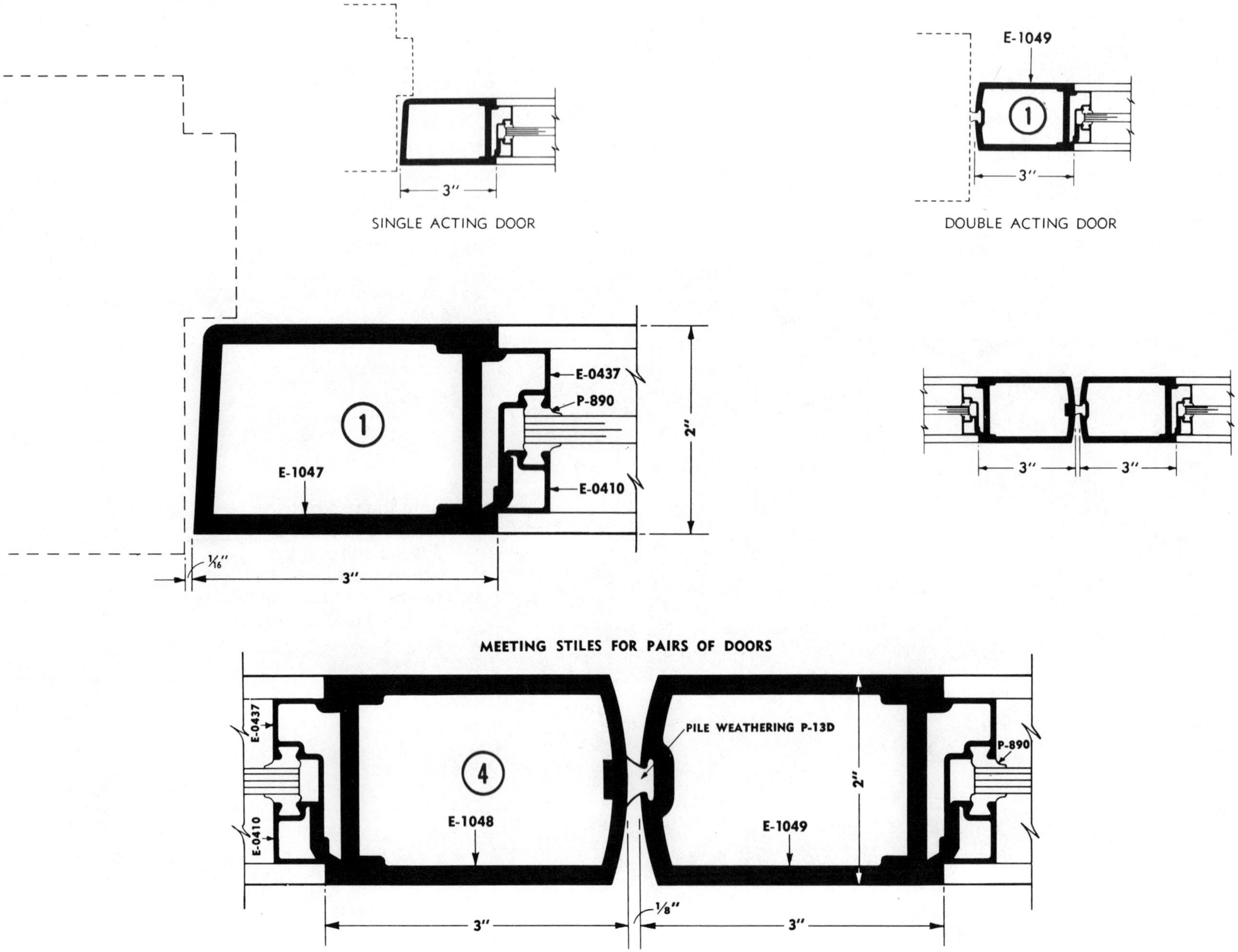
3″
SINGLE ACTING DOOR
E-1049
1
3″
DOUBLE ACTING DOOR
1
E-0437
P-890
E-1047
E-0410
2″
1/16″
3″
3″
3″
MEETING STILES FOR PAIRS OF DOORS
E-0437
E-0410
4
E-1048
PILE WEATHERING P-13D
2″
P-890
E-1049
3″
1/8″
3″

Fig. 8-16 *(cont.)*

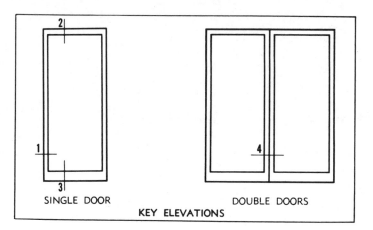

SINGLE DOOR

DOUBLE DOORS

KEY ELEVATIONS

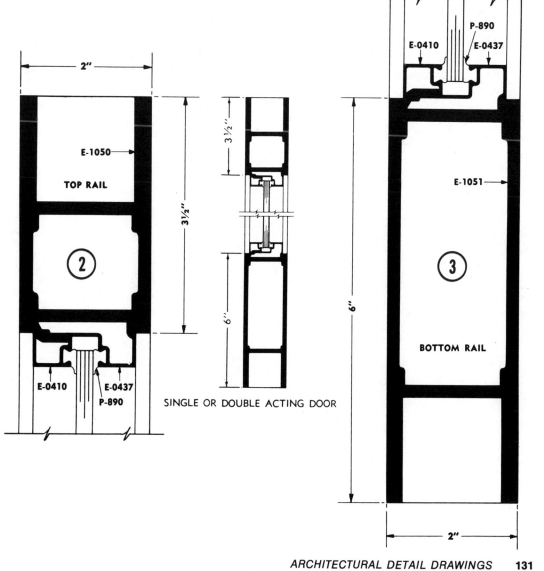

2″

E-1050

TOP RAIL

3½″

②

E-0410   E-0437

P-890

3½″

6″

SINGLE OR DOUBLE ACTING DOOR

P-890

E-0410   E-0437

E-1051

③

BOTTOM RAIL

6″

2″

Fig. 8-17 *Set of Details for Fixed-Wall Systems (Courtesy of Vaughan Walls, Inc.)*

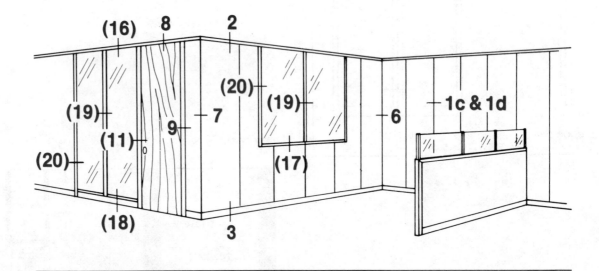

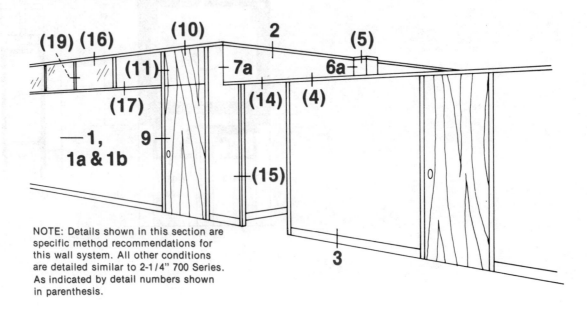

NOTE: Details shown in this section are specific method recommendations for this wall system. All other conditions are detailed similar to 2-1/4" 700 Series. As indicated by detail numbers shown in parenthesis.

Fig. 8-17 *(cont.)*

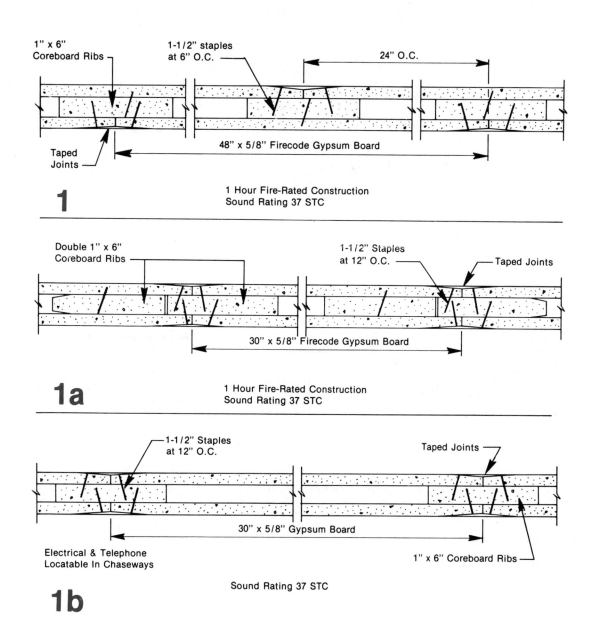

1" x 6"
Coreboard Ribs

1-1/2" staples
at 6" O.C.

24" O.C.

Taped
Joints

48" x 5/8" Firecode Gypsum Board

1

1 Hour Fire-Rated Construction
Sound Rating 37 STC

Double 1" x 6"
Coreboard Ribs

1-1/2" Staples
at 12" O.C.

Taped Joints

30" x 5/8" Firecode Gypsum Board

1a

1 Hour Fire-Rated Construction
Sound Rating 37 STC

1-1/2" Staples
at 12" O.C.

Taped Joints

30" x 5/8" Gypsum Board

Electrical & Telephone
Locatable In Chaseways

1" x 6" Coreboard Ribs

1b

Sound Rating 37 STC

Fig. 8-17 *(cont.)*

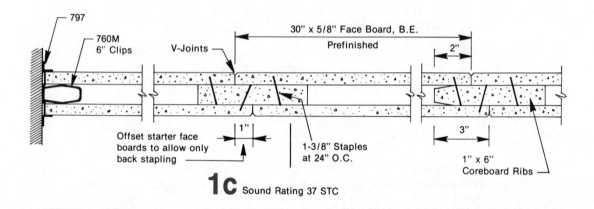

797

760M
6" Clips

V-Joints

30" x 5/8" Face Board, B.E.

Prefinished

2"

Offset starter face
boards to allow only
back stapling

1"

1-3/8" Staples
at 24" O.C.

3"

1" x 6"
Coreboard Ribs

1c Sound Rating 37 STC

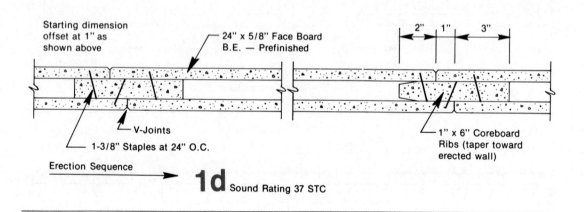

Starting dimension
offset at 1" as
shown above

24" x 5/8" Face Board
B.E. — Prefinished

2" 1" 3"

V-Joints

1-3/8" Staples at 24" O.C.

1" x 6" Coreboard
Ribs (taper toward
erected wall)

Erection Sequence

1d Sound Rating 37 STC

Electrical & Telephone
Services Locatable In
Chaseways

Fig. 8-17 *(cont.)*

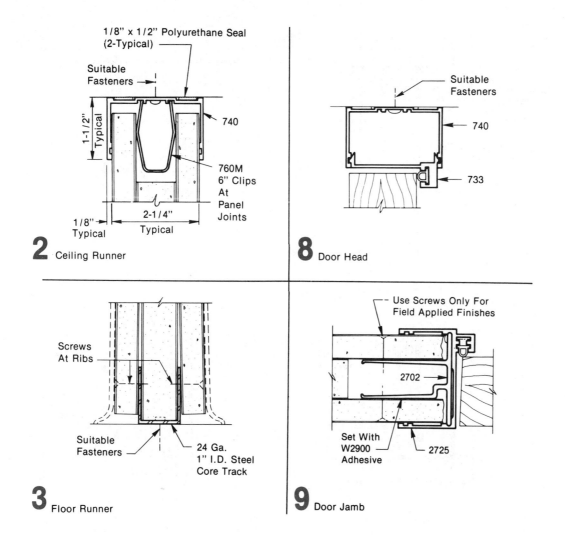

1/8" x 1/2" Polyurethane Seal
(2-Typical)

Suitable
Fasteners

1-1/2"
Typical

740

760M
6" Clips
At
Panel
Joints

1/8"
Typical

2-1/4"
Typical

2 Ceiling Runner

Suitable
Fasteners

740

733

8 Door Head

Screws
At Ribs

Suitable
Fasteners

24 Ga.
1" I.D. Steel
Core Track

3 Floor Runner

Use Screws Only For
Field Applied Finishes

2702

Set With
W2900
Adhesive

2725

9 Door Jamb

Fig. 8-17 *(cont.)*

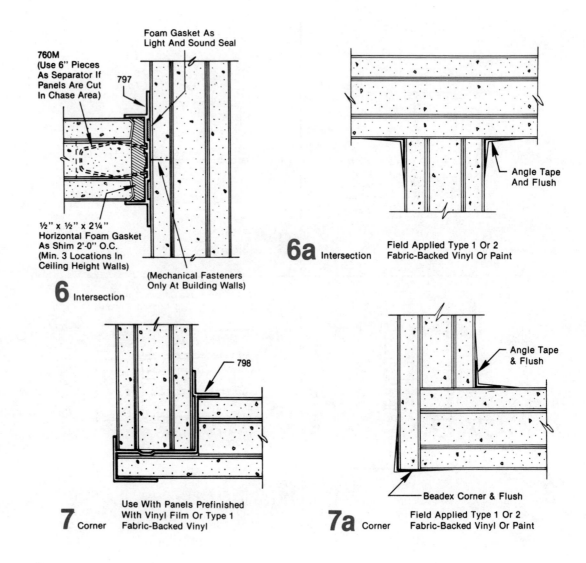

760M
(Use 6" Pieces As Separator If Panels Are Cut In Chase Area)

797

Foam Gasket As Light And Sound Seal

½" x ½" x 2¼" Horizontal Foam Gasket As Shim 2'-0" O.C. (Min. 3 Locations In Ceiling Height Walls)

(Mechanical Fasteners Only At Building Walls)

6 Intersection

6a Intersection — Field Applied Type 1 Or 2 Fabric-Backed Vinyl Or Paint

Angle Tape And Flush

798

7 Corner — Use With Panels Prefinished With Vinyl Film Or Type 1 Fabric-Backed Vinyl

Angle Tape & Flush

Beadex Corner & Flush

7a Corner — Field Applied Type 1 Or 2 Fabric-Backed Vinyl Or Paint

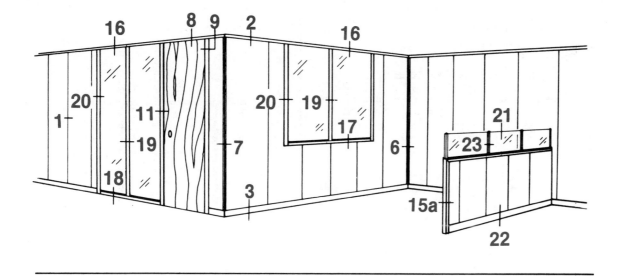

Fig. 8-18A *Set of Details for Dismountable-Wall Systems (Courtesy of Vaughan Walls, Inc.)*

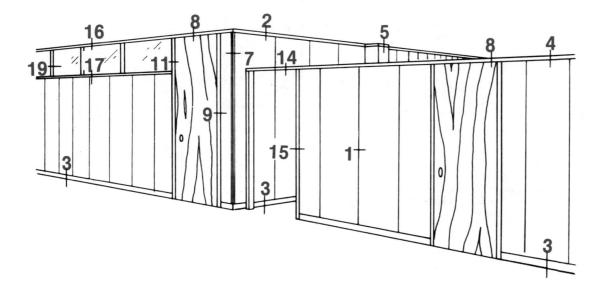

Fig. 8-18A *(cont.)*

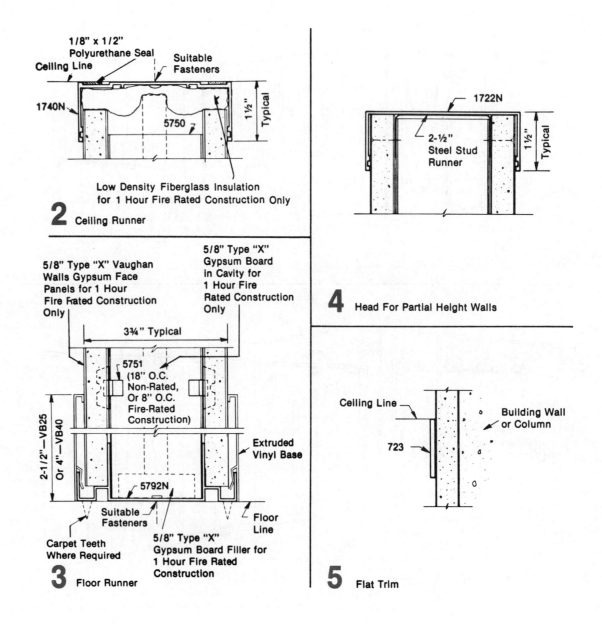

1/8" x 1/2" Polyurethane Seal

Ceiling Line

Suitable Fasteners

1740N

5750

1½" Typical

Low Density Fiberglass Insulation for 1 Hour Fire Rated Construction Only

2 Ceiling Runner

1722N

2-½" Steel Stud Runner

1½" Typical

4 Head For Partial Height Walls

5/8" Type "X" Vaughan Walls Gypsum Face Panels for 1 Hour Fire Rated Construction Only

5/8" Type "X" Gypsum Board In Cavity for 1 Hour Fire Rated Construction Only

3¾" Typical

5751 (18" O.C. Non-Rated, Or 8" O.C. Fire-Rated Construction)

2-1/2"—VB25 Or 4"—VB40

Extruded Vinyl Base

5792N

Suitable Fasteners

Floor Line

Carpet Teeth Where Required

5/8" Type "X" Gypsum Board Filler for 1 Hour Fire Rated Construction

3 Floor Runner

Ceiling Line

723

Building Wall or Column

5 Flat Trim

Fig. 8-18A *(cont.)*

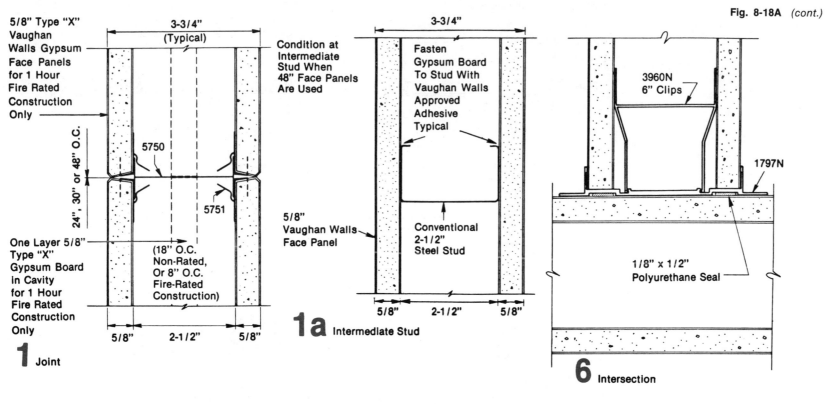

5/8" Type "X" Vaughan Walls Gypsum Face Panels for 1 Hour Fire Rated Construction Only

3-3/4" (Typical)

5750

5751

One Layer 5/8" Type "X" Gypsum Board in Cavity for 1 Hour Fire Rated Construction Only

24", 30" or 48" O.C.

(18" O.C. Non-Rated, Or 8" O.C. Fire-Rated Construction)

5/8"   2-1/2"   5/8"

1 Joint

Condition at Intermediate Stud When 48" Face Panels Are Used

3-3/4"

Fasten Gypsum Board To Stud With Vaughan Walls Approved Adhesive Typical

5/8" Vaughan Walls Face Panel

Conventional 2-1/2" Steel Stud

5/8"   2-1/2"   5/8"

1a Intermediate Stud

3960N 6" Clips

1797N

1/8" x 1/2" Polyurethane Seal

6 Intersection

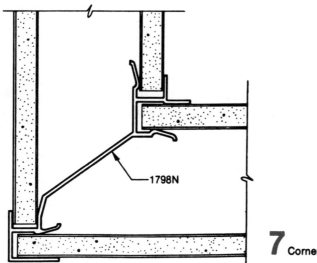

1798N

7 Corner

ARCHITECTURAL DETAIL DRAWINGS   **139**

Fig. 8-18A *(cont.)*

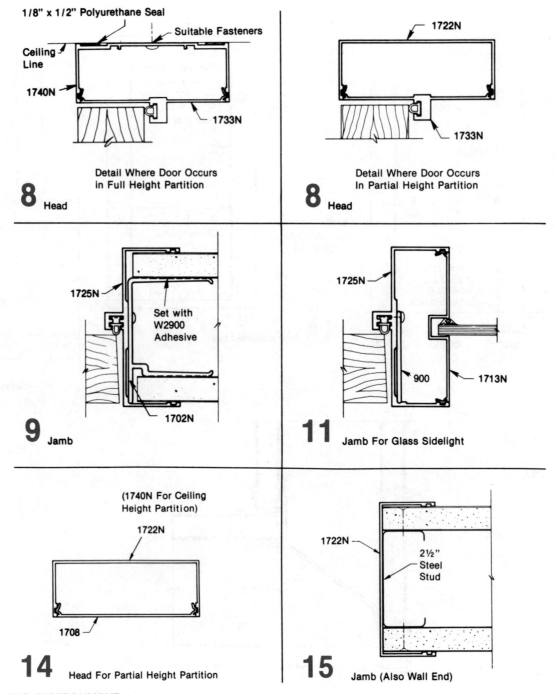

1/8" x 1/2" Polyurethane Seal

Suitable Fasteners

Ceiling Line

1740N

1733N

Detail Where Door Occurs in Full Height Partition

8 Head

1722N

1733N

Detail Where Door Occurs In Partial Height Partition

8 Head

1725N

Set with W2900 Adhesive

1702N

9 Jamb

1725N

900

1713N

11 Jamb For Glass Sidelight

(1740N For Ceiling Height Partition)

1722N

1708

14 Head For Partial Height Partition

1722N

2½" Steel Stud

15 Jamb (Also Wall End)

Fig. 8-18A *(cont.)*

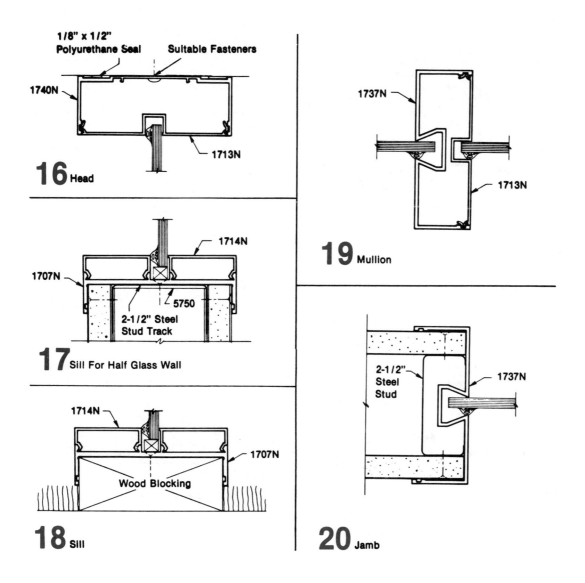

1/8" x 1/2" Polyurethane Seal **Suitable Fasteners**

1740N

1713N

16 Head

1714N

1707N

5750

2-1/2" Steel Stud Track

17 Sill For Half Glass Wall

1714N

1707N

Wood Blocking

18 Sill

1737N

1713N

19 Mullion

2-1/2" Steel Stud

1737N

20 Jamb

Fig. 8-18A *(cont.)*

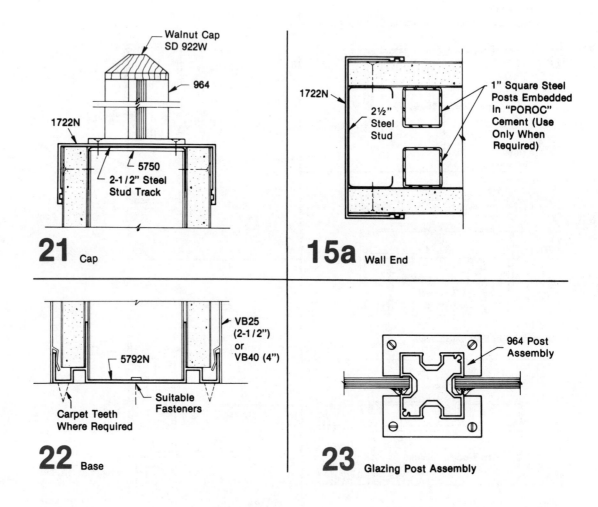

Walnut Cap
SD 922W

964

1722N

5750
2-1/2" Steel
Stud Track

21 Cap

1722N

2½"
Steel
Stud

1" Square Steel
Posts Embedded
In "POROC"
Cement (Use
Only When
Required)

15a Wall End

VB25
(2-1/2")
or
VB40 (4")

5792N

Suitable
Fasteners

Carpet Teeth
Where Required

22 Base

964 Post
Assembly

23 Glazing Post Assembly

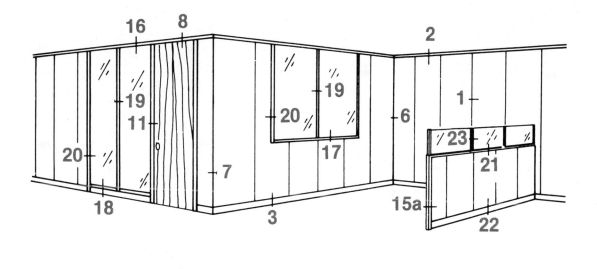

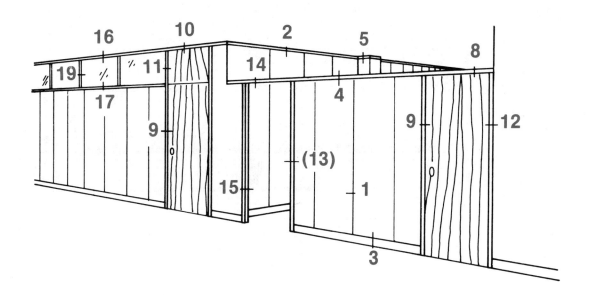

Fig. 8-18B *(cont.)*

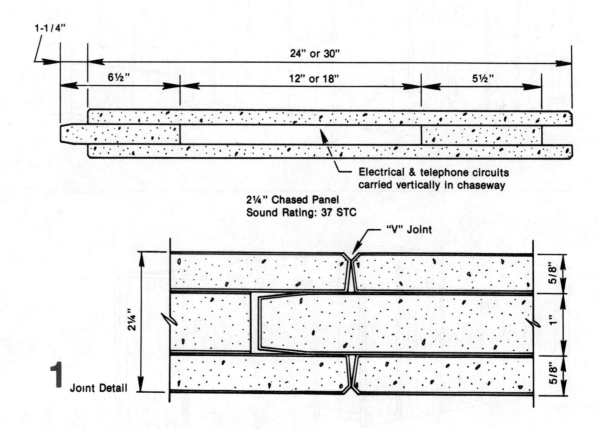

2¼" Chased Panel
Sound Rating: 37 STC

Electrical & telephone circuits
carried vertically in chaseway

1 Joint Detail

Fig. 8-18B *(cont.)*

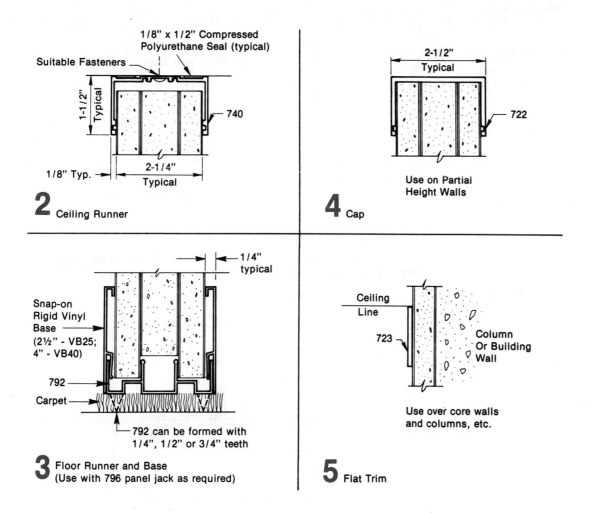

1/8" x 1/2" Compressed
Polyurethane Seal (typical)

Suitable Fasteners

1-1/2"
Typical

740

1/8" Typ.

2-1/4"
Typical

2 Ceiling Runner

2-1/2"
Typical

722

Use on Partial
Height Walls

4 Cap

1/4"
typical

Snap-on
Rigid Vinyl
Base
(2½" - VB25;
4" - VB40)

792

Carpet

792 can be formed with
1/4", 1/2" or 3/4" teeth

3 Floor Runner and Base
(Use with 796 panel jack as required)

Ceiling
Line

723

Column
Or Building
Wall

Use over core walls
and columns, etc.

5 Flat Trim

Fig. 8-18B *(cont.)*

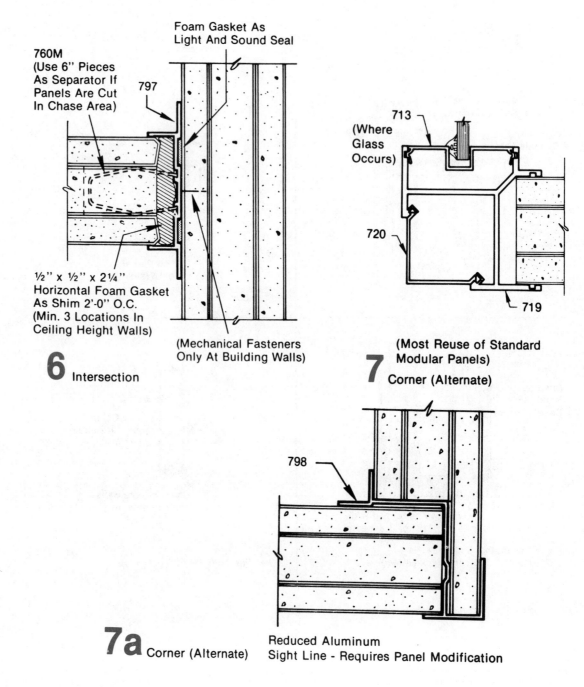

760M
(Use 6" Pieces
As Separator If
Panels Are Cut
In Chase Area)

797

Foam Gasket As
Light And Sound Seal

½" x ½" x 2¼"
Horizontal Foam Gasket
As Shim 2'-0" O.C.
(Min. 3 Locations In
Ceiling Height Walls)

(Mechanical Fasteners
Only At Building Walls)

6 Intersection

713
(Where
Glass
Occurs)

720

719

(Most Reuse of Standard
Modular Panels)

7 Corner (Alternate)

798

7a Corner (Alternate)

Reduced Aluminum
Sight Line - Requires Panel Modification

Fig. 8-18B *(cont.)*

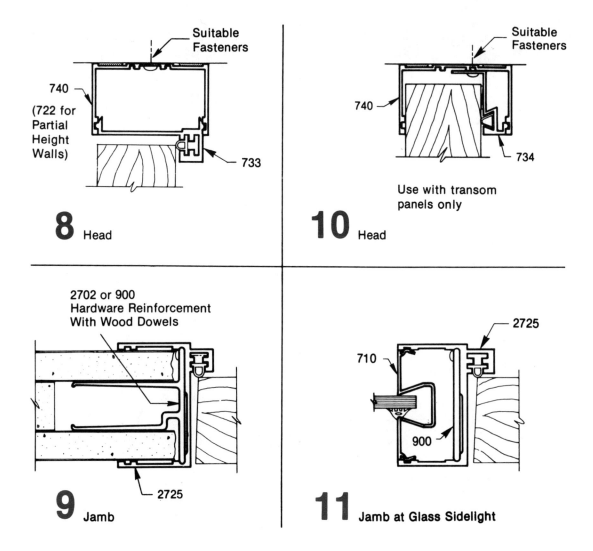

Suitable
Fasteners

740

(722 for
Partial
Height
Walls)

733

8 Head

Suitable
Fasteners

740

734

Use with transom
panels only

10 Head

2702 or 900
Hardware Reinforcement
With Wood Dowels

2725

9 Jamb

2725

710

900

11 Jamb at Glass Sidelight

Fig. 8-18B *(cont.)*

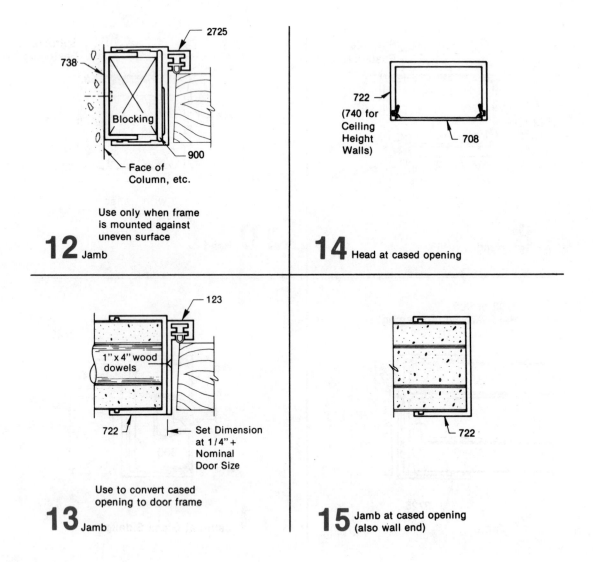

2725

738

Blocking

900

Face of
Column, etc.

Use only when frame
is mounted against
uneven surface

12 Jamb

722
(740 for
Ceiling
Height
Walls)

708

14 Head at cased opening

123

1" x 4" wood
dowels

722

Set Dimension
at 1/4" +
Nominal
Door Size

Use to convert cased
opening to door frame

13 Jamb

722

15 Jamb at cased opening
(also wall end)

need to dimension the elevation. If a detailed wall section is not provided, however, then the elevation should be dimensioned. This follows the basic rule that dimensions are not to be repeated on the same sheet. A typical technique for dimensioning elevations is to use the grade line as the *benchmark* or reference point. That is, all height dimensions begin from the grade line. Above-ground height dimensions are measured from the grade line up, and measurements in the foundation are from the grade line down. Where the grade line is not used as the benchmark, the reference point or line is drawn as a center line and identified as in a note as the benchmark or *zero-elevation* point.

When drawing elevations, it is good practice to standardize all material symbols, hatchings, and notations. Section markers should be drawn in the same fashion throughout the drawing; elevation scales and titles should remain constant; and all hardware, material, and hatchings should be drawn with approved AIA symbols. Remember, the primary purpose of the exterior elevation is to show all the important parts of the building. The dimensional proportions and construction considerations should be as close to reality as possible.

DRAWING ELEVATIONS

Elevations can be prepared by using floor plans and detailed wall sections. If properly drawn, the floor

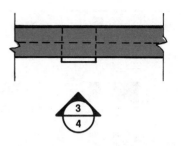

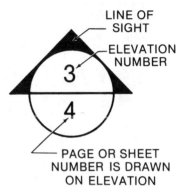

LINE OF SIGHT

ELEVATION NUMBER

PAGE OR SHEET NUMBER IS DRAWN ON ELEVATION

Fig. 9-3 *Interior Elevation Notation System*

Fig. 9-4 *Typical Exterior Elevation. Most elevations are drawn as two-dimensional orthographic drawings. This example is typical.*

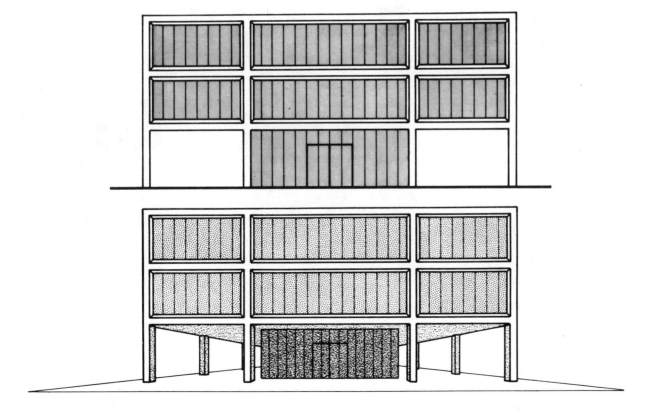

Fig. 9-5 *Perspective Elevation. This is a perspective elevation of the building in Fig. 9-4. The use of perspective adds to the understanding of building design and layout.*

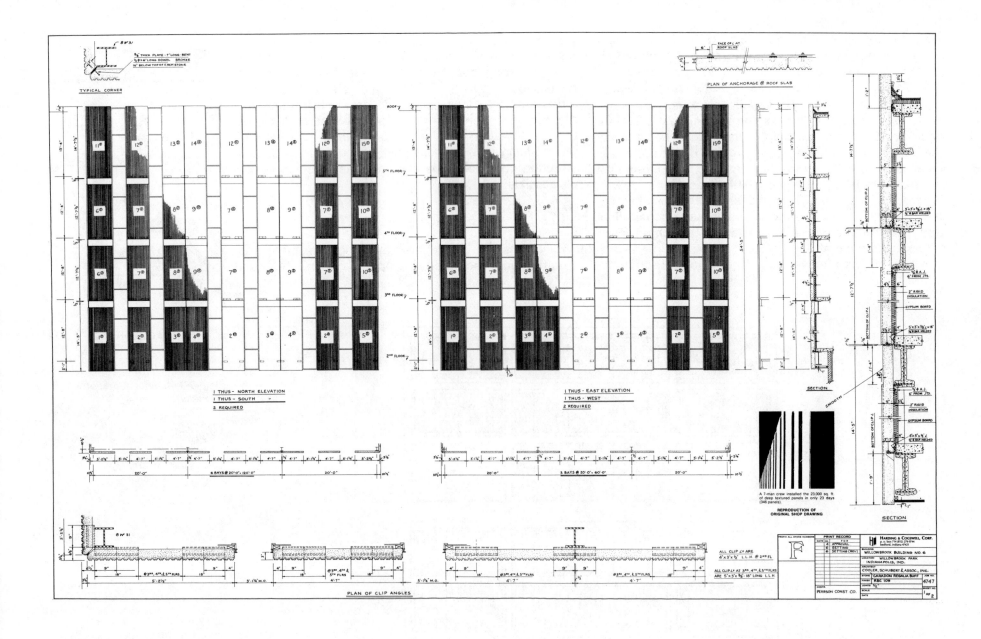

Fig. 9-6 *Exterior Elevation in Combination with Detailed Sections.
Detailed section drawings are frequently presented along with elevation
drawings. This is an integration of the two drawings. (Courtesy of
Harding & Cogswell Corporation)*

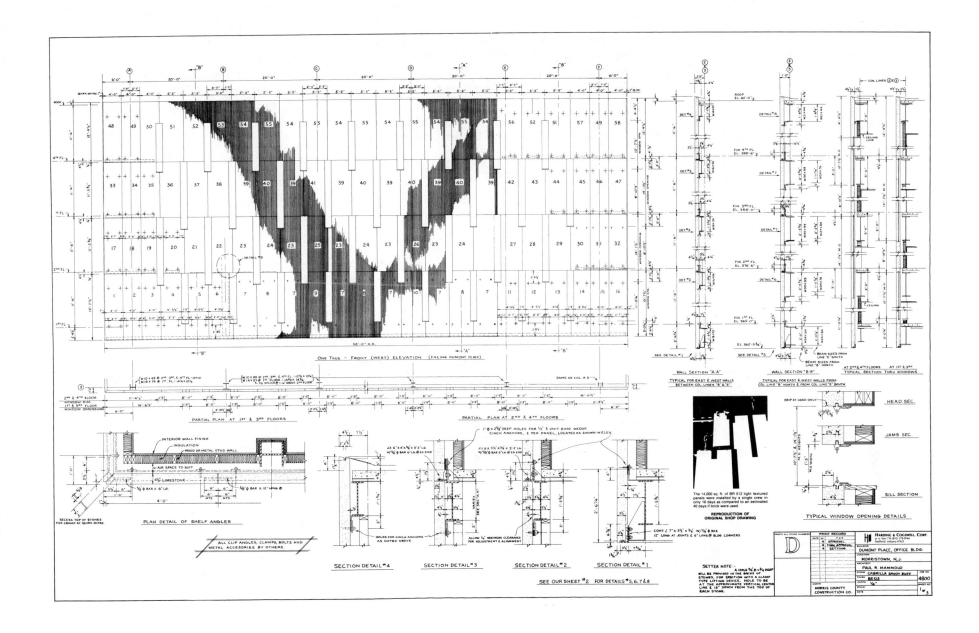

Fig. 9-6 *(cont.)*

ELEVATIONS **167**

plans provide all length and width dimensions, and the detailed wall section supplies all heights. Elevations therefore should be drawn to the same scale as the floor plans: it is easier to transfer distances from one drawing to another than it is to translate a distance from one scale to another. Detailed wall sections, however, are frequently drawn to larger scales than are floor plans.

An eight-step process can aid drafters in drawing both interior and exterior elevations. These eight steps are not the only way of drawing elevations, but they provide the beginning drafter with a logical progression in starting, completing, and evaluating elevations.

STEP 1: ESTABLISH SCALE AND USE PLANS

In drawing elevations, use the same scale you used in the floor plans. Usually this is $1/4'' = 1'-0''$ or $1/8'' = 1'-0''$ (SI 1:50 or 1:100). When using the floor plan to establish elevation lengths and widths, be sure the drawing surface is large enough to handle two sheets of drawing paper adequately. The floor plan is taped directly above the elevation, and the dimensions are brought down from the floor plan to the elevation. If the detailed wall section was drawn separately from the elevation and to the same scale as the floor plan, it can be used in developing the elevation. In this case, the drawing surface must be large enough to handle three sheets of drawing paper. The detailed wall section is taped to one side of the elevation drawing sheet, and all height measurements are brought directly across to the elevation.

STEP 2: ESTABLISH REFERENCE LINES

The first reference line drawn is the grade line. This is only logical: all heights are drawn and dimensioned from it. The next reference lines drawn are the floor and ceiling lines. These normally appear as center lines on the finished drawing. Ceiling heights are typically 8'-1'' (2464 mm) from the floor. This distance varies in commercial buildings and is noted in the design specifications.

After the horizonatal reference lines are drawn, locate and draw all vertical reference lines. These lines are drawn from the floor plan and locate all exterior walls, edges, and cut-ins. See Fig. 9-7A.

STEP 3: DRAW ROOF LINES

Locate and draw the peak height of the roof. If the building has a flat roof, calculate the distance between the ceiling on the top floor and the top of the roof, taking into consideration all structural supports. For sloping roofs, make sure enough space is allowed for the width of rafters or truss construction. After the roof line has been drawn, locate and mark the heights of all cornices.

Sloping roof lines should be drawn beyond the walls, to allow for overhang. Flat roofs are usually drawn flush to the building walls. Refer to the design specifications to locate the actual distance of the roof overhang. If a roof layout was drawn on the floor plan, simply bring down the overhang measurement. See Fig. 9-7B.

STEP 4: ESTABLISH WINDOW AND DOOR HEIGHTS

Exterior doors are measured from the floor line. These are available in standard stock heights of from 6'-8'' (2032 mm) to 7'-0'' (2134 mm). In many cases, the door height is used to establish window heights. Where the window heights vary, such as for window-walls, design specifications and floor-plan notations give exact window locations and dimensions.

Building elevations with many windows and doors of the same variety and size can be drawn easily. There are three shortcut techniques. These are the use of *transfer overlays*, *standardized* or *custom-made templates*, and *previously drawn windows and doors*. These last are drawn on small pieces of paper, preferably polyester film, that can easily be moved under the drawing sheet itself and traced. See Fig. 9-7C.

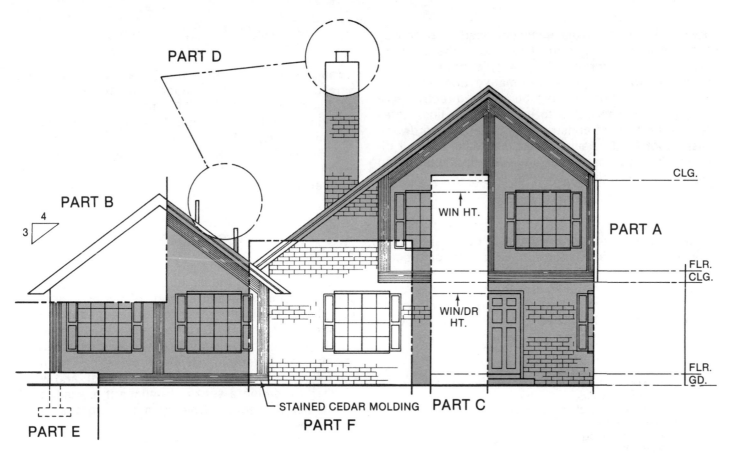

PART D

PART B

4
3

PART A

CLG.

WIN HT.

FLR.
CLG.

WIN/DR
HT.

FLR.
GD.

STAINED CEDAR MOLDING

PART C

PART F

PART E

Fig. 9-7 *Component Parts in Drawing. A. Establish Grade, Floor, and Ceiling. B. Determine Roof Height and Pitch. C. Establish Window and Door Height. D. Locate Chimneys and Stacks and Calculate Appropriate Heights. E. Draw in Necessary Foundation Indicators. F. Draw in Details, Symbols, Notations, and Needed Dimensions.*

STEP 5: PROJECT CHIMNEY AND STACK HEIGHTS

The locations of chimneys and stacks can be projected from the floor plan. If a detailed section drawing was prepared for a fireplace, furnace, or boiler, height dimensions may be taken from it. Stack heights vary depending upon their location. Chimneys, however, should extend at least 2'-0'' (610 mm) above the ridge line of the roof. If the chimney height is less than this, the flue will not draw smoke properly. See Fig. 9-7D.

STEP 6: DRAW FOOTING, FOUNDATION, AND OTHER ELEVATION LINES

It is sometimes advisable to draw in the footing and foundation lines. Since these lines are below grade level, they should be drawn as hidden lines. Sometimes this portion of the elevation is done as a sectional drawing, for example, when additional information and specifications are needed. Footing and foundation heights are taken directly from the detailed sections in the foundation plan. If a basement is to be included, remember that most basements are 7'-0'' (2134 mm) to 7'-6'' (2286 mm) in depth. At this time, all other lines should be darkened to their appropriate weights. See Fig. 9-7E.

STEP 7: ADD MATERIAL HATCHINGS AND NEEDED DIMENSIONS

Material hatchings and symbols should be done last. It is not necessary to hatch all surfaces. Hatching should be limited to the minimum needed to convey all necessary information. This keeps the drawing clear and uncluttered. Often, simple notations can make the drawing more informative and easier to understand. Notations may be made directly on a component or connected to it by a leader line. Notes identify the type of construction, materials, hardware, finish, floor levels, ceiling lines, etc. Make sure all dimensions used are consistent with floor plans and building specifications. See Fig. 9-7.

STEP 8: CHECK ELEVATION PLANS

The last step is to check all components of the elevation. As with other drawings, drafters should be prepared to make changes in elevations before the final set of drawings is accepted. This does *not* mean changes caused by carelessness. It is always good practice to make sure that the major aspects of an elevation drawing have been included. The following checklist contains points that should be reviewed:

1. Dimensions (as needed)

   a. Floor-to-ceiling heights
   b. Door and window heights
   c. Chimney and stack heights
   d. Tower heights
   e. Roof overhang
   f. Roof pitch
   g. Footing depth
   h. Foundation and basement depth
   i. Special construction

2. Grade line
3. Floor and ceiling lines
4. Identification of doors, windows, and louvers
5. Foundation lines
6. Dormers
7. Columns
8. Shutters
9. Material hatching symbols
10. Notations for materials, hardware, and construction
11. Detailed wall sections or references to them
12. Steps, stoops, and railings
13. Flashings, gutters, and downspouts
14. Chimneys and stacks
15. Scale of drawing
16. Title

SAMPLE ELEVATIONS

Four sample elevations are presented here. These were developed from the floor plans shown in Chapter 7. See Figs. 7-4, 7-5, 7-6, and 7-7. Fig. 9-8 is the elevations for the residential building; Fig. 9-9 is the commercial bank; Fig. 9-10 is the industrial building; and Fig. 9-11 is the steamboat. Though by no means exactly alike, these elevations are examples of good architectural drafting practice.

SUMMARY

Elevations show the components and design concepts in the interior and exterior of the building. Interior elevations illustrate inside constructional and design characteristics. Exterior elevations show the building from the outside. Exterior elevations are by far the most common type of elevation, normally consisting of four views: north, south, east, and west.

When preparing a set of elevations it is wise to follow a set procedure. One such has eight steps or processes:

1. Establish proper scale and use other plans
2. Establish reference lines
3. Draw roof lines
4. Establish window and door heights
5. Project chimney and stack heights
6. Draw footing, foundation, and other elevation lines
7. Draw in material hatchings and needed dimensions
8. Check elevation plans

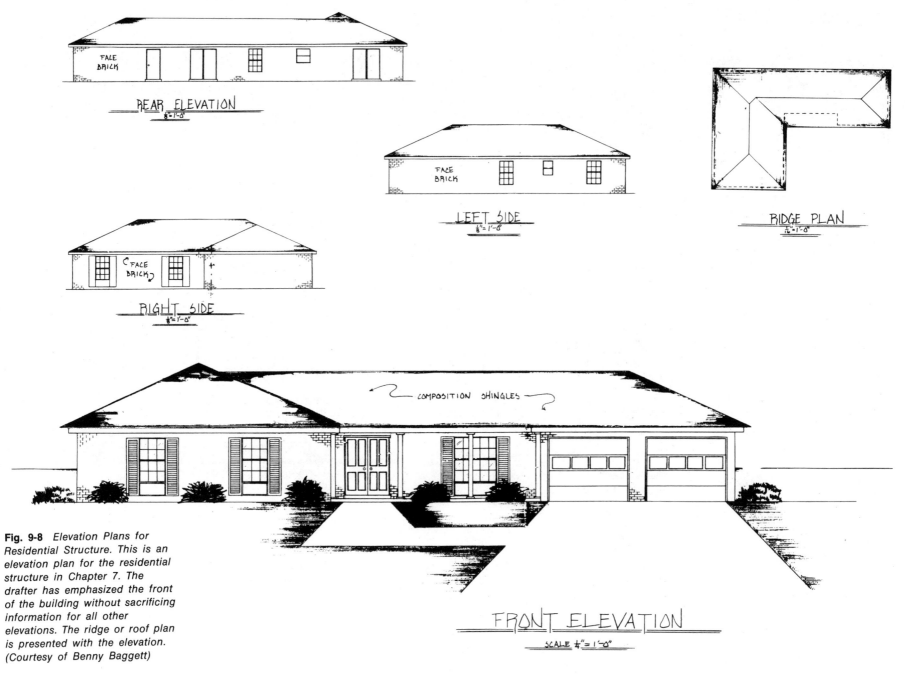

REAR ELEVATION

FACE BRICK

LEFT SIDE

FACE BRICK

RIDGE PLAN

RIGHT SIDE

FACE BRICK

COMPOSITION SHINGLES

FRONT ELEVATION

SCALE ¼"= 1'-0"

Fig. 9-8 *Elevation Plans for Residential Structure. This is an elevation plan for the residential structure in Chapter 7. The drafter has emphasized the front of the building without sacrificing information for all other elevations. The ridge or roof plan is presented with the elevation. (Courtesy of Benny Baggett)*

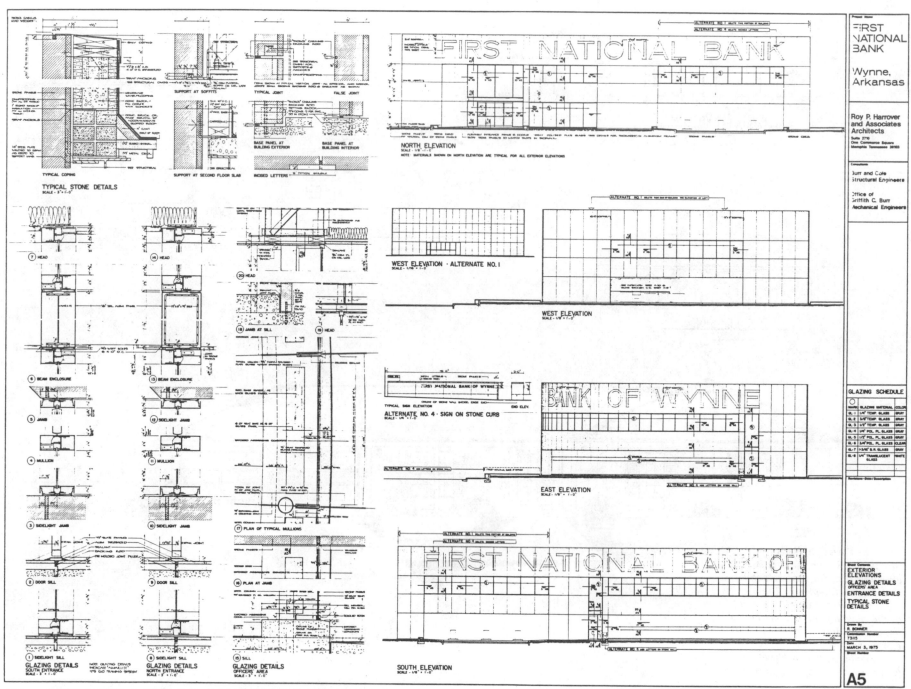

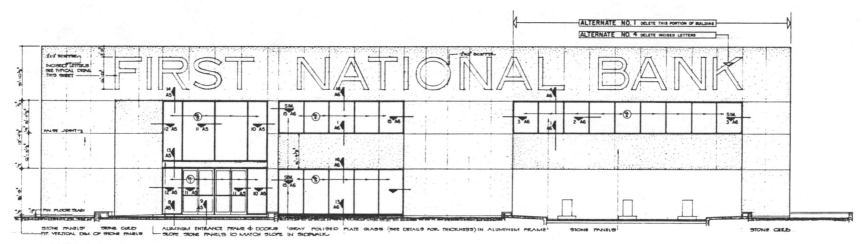

NORTH ELEVATION
SCALE - 1/8" - 1'-0"

NOTE: MATERIALS SHOWN ON NORTH ELEVATION ARE TYPICAL FOR ALL EXTERIOR ELEVATIONS

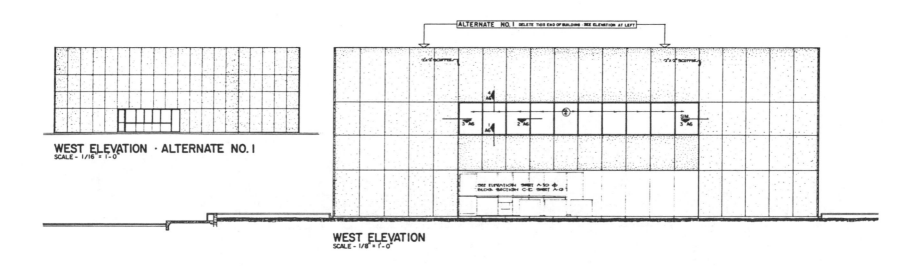

WEST ELEVATION · ALTERNATE NO. 1
SCALE - 1/16" = 1'-0"

WEST ELEVATION
SCALE - 1/8" = 1'-0"

Pages 172–174
Fig. 9-9 *Elevations for a Commercial Bank (Courtesy of Roy P. Harrover and Associates, Architects)*

Fig. 9-9 *(cont.)*

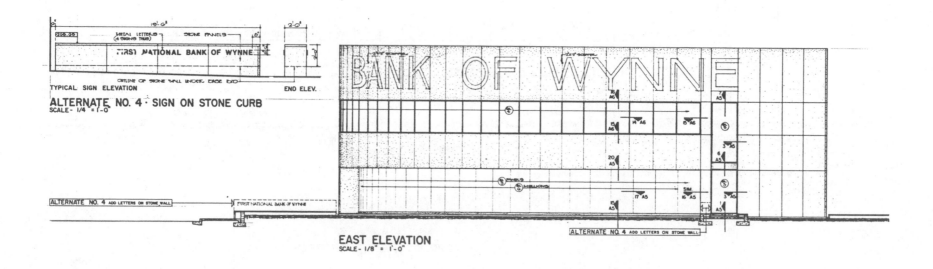

TYPICAL SIGN ELEVATION

ALTERNATE NO. 4 · SIGN ON STONE CURB
SCALE - 1/4" = 1'-0"

END ELEV.

FIRST NATIONAL BANK OF WYNNE

ALTERNATE NO. 4 ADD LETTERS ON STONE WALL

BANK OF WYNNE

ALTERNATE NO. 4 ADD LETTERS ON STONE WALL

EAST ELEVATION
SCALE - 1/8" = 1'-0"

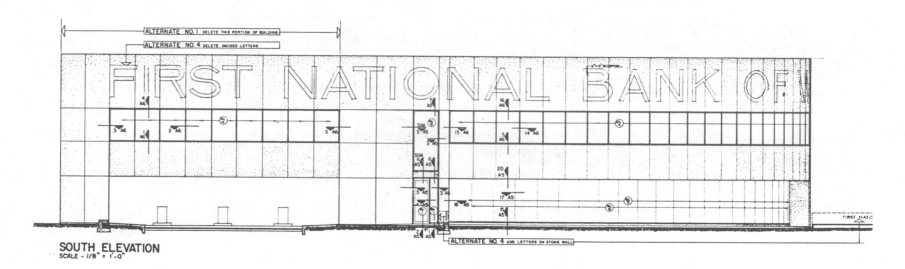

ALTERNATE NO. 1 DELETE THIS PORTION OF BUILDING

ALTERNATE NO. 4 DELETE INCISED LETTERS

FIRST NATIONAL BANK OF

ALTERNATE NO. 4 ADD LETTERS ON STONE WALL

SOUTH ELEVATION
SCALE - 1/8" = 1'-0"

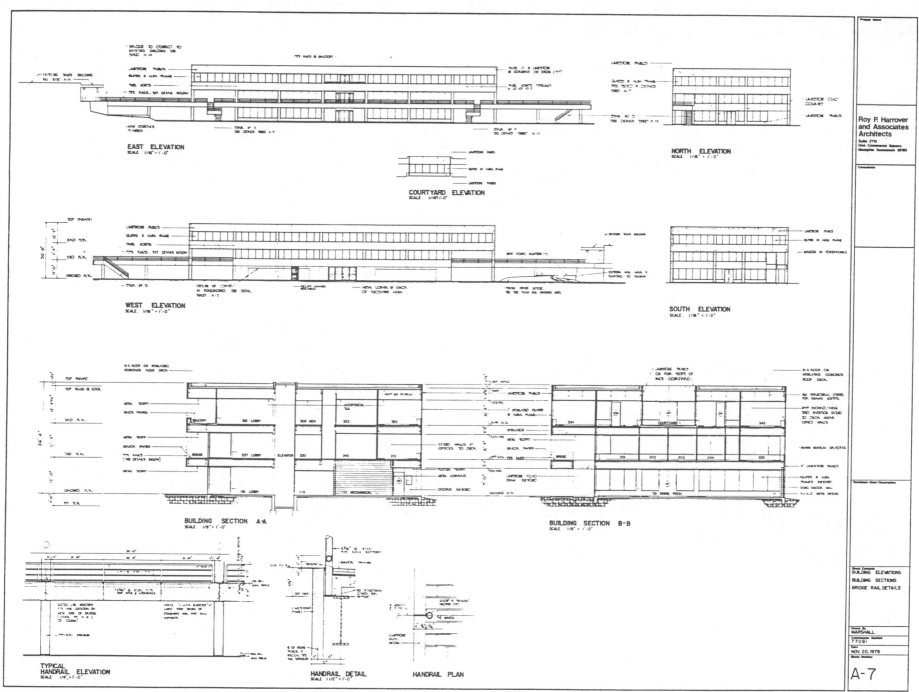

EAST ELEVATION
SCALE: 1/16" = 1'-0"

COURTYARD ELEVATION
SCALE: 1/16" = 1'-0"

NORTH ELEVATION
SCALE: 1/16" = 1'-0"

WEST ELEVATION
SCALE: 1/16" = 1'-0"

SOUTH ELEVATION
SCALE: 1/16" = 1'-0"

BUILDING SECTION A-A
SCALE: 1/8" = 1'-0"

BUILDING SECTION B-B
SCALE: 1/8" = 1'-0"

TYPICAL HANDRAIL ELEVATION
SCALE: 1/4" = 1'-0"

HANDRAIL DETAIL
SCALE: 1 1/2" = 1'-0"

HANDRAIL PLAN

Roy P. Harrover
and Associates
Architects

Suite 2770
One Commerce Square
Memphis Tennessee 38103

Consultants

Revisions Date / Description

Sheet Contents
BUILDING ELEVATIONS
BUILDING SECTIONS
BRIDGE RAIL DETAILS

Drawn By
MARSHALL
Commission Number
77091
Date
NOV. 20, 1978
Sheet Number

A-7

ELEVATIONS   **175**

Fig. 9-10 *Elevations for an Industrial Building (Courtesy of Roy P. Harrover and Associates, Architects)*

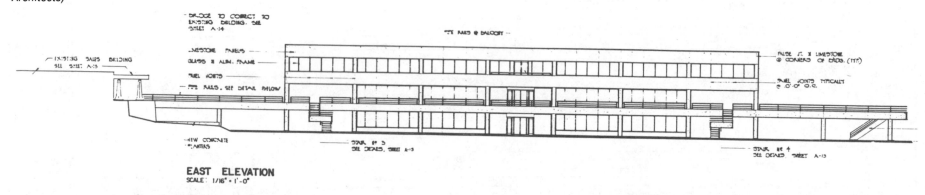

EAST ELEVATION
SCALE: 1/16" = 1'-0"

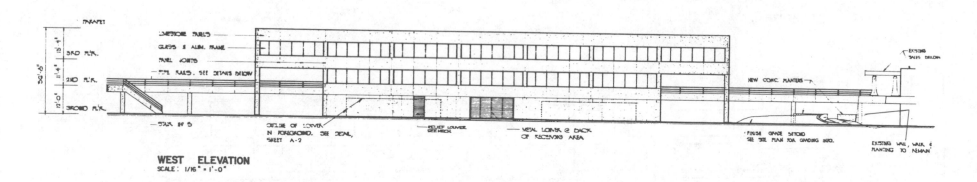

WEST ELEVATION
SCALE: 1/16" = 1'-0"

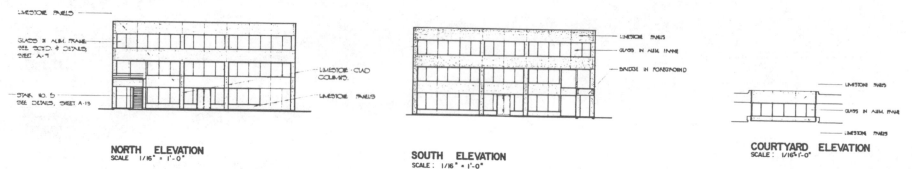

NORTH ELEVATION
SCALE: 1/16" = 1'-0"

SOUTH ELEVATION
SCALE: 1/16" = 1'-0"

COURTYARD ELEVATION
SCALE: 1/16" = 1'-0"

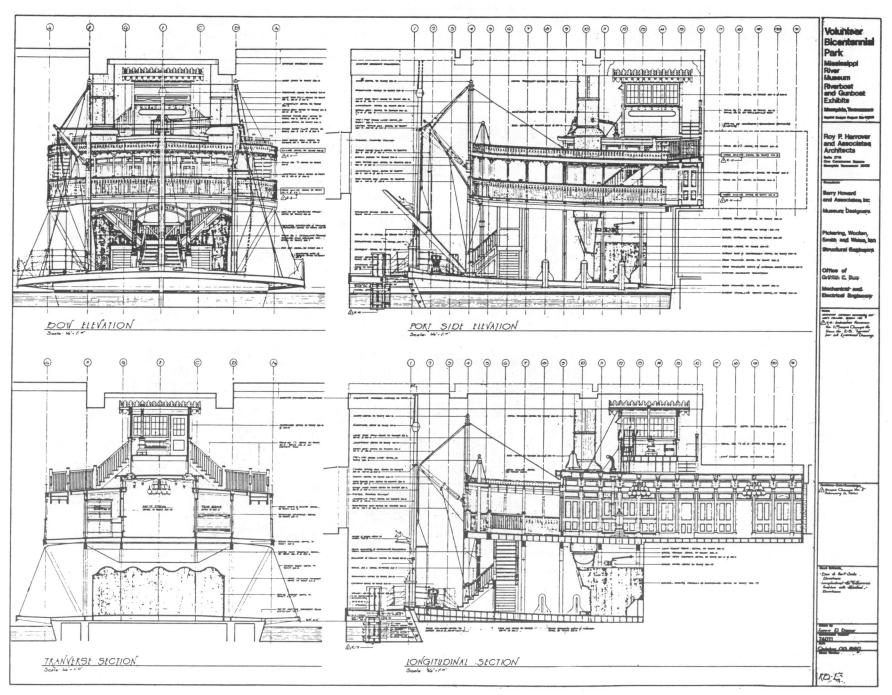

ROW ELEVATION
Scale: ¼"=1'-0"

PORT SIDE ELEVATION
Scale: ¼"=1'-0"

TRANVERSE SECTION
Scale: ¼"=1'-0"

LONGITUDINAL SECTION
Scale: ¼"=1'-0"

Volunteer
Bicentennial
Park

Mississippi
River
Museum

Riverboat
and Gunboat
Exhibits

Memphis, Tennessee

Roy P. Harrover
and Associates
Architects

Barry Howard
and Associates, Inc.

Museum Designers

Pickering, Wooten,
Smith and Weiss, Inc.

Structural Engineers

Office of
Griffith C. Burr

Mechanical and
Electrical Engineers

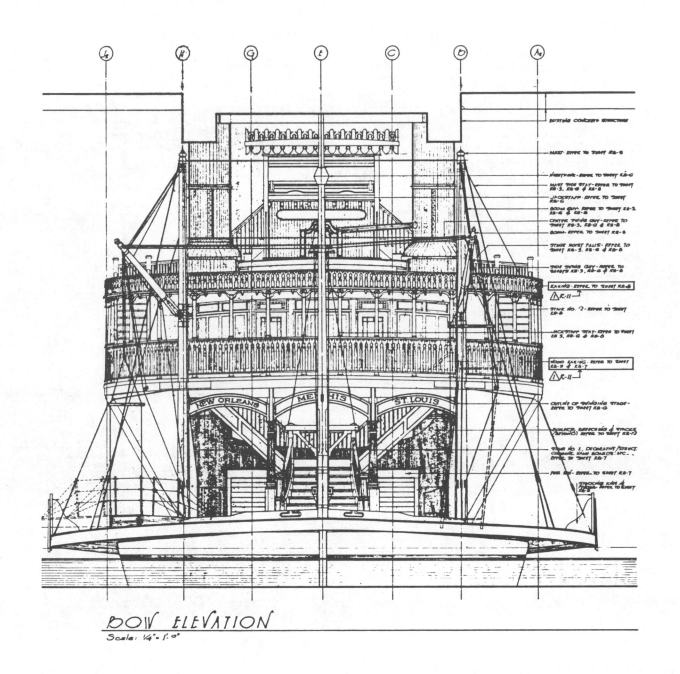

BOW ELEVATION
Scale: ¼" = 1'-0"

Pages 177–179
Fig. 9-11 *Elevations of a Steamboat (Courtesy of Roy P. Harrover and Associates, Architects)*

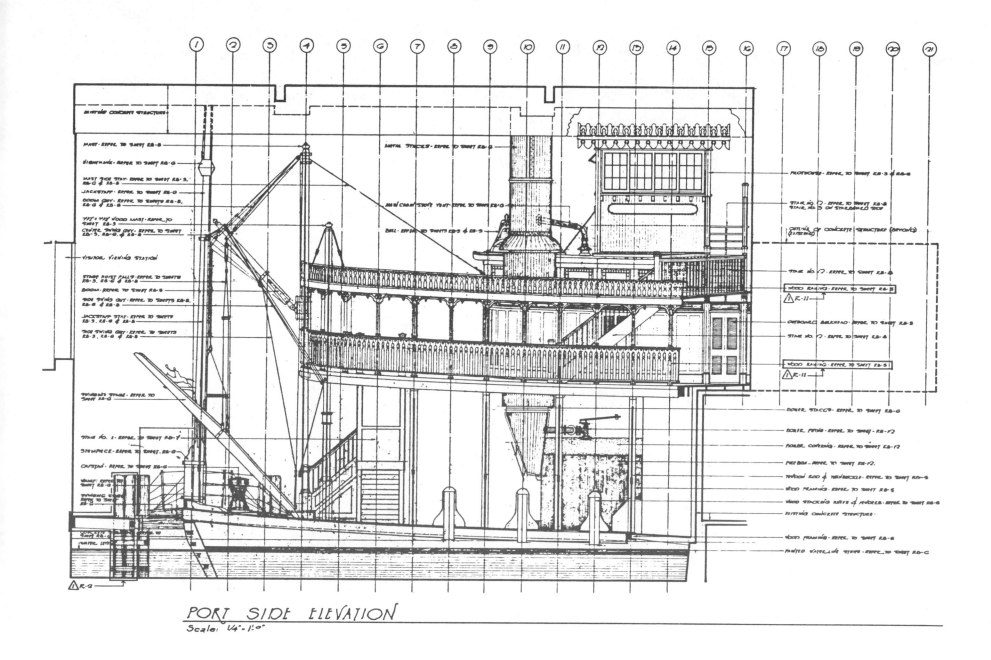

PORT SIDE ELEVATION
Scale: 1/4" = 1'-0"

REVIEW QUESTIONS

1. What are elevations?
2. What are the two types of elevation plans? What is the difference?
3. Why is perspective not used in elevations?
4. Explain why more than four exterior elevations might be needed.
5. Why draw elevations to the same scale as floor plans?
6. Explain each of the following:

   a. Grade line
   b. Floor line
   c. Ceiling line
   d. Roof line

7. What is the relationship between window and exterior door heights?
8. Explain the need for proper chimney height.
9. Are footing and foundation lines always drawn in elevations?
10. Should material hatching be used throughout the building surface? Why?

EXERCISES

1. Draw elevations of the building you developed floor plans for in Chapter 7.
2. Draw an interior elevation, showing one special feature of the building.
3. Get a set of working drawings for an existing building. Prepare a new set of elevations, so that the exterior will be different from the original. Check that information on the new building corresponds with that on the old. If there *is* a difference, either defend or change the drawing.

FRAMING AND ROOF PLANS

GLOSSARY

Framing plans drawings illustrating the building skeleton—the beams and other support

Phantom line a long line followed by two short dashes, used to show the movement or the position of a particular structural component

Splash blocks blocks made of structural material, such as concrete, to collect or guide water from various parts of the building

Framing and roof plans are drawn when additional structural and design parameters need to be specified for construction purposes. These plans, however, are not typically part of the set of working drawings prepared for simple commercial and residential structures. Architectural firms frequently subcontract with structural engineering firms to design, develop, and draw these specialized specifications for large and complex projects.

FRAMING PLANS

Framing plans show the completed structural configuration of a building. In other words, they show the skeletal system of the building. Special structural considerations, such as load bearings, structural dynamics, and stress points frequently require the use of the special talents of structural or civil engineers. This is usually done through subcontracting. Small firms are not likely to have staff members experienced in structural engineering, so these find it especially economical and practical to subcontract such designs to specialized outside firms. For less complex structures or if the firm has in-house engineers, architectural drafters should be prepared to draw framing plans.

CHARACTERISTICS OF FRAMING PLANS

Framing plans are often drawn for floor, roof, and walls. The use of floor plans and elevations is an integral part of the process. Framing plans are layout drawings rather than details. Some detailing may be required to show structural and mechanical fastening arrangements. Typical framing plans locate and give specifications for structural support features, such as columns, beams, plates, girders, studs, and joists.

It is important to realize that framing plans enhance the quality and completeness of the architectural design. The plans are prepared so as to show the unique features of the structural system. There are three basic structural systems: *wood, steel,* and *concrete.* Any one or a combination of these can be used in the building's skeletal system.

DRAWING FRAMING PLANS

The most efficient approach to drawing framing plans is to trace the supporting elements from the foundation plan, floor plan, or elevation. Foundation and floor plans are drawn at a theoretical horizontal section height, showing no windows, doors, or mechanical hardware openings that are part of the structural support system. The framing system itself is of primary importance; the initial layout should be drawn in lightly and remain a light-weight line in the final drawing.

Once the layout has been traced, locate each structural member. A member may be illustrated as a solid, center, or phantom line. In any case, notations give structural member specifications. See Figs. 10-1 through 10-6. Table 10-1 presents the former and current standards for designating various types of common structural steel shapes. Some individual members are actually drawn to scale rather than in the simplified form. See Fig. 10-7.

After each member is located, drawn, and noted, details for the appropriate cutting planes are drawn. These show how the members are fastened to columns, walls, and each other. Figs. 10-8 and 10-9 are examples of framing plan details.

Pages 183–185
Fig. 10-1 *Second-Floor Framing Plan for an Industrial Building. The first-floor framing plan is part of the foundation framing-plan system. (Courtesy of Roy P. Harrover and Associates, Architects)*

ROOF PLANS

Roof plans show the overall arrangement of the roof system. The plan also shows each part of the building that rises through the roof, such as chimneys and stacks, or rests on it, such as flagpoles and fire dampers. Of all the different types of plans, perhaps the roof plan is the least often included in working drawings. All information needed to construct a roof is usually given in the elevations, framing plans, and related detail drawings. However, architectural drafters need to be competent in preparing such drawings when necessary.

CHARACTERISTICS OF ROOF PLANS

Roof plans show how the entire system appears from above; that is, they give a bird's-eye view of the building. The plans show the contractor and tradesmen all roof components that affect construction procedures.

Table 10-1 Designations of Common Structural Steel Shapes

Structural Shapes	New Designation	Old Designation
American Standard Channel	C	Ϲ
HP Shape	HP	BP
Flat Bar	Bar	Bar
Round Bar	Bar	Bar ◌
Square Bar		Bar ▢
Equal Leg Angle	L	∠
Unequal Leg Angle	L	∠
M Shape	M	M, JR
Misc. Channel	MC	Ϲ, JR
Pipe	Pipe	Pipe
S Shape	S	I
Structural Tee Cut from M Shape	MT	ST M, ST JR
Structural Tee Cut from S Shape	ST	ST I
Structural Tee Cut from W Shape	WT	ST WF, ST B
Structural Tubing	TS	Tube
W Shape	W	WF, B

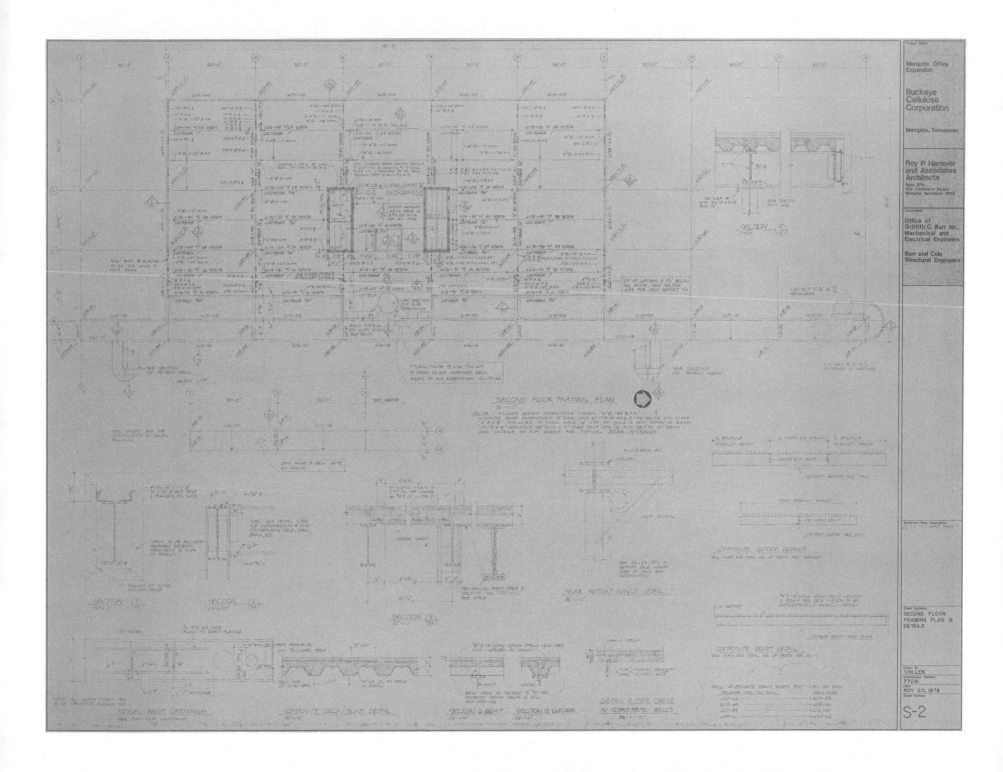

Memphis Office
Expansion

Buckeye
Cellulose
Corporation

Memphis, Tennessee

Roy P. Harrover
and Associates
Architects
Suite 2710
One Commerce Square
Memphis, Tennessee 38103

Office of
Griffith C. Burr Inc.,
Mechanical and
Electrical Engineers

Burr and Cole
Structural Engineers

Sheet Contents
SECOND FLOOR
FRAMING PLAN &
DETAILS

Drawn By
THILLEN
Commission Number
77091
Date
NOV. 20, 1978
Sheet Number

S-2

Fig. 10-1 *(cont.)*

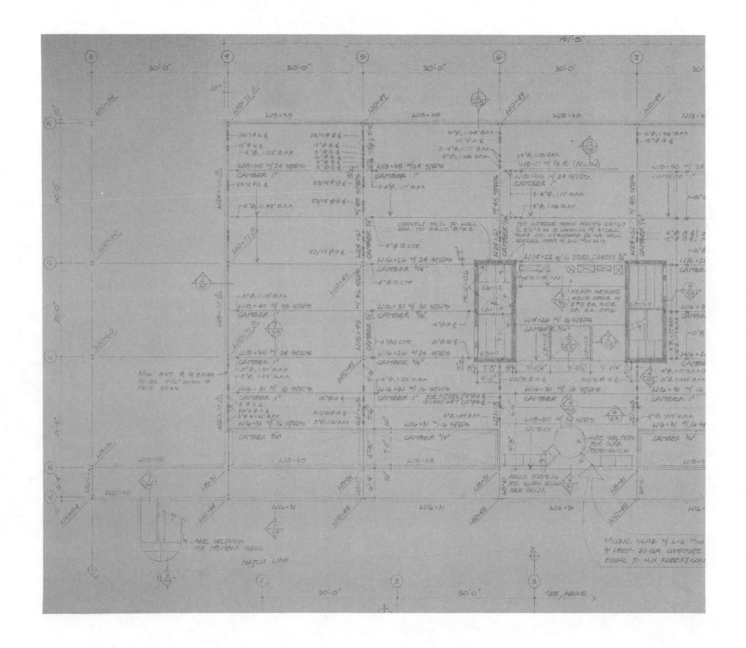

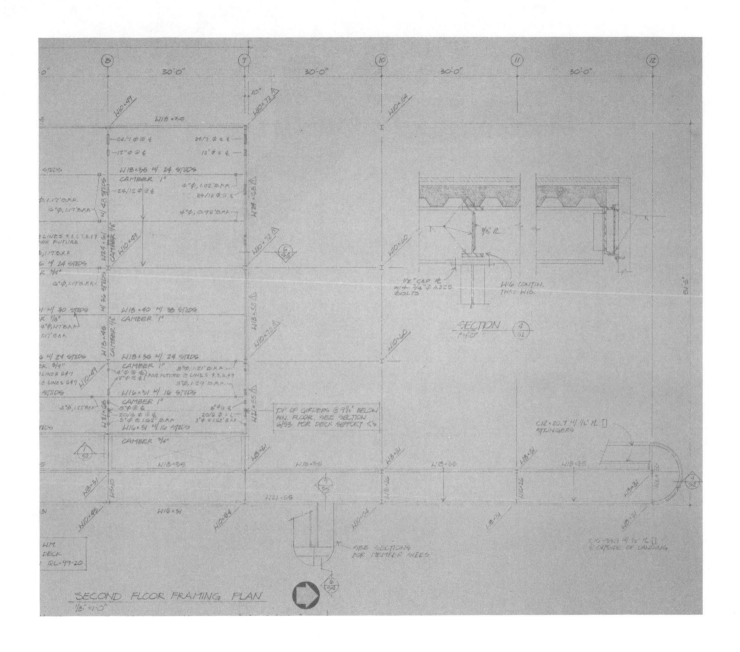

SECOND FLOOR FRAMING PLAN
1/8"=1'-0"

SECTION 4/52
1'=1'-0"

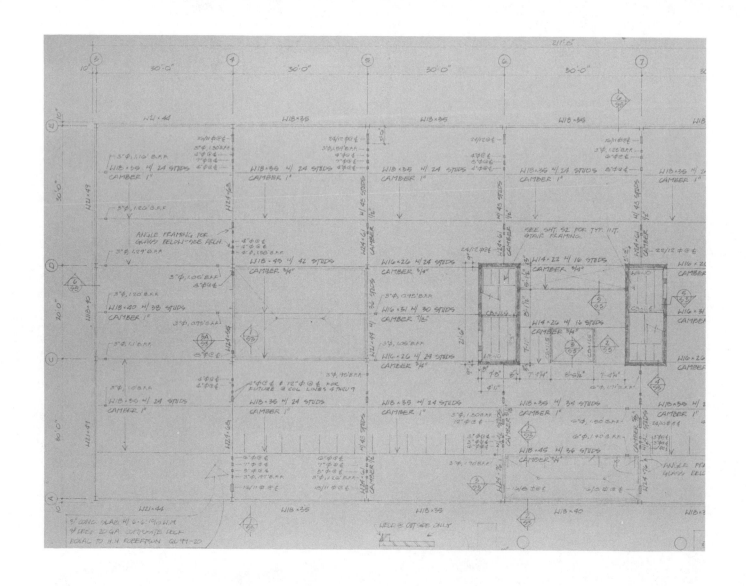

Pages 186–188
Fig. 10-2 *Third-Floor Framing Plan. This is the building in Fig. 10-1. Note the relationship between the drawings. (Courtesy of Roy P. Harrover and Associates, Architects)*

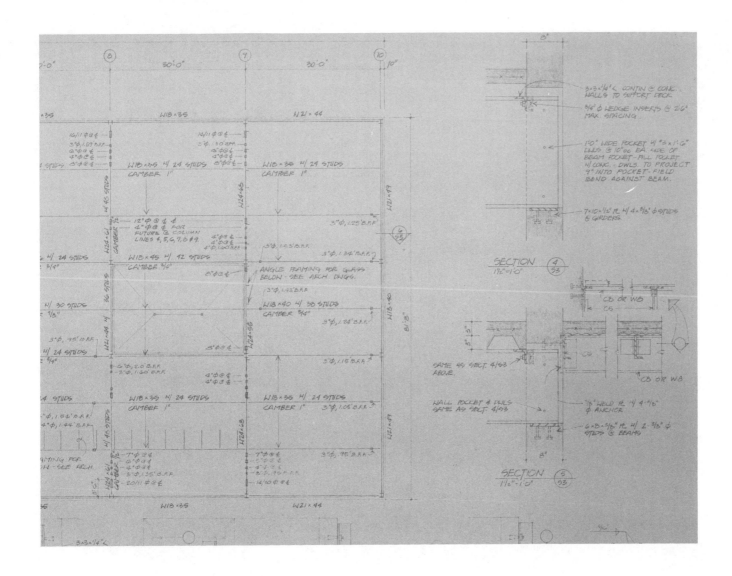

SECTION $\frac{4}{S3}$
$1\frac{1}{2}"=1'-0"$

SECTION $\frac{5}{S3}$
$1\frac{1}{2}"=1'-0"$

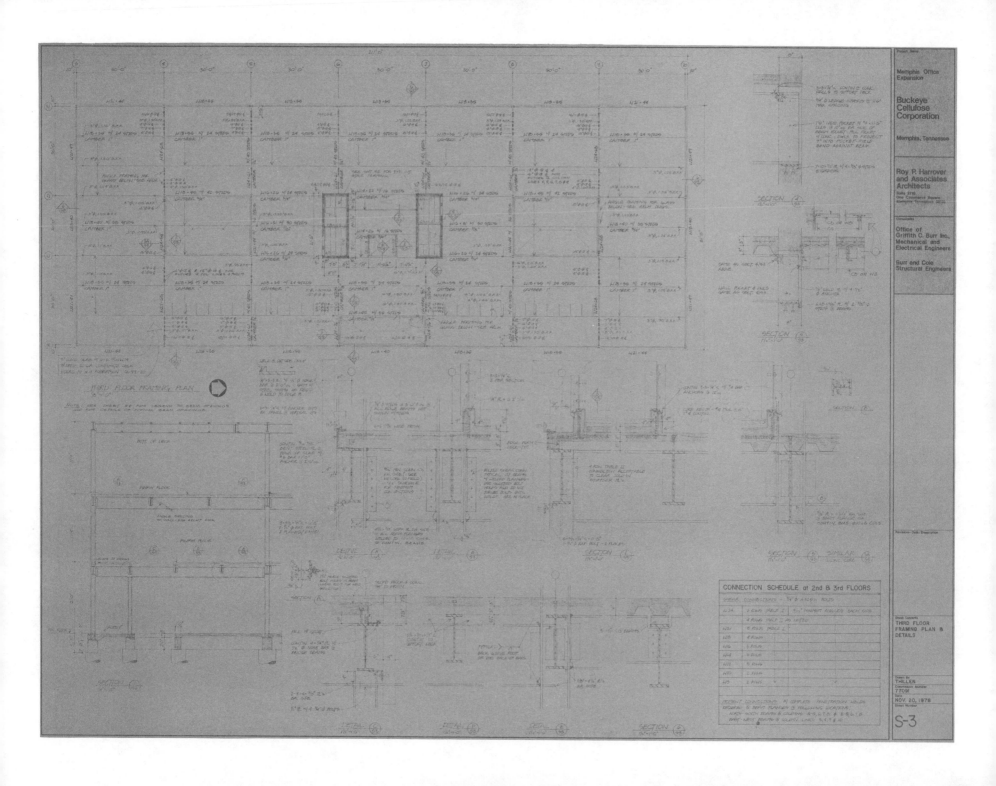

Project Name

Memphis Office
Expansion

Buckeye
Cellulose
Corporation

Memphis, Tennessee

Roy P. Harrover
and Associates
Architects

Suite 2210
One Commerce Square
Memphis, Tennessee 38103

Consultants

Office of
Griffith C. Burr Inc,
Mechanical and
Electrical Engineers

Burr and Cole
Structural Engineers

Revisions · Date · Description

Sheet Contents
THIRD FLOOR
FRAMING PLAN &
DETAILS

Drawn By
THILLEN

Commission Number
7709I

Date
NOV. 20, 1978

Sheet Number
S-3

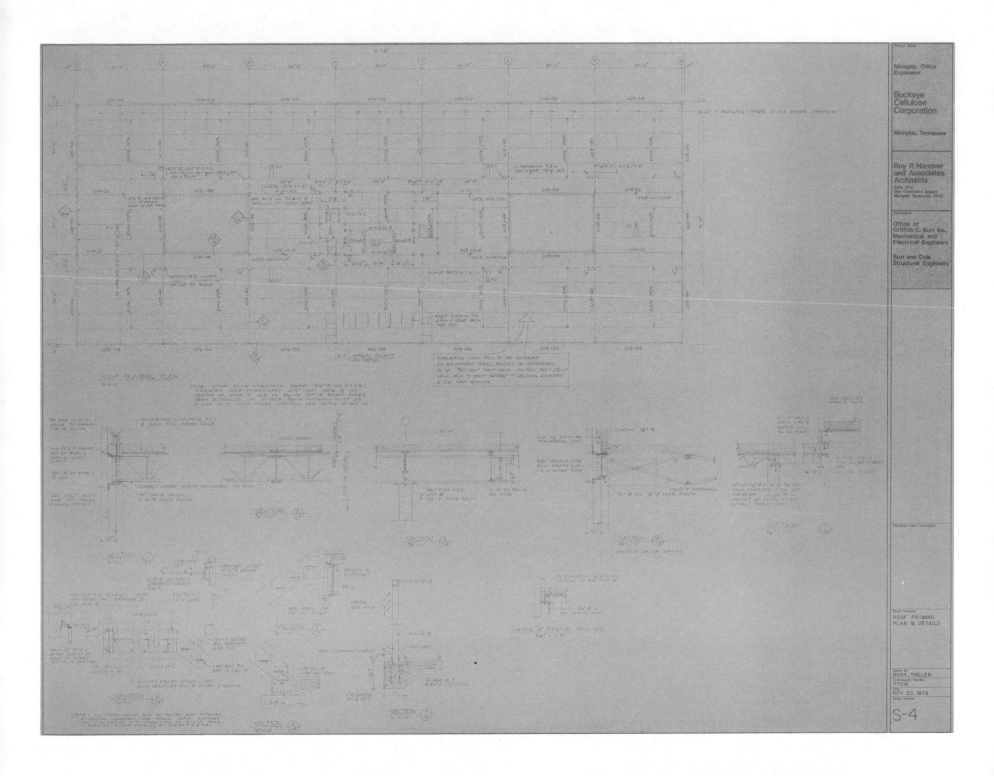

ROOF FRAMING PLAN

Memphis Office
Expansion

Buckeye
Cellulose
Corporation

Memphis, Tennessee

Roy P. Harrover
and Associates
Architects
Suite 2718
One Commerce Square
Memphis Tennessee 38103

Office of
Griffith C. Burr Inc.
Mechanical and
Electrical Engineers

Burr and Cole
Structural Engineers

ROOF FRAMING
PLAN & DETAILS

Drawn By
BURR, THILLEN
Commission Number
77091
Date
NOV. 20, 1978
Sheet Number

S-4

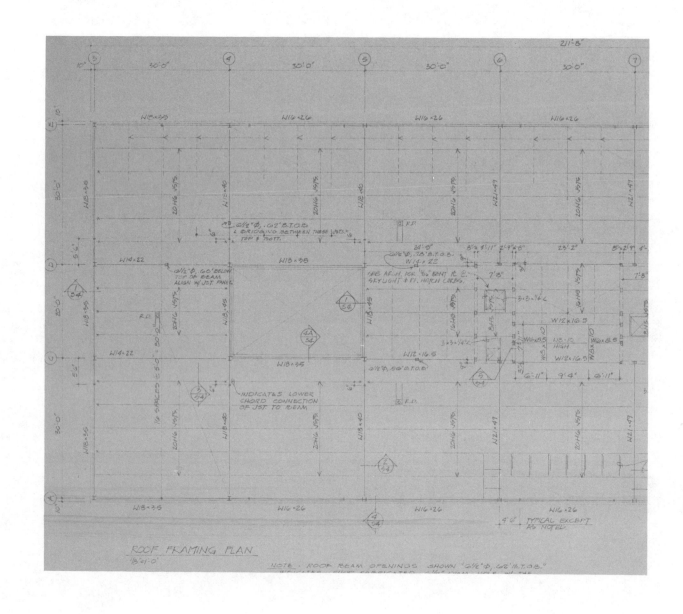

ROOF FRAMING PLAN
1/8"=1'-0"

Pages 189–191

Fig. 10-3 *Roof-Framing Plan.
This is the building in Figs. 10-1
and 10-2. (Courtesy of Roy P.
Harrover and Associates,
Architects)*

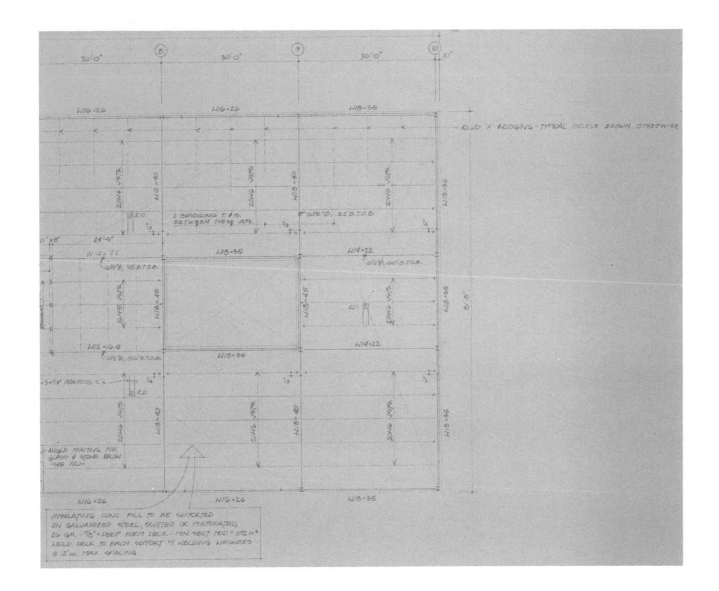

Page 192
Fig. 10-4 *Framing Plan for the Second Floor of a Commercial Building. Observe the notation and overall configuration of the system. (Courtesy of Roy P. Harrover and Associates, Architects)*

Page 193
Fig. 10-5 *Roof-Framing Plan. This is the building in Fig. 10-4. Note the relationship between the two framing plans. (Courtesy of Roy P. Harrover and Associates, Architects)*

FRAMING AND ROOF PLANS   191

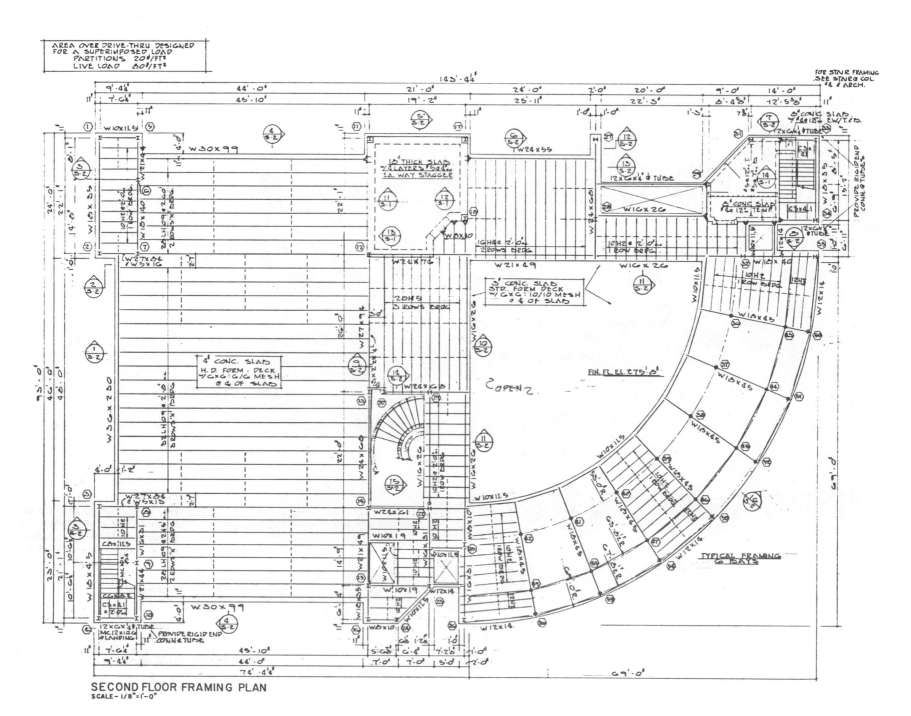

AREA OVER DRIVE-THRU DESIGNED
FOR A SUPERIMPOSED LOAD
PARTITIONS 20#/FT²
LIVE LOAD 80#/FT²

SECOND FLOOR FRAMING PLAN
SCALE- 1/8"=1'-0"

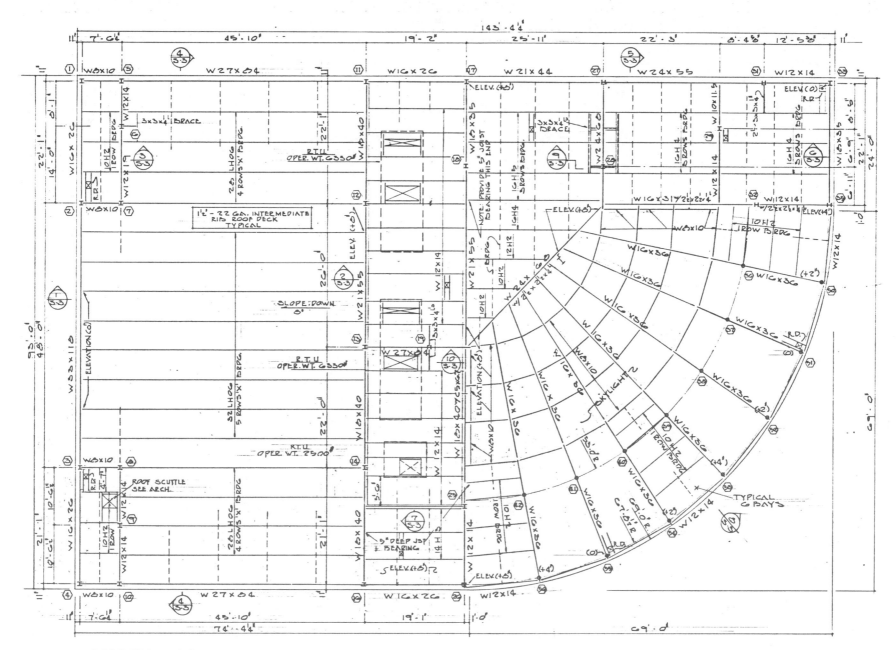

ROOF FRAMING PLAN
SCALE-1/8"=1'-0"

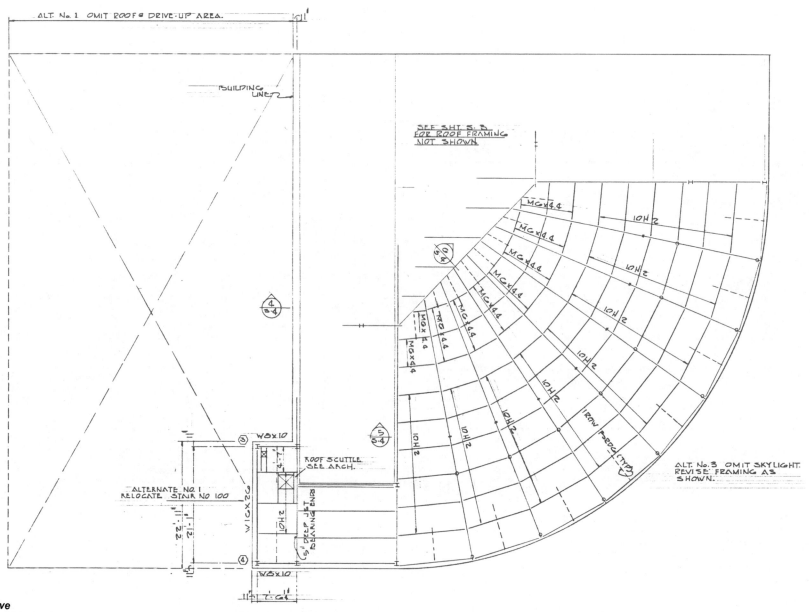

ROOF FRAMING PLAN (ALT. NO. 1 & 3)
SCALE 1/8"=1'-0"

Fig. 10-6 *Alternative Roof-Framing Plan. This is the commercial building in Figs. 10-4 and 10-5. (Courtesy of Roy P. Harrover and Associates, Architects)*

The roof plans identify the type of roof design and all dimensional considerations. Slope, positions of high and low points, and the location of such system components as valleys, drains, and stacks are drawn. In a few instances, the type of structural grid system used is included. All mechanical mountings to be built onto the roof, such as antennas, air-conditioning units, and water towers, are drawn in position and given the appropriate specifications.

DRAWING ROOF PLANS

To maintain consistency, draw roof plans at the same scale as the floor plans. It is usually best to start with the top-floor plan of the building. If there is a series of roofs on several levels of the building, several floor plans may be used. The outline of the floor plans should be drawn in lightly, to locate the configuration of the roof.

Once the top-floor layout is drawn, locate and draw the roof system itself. See Figs. 10-10 and 10-11. The following aspects of the roof should be taken into consideration when drawing the roof plan:

1. Dimensional positioning and references of the roof to the building itself
2. Overhang, canopies, and roof design
3. Direction of slope for drainage and position of such drainage components as overflow pipes, gutters, and saddles
4. Location of all mechanical mountings
5. Dimensioning to walls, columns, and other structural features
6. Location and notation of special roof features, such as fences, stacks, bulkheads, ladders, stairs, splash blocks, and roofing material
7. Cutting planes and references to needed detail drawings

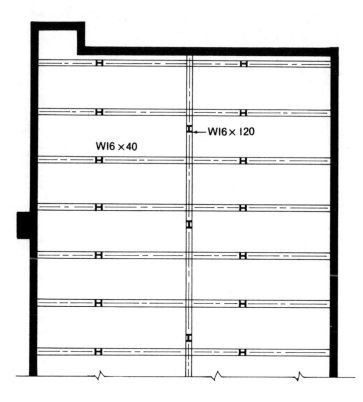

WI6 × 40

WI6 × 120

Fig. 10-7 *Frame Members Drawn to Scale*

SUMMARY

Framing and roof plans are not always included in the architectural working drawings. For especially complex structural designs and roof systems, however, framing and roof plans can be very useful to the contractor.

Framing plans show the structural configuration of a building; roof plans show the roof design. Framing plans dimensionally locate and give specifications for each structural member of the building. They are drawn for the foundation, floor plans, elevations, and roof plans. Roof plans show how the roof appears in the horizontal plane. They locate all roof components, including any part of the building that rises above or through the roof.

Fig. 10-8 *Sectional Details for Framing Plan. Note the use of detailing to show the relationship between the structural system and the foundation system, as well as the mechanical fastening methods. (Courtesy of Roy P. Harrover and Associates, Architects)*

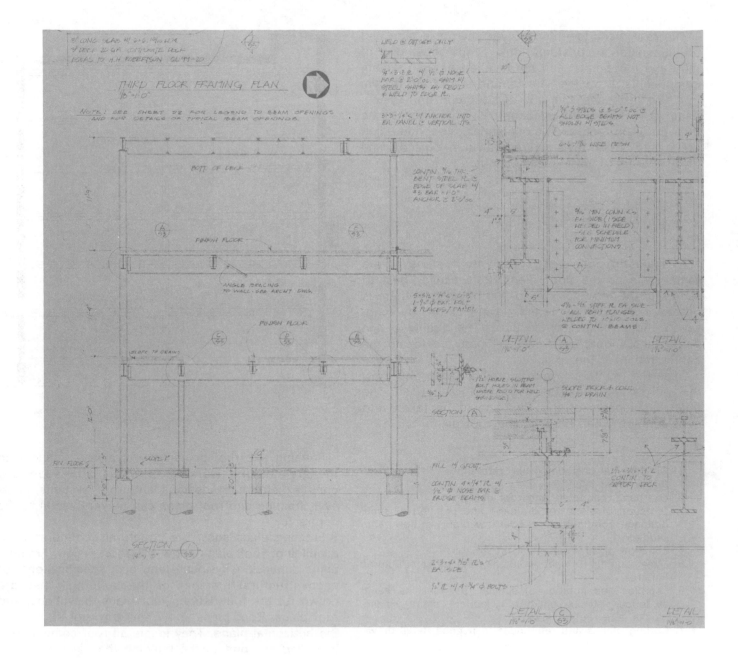

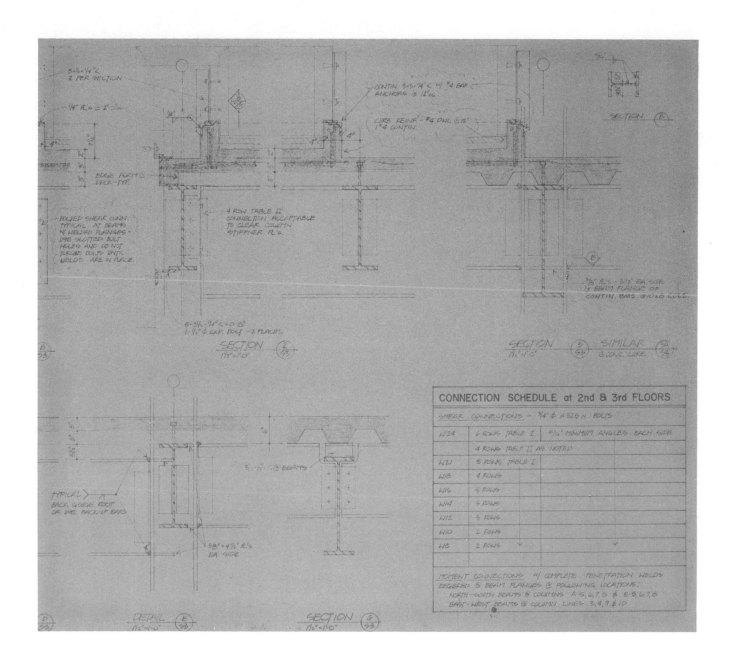

CONNECTION SCHEDULE at 2nd & 3rd FLOORS

SHEAR CONNECTIONS — ¾" ⌀ A325 N. BOLTS

W24	6 ROWS TABLE I	5/16" MINIMUM ANGLES EACH SIDE
	4 ROWS TABLE II AS NOTED	
W21	5 ROWS TABLE I	
W18	4 ROWS	
W16	3 ROWS	
W14	3 ROWS	
W12	3 ROWS	
W10	2 ROWS	
W8	2 ROWS	

MOMENT CONNECTIONS W/ COMPLETE PENETRATION WELDS
REQUIRED @ BEAM FLANGES @ FOLLOWING LOCATIONS:
NORTH-SOUTH BEAMS @ COLUMNS A-5,6,7,8 & E-5,6,7,8
EAST-WEST BEAMS @ COLUMN LINES 3,4,9 & 10

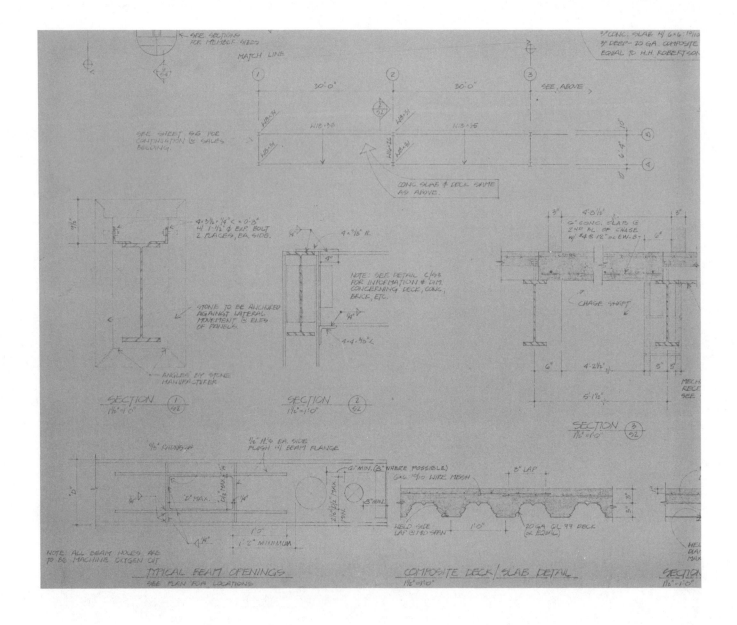

Fig. 10-9 *Framing Plan Details for Industrial Building. The details clearly show the structure of the methods of fastening and system configuration. (Courtesy of Roy P. Harrover and Associates, Architects)*

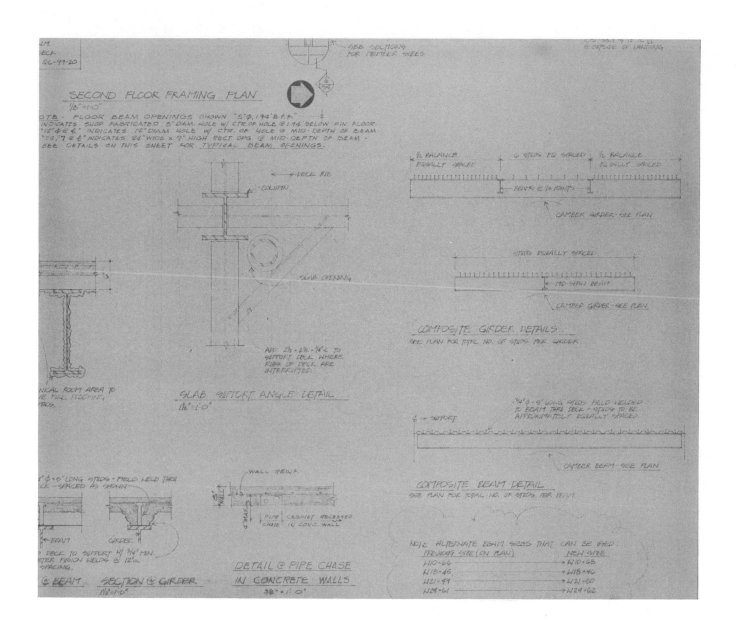

SECOND FLOOR FRAMING PLAN
1/8" = 1'-0"

NOTE - FLOOR BEAM OPENINGS SHOWN "5"∅, 1.94' B.F.F."
INDICATES SHOP FABRICATED 5" DIAM. HOLE W/ CTR. OF HOLE @ 1.94' BELOW FIN. FLOOR.
"12"∅ @ ₵" INDICATES 12" DIAM HOLE W/ CTR. OF HOLE @ MID-DEPTH OF BEAM.
"24, 7 @ ₵" INDICATES 24" WIDE × 7" HIGH RECT. OPG. @ MID-DEPTH OF BEAM -
SEE DETAILS ON THIS SHEET FOR TYPICAL BEAM OPENINGS.

DECK RIB

COLUMN

SLAB OPENING

ADD 2½ × 2½ × ¼"L TO
SUPPORT DECK WHERE
RIBS OF DECK ARE
INTERRUPTED.

SLAB SUPPORT ANGLE DETAIL
1½" = 1'-0"

WALL REINF.

PIPE   CABINET RECESSED
CHASE   IN CONC. WALL

DETAIL @ PIPE CHASE
IN CONCRETE WALLS
¾" = 1'-0"

¼" × 5" LONG STUDS - FIELD WELD THRU
DECK - SPACED AS SHOWN

BEAM   GIRDER

DECK TO SUPPORT W/ ¾" MIN.
DIAMETER FUSION WELDS @ 12" OC
SPACING.

@ BEAM   SECTION @ GIRDER
1½" = 1'-0"

½ BALANCE   6 STUDS EQ. SPACED   ½ BALANCE
EQUALLY SPACED   EQUALLY SPACED

BEAMS @ ⅓ POINTS

CAMBER GIRDER - SEE PLAN

STUDS EQUALLY SPACED

MID-SPAN BEAM

CAMBER GIRDER - SEE PLAN

COMPOSITE GIRDER DETAILS
SEE PLAN FOR TOTAL NO. OF STUDS PER GIRDER.

¾"∅ × 5" LONG STUDS FIELD WELDED
TO BEAM THRU DECK - STUDS TO BE
APPROXIMATELY EQUALLY SPACED.

₵ OF SUPPORT

CAMBER BEAM - SEE PLAN

COMPOSITE BEAM DETAIL
SEE PLAN FOR TOTAL NO. OF STUDS PER BEAM.

NOTE: ALTERNATE BEAM SIZES THAT CAN BE USED:

PREVIOUS SIZE (ON PLAN)	NEW SIZE
W10×66	W10×68
W18×46	W18×46
W21×49	W21×50
W24×61	W24×62

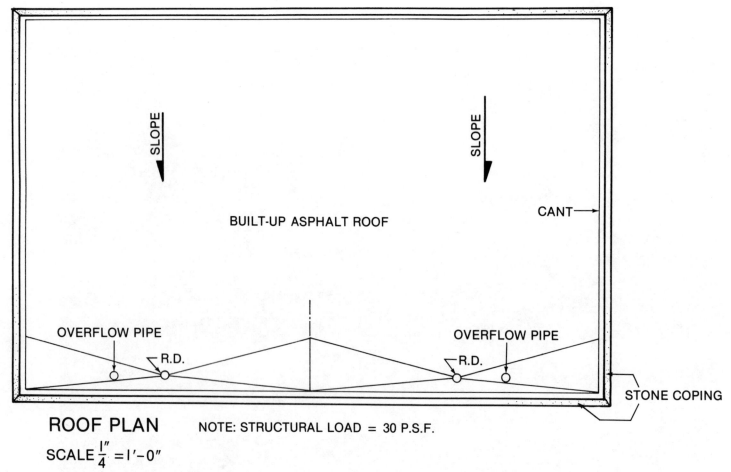

Fig. 10-10 *Roof Plan for a Small Commercial Building. Note the roof drain (RD) indicators, as well as the overflow pipe. Any mechanical devices to be installed on the roof would be drawn in place and dimensionally located.*

SLOPE

SLOPE

BUILT-UP ASPHALT ROOF

CANT

OVERFLOW PIPE

R.D.

OVERFLOW PIPE

R.D.

STONE COPING

ROOF PLAN

NOTE: STRUCTURAL LOAD = 30 P.S.F.

SCALE $\frac{1''}{4} = 1'-0''$

REVIEW QUESTIONS

1. When are framing plans prepared as part of a set of architectural working drawings?
2. Identify the specific typical features in framing plans that would not be found in any other drawings.
3. What three basic structural systems can be used in a building?
4. Identify four of the major features illustrated in roof plans.
5. Briefly explain the most efficient method for drawing roof plans.

EXERCISES

1. Draw framing plans for one floor and one wall of the building(s) you have already prepared floor plans and elevations for.
2. Get a set of framing plans for a small commercial building and compare the designations of common structural steel shapes to those in Table 10-1. Convert from the old to the new designations.
3. Draw roof framing plans for the structure in Exercise 1.

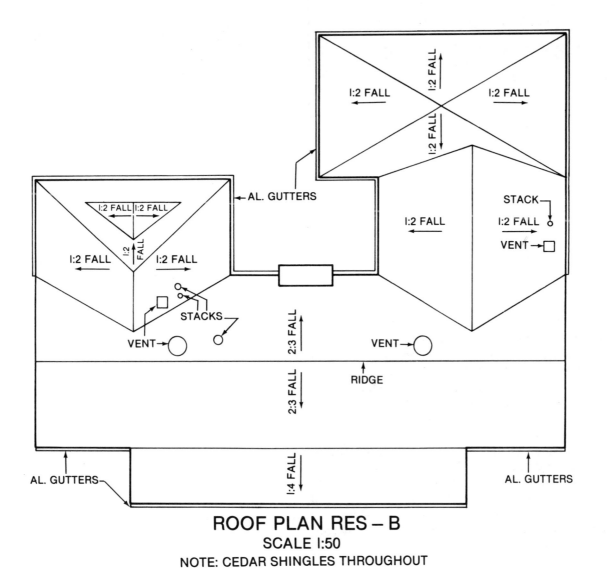

Fig. 10-11 *Plan for a Residential Structure. Note that, in this fairly complex plan, the direction of slope is identified by a rise-to-run ratio, followed by the term fall. All l-structure components that rise above the roof surface are also shown here.*

I:2 FALL

I:2 FALL

I:2 FALL

I:2 FALL

I:2 FALL I:2 FALL

I:2 FALL

I:2 FALL

I:2 FALL

I:2 FALL

AL. GUTTERS

STACK

VENT

STACKS

VENT

2:3 FALL

2:3 FALL

VENT

RIDGE

AL. GUTTERS

I:4 FALL

AL. GUTTERS

ROOF PLAN RES – B
SCALE I:50
NOTE: CEDAR SHINGLES THROUGHOUT

11

PLUMBING-SYSTEM PLANS

Plumbing-system plans are used by the plumbing contractor to determine the general design, layout, and component parts of the building's plumbing system. They may or may not be drawn to scale and are therefore rather different from most architectural working drawings. *Layouts* of the system are usually drawn to scale and show required dimensional locations for various parts of the system. "Three-dimensional" *isometric drawings* usually are not drawn to scale, since the configuration of the system is more important than exact component location.

Both layout and isometric plumbing-system drawings are single-line drawings. Each line represents the center of the pipe, supply line, or other unit. Most plumbing-system drawings provide information about hot-water supply, cold-water supply, and waste-material flow and disposal. Buildings supplied with natural or propane gas lines include these lines in the plumbing drawings. It is common for architectural firms to subcontract engineering firms to design the plumbing system, and other parts of the environmental system, such as the electrical, heating, ventilation, and air-conditioning systems. Subcontracting is most frequent for complex, specialized plumbing systems, such as that in an industrial plant requiring the movement of chemicals or toxic gases, the removal of industrial wastes, and special waste treatment.

GLOSSARY

Exterior plumbing fixtures, such as showers, lavatories, water heaters, water closets, tubs, and so forth
Interior plumbing parts located in the walls or floors of a building, such as pipes

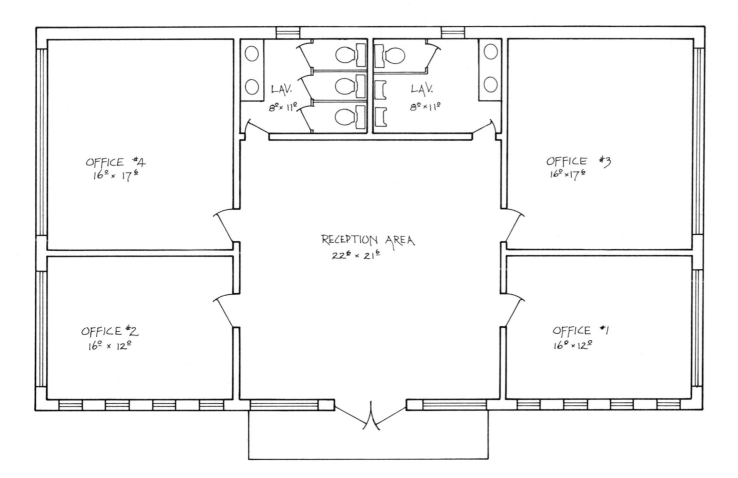

Fig. 11-1 *Simple Commercial Building Not Requiring Plumbing-System Drawing (Courtesy of Benny Baggett)*

OFFICE #4
16⁰ × 17⁶

OFFICE #3
16⁰ × 17⁶

LAV.
8⁰ × 11⁰

LAV.
8⁰ × 11⁰

RECEPTION AREA
22⁶ × 21⁶

OFFICE #2
16⁰ × 12⁰

OFFICE #1
16⁰ × 12⁰

CHARACTERISTICS OF PLUMBING-SYSTEM DRAWINGS

The plumbing system may be drawn directly on the floor plans of simple buildings. They may not even be required, if the plumber would be able to figure out the design of the plumbing system by knowing the location of all exterior plumbing fixtures, such as tubs, shower heads, water closets, lavatories, and water heaters.

In contrast, layout drawings for more complex buildings show all interior aspects of the plumbing system—components located in the walls or floors of the building. Fig. 11-1 shows a simple commercial building that does not require plumbing-system drawings.

When plumbing-system drawings are prepared for the plumber, they are used along with the floor plans. Together, these give the plumber an idea of how the plumbing system is to be constructed. Both sets of drawings let the plumber locate and position each fixture and related supply line in accordance with the desired appearance of the building. For example, piping obviously should not pass through window and door spaces. Layout or isometric plumbing-system drawings usually do not show the exterior plumbing

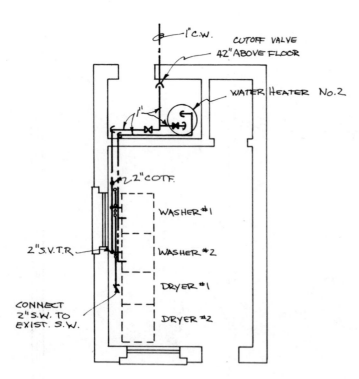

Fig. 11-2 *Simple Plumbing Layout for Residential Laundry Room. Note how the heavier lines are used to denote the plumbing system itself. (Layout courtesy of MMH/Hall, Architects, Planners)*

1" C.W.

CUTOFF VALVE
42" ABOVE FLOOR

WATER HEATER No. 2

2 2" C.O.T.F.

WASHER #1

WASHER #2

2" S.V.T.R.

DRYER #1

DRYER #2

CONNECT
2" S.W. TO
EXIST. S.W.

fixtures. These single-line drawings use symbols and notations to explain the contents of the pipe, the size of the pipe, the types of connections, and the directions of flow. See Fig. 11-2.

Not every length of pipe and connection need be indicated on the plumbing drawings. Plumbers often have a lot of leeway in determining what is best for the building. Only the essential parts and configuration of the system are drawn.

Even if many decisions are left up to the plumber, the plumbing-system drawings are still very important. They contain information about the arrangement and connection of risers, vents, and fixtures. Even in simple single-story floor plans, plumbing drawings explain the interconnections of fixtures, floor-drain connections, and related system specifications. See Figs. 11-3 through 11-5 for examples.

DRAWING THE PLUMBING SYSTEM

To draw a plumbing system properly, check *all* system specifications with those in both the National

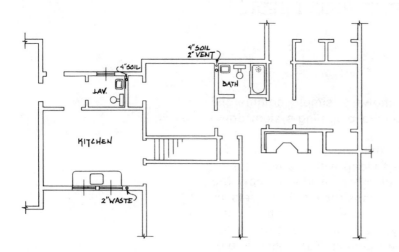

4" SOIL
2" VENT

4" SOIL

LAV.

BATH

KITCHEN

2" WASTE

FIRST FLOOR PLUMBING LAYOUT

4" FRESH AIR INLET

PERFORATED PLATE
OR RETURN BEND

2'-6" MIN.

4" SOIL
2" VENT
CLEANOUTS

WASH TUBS

4" HOUSE TRAP

6" VITRIFIED CLAY
OR E.H.C.I. HOUSE
SEWER TO
PUBLIC SEWER.

4" SOIL
C.O.

4" HOUSE DRAIN

TRAP PIT WITH IRON
FRAME & COVER OVER

2'

2" WASTE

BASEMENT PLUMBING LAYOUT

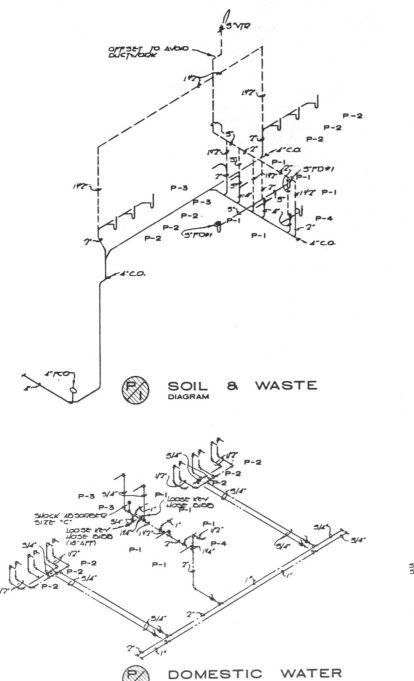

Fig. 11-3 *Isometric Plumbing-System Drawings for a Commercial Building. One system is for soil and waste; the other is for domestic water. (Courtesy of Roy P. Harrover and Associates, Architects)*

(P-1) SOIL & WASTE DIAGRAM

(P-2) SOIL & WASTE DIAGRAM

(P-1) DOMESTIC WATER DIAGRAM

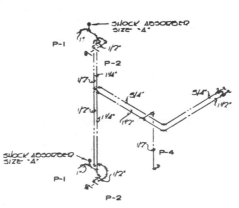

(P-2) DOMESTIC WATER DIAGRAM

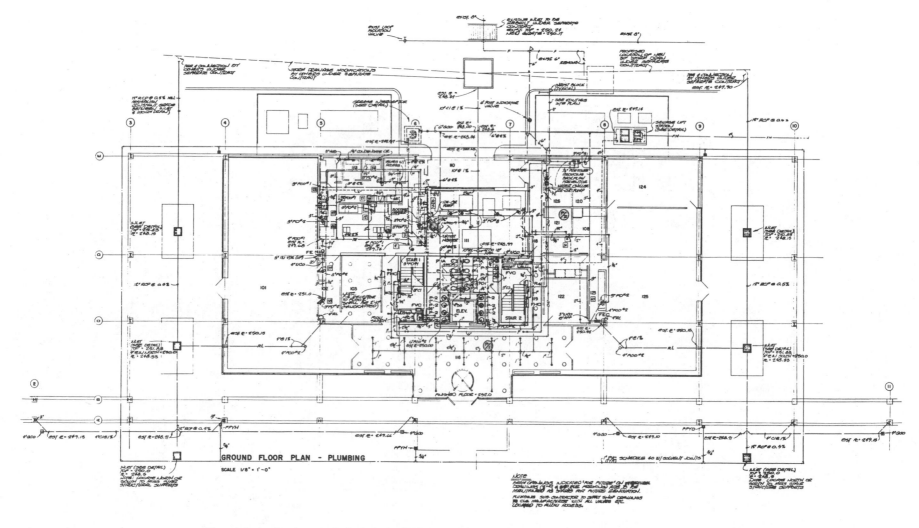

GROUND FLOOR PLAN - PLUMBING

SCALE 1/8" = 1'-0"

Fig. 11-4 *Plumbing Layout for the Ground Floor of an Industrial Complex. Note how the layout shows the specific locations of the internal and external components of the plumbing system. (Courtesy of Roy P. Harrover and Associates, Architects)*

Plumbing Code and local building codes. Though plumbing-system drawings are often prepared by an outside engineering firm, the drafter may have to redraw the system according to the architectural firm's standards and style. Redrawing often provides a quality control, a way of double-checking specifications. Whether the architectural or the engineering firm designs the system, the architectural drafter must have a clear understanding of how the plumbing-system drawings are prepared.

PLUMBING LAYOUT DRAWINGS

Layouts are also referred to as *plumbing floor plans.* Unlike an isometric drawing, the layout is drawn on the floor plan, which includes various parts of the building. It is used to show how the plumbing system fits into the building. The floor plan, however, is secondary in importance and is therefore drawn in a lighter line weight than the system layout itself.

Plumbing-layout drawings are drawn to scale. The

scale used in the floor plans is also used in the layout. Consistency in scaling eliminates a lot of confusion for the plumber. When drawing the plumbing layout:

1. Use all appropriate plumbing-system symbols.
2. Dimensionally locate the water-supply line with respect to the main feeder line.
3. Lay out cold water lines with all outlets.
4. Specify all valve, fitting, and pipe sizes.
5. Locate and position the water heater.
6. Lay out hot-water lines, with all outlets.
7. Note hot-water lines with the appropriate symbol and specify valves, fittings, and pipe sizes.
8. Locate and draw the building drain with sewer connections or septic system.
9. Lay out soil lines, with a heavy, dark line.
10. Specify pipe sizes and fixtures.
11. Identify all vents and note with clean-out symbols.
12. Locate gas-supply lines.
13. Lay out gas line, with all outlets.
14. Specify all fittings, pipe sizes, and valves.
15. Darken in all of the plumbing system, so that it will stand out from the floor plan.

ISOMETRIC PLUMBING DRAWINGS

Isometric plumbing drawings are frequently called *plumbing schematics.* They do not show any part of the building itself, usually only the interior plumbing system. However, a few exterior fixtures may be drawn in, for example, the water heater and the piping leading to it. In most cases, isometrics are not drawn to scale, since their primary purpose is to give not dimensional reference but rather an indication of how the system looks in three-dimensions. Hence, it is good practice to draw *both* layout and isometric plumbing drawings. When drawing the isometric plumbing drawing:

1. Use all appropriate plumbing-system symbols, to scale if required
2. Lay out the configuration of the cold water lines.
3. Specify valves, fittings, and pipe sizes.
4. Position the water heater in relationship to the cold water supply.

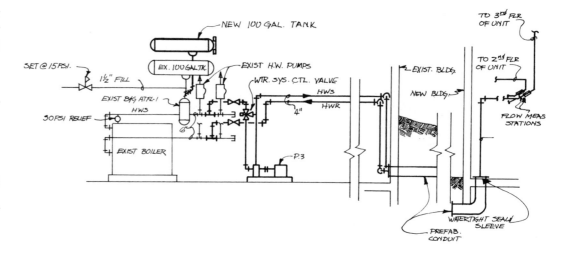

5. Lay out the hot water supply lines.
6. Specify valves, fittings, and pipe sizes.
7. Arrange the drainage and waste-disposal configuration, in relationship to the cold and hot-water lines.
8. For multiple-story buildings, draw a section through the stack and vent lines.
9. Locate the relative position of gas-supply lines.
10. Lay out the configuration of the gas lines.
11. Note all specifications essential to the schematic.

SUMMARY

Plumbing-system drawings are prepared as layouts, isometrics, or both. Layouts use floor plans to show how the plumbing system fits into the building; they are drawn to scale. Isometrics, on the other hand, are usually not drawn to scale; they show no part of the building. Rather, they show the general configuration of the system.

Often, the layout and isometric are used together to show the plumber how the system is to be laid out and constructed. It should be noted, however, that they serve more as a guide to the plumber than as a specific construction plan.

Pages 207–210

Fig. 11-5 *Hot-Water System for an Industrial Complex. Note how the heavier lines in this drawing identify new additions to the existing system. (Layout design courtesy of Roy P. Harrover and Associates, Architects)*

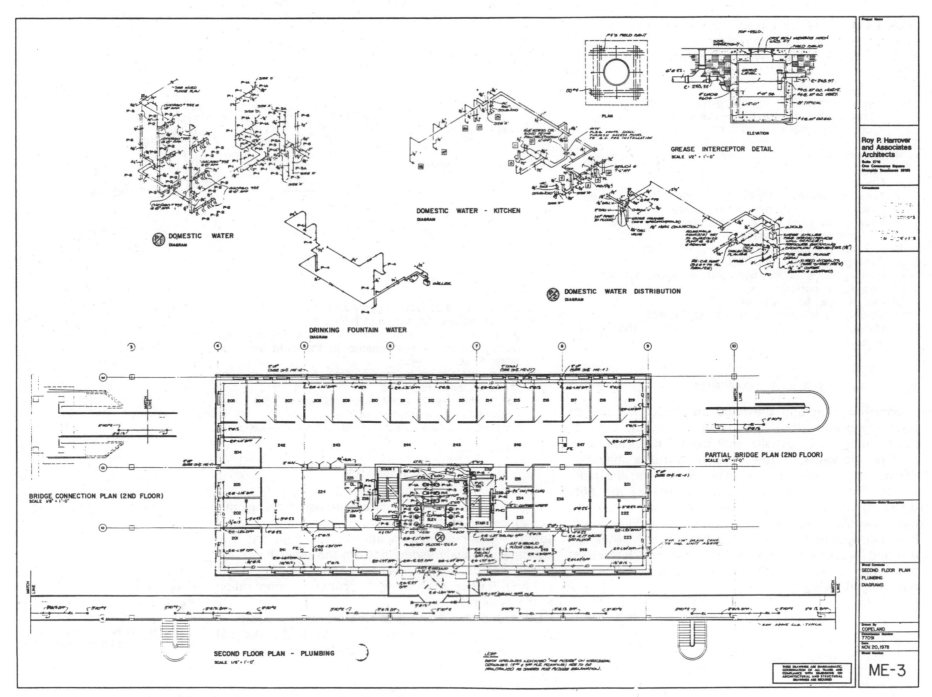

DOMESTIC WATER
DIAGRAM

DOMESTIC WATER - KITCHEN
DIAGRAM

GREASE INTERCEPTOR DETAIL
SCALE 1/2" = 1'-0"

PLAN

ELEVATION

DOMESTIC WATER DISTRIBUTION
DIAGRAM

DRINKING FOUNTAIN WATER
DIAGRAM

BRIDGE CONNECTION PLAN (2ND FLOOR)
SCALE 1/8" = 1'-0"

PARTIAL BRIDGE PLAN (2ND FLOOR)
SCALE 1/8" = 1'-0"

SECOND FLOOR PLAN - PLUMBING
SCALE 1/8" = 1'-0"

Roy P. Harrover
and Associates
Architects

Suite 2718
One Commerce Square
Memphis Tennessee 38103

SECOND FLOOR PLAN
PLUMBING
DIAGRAMS

Drawn By
COPELAND
77091
Date
NOV. 20, 1978
Sheet Number

ME-3

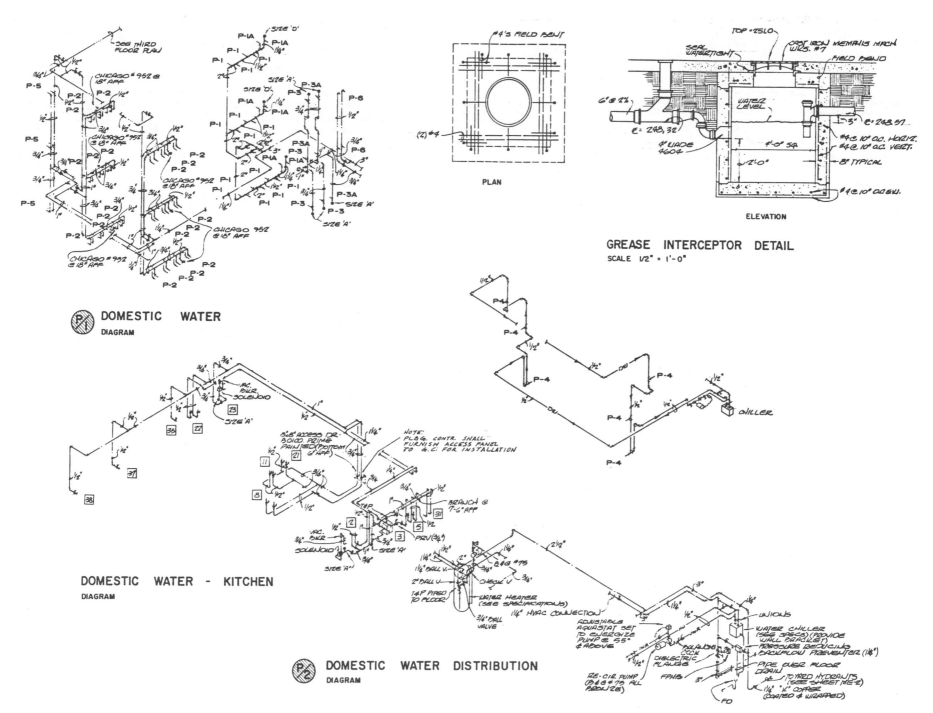

PLAN

GREASE INTERCEPTOR DETAIL
SCALE 1/2" = 1'-0"

ELEVATION

P-1 DOMESTIC WATER
DIAGRAM

DOMESTIC WATER - KITCHEN
DIAGRAM

P-2 DOMESTIC WATER DISTRIBUTION
DIAGRAM

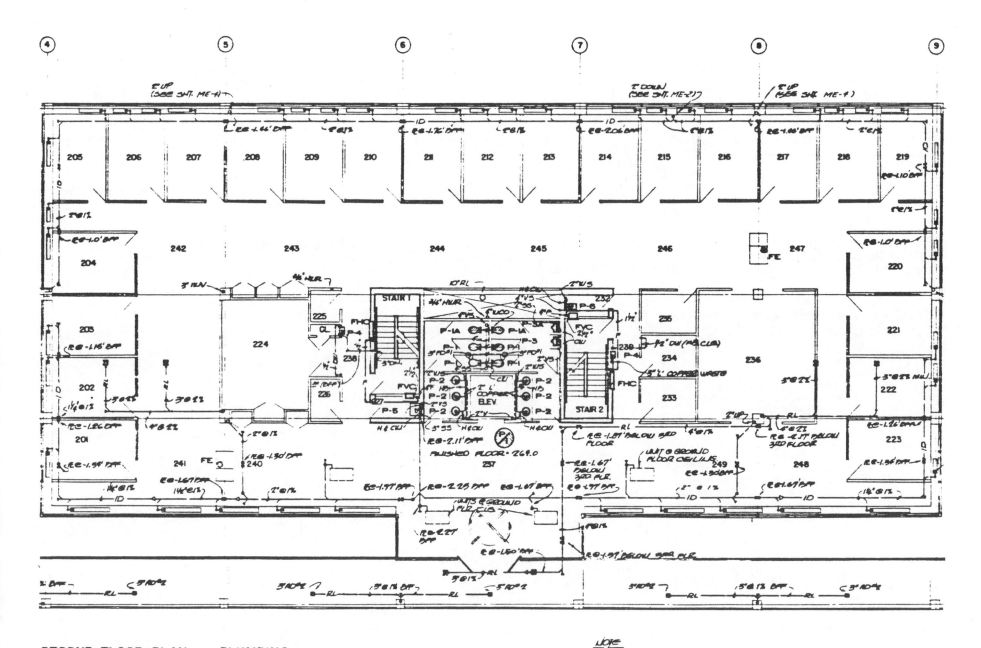

SECOND FLOOR PLAN - PLUMBING

SCALE 1/8" = 1'-0"

Fig. 11-5 *(cont.)*

NOTE

BEAM OPENINGS INDICATED "FOR FUTURE" ON STRUCTURAL
DRAWINGS (2ND & 3RD FLR. FRAMING) ARE TO BE
MAINTAINED AS SPARES FOR FUTURE RENOVATION.

REVIEW QUESTIONS

1. What is the difference between a plumbing floor plan and plumbing layout drawing?
2. What are the differences between a layout and a schematic of the plumbing system?
3. What is included in the plumbing system?
4. When might a plumbing-system drawing not be required for a building?
5. What is interior plumbing? Exterior?

EXERCISES

1. Prepare plumbing layout drawings for the building(s) you have prepared floor plans and elevations for; indicate flow of water.
2. Prepare isometric plumbing drawings for the same building(s).

12

ELECTRICAL SYSTEM AND REFLECTIVE CEILING PLANS

GLOSSARY

Electrical plans drawings that show the layout and position of electrical components

Power drawings drawings that show the wiring of electrical panels

Reflective ceiling plans drawings that show all features of the ceiling, drawn as if viewed in a mirror on the floor

Electrical plans show the location and types of electrical fixtures to be installed in a building. Like plumbing-system plans, electrical drawings are drawn schematically. They are not detailed pictorial drawings of electrical fixtures. The electrical plan gives the electrician an idea of the electrical layout and system configuration for the building. In larger, complex projects, the architectural firm often subcontracts the electrical plans to an engineering firm.

The word *reflective* in the term *reflective ceiling plan* comes from the idea that the floor is a mirror that reflects the ceiling. The floor plan is used to draw the ceiling plans. If the ceiling were drawn as if seen from below, it would be a right-to-left reversal of the floor. A reflective ceiling plan shows all components in correct relationship, but as a *mirror image* of the ceiling. The reflective ceiling plan shows all features of the ceiling.

In many ways, the reflective ceiling plan has a close tie with the electrical-system plan, in that the ceiling is the source of most room lighting. Reflective plans usually show the total environmental system.

CHARACTERISTICS OF ELECTRICAL SYSTEM PLANS

No matter how simple a building may be, the architectural drafter should prepare an electrical system plan. The actual wiring of outlets, lights, meters, and electrical panels is usually left to the electrician. Like the plumber with the plumbing system, the electrician has considerable latitude in determining what is best in the installation of the electrical system.

Because of advances and the development of new, sophisticated equipment in the field, the electrical systems of many commercial and industrial buildings are complex. Plans for these systems may be developed by the architect or by an engineer specializing in electrical systems. Architectural and engineering firms frequently divide their electrical-system plans into two broad categories: *electrical* and *power* drawings.

ELECTRICAL DRAWINGS

Electrical drawings show the general location of fixtures and components. Specific fixtures are designated by their appropriate symbols, and curved lines show where connections are to be made. Fig. 12-1 gives an example. The actual path of the conduit is not shown in the drawing; this is left to the judgment of the electrician. When drawing an electrical fixture, show it as close as possible to where it is to be installed. Where the position is critical, give exact directions about the location of the fixture.

Some simple electrical systems may be drawn on the floor plan itself. It is better practice, however, to prepare a separate electrical drawing. This helps avoid confusion at the job site. When separate electrical drawings are prepared, they are drawn on top of the floor-plan layout with a heavier line weight than the floor plan itself. See Figs. 12-2 through 12-4 for examples of electrical drawings.

POWER DRAWINGS

Power drawings show the power supply and distribution for a building. They provide detailed information about how the electrical lines are to be hooked up to the building, about wiring for control panels, and about other circuitry. These drawings include such information as location of service wires, conduit specifications, meter hook-ups, service-panel wiring,

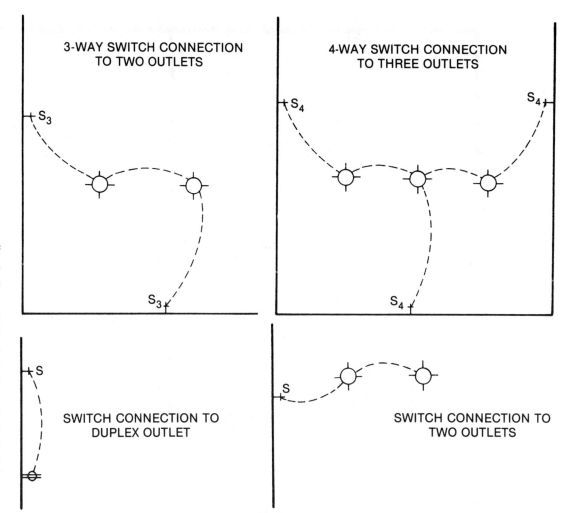

Fig. 12-1 *Four Common Types of Electrical Connection Drawings*

amperage rating, circuit numbering, grounding, and sub-panels for remote circuitry.

Power drawings may not be entirely in schematic form. Details of various electrical equipment are drawn to show how and where leads are connected. Power drawings are usually confined to commercial and industrial buildings with rather complex, specialized electrical hook-ups and equipment. For this reason, these drawings are not included in the working drawings for residential structures. See Fig. 12-5.

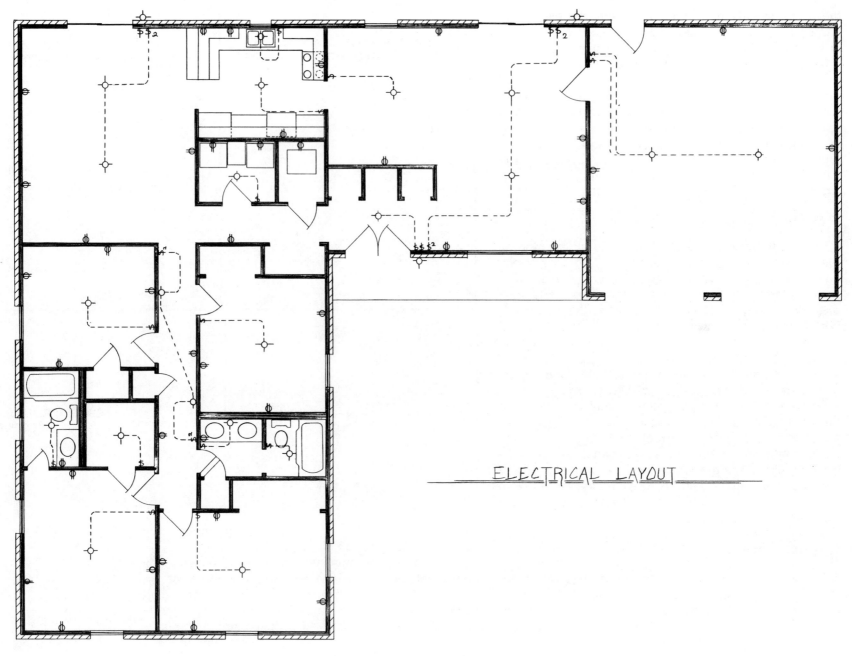

ELECTRICAL LAYOUT

Fig. 12-2 *Electrical Layout for a
Residential Structure*

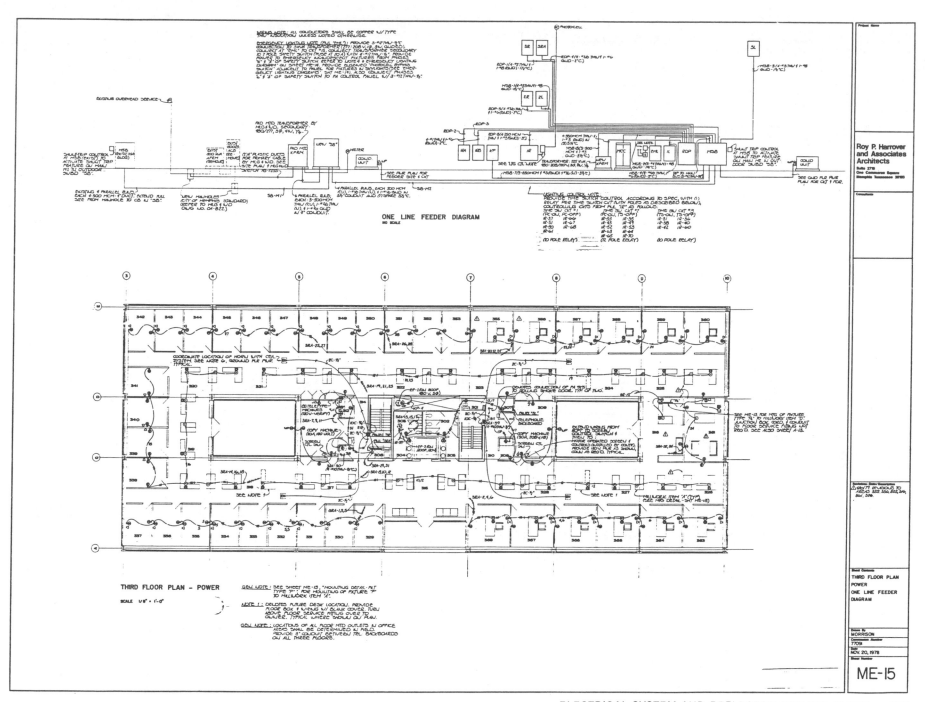

ONE LINE FEEDER DIAGRAM
NO SCALE

THIRD FLOOR PLAN - POWER

SCALE 1/8" = 1'-0"

Roy P. Harrover
and Associates
Architects

Suite 2716
One Commerce Square
Memphis Tennessee 38103

THIRD FLOOR PLAN
POWER
ONE LINE FEEDER
DIAGRAM

Drawn By
MORRISON

Commission Number
77091

Date
NOV. 20, 1978

ME-15

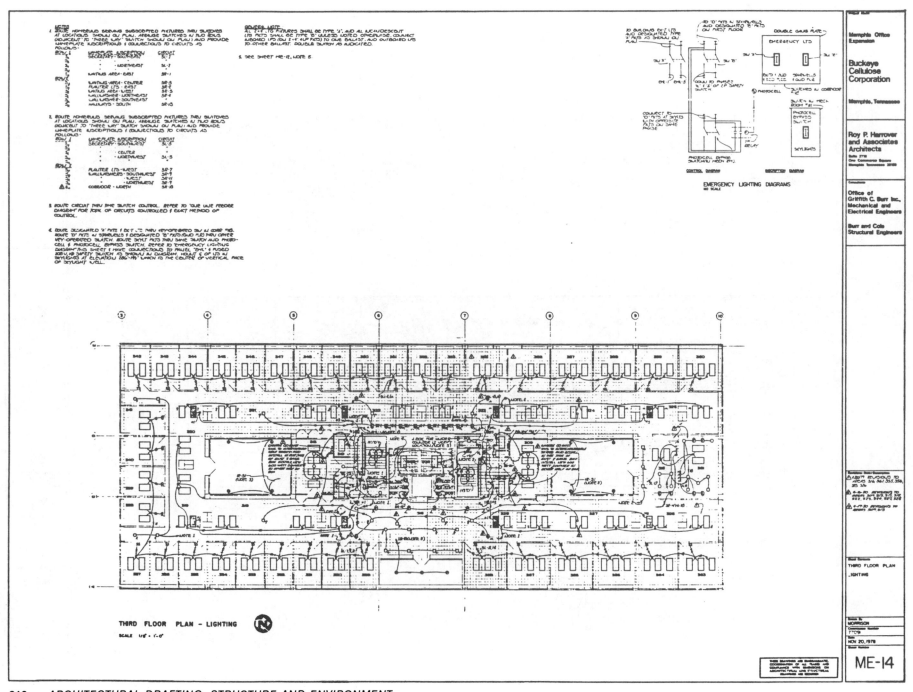

THIRD FLOOR PLAN - LIGHTING

SCALE 1/8" = 1'-0"

EMERGENCY LIGHTING DIAGRAMS
NO SCALE

Memphis Office
Expansion

Buckeye
Cellulose
Corporation

Memphis, Tennessee

Roy P. Harrover
and Associates
Architects

Office of
Griffith C. Burr Inc.,
Mechanical and
Electrical Engineers

Burr and Cole
Structural Engineers

THIRD FLOOR PLAN
LIGHTING

MORRISON

NOV 20, 1978

ME-14

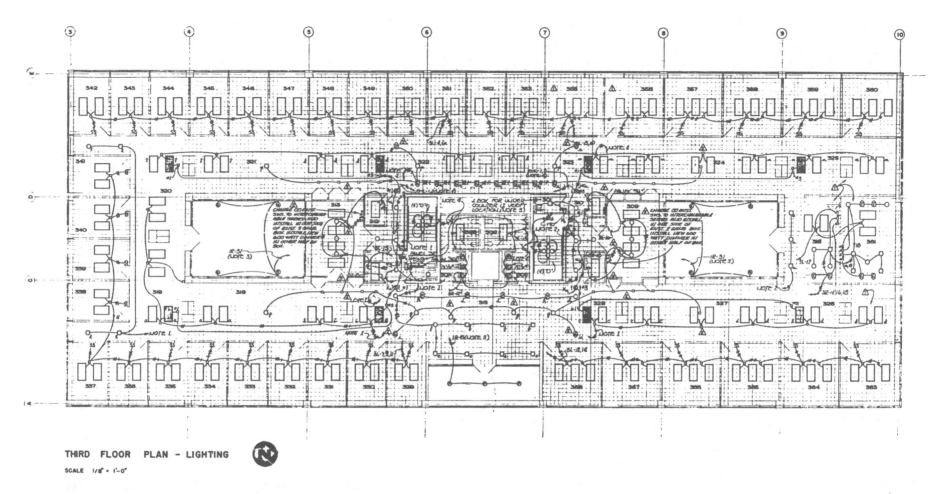

THIRD FLOOR PLAN - LIGHTING

SCALE 1/8" = 1'-0"

DRAWING ELECTRICAL PLANS

Though simple electrical-system drawings may be drawn directly on the floor plans, it is always better to prepare them separately. Before beginning to draw, always check the electrical specifications against the National Electrical Code and the local building regulations. When drawing the electrical system:

1. Locate the service panel.
2. Indicate amperage information for each circuit.
3. Locate and identify all required high-voltage outlets (over 110/120).
4. Locate and identify all wall and ceiling outlets.
5. Locate and identify telephone, door bells, alarms and other special outlets.
6. Locate and identify all switches, outlet and fixture connections with curved lines.
7. Complete the electrical schedule.
8. Prepare details required for power drawings.
9. Identify all circuits and show appropriate hook-ups.
10. Give all circuitry specifications.
11. Darken all lines in the electrical plan, so that they are heavier than non-electrical features.

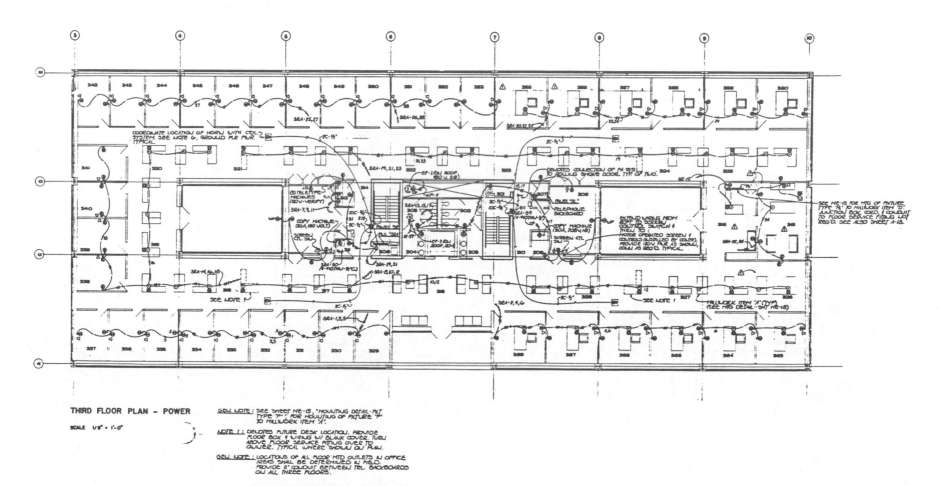

THIRD FLOOR PLAN – POWER

SCALE 1/8" = 1'-0"

Fig. 12-4 *(cont.)*

CHARACTERISTICS OF REFLECTIVE CEILING PLANS

Reflective ceiling plans are mirror images of the ceiling. That is, the plans would be drawn as if the floor were a mirror and the viewer were looking down into it. Ceiling plans show every detail of the ceiling. See Figs. 12-6 through 12-8.

A reflective ceiling plan is prepared like a floor plan, at the same scale, with all notations and dimensions on the plan itself. Some ceiling plans carry acoustical and illumination information about the ceiling. They give specifications for type of lighting

fixtures, finishing materials, air diffusers, return-air ducts, sound system fixtures, and columns or structural supports.

DRAWING REFLECTIVE CEILING PLANS

The drafter should always remember that the reflective ceiling plan is a mirror image of and drawn to the same scale as the floor plan. When drawing the reflective ceiling plan:

1. Locate and draw structural components that touch or go through the ceiling.

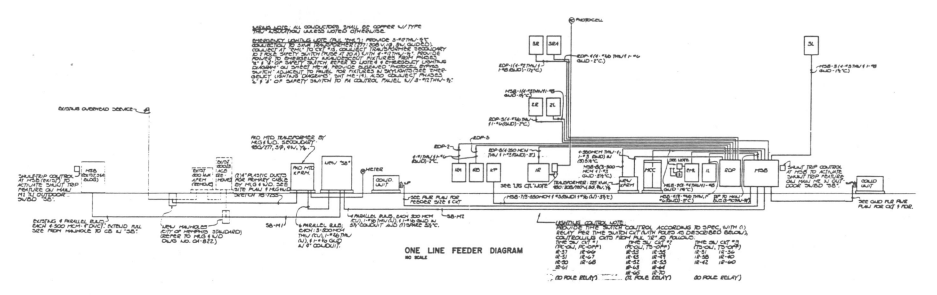

ONE LINE FEEDER DIAGRAM

Fig. 12-5 *Power Drawing for an Industrial Building. (Courtesy of Roy P. Harrover and Associates, Architects)*

2. Locate and draw with hidden lines any stairways or other special features under the ceiling.
3. Locate and draw all light fixtures, air diffusers, skylights, return-air ducts and grills, sound-system fixtures, access panels, and other ceiling components.
4. Draw all moldings, special design features, and any pattern to be in the ceiling.
5. Give all required specifications and schedules.
6. Dimension and note all other features of the ceiling.

SUMMARY

Electrical-system plans should be prepared for all buildings, regardless of their simplicity. Buildings with sophisticated, complex designs frequently require two types of electrical system drawings: electrical drawings and power drawings. Electrical drawings show schematically the locations of all electrical fixtures and components. Power drawings show details of power supply and distribution.

Reflective ceiling plans are drawings that show the ceiling as it would be seen if reflected by the floor.

They are drawn to the same scale as the floor plan, and show all characteristics of the ceiling. They locate all mechanical and electrical devices on the ceiling itself. Reflective ceiling plans also explain the illumination and acoustical qualities of the ceiling.

REVIEW QUESTIONS

1. What is the major purpose of electrical-system plans?
2. How does the electrician use electrical-system plans?
3. What are the two categories of electrical-system plans?
4. Which electrical system plan is used in drawing power supplies?
5. What two references should be checked to assure proper specifications before one begins to draw the electrical system?
6. What principle is used when drawing reflective ceiling plans?
7. What is the purpose of reflective ceiling plans?
8. What are some of the items included in reflective ceiling plans?

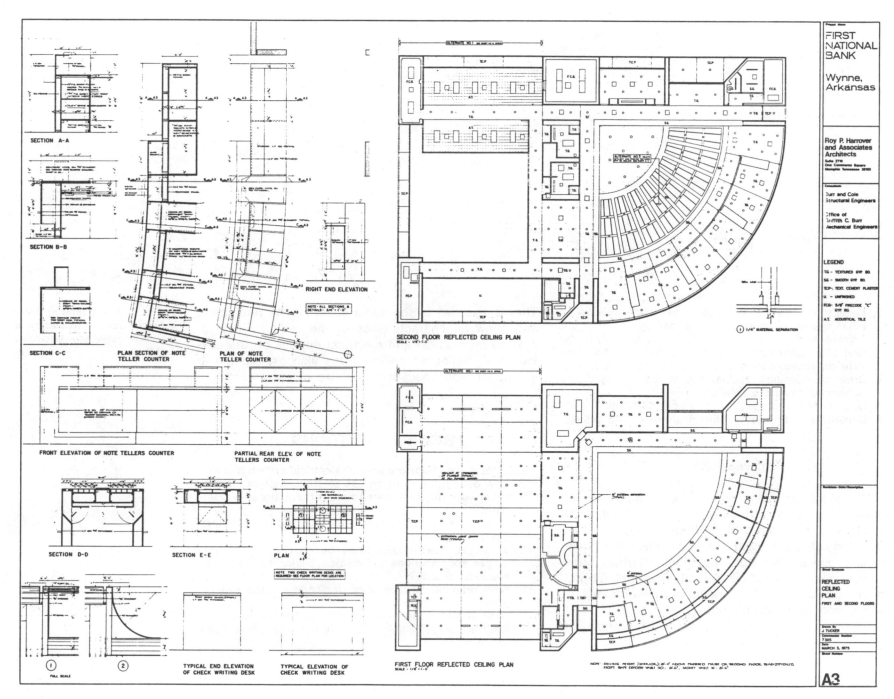

SECTION A-A

SECTION B-B

SECTION C-C

RIGHT END ELEVATION

NOTE - ALL SECTIONS &
DETAILS - 3/4" = 1'-0"

PLAN SECTION OF NOTE
TELLER COUNTER

PLAN OF NOTE
TELLER COUNTER

FRONT ELEVATION OF NOTE TELLERS COUNTER

PARTIAL REAR ELEV. OF NOTE
TELLERS COUNTER

SECTION D-D

SECTION E-E

PLAN

NOTE TWO CHECK WRITING DESKS ARE
REQUIRED - SEE FLOOR PLAN FOR LOCATION

TYPICAL END ELEVATION
OF CHECK WRITING DESK

TYPICAL ELEVATION OF
CHECK WRITING DESK

FULL SCALE

SECOND FLOOR REFLECTED CEILING PLAN
SCALE - 1/8" = 1'-0"

1/4" MATERIAL SEPARATION

FIRST FLOOR REFLECTED CEILING PLAN
SCALE - 1/8" = 1'-0"

FIRST NATIONAL BANK

Wynne, Arkansas

Roy P. Harrover and Associates Architects
Suite 2710
One Commerce Square
Memphis Tennessee 38103

Burr and Cole
Structural Engineers

Office of
Griffith C. Burr
Mechanical Engineers

LEGEND

T.G. - TEXTURED GYP. BD.
S.G. - SMOOTH GYP. BD.
T.C.P. - TEXT. CEMENT PLASTER
U. - UNFINISHED
F.C.B - 5/8" FIRECODE "C"
GYP. BD.
A.T. - ACOUSTICAL TILE

Revisions - Date / Description

Sheet Contents

REFLECTED
CEILING
PLAN
FIRST AND SECOND FLOORS

Drawn By
J. TUCKER

7365

MARCH 3, 1975

A3

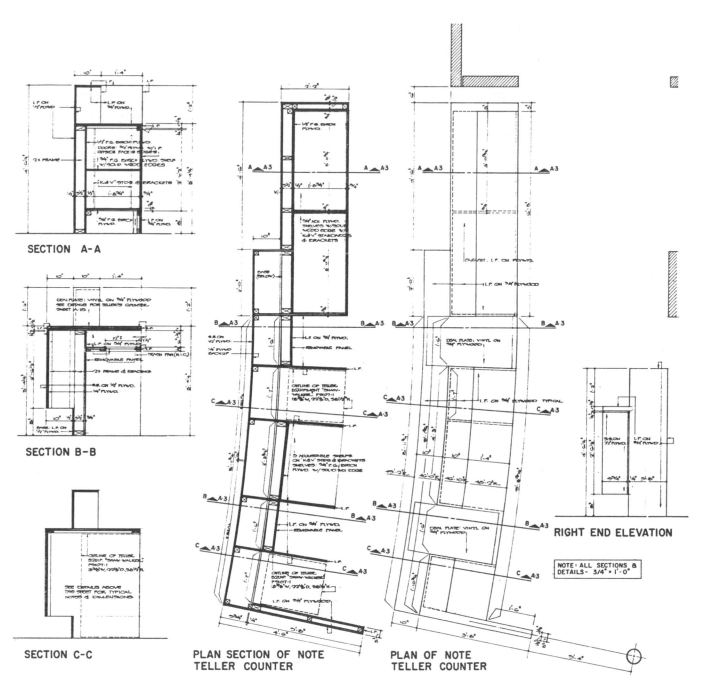

SECTION A-A

SECTION B-B

SECTION C-C

PLAN SECTION OF NOTE
TELLER COUNTER

PLAN OF NOTE
TELLER COUNTER

RIGHT END ELEVATION

NOTE: ALL SECTIONS &
DETAILS- 3/4" = 1'-0"

Fig. 12-6 *(cont.)*

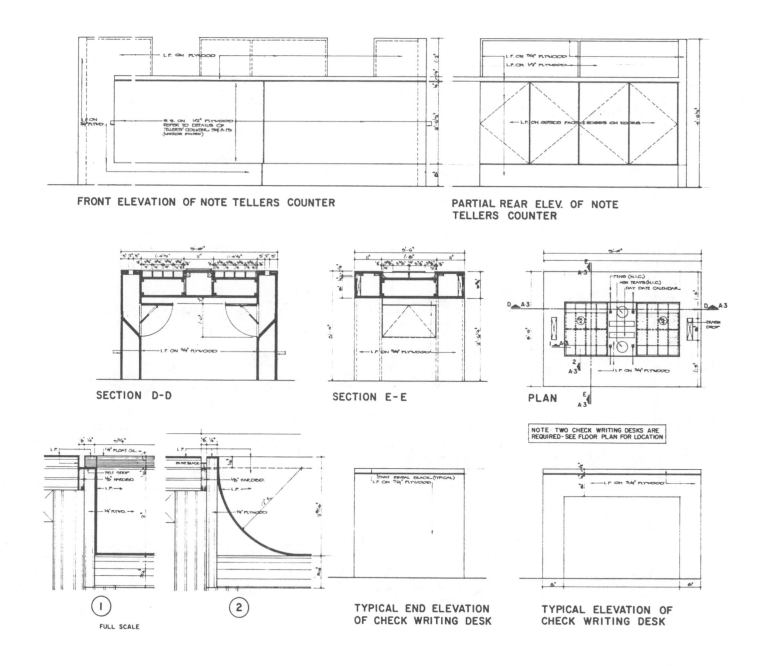

FRONT ELEVATION OF NOTE TELLERS COUNTER

PARTIAL REAR ELEV. OF NOTE TELLERS COUNTER

SECTION D-D

SECTION E-E

PLAN

FULL SCALE

TYPICAL END ELEVATION OF CHECK WRITING DESK

TYPICAL ELEVATION OF CHECK WRITING DESK

NOTE: TWO CHECK WRITING DESKS ARE REQUIRED-SEE FLOOR PLAN FOR LOCATION

Fig. 12-6 *(cont.)*

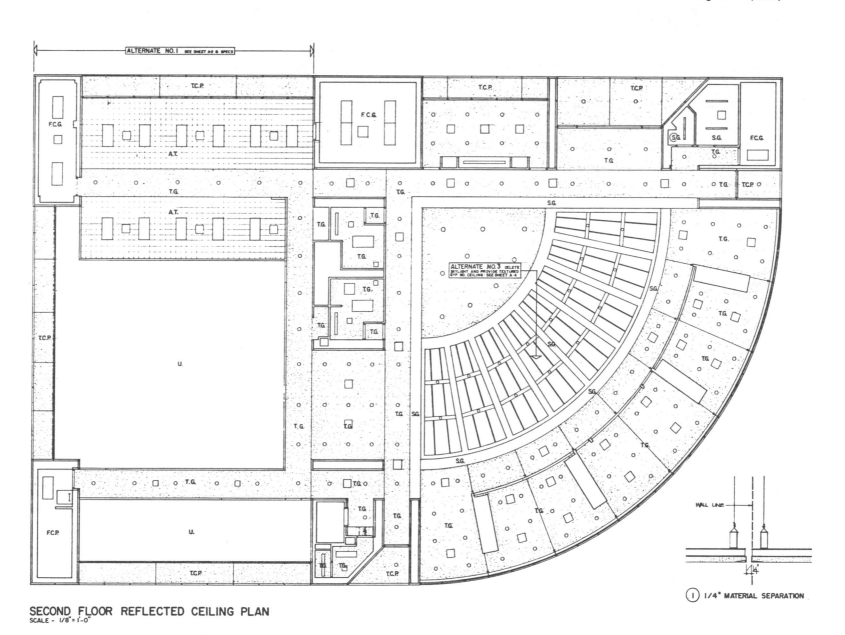

SECOND FLOOR REFLECTED CEILING PLAN
SCALE - 1/8" = 1'-0"

① 1/4" MATERIAL SEPARATION

Fig. 12-6 *(cont.)*

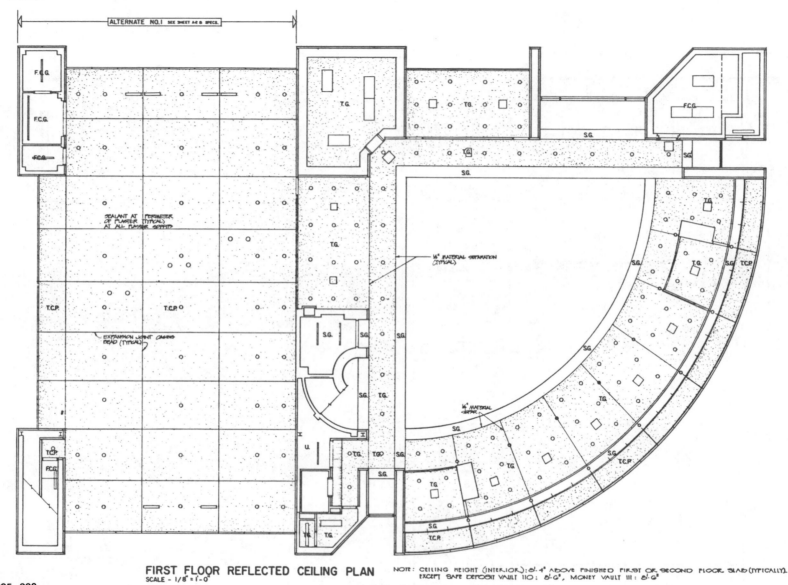

FIRST FLOOR REFLECTED CEILING PLAN
SCALE - 1/8" = 1'-0"

NOTE: CEILING HEIGHT (INTERIOR): 8'-4" ABOVE FINISHED FIRST OR SECOND FLOOR SLAB (TYPICALLY).
EXCEPT SAFE DEPOSIT VAULT 110: 8'-6", MONEY VAULT III: 8'-6"

Pages 225–228
Fig. 12-7 *Partial Reflective Ceiling Plan for Industrial Building (Courtesy of Roy P. Harrover and Associates, Architects)*

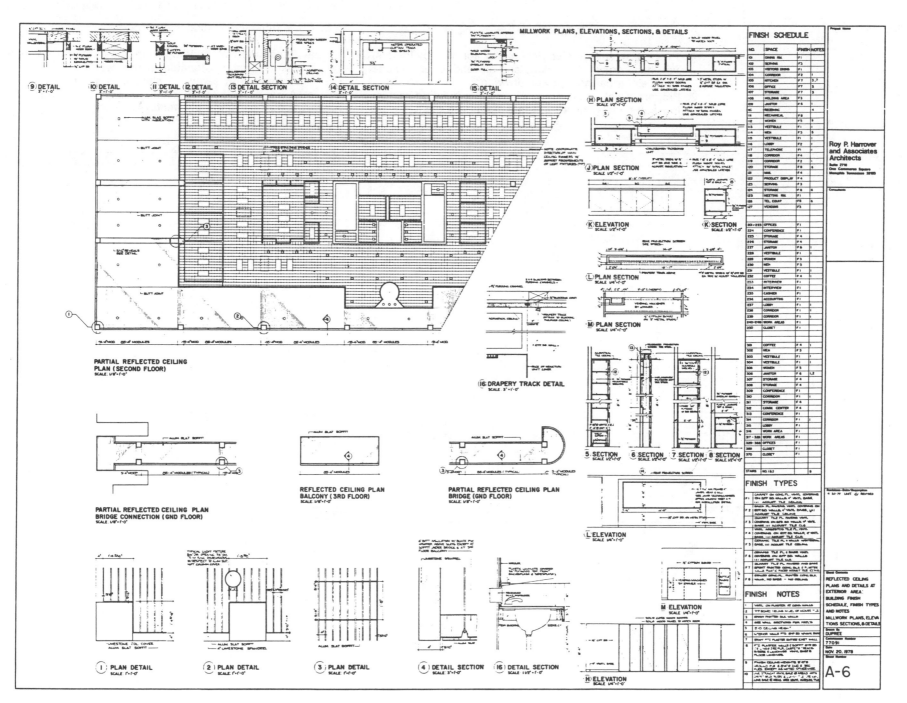

MILLWORK PLANS, ELEVATIONS, SECTIONS, & DETAILS

(9) DETAIL
(10) DETAIL
(11) DETAIL
(12) DETAIL
(13) DETAIL SECTION
(14) DETAIL SECTION
(15) DETAIL

PARTIAL REFLECTED CEILING
PLAN (SECOND FLOOR)
SCALE 1/8"=1'-0"

(16) DRAPERY TRACK DETAIL
SCALE 3"=1'-0"

REFLECTED CEILING PLAN
BALCONY (3RD FLOOR)
SCALE 1/8"=1'-0"

PARTIAL REFLECTED CEILING PLAN
BRIDGE (GND FLOOR)
SCALE 1/8"=1'-0"

PARTIAL REFLECTED CEILING PLAN
BRIDGE CONNECTION (GND FLOOR)
SCALE 1/8"=1'-0"

(H) PLAN SECTION
SCALE 1/2"=1'-0"

(J) PLAN SECTION
SCALE 1/2"=1'-0"

(K) ELEVATION
SCALE 1/2"=1'-0"

(K) SECTION
SCALE 1/2"=1'-0"

(L) PLAN SECTION
SCALE 1/4"=1'-0"

(M) PLAN SECTION
SCALE 1/4"=1'-0"

(5) SECTION
SCALE 1/2"=1'-0"
(6) SECTION
SCALE 1/2"=1'-0"
(7) SECTION
SCALE 1/2"=1'-0"
(8) SECTION
SCALE 1/2"=1'-0"

(L) ELEVATION
SCALE 1/4"=1'-0"

(M) ELEVATION
SCALE 1/4"=1'-0"

(H) ELEVATION
SCALE 1/4"=1'-0"

(1) PLAN DETAIL
SCALE 1"=1'-0"
(2) PLAN DETAIL
SCALE 1"=1'-0"
(3) PLAN DETAIL
SCALE 1"=1'-0"
(4) DETAIL SECTION
SCALE 3"=1'-0"
(16) DETAIL SECTION
SCALE 1 1/2"=1'-0"

FINISH SCHEDULE

NO.	SPACE	FINISH	NOTES
101	DINING RM.	F1	
102	SERVING	F3	
103	VISITORS DINING	F1	
104	CORRIDOR	F1	
105	KITCHEN	F7	3,7
106	OFFICE	F7	3
107	STORAGE	F7	3
108	HOLDING AREA	F3	
109	JANITOR	F6	6
110	RECEIVING	F7	
111	MECHANICAL	F8	
112	WOMEN	F5	5
113	VESTIBULE	F1	
114	MEN	F5	5
115	VESTIBULE	F1	
116	LOBBY	F2	
117	TELEPHONE	F1	
118	CORRIDOR	F1	
119	CORRIDOR	F2	
120	STORAGE	F6	6
121	MAIL	F1	
122	PRODUCT DISPLAY	F1	
123	SERVING	F3	
124	STORAGE	F6	6
125	MEETING RM.	F1	
126	TEL. EQUIP.	F6	6
127	VENDING	F3	
201-223	OFFICES	F1	
224	CONFERENCE	F1	
225	STORAGE	F4	
226	STORAGE	F4	
227	JANITOR	F6	6
228	VESTIBULE	F1	
229	WOMEN	F5	
230	MEN	F5	
231	VESTIBULE	F1	
232	COFFEE	F4	
233	INTERVIEW	F1	
234	INTERVIEW	F1	
235	CASHIER	F1	
236	ACCOUNTING	F1	
237	LOBBY	F1	
238	CORRIDOR	F1	
239	CORRIDOR	F1	
240-249	WORK AREAS	F1	
250	CLOSET	F1	
301	COFFEE	F4	
302	MEN	F3	
303	VESTIBULE	F1	
304	VESTIBULE	F1	
305	WOMEN	F3	
306	JANITOR	F6	1,2
307	STORAGE	F4	
308	STORAGE	F4	
309	CONFERENCE	F1	
310	CORRIDOR	F1	
311	STORAGE	F4	
312	COMM. CENTER	F1	
313	CONFERENCE	F1	
314	LOBBY	F1	
315	CORRIDOR	F1	
316	WORK AREA	F1	
317-328	WORK AREAS	F1	
329-368	OFFICES	F1	
369	CLOSET	F1	
370	CLOSET	F1	
STAIRS	NO. 1 & 2		

FINISH TYPES

F1 CARPET ON CONC. FL. VINYL COVERING ON GYP. BD. WALLS, 4" VINYL BASE, (1) ACOUST TILE CEILING

F2 BRICK FL. PAVERS VINYL COVERING ON GYP. BD. WALLS, 4" VINYL BASE, (1) ACOUST TILE CEILING

F3 QUARRY TILE FL. PAVERS VINYL COVERING ON GYP. BD. WALLS & VINYL BASE, (1) ACOUST TILE CLG.

F4 VINYL ASBESTOS TILE FL. VINYL COVERING ON GYP. BD. WALLS, 4" VINYL BASE, (1) ACOUST TILE CEILING

F5 CERAMIC TILE FL. & WALLS WITH VINYL BASE, (1) ACOUST TILE CEILING

F6 EXPOSED CONC. FL. & BARE WALLS, CONC. BLK. & PLASTER

F7 QUARRY TILE FL. PAVERS AND BASE, EPOXY PAINTED CONC. BLK. & PLASTER WALLS, ACOUST TILE CLG.

F8 SEALED CONC. FL. PAINTED CONC. BLK. WALLS, NO BASE - NO CEILING

FINISH NOTES

1 VINYL ON PLASTER AT CONC. WALLS
2 GYP. BOARD CEILING IN LIEU OF ACOUST. TILE
3 EPOXY PAINTED BLK. WALLS
4 SEE WALL SECTIONS FOR HEIGHTS
5 9'-0" CEILING HEIGHT
6 INTERIOR WALLS FT'G GYP. BD. ON WOOD. STUD
7 STAIN (1) PLASTER ENTIRE EAST WALL
8
9 FINISH CEILING HEIGHTS 9'-0"
10

Roy P. Harrover
and Associates
Architects
Suite 2710
One Commerce Square
Memphis, Tennessee 38103

Commission Number
77091
Date
NOV. 20, 1978
Sheet Number

REFLECTED CEILING
PLANS AND DETAILS AT
EXTERIOR AREA:
BUILDING FINISH
SCHEDULE, FINISH TYPES
AND NOTES
MILLWORK PLANS, ELEVA-
TIONS SECTIONS, & DETAILS
Drawn By
DUPREE

A-6

Fig. 12-7 *(cont.)*

EXERCISES

1. Prepare a set of electrical plans for the building(s) you have drawn floor plans and elevations for. Include both electrical and power drawings.
2. Prepare a set of electrical plans for a building requiring sub-panels for an outdoor lighting system.

3. Draw reflective ceiling plans for:

   a. A commercial building with most of the environmental systems located in the ceiling.
   b. A room with a built-in speaker system.
   c. A room with a specially designed ceiling, with acoustical and light features.

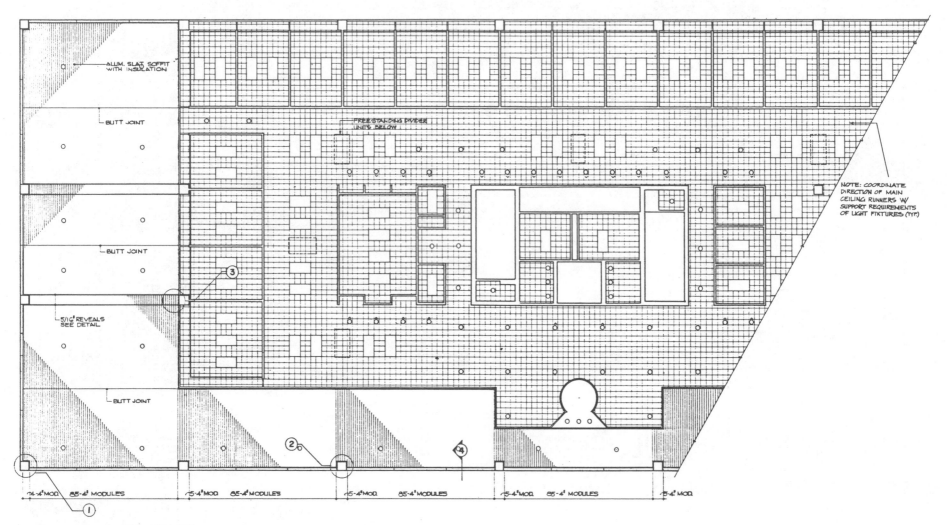

PARTIAL REFLECTED CEILING PLAN (SECOND FLOOR)
SCALE: 1/8"=1'-0"

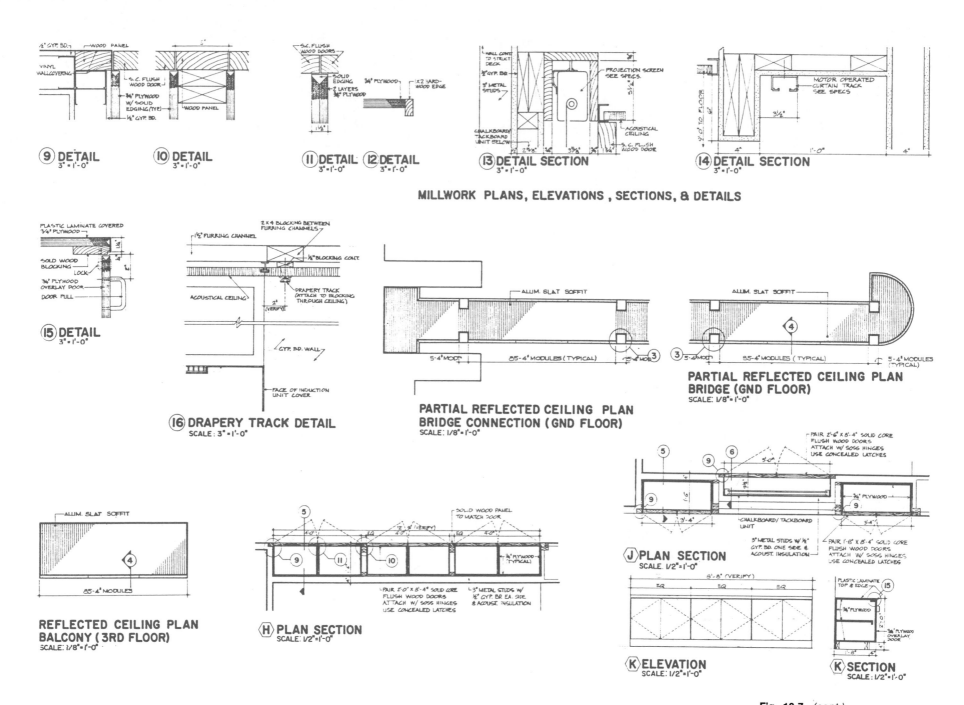

MILLWORK PLANS, ELEVATIONS, SECTIONS, & DETAILS

(9) **DETAIL** 3" = 1'-0"

(10) **DETAIL** 3" = 1'-0"

(11) **DETAIL** 3" = 1'-0"

(12) **DETAIL** 3" = 1'-0"

(13) **DETAIL SECTION** 3" = 1'-0"

(14) **DETAIL SECTION** 3" = 1'-0"

(15) **DETAIL** 3" = 1'-0"

(16) **DRAPERY TRACK DETAIL** SCALE: 3" = 1'-0"

PARTIAL REFLECTED CEILING PLAN BRIDGE CONNECTION (GND FLOOR) SCALE: 1/8" = 1'-0"

PARTIAL REFLECTED CEILING PLAN BRIDGE (GND FLOOR) SCALE: 1/8" = 1'-0"

REFLECTED CEILING PLAN BALCONY (3RD FLOOR) SCALE: 1/8" = 1'-0"

(H) **PLAN SECTION** SCALE: 1/2" = 1'-0"

(J) **PLAN SECTION** SCALE: 1/2" = 1'-0"

(K) **ELEVATION** SCALE: 1/2" = 1'-0"

(K) **SECTION** SCALE: 1/2" = 1'-0"

Fig. 12-7 *(cont.)*

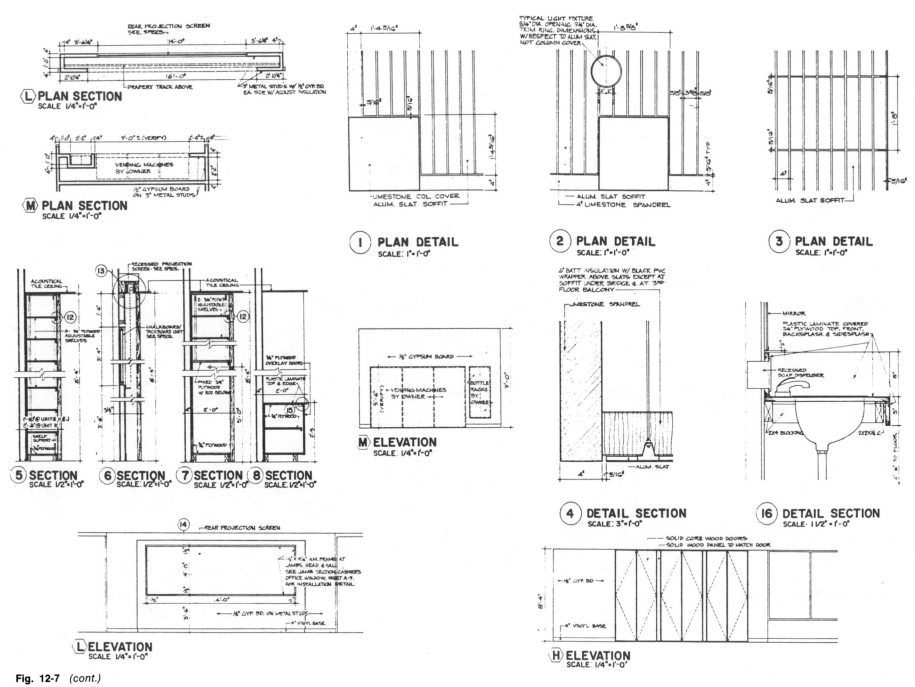

Fig. 12-7 *(cont.)*

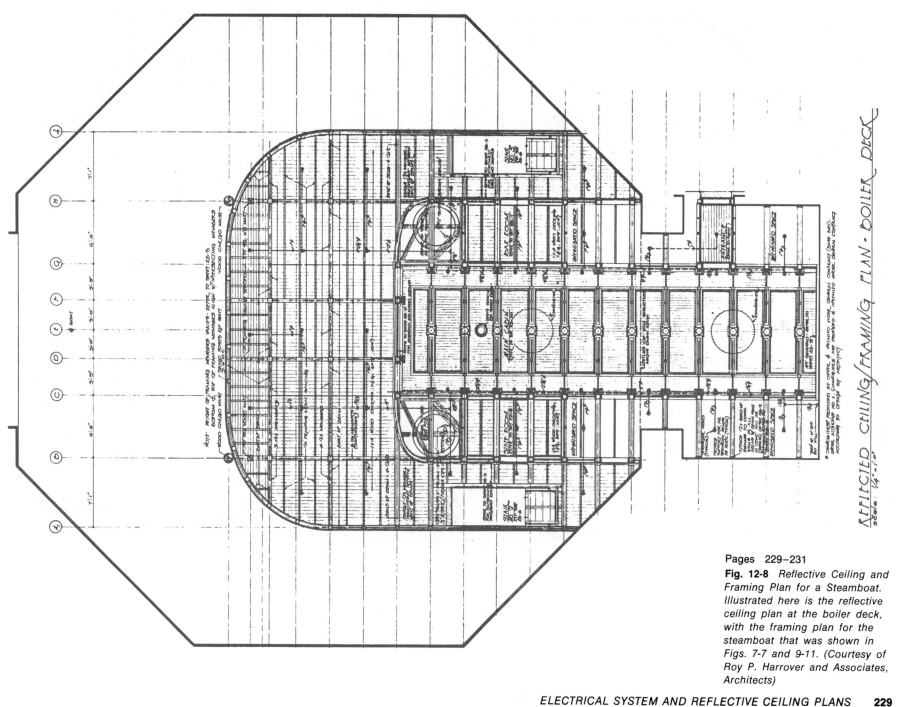

REFLECTED CEILING/FRAMING PLAN · BOILER DECK
Scale: 1/4" = 1'-0"

Pages 229–231

Fig. 12-8 *Reflective Ceiling and Framing Plan for a Steamboat. Illustrated here is the reflective ceiling plan at the boiler deck, with the framing plan for the steamboat that was shown in Figs. 7-7 and 9-11. (Courtesy of Roy P. Harrover and Associates, Architects)*

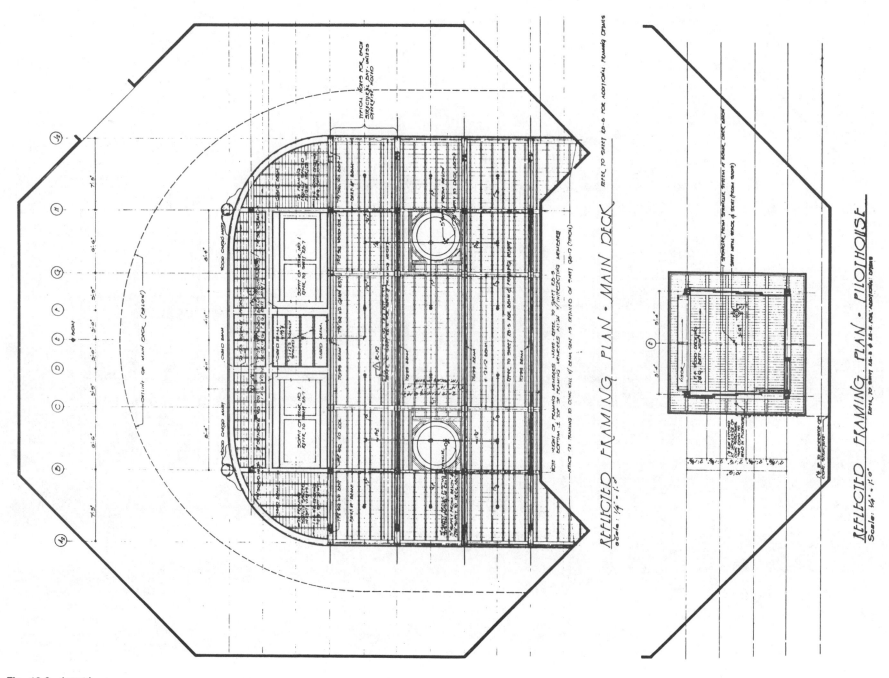

REFLECTED FRAMING PLAN · MAIN DECK
Scale: 1/4" = 1'-0"

REFLECTED FRAMING PLAN · PILOTHOUSE
Scale: 1/4" = 1'-0"

Fig. 12-8 *(cont.)*

230   ARCHITECTURAL DRAFTING: STRUCTURE AND ENVIRONMENT

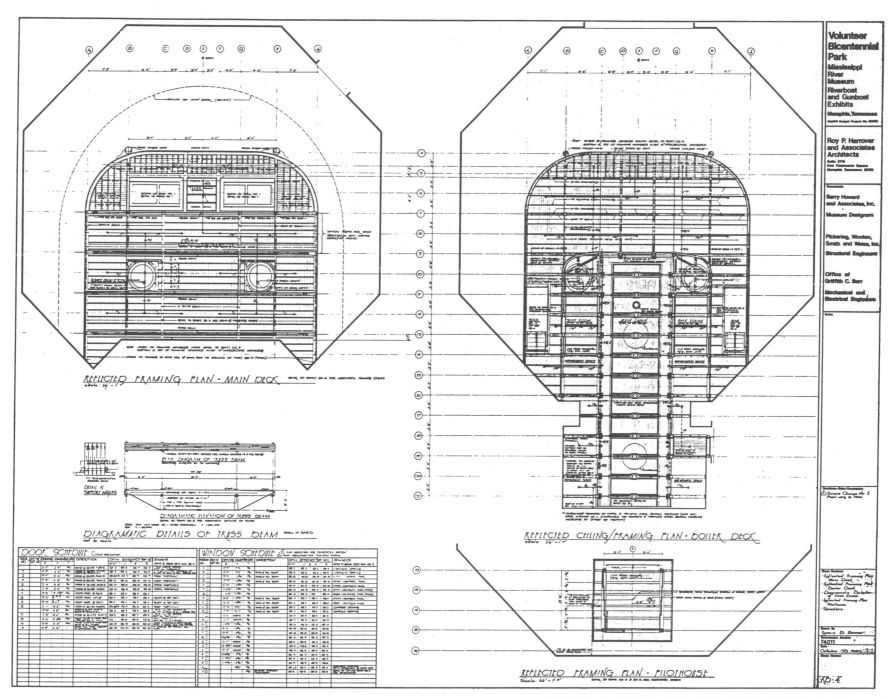

REFLECTED FRAMING PLAN - MAIN DECK

DIAGRAMATIC DETAILS OF TRUSS BEAM

REFLECTED CEILING/FRAMING PLAN - BOILER DECK

REFLECTED FRAMING PLAN - PILOTHOUSE

DOOR SCHEDULE

WINDOW SCHEDULE

Volunteer
Bicentennial
Park

Mississippi
River
Museum
Riverboat
and Gunboat
Exhibits

Memphis, Tennessee

Roy P. Harrover
and Associates
Architects

Barry Howard
and Associates, Inc.

Museum Designers

Pickering, Wooten,
Smith and Weiss, Inc.

Structural Engineers

Office of
Griffith C. Burr

Mechanical and
Electrical Engineers

74011

October 70, 1980

13

HEATING, VENTILATION, AND AIR-CONDITIONING (HVAC) SYSTEM PLANS

GLOSSARY

HVAC abbreviation for *Heating, Ventilation, and Air-Conditioning*

The heating, ventilation, and air-conditioning system is perhaps the most complex of all environmental-control systems. The plumbing and electrical drawings are basically single-line schematics, but this will not suffice for most HVAC plans. Drafters frequently have to draw the configuration of the ductwork that services the HVAC system. These drawings must be drawn to scale, and the size and location of the ductwork must be dimensionally correct.

Accuracy and true representation are critical in HVAC-system plans. If the plans are not accurate, they give a false idea of how much space has been allowed for the ductwork. Since tradespeople follow these plans closely, erroneous representation adds to the computations required on the project. This in turn slows down work and adds to the expenses. For designs with special HVAC-system considerations, architectural firms often contract with specialized engineering firms.

CHARACTERISTICS OF HVAC SYSTEM PLANS

HVAC drawings show how warmed, cooled, and ambient (existing) air is circulated throughout a building. These drawings give specifications for the heating and cooling units in the system. In some commercial, industrial, and—in recent years—residential structures, architects have designed central vacuum systems to be included in the building. If this is the case, the vacuum system too should be shown as part of the HVAC system.

All aspects of the HVAC system are superimposed on a floor-plan layout. See Figs. 13-1 through 13-3. It is sometimes necessary to show how the ductwork is viewed through a sectional elevation, as in Fig. 13-4. Heating, cooling, and vacuum details are not always required; whether they are done is often left to the discretion of the drafter or depends on the common operating practices of the architectural firm.

HVAC-system plans include drawings for each floor serviced by the system, giving required dimensions, specifications, and details for construction. Good drafting practice is to prepare HVAC drawings separately from the floor plans, thereby avoiding confusion about dimensions and specifications. These HVAC plans show the location and specifications of dampers, thermostats, related controls, all sheet-metal configurations, the ductwork, distributors, diffusers, heating and air-conditioning units, vacuum pumps, and other components. In addition to these drawings, schedules are also prepared for various units in the system.

DRAWING HVAC SYSTEM PLANS

Drawing the HVAC plans is a complicated process, which can be complicated even more if a logical method is not used. These plans must show the tradespeople how the air moves from the heating and air-conditioning units to each room. Complications arise with a two-duct system: one with a set of ducts that carry air into the rooms and separate ducts that take air back out of the rooms. With such a design, the drafter not only must be aware of width and length dimensions, but also must be sensitive to

height, especially in places where the systems would cross.

The capacity of each room outlet, as well as of the heating and cooling units, are specified on the floor-plan layout. See Fig. 13-5. Combined heating and cooling ductwork capacity is usually measured in *cubic feet per minute* of air flow, abbreviated *CFM*. In addition to system capacity, the drawings show the various sizes of ductwork, reduction fittings, turns, grills, and other aspects of the system.

Before beginning to draw the HVAC system, check all specifications against the *Heating, Ventilating, Air-Conditioning Guide.* All symbols and notations should conform to the standards set forth by the American Standards Association, Inc. (ASA). When drawing the HVAC system:

1. Draw the floor-plan layout for every level serviced by the HVAC system.
2. Dimensionally locate and draw such central units as heating, air-conditioning, and vacuum.
3. Locate and specify all outlets and their capacity.
4. Coordinate ceiling outlets with other environmental control systems.
5. Lay out ducts for each room, checking the *Heating, Ventilating, Air-Conditioning Guide* for proper sizes.
6. Draw in all rectangular ducts and give dimensions.
7. Draw in all circular ducts with single-line symbols, and give sizes.
8. Locate and draw the smoke pipes to the chimneys or appropriate vents.
9. Locate and draws risers for second- and multiple-story outlets.
10. Draw all gaseous and liquid heating or cooling systems that use pipes, as single-line schematics.
11. Identify feeder lines for pipe HVAC systems, with single solid lines, and show return lines as single hidden lines.
12. Darken in all of the HVAC system, so that it is of heavier line weight than the floor-plan layout or section.
13. Draw and specify all structural details needed for the HVAC system.
14. Include all necessary notations and schedules.

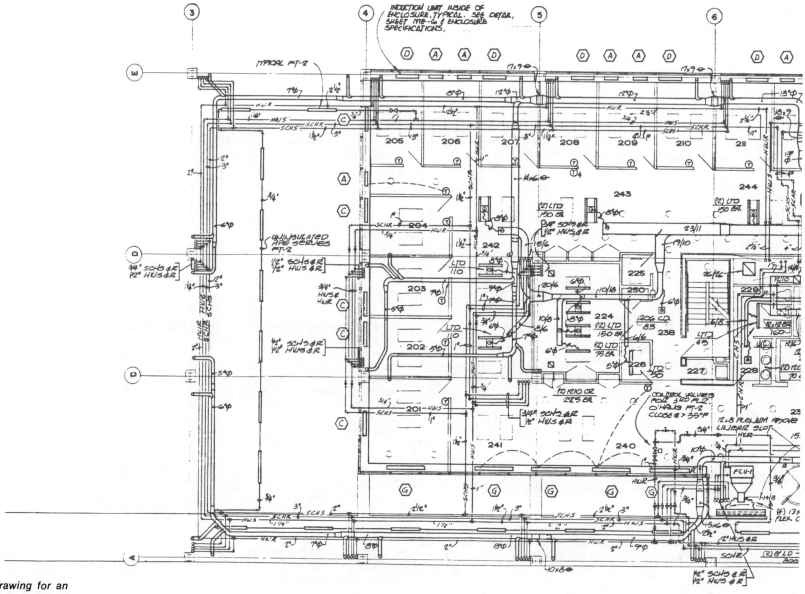

SECOND FLOOR PLAN - HVAC

SCALE 1/8" = 1'-0"

Pages 234-236

Fig. 13-1 *HVAC Drawing for an Industrial Building. Note the method for identifying the size of the ductwork to be installed in the building. (Courtesy of Roy P. Harrover and Associates, Architects)*

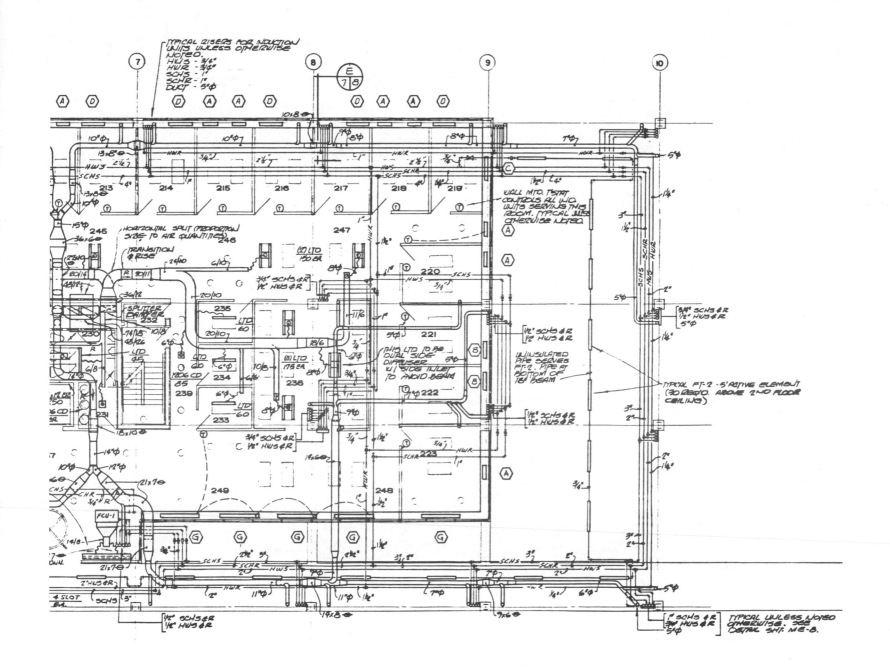

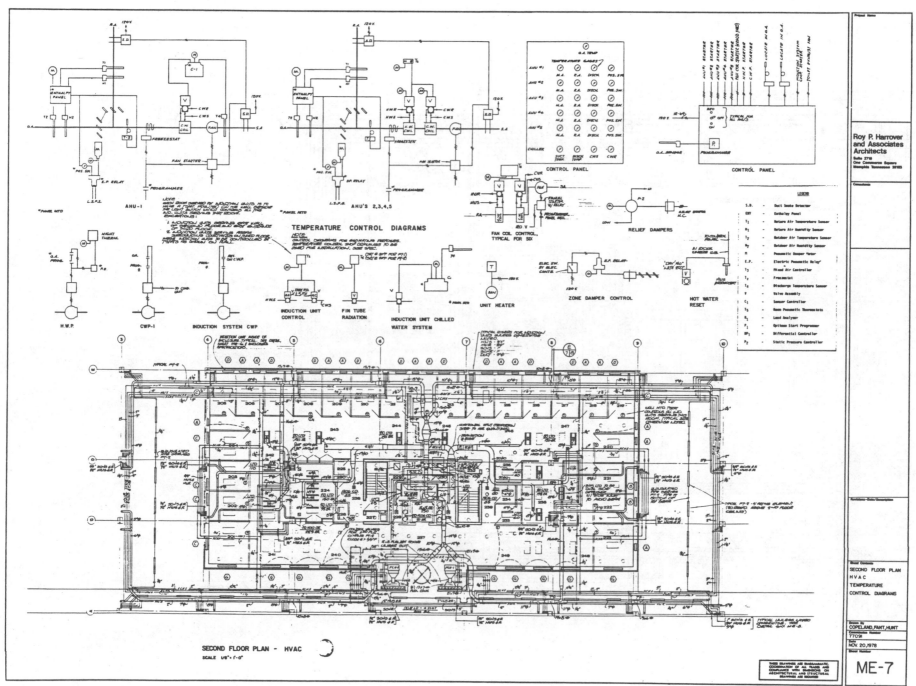

TEMPERATURE CONTROL DIAGRAMS

CONTROL PANEL

CONTROL PANEL

LEGEND

SECOND FLOOR PLAN - HVAC

SCALE 1/8" = 1'-0"

Roy P. Harrover and Associates Architects
Suite 2710
One Commerce Square
Memphis Tennessee 38103

SECOND FLOOR PLAN
HVAC
TEMPERATURE
CONTROL DIAGRAMS

Drawn By
COPELAND, FANT, HUNT

77091

Date
NOV. 20, 1978

ME-7

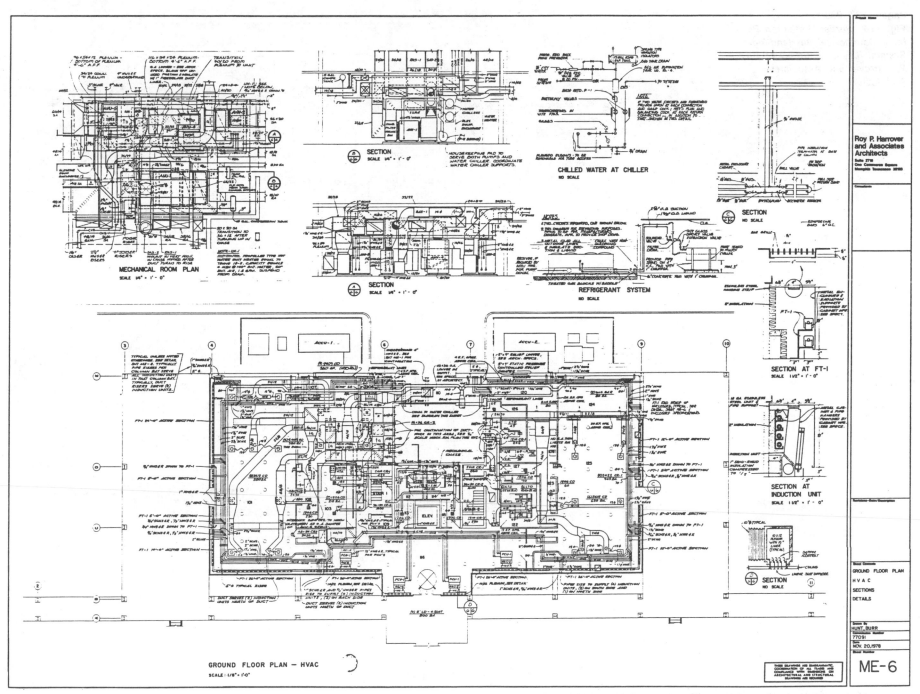

MECHANICAL ROOM PLAN
SCALE 1/4" = 1'-0"

SECTION
SCALE 1/4" = 1'-0"

SECTION
SCALE 1/4" = 1'-0"

CHILLED WATER AT CHILLER
NO SCALE

REFRIGERANT SYSTEM
NO SCALE

SECTION
NO SCALE

SECTION
NO SCALE

SECTION AT FT-1
SCALE 1 1/2" = 1'-0"

SECTION AT
INDUCTION UNIT
SCALE 1 1/2" = 1'-0"

SECTION
NO SCALE

GROUND FLOOR PLAN — HVAC
SCALE : 1/8" = 1'-0"

Roy P. Harrover
and Associates
Architects
Suite 2718
One Commerce Square
Memphis Tennessee 38103

Consultants

Sheet Contents
GROUND FLOOR PLAN
HVAC
SECTIONS
DETAILS

Drawn By
HUNT, BURR
Commission Number
77091
Date
NOV. 20, 1978
Sheet Number

ME-6

Fig. 13-2 *Partial Ventilation Plan for a Commercial Air-Handling System. (Layout courtesy of Roy P. Harrover and Associates, Architects)*

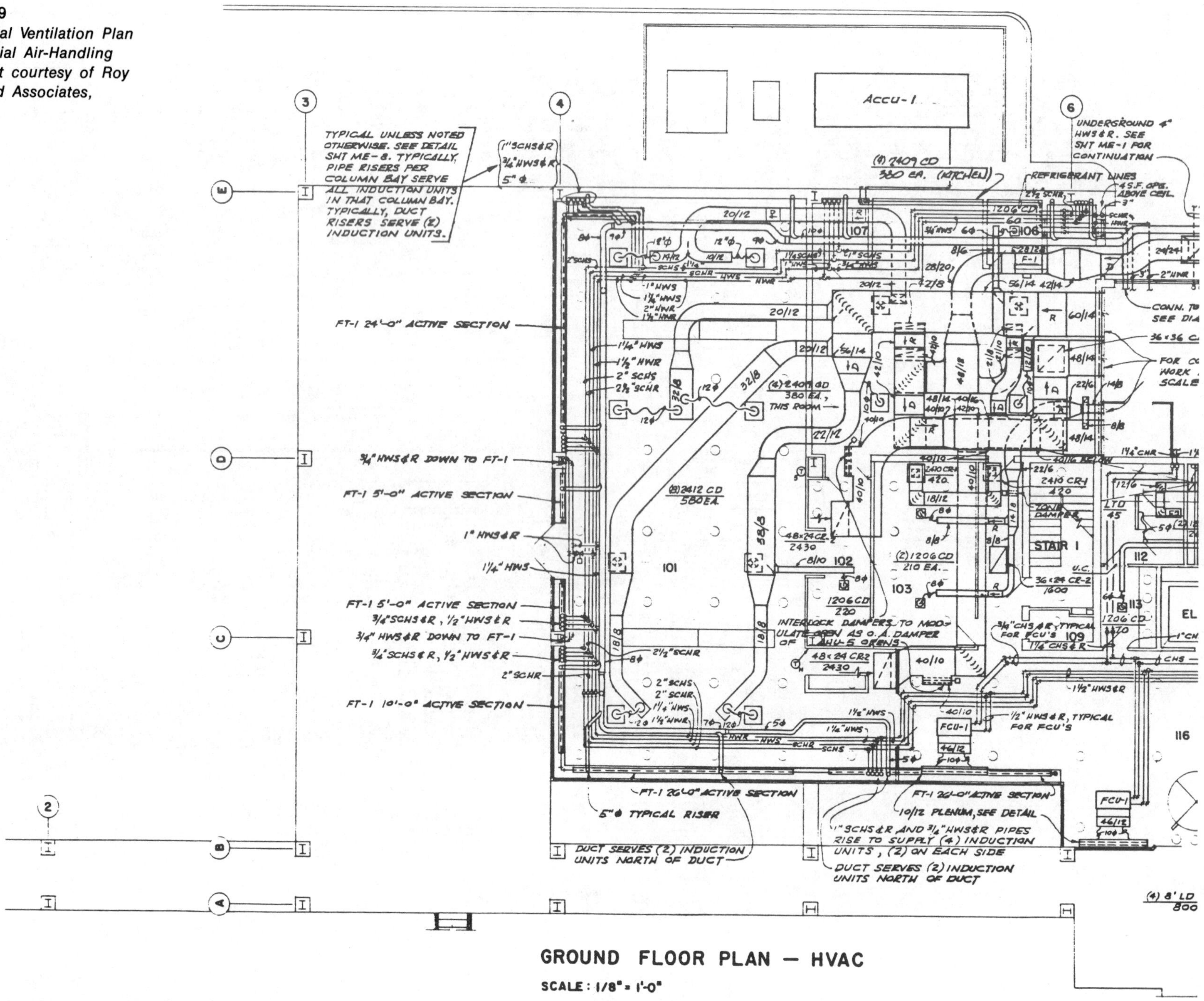

GROUND FLOOR PLAN — HVAC

SCALE: 1/8" = 1'-0"

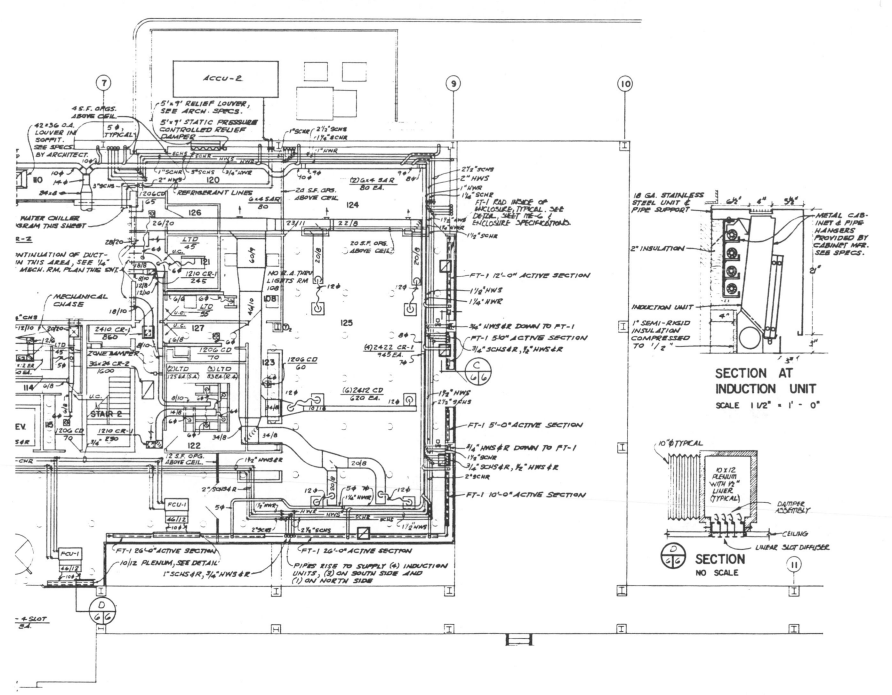

SECTION AT
INDUCTION UNIT

SCALE 1 1/2" = 1'- 0"

SECTION

NO SCALE

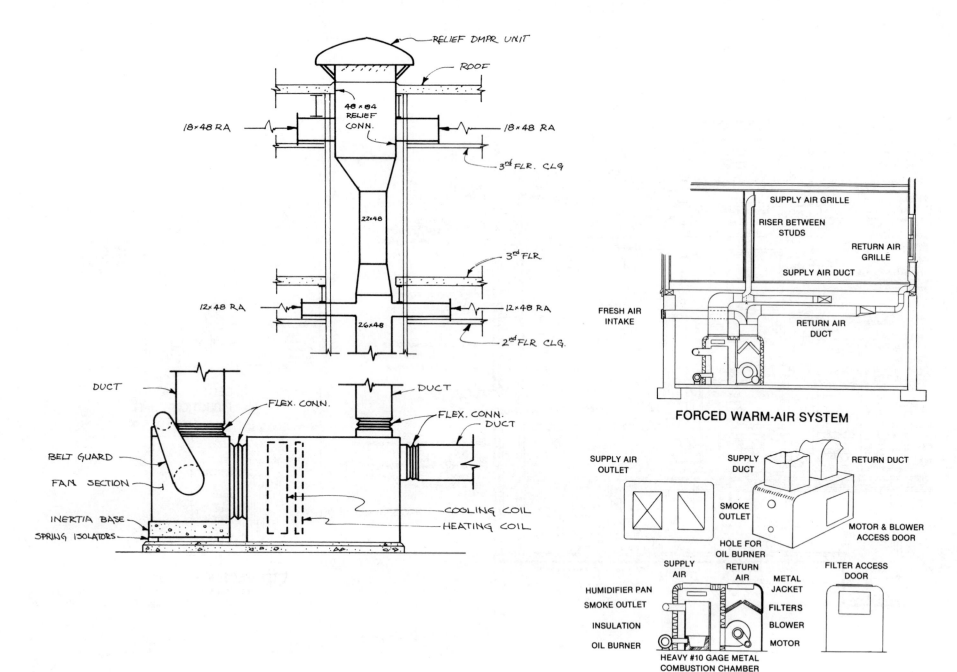

RELIEF DMPR UNIT

ROOF

48 x 84 RELIEF CONN.

18 x 48 RA

18 x 48 RA

3rd FLR. CLG.

22 x 48

3rd FLR

12 x 48 RA

12 x 48 RA

26 x 48

2nd FLR. CLG.

DUCT

DUCT

FLEX. CONN.

FLEX. CONN.

DUCT

BELT GUARD

FAN SECTION

INERTIA BASE

SPRING ISOLATORS

COOLING COIL

HEATING COIL

Fig. 13-3 *Typical Detailing in HVAC Drawings*

SUPPLY AIR GRILLE

RISER BETWEEN STUDS

RETURN AIR GRILLE

SUPPLY AIR DUCT

FRESH AIR INTAKE

RETURN AIR DUCT

FORCED WARM-AIR SYSTEM

SUPPLY AIR OUTLET

SUPPLY DUCT

RETURN DUCT

SMOKE OUTLET

MOTOR & BLOWER ACCESS DOOR

HOLE FOR OIL BURNER

FILTER ACCESS DOOR

SUPPLY AIR

RETURN AIR

METAL JACKET

HUMIDIFIER PAN

SMOKE OUTLET

FILTERS

INSULATION

BLOWER

OIL BURNER

MOTOR

HEAVY #10 GAGE METAL COMBUSTION CHAMBER

DETAILS OF A TYPICAL WARM-AIR BLOWER-BURNER FURNACE UNIT

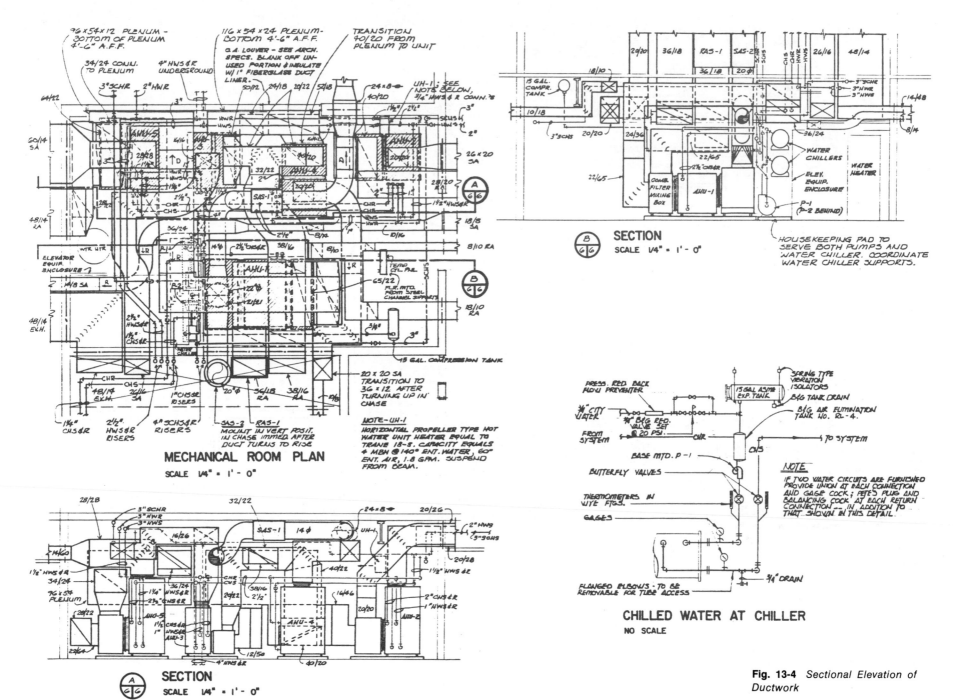

MECHANICAL ROOM PLAN
SCALE 1/4" = 1'-0"

SECTION
B 6/6
SCALE 1/4" = 1'-0"

HOUSEKEEPING PAD TO
SERVE BOTH PUMPS AND
WATER CHILLER. COORDINATE
WATER CHILLER SUPPORTS.

NOTE—UH-1
HORIZONTAL PROPELLER TYPE HOT
WATER UNIT HEATER EQUAL TO
TRANE 18-S. CAPACITY EQUALS
4 MBH @ 140° ENT. WATER, 60°
ENT. AIR, 1.8 GPM. SUSPEND
FROM BEAM.

CHILLED WATER AT CHILLER
NO SCALE

NOTE
IF TWO WATER CIRCUITS ARE FURNISHED
PROVIDE UNION AT EACH CONNECTION
AND GAGE COCK; PETE'S PLUG AND
BALANCING COCK AT EACH RETURN
CONNECTION — IN ADDITION TO
THAT SHOWN IN THIS DETAIL.

SECTION
A 6/6
SCALE 1/4" = 1'-0"

Fig. 13-4 *Sectional Elevation of Ductwork*

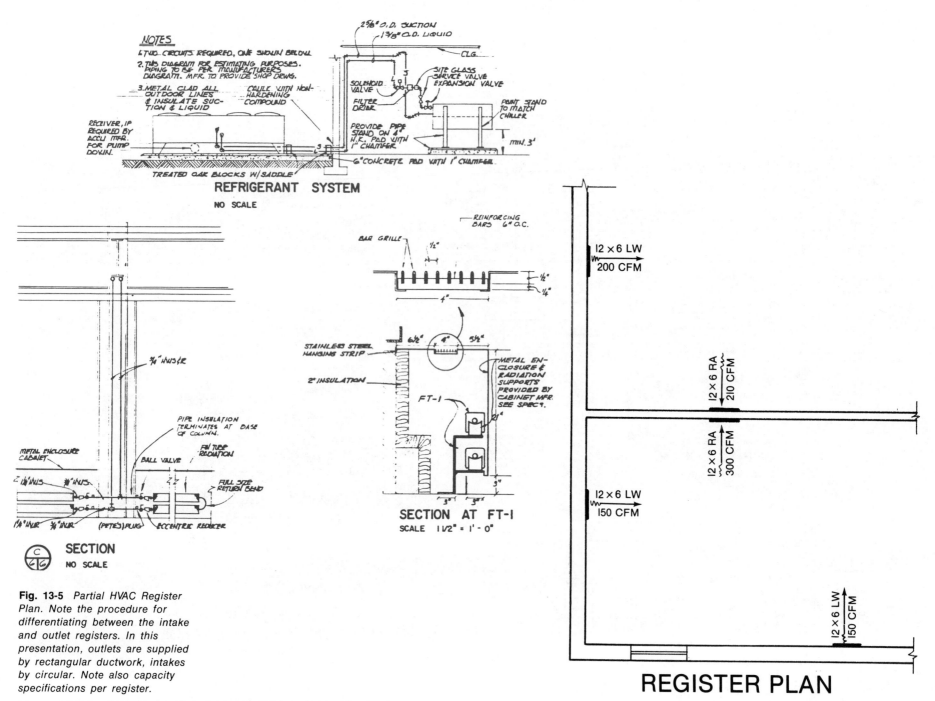

NOTES
1. TWO CIRCUITS REQUIRED, ONE SHOWN BELOW
2. THIS DIAGRAM FOR ESTIMATING PURPOSES. PIPING TO BE PER MANUFACTURERS DIAGRAM. MFR. TO PROVIDE SHOP DWGS.
3. METAL CLAD ALL OUTDOOR LINES & INSULATE SUCTION & LIQUID

2⅝" O.D. SUCTION
1⅜" O.D. LIQUID
CLG.

SITE GLASS
SERVICE VALVE
EXPANSION VALVE

CAULK WITH NON-HARDENING COMPOUND

SOLENOID VALVE

FILTER DRIER

PAINT STAND TO MATCH CHILLER

RECEIVER, IF REQUIRED BY ACCU MFR. FOR PUMP DOWN.

PROVIDE PIPE STAND ON 4" H.K. PAD WITH 1" CHAMFER

MIN. 3'

6" CONCRETE PAD WITH 1" CHAMFER

TREATED OAK BLOCKS W/SADDLE

REFRIGERANT SYSTEM
NO SCALE

REINFORCING BARS 6" O.C.

BAR GRILLE

½"
½"
¼"
1"

STAINLESS STEEL HANGING STRIP

6½"   4"   5½"

2" INSULATION

FT-1

METAL ENCLOSURE & RADIATION SUPPORTS PROVIDED BY CABINET MFR. SEE SPECS.

2"

3"   3"   3"

SECTION AT FT-1
SCALE 1½" = 1'-0"

¾" INSUL.

PIPE INSULATION TERMINATES AT BASE OF COLUMN

FIN TUBE RADIATION

METAL ENCLOSURE CABINET

BALL VALVE

FULL SIZE RETURN BEND

2 ½" INSUL.   ¾" INSUL.

1¼" INSUL.   ¾" INSUL.   (PETES) PLUG   ECCENTRIC REDUCER

(C/6) **SECTION**
NO SCALE

Fig. 13-5 *Partial HVAC Register Plan. Note the procedure for differentiating between the intake and outlet registers. In this presentation, outlets are supplied by rectangular ductwork, intakes by circular. Note also capacity specifications per register.*

12 × 6 LW
200 CFM

12 × 6 RA
210 CFM

12 × 6 RA
300 CFM

12 × 6 LW
150 CFM

12 × 6 LW
150 CFM

REGISTER PLAN

SUMMARY

Heating, ventilation, and air-conditioning plans not only show the configuration of the system, they show the system *to scale.* These drawings show how warm, cool, and existing air is circulated throughout the building. They are superimposed on floor-plan layouts and sectional elevations. Plans should be drawn for each floor serviced by the HVAC system.

REVIEW QUESTIONS

1. What three types of systems are usually included in the HVAC system?
2. How do HVAC-system plans differ from other environmental-control plans?
3. What components are specified in HVAC-system plans?
4. Why should HVAC-system drawings not be drawn on the floor plan?
5. What does *CFM* stand for? Where is it used?
6. What reference should be used when checking HVAC specifications?
7. Explain what a two-duct system is and the complications it can cause the drafter.

EXERCISES

1. For the plans and elevations already developed, illustrate how the air will be distributed throughout the building.
2. Incorporate a central vacuum system for a building with an existing HVAC system, and schematically show how materials are carried in it.
3. Prepare HVAC-system plans for a building requiring a two-duct system. Include cross-section elevations with these plans where required.

14 ARCHITECTURAL PLANS FOR RECYCLED BUILDINGS

Recycling buildings through remodeling and renovation has recently taken on great importance in the architectural field. Many businesses and families have found it both economical and satisfying to recycle an existing building, rather than to construct a new one. Today, considerable emphasis is placed on the preservation and maintenance of viable communities and local business districts. "Bigger is better" and "newer is best" have given way to a philosophy of retaining our past. Recycling architectural structures that once might have been thought to have outlived their usefulness is an especially efficient way of using resources.

The term *recycling* assumes that there is an existing structure. It may be new or old; the proposed activities for the building may be the same as or different from the original intent. Recycling means remodeling and renovating buildings to return them to further use.

THE NATURE OF RECYCLING PLANS AND SPECIFICATIONS

In preparing architectural working drawings and specifications for recycled buildings, a specific set of procedures and techniques should be followed. Before approaching a recycling project, one should have a clear understanding of just what is to be done with the building(s). Several terms must be defined. To

GLOSSARY

Keynoting a notation system that uses a letter or number *keyed,* or referenced, to drawing specifications

Recycling buildings renovating or restoring existing buildings for further use

Renovation the process of making older structures appear new by replacing and repairing worn and broken parts

Restoration the process of returning a structure to its original form

remodel is to make over, rebuild, and perhaps add on to an existing structure. To *renovate* means to make older structures appear new by replacing or repairing worn and broken parts of the building. In historical *restoration,* in which buildings with historical value are returned to their original state, renovation, not remodeling, is the object. The architectural firm usually follows essentially the same process in preparing plans and specifications.

The process of a recycling project may be divided into three broad areas: *project study; preparing plans and specifications;* and *bidding and contract.* As can be seen, this process is the same as for any other architectural project. However, the goal and application is improving an existing structure, rather than building a new structure.

PROJECT STUDY

The depth and breadth of the project study varies, depending upon the size of the project and the number of buildings. The first step is to conduct a survey in three areas. These include *an analysis of the marketing of the project, the suitability of the neighborhood,* and *the condition of the building(s).*

A marketing study determines whether the recycling will be profitable for the owner. Suppose that a building is to be recycled as an office building. For such a project, an analysis is made of how many office buildings there are in the area and of the demand for office space in and beyond the neighborhood. Determining the supply of and demand for office space shows the reasonable potential for renting all or part of the building.

The second survey studies the character of the neighborhood. A study of the *viability*—the "health"—of the neighborhood and surrounding areas is important. Such a study looks at availability of public transportation, shopping centers and areas, location of schools and libraries, and the types of public services (e.g., fire and police protection, sanitation, sewer systems, and utility hook-ups) both cur-

rent and proposed. The final aspect of this survey involves examining the zoning. Existing zoning either conforms to the desired use of the building (in our example, a zoning of either *O* or *C* would be appropriate) or requires change (in our example, this might mean an upgrade from *A* or *R* to *O* or *C*). In the second case, the client must petition the local planning commission or government for a zoning change.

The last project study is a survey of the building itself to determine if it is suitable for recycling. The building survey addresses the condition of the exterior, the condition of the interior, and the adaptability of the building to recycled use. An exterior examination of the building helps the firm decide whether the building needs a new facade or requires repair of the old one. Inspection of the interior of the building shows the type of construction (e.g., wall bearing, foundation, floors and ceilings, cornices, and parapets) and the condition of each building system (heating, electrical, plumbing, ventilation, elevators, stairs, etc.). The inspection usually includes both on-site inspection and review of photographs. With the information gathered in the building survey, the architect can accurately calculate the amount of work required for the project and therefore the cost of the project.

PLANS AND SPECIFICATIONS

If it appears that the recycling project is a good one, the firm proceeds to the next step: develop building plans and specifications.

Architectural Plans The set of architectural plans prepared for a recycling project contains the same information typically found in other architectural working drawings, and more. The difference is that the drafter not only prepares a set of plans showing what the building will look like when completed, but he or she also draws a set of plans showing what the building looked like before recycling. Fig. 14-1 gives an example of before-and-after drawings. The drawing

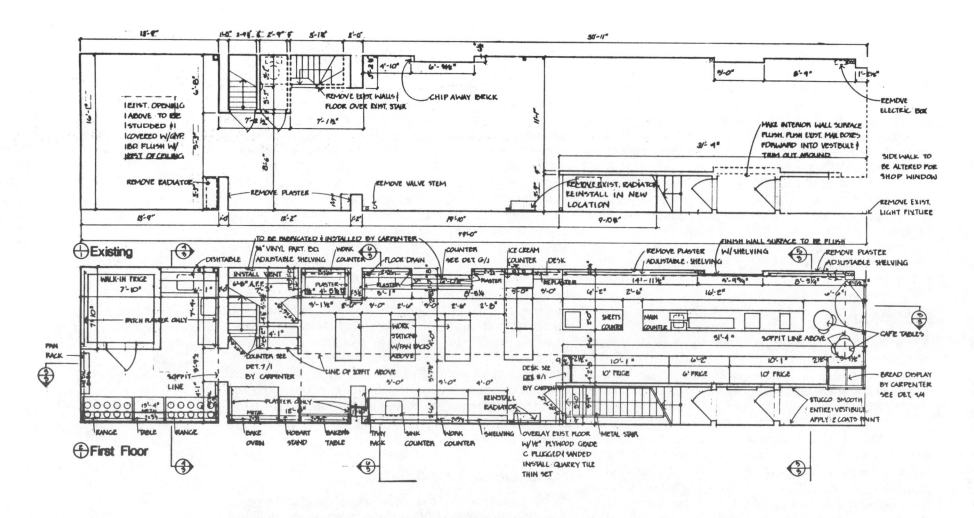

Fig. 14-1 *Before-and-After Drawings in a Recycling Project. Note the difference between the existing floor plan and the first floor plan. The "after" drawing is extensively notated and detailed to show what work has to be done to meet project requirements. (Courtesy of Alfredo De Vido Associates, Architects)*

labeled "1/1 Existing" is a floor plan showing the building before recycling; the drawing "2/1 First Floor" is the same floor as it will appear.

Other drawings usually included in the plans for recycling projects are the site-plan elevations, the foundation-system, environmental-system, and floor plans, and the exterior and interior elevations. Additional details and notations may explain how certain construction is to be done and what materials are to be used. Specific drawing practices are covered in this chapter under "Graphic Procedures and Tech-

niques for Recycling Projects."

Project Specifications Project specifications prepared for both the contractor and the client inform them of what is to be constructed or reconstructed and of the materials and hardware to be used. These specifications are frequently referred to as *trade specifications*, because they are divided up according to the areas (per specification heading) that require work. The specifications for some projects are quite detailed and lengthy.

BIDDING AND CONTRACT

Plans and specifications for recycling projects tend to be even more detailed and extensive than those for new buildings. The reason is obvious: there are *two* buildings, one "before" and one "after." Specific instructions for restoration of existing components are required. The architectural firm must spell out in the bidding process exactly what is to be constructed and what is to be reconstructed. Documents are assembled and submitted to provide a justification for the cost of the project. These are carefully reviewed by the potential client. Among those usually submitted for bidding are

1. Drawings and presentations
2. Complete list of all working drawings, by number
3. General conditions of the contract (See AIA Document Form A201.)
4. List of addenda to plans and specifications, identifying any changes in the original plans and specifications
5. Cost break-outs, by item (removal of existing walls, replacement of hardware, etc.)
6. Proposal form, signed by the architect

Generally, bids must be submitted by a given date. A thirty-day evaluation period follows. When a plan is chosen, the architect and the client (and normally also their legal representatives) draw up a legal contract, which is then signed by both parties. Work on the project can now begin. Some contract considerations are

1. Names and addresses of client and contractor
2. Date of contract
3. Location of work
4. Description of the work
5. Performance bonding, to assure minimum level of work
6. Proposed target dates for completion
7. What the contractor is to furnish
8. Price of the work, including alternates
9. How payments are to be made
10. Miscellaneous provisions

GRAPHIC PROCEDURES AND TECHNIQUES FOR RECYCLING PROJECTS

The basic techniques and graphic procedures are similar to those used in other drawings. The difference is in their application. The line weights and expressions, notations, and other techniques are the same as those in traditional drawings, but their use and adaptation in specific drawings are somewhat different.

LINE WEIGHTS AND EXPRESSIONS

The lines and expressions are interpretive tools in architectural drawings, as in drawings for recycled buildings. Certain practices help the contractor and tradespeople understand what is to be accomplished in the recycling process. Emphasis is given to areas involving removing, replacing, construction, or reconstruction by the contractor.

Remember that, when recycling drawings are prepared, emphasize those areas of the building where work is to be done, by using heavier-weight lines. If an addition is planned, present it in heavier lines than the rest of the building. Lighter line weights are used for those areas not affected by the construction. This focuses attention on the remodeling or renovation.

In preparing working drawings for the recycled parts of the building, line weights follow the standards for other architectural drawings. Note in Fig. 14-2 how the addition or recycled part of the building is drawn as in a typical working drawing, but the main building is drawn lighter. In some cases, the unaffected part of the building is presented as a *screened* drawing that has the quality of a halftone, a reproduced photograph. See "Screening and Photographs."

Draw broken lines to indicate where old construction and hardware are to be removed. These should be the same presentation and weight as hidden lines. Fig. 14-3 shows this technique. All old construction to be eliminated is drawn with broken lines, with nota-

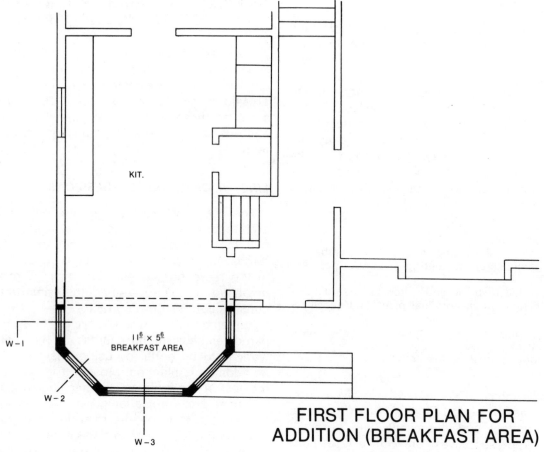

Fig. 14-2 *Addition on Recycled Building. Note how the addition (breakfast area) stands out, being drawn in a much heavier line weight.*

KIT.

W—1

$11^{6} \times 5^{6}$
BREAKFAST AREA

W—2

W—3

FIRST FLOOR PLAN FOR
ADDITION (BREAKFAST AREA)

SCALE: $\frac{1''}{4} = 1'-0''$

tions indicating its removal. New construction is identified by crosshatching, accompanied by notations.

The symbols used in recycling drawings vary within the profession. The use of broken lines for removal of old construction is fairly standard, although not always used. Methods of showing construction vary widely. It is therefore exceptionally important to include a *legend* to indicate what each symbol is to represent. Once the legend has been prepared, it is the standard for the entire set of drawings. In fact, to avoid confusion, architectural firms almost always use the same expressions and symbols in all their drawings, rather than changing from project to project.

KEYNOTING

Keynoting is not limited strictly to recycling drawings, but it lends itself more readily to this area than to others. As shown in Fig. 14-4, keynoting is a notation system *keyed* to a number or letter. Instead of writing long notations and specifications for each particular part of the building, a number or letter is

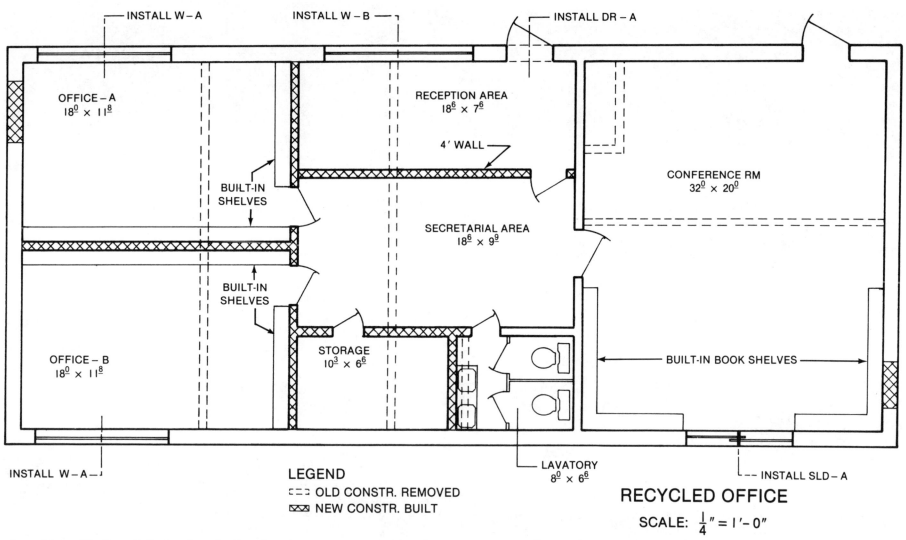

INSTALL W – A   INSTALL W – B   INSTALL DR – A

OFFICE – A
$18^0 \times 11^8$

RECEPTION AREA
$18^6 \times 7^6$

4' WALL

CONFERENCE RM
$32^0 \times 20^0$

BUILT-IN SHELVES

SECRETARIAL AREA
$18^6 \times 9^9$

BUILT-IN SHELVES

OFFICE – B
$18^0 \times 11^8$

STORAGE
$10^3 \times 6^6$

BUILT-IN BOOK SHELVES

INSTALL W – A

LEGEND

⊏⊐⊐ OLD CONSTR. REMOVED
⋈⋈⋈ NEW CONSTR. BUILT

LAVATORY
$8^0 \times 6^6$

INSTALL SLD – A

RECYCLED OFFICE

SCALE: $\frac{1}{4}" = 1'-0"$

placed in a "balloon" that refers to the drawing specifications. These notations and specifications can then be typed and attached to the master drawing. This cuts down on the time required for extensive hand lettering.

SCREENING AND PHOTOGRAPHS

The use of screening and photographs has become popular in recent years. Screening can be used to show both old construction to be removed and the parts of the building that are not affected by the recycling process. Fig. 14-5 shows how this technique can be used for unaffected parts of the building; Fig. 14-6 illustrates its use for old construction to be removed.

Photographs can also be used effectively. A common and easy technique is to take a high-contrast

Fig. 14-3 *Recycled Building, Showing Location of Old and New Construction*

TYPICAL 2-STORY BUILDINGS CONTAINING 2-BR TOWNHOUSE UNITS

1-STORY 1-BR UNIT / 2-STORY 2-BR UNITS   1-BR UNIT   1-BR UNIT

TYPICAL 2-STORY BUILDINGS

Fig. 14-4 *Application of Keynoting. The typed—not lettered—notations in the lower part of the sheet are keynoted to the illustrations. Color is used in this figure for emphasis only; the actual drawing does not include color. (Courtesy of MMH/Hall, Architects, Planners)*

(BLDG. L-2) LAUNDRY-2/MAINTENANCE BLDG.

NOTES TO NUMBERED KEYS

28 Repair or replace flashing to make weathertight and sound.

27 Replace siding with 3/8" plywood siding.

30 Repair or replace porch roof (see Note 27 on Sheet A3).

31 Replace all unsound trim.

32 Repair or replace louvers.

33 Remove existing roofs on buildings on west side of street. Repair decking as necessary. Install new 15# roofing felt and new shingles.

34 Replace all doors and windows.

35 Sandblast painted buildings to remove paint, then tuckpoint.

36 Replace all missing or damaged bricks.

37 Remove frame addition.

38 Repair or replace gutters and downspouts - add splash blocks of precast concrete.

39 Remove any unnecessary vents, pipes, etc.

40 Repair flashing at all roof penetrations as necessary.

41 Inspect and repair roofs on east side of street, replacing missing or damaged shingles to match the existing.

BWB Associates Inc
Architects
825 Ridge Lake Blvd
Memphis TN 38138 USA

CONSULTING ARCHITECTS
MMH Hall, Architects/Planners
CONSULTING ENGINEERS
Herschel L. Powell and Associates

REHABILITATION OF
SAINTS COURTS APARTMENTS
MEMPHIS, TENNESSEE

Project No. FHA No. 086-35150-PM-L8

Date 8/20/80

A-4

black and white photograph of the building and reproduce the picture on a translucent medium, using Xerography. The Xerographic reproduction is then attached to the master drawing for keynoting or other forms of notation. Fig. 14-7 shows this technique. This illustration demonstrates the amount of drawing time saved by using the photograph instead of a hand-drawn elevation.

DRAWING PLANS FOR RECYCLED BUILDINGS

Drawing plans for recycling projects can be divided into a two-step process: drawing the existing structure and drawing the recycled structure. The first presents plans, elevations, and required details of the building *before* recycling; the second includes all the drawings needed for the finished project. These before-and-after drawings are necessary for the architect, contractor, and client to see the required changes needed for the recycling process.

DRAWINGS OF EXISTING STRUCTURES

Architectural drawings of the existing structure usually require only three types of drawings. These are site plans, floor plans, and elevations. In more complicated projects, it may be necessary to include all system, foundation, and detail drawings. To help save time and money, the architect tries to secure the original plans of the building. If possible, the original plans are checked, so that the fewest drawings of the existing structure need be done.

Presentations for existing buildings are usually prepared in the format shown in Figs. 14-8 through 14-10. These are plans for a residential structure to be

Fig. 14-5 *Use of Screening to Indicate Unaffected Part of Recycling Project*

Fig. 14-6 *Use of Screening to Show Removal of Old and Addition of New Construction*

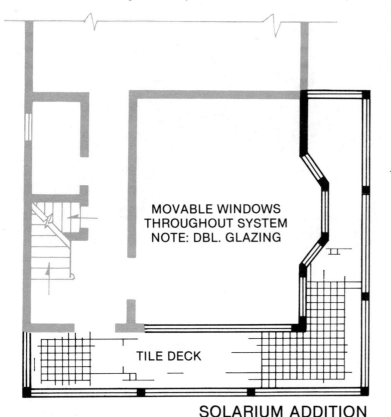

MOVABLE WINDOWS
THROUGHOUT SYSTEM
NOTE: DBL. GLAZING

TILE DECK

SOLARIUM ADDITION

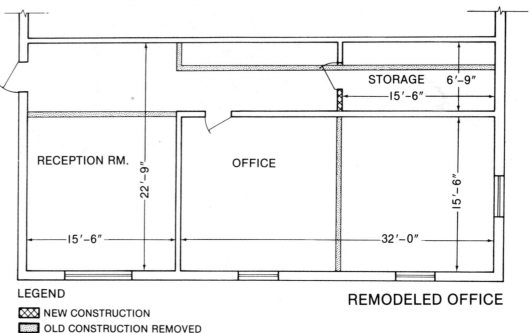

STORAGE   6'-9"
15'-6"

RECEPTION RM.   22'-9"

OFFICE   15'-6"

15'-6"   32'-0"

LEGEND
⊠ NEW CONSTRUCTION
▒ OLD CONSTRUCTION REMOVED

REMODELED OFFICE

8. REMOVE FIXED SHUTTERS & SIDING. OPEN DOORWAY

(SEE KEYNOTES ⑪ & ⑬ ON THIS SHEET)

recycled for commercial use as a doctor's office. Since not all recycling projects involve entire buildings (e.g., bridges and towers), drawings are not always the best technique. Fig. 14-11 shows the use of photography in a park-renovation project.

DRAWINGS OF RECYCLED STRUCTURES

After the existing structure has been drawn or the drawings have been secured, there is usually some lag time until the recycled drawings are prepared. During the early stages of the project, the existing structure drawings aid the architect in the redesign. After it is determined what the finished product will be, the drafter prepares drawings of the recycled structure.

Figs. 14-12 through 14-14 are the drawings for the recycled doctor's office building. Note the special de-

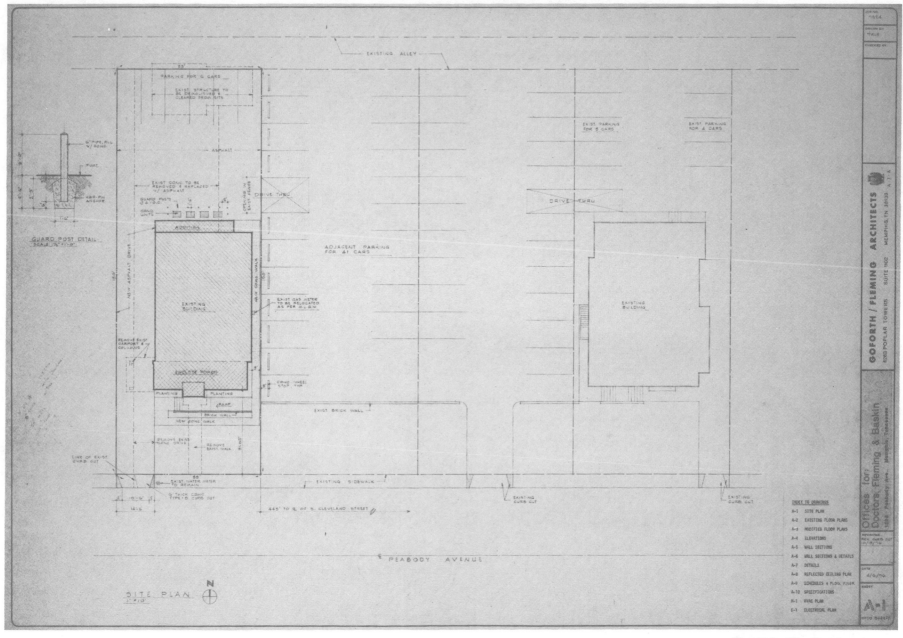

Fig. 14-8 *Site Plan for an Existing Building (Courtesy of Goforth/Fleming, Architects)*

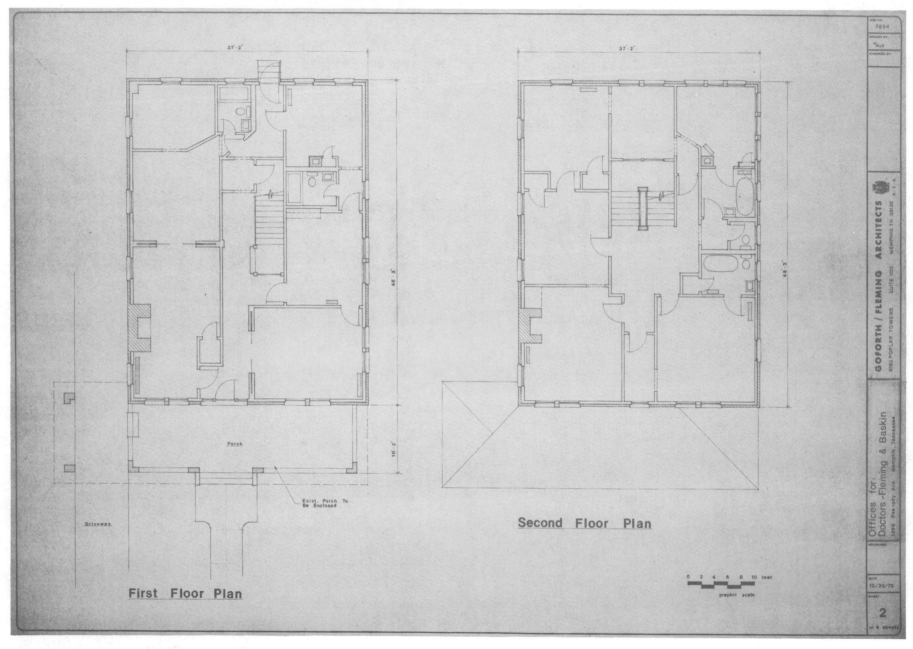

First Floor Plan

Second Floor Plan

graphic scale

Fig. 14-9 *Floor Plan of a Building to Be Recycled Before Renovation (Courtesy of Goforth/Fleming, Architects)*

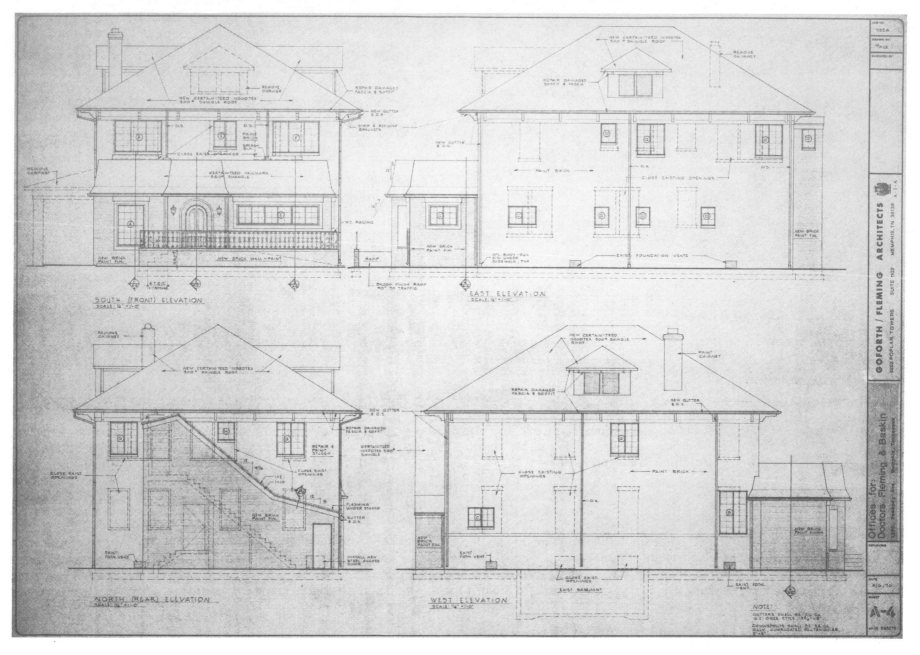

Fig. 14-10 *Elevation of a Building, Showing Changes in Exterior Appearance (Courtesy of Goforth/Fleming, Architects)*

ARCHITECTURAL PLANS FOR RECYCLED BUILDINGS **255**

6. CONCRETE PICNIC TABLES TO REMAIN (SEE KEYNOTE ⑩ SHEET A-1 & DETAILS 11 & 16 ON THIS SHEET)

Fig. 14-11 *Photographic Presentation of Park Benches to Be Renovated (Courtesy of MMH/Hall, Architects, Planners)*

tails and notations about new construction, old construction, and removal of existing construction. Fig. 14-15, by comparison, is the drawing for the recycled structure in the park-renovation project.

SUMMARY

The recent interest in preserving the past and the need to maintain viable neighborhoods and business communities have produced an increase in recycling projects. Architectural firms conduct project studies, prepare plans and specifications, and bid on con-

tracts for recycling projects.

The graphic procedures and techniques in recycling projects are based upon standard architectural drafting procedures, but there are differences. Line weights are usually heavier for the recycled parts of the building, and legends are used to interpret the various information. Other techniques, such as keynoting, screening, and photography, are readily adapted to recycling projects.

When preparing recycling plans, remember that these plans present two sets of information: how the structure appeared before recycling and how the structure will appear.

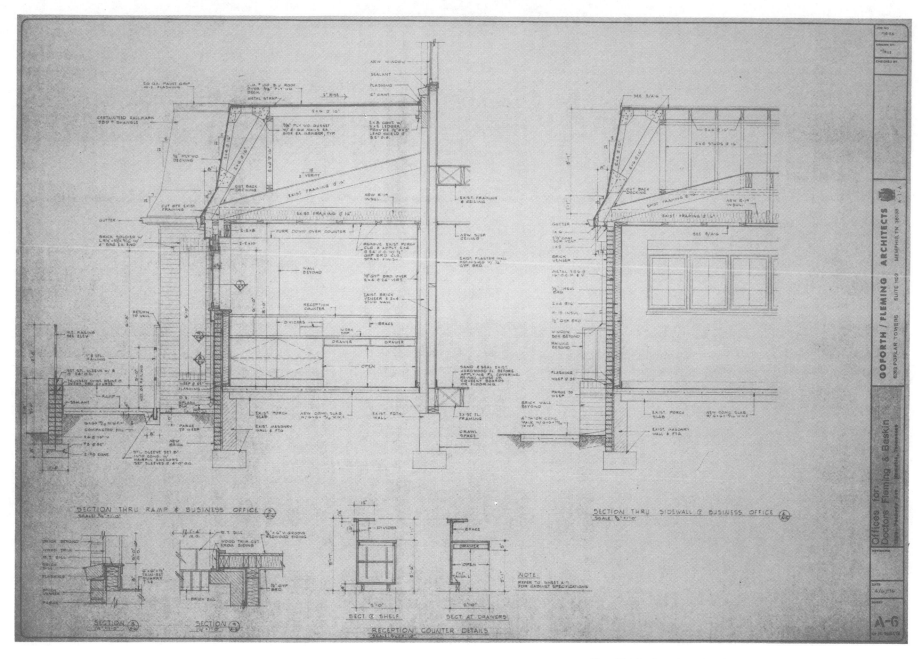

Fig. 14-12 *Drawings for Doctor's Office Building in Figs. 14-8 through 14-10. (Courtesy of Goforth/Fleming, Architects)*

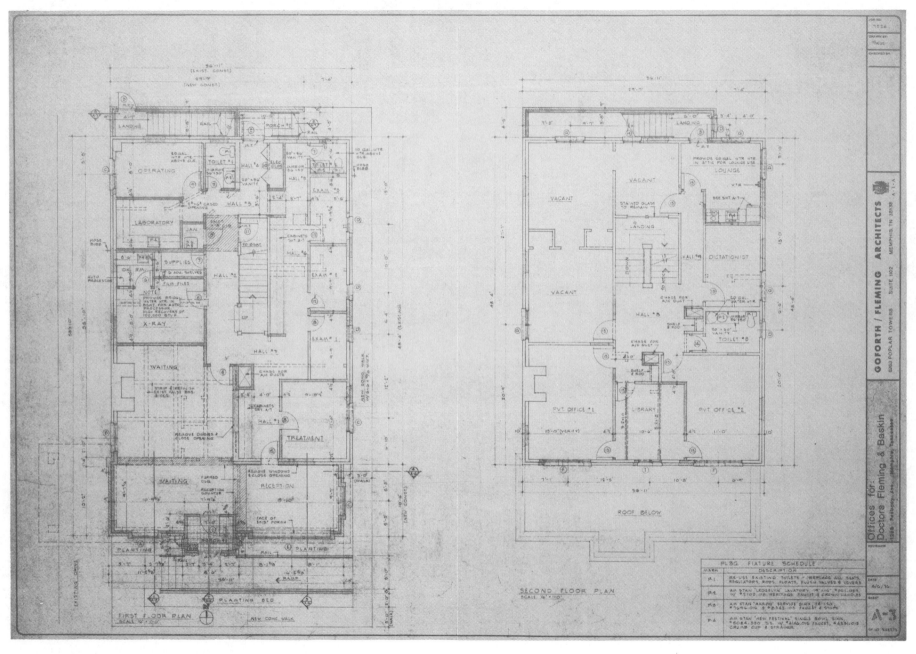

Fig. 14-13 *Drawings for Doctor's Office Building in Figs. 14-8 through 14-10. (Courtesy of Goforth/Fleming, Architects)*

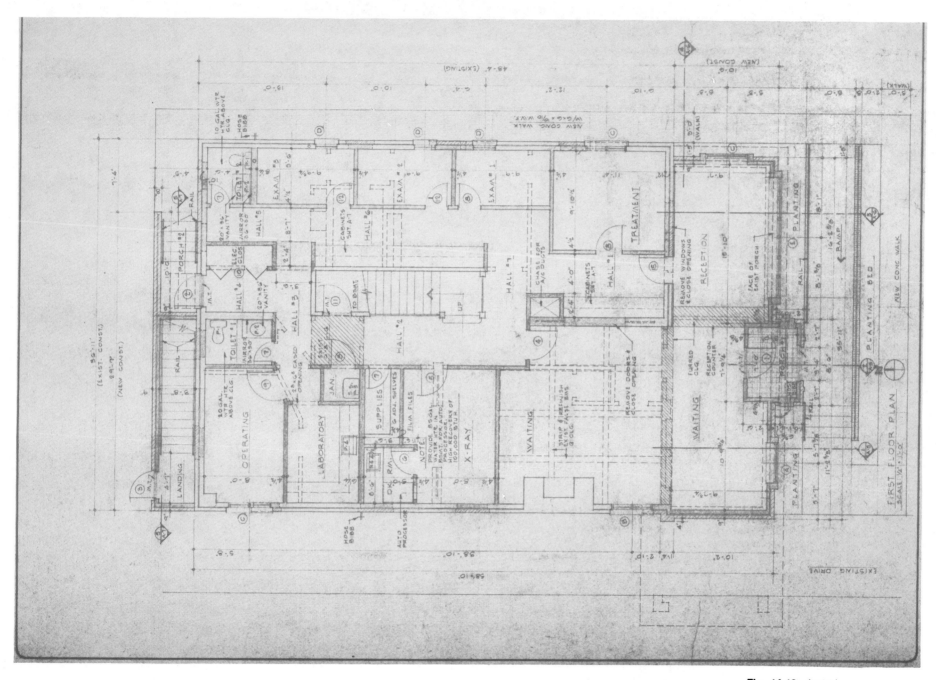

Fig. 14-13 *(cont.)*

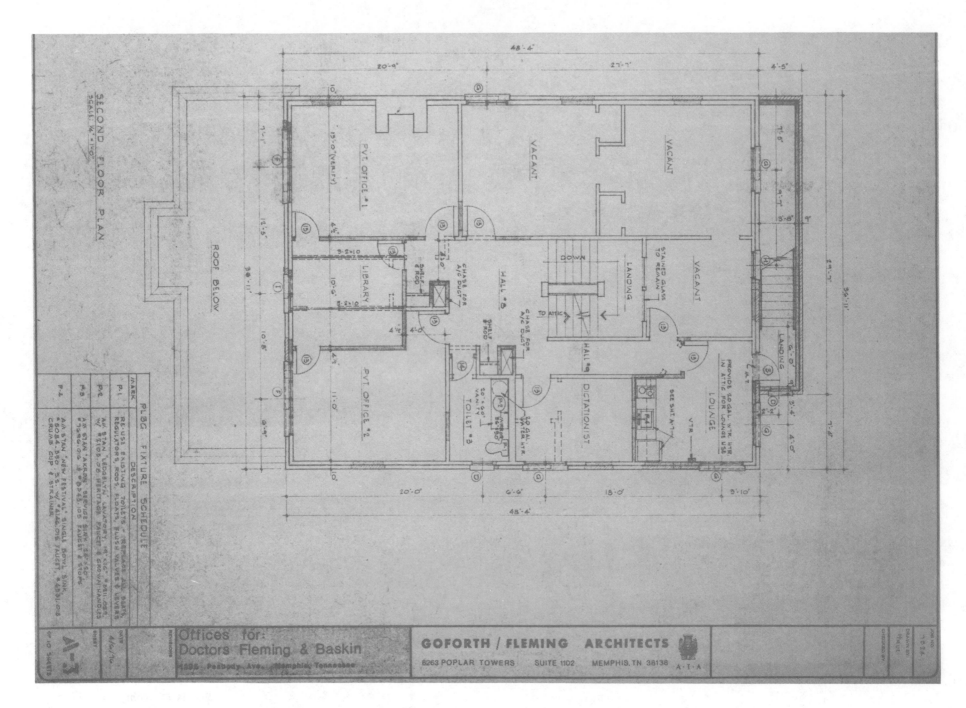

REVIEW QUESTIONS

1. Explain the meaning of the following terms:

   a. recycling
   b. remodeling
   c. renovation
   d. restoration

2. Explain the importance of the following in a recycling project:

   a. marketing analysis
   b. neighborhood suitability study
   c. condition of existing building

3. Describe the two types of architectural drawings required in a recycling project.
4. What does the term *trade specifications* mean?
5. Explain how the following are used in recycling plans:

   a. keynoting
   b. legends
   c. screening
   d. photographs

EXERCISES

1. Secure plans for an existing residence of approximately 1200–1400 square feet, and prepare plans to add on a general-purpose office of approximately 120 square feet.
2. Using plans for a commercial building originally designed for retailing activities, draw plans to recycle the building into rental space for general offices.
3. Take the dimensions of an existing residential structure; develop a set of plans for that building.
4. Draw a set of recycling plans based upon the plans drawn in Exercise 3, to convert that residential structure into office space for a law practice.

Page 260
Fig. 14-14 *Drawings for Doctor's Office Building in Figs. 14-8 through 14-10. (Courtesy of Goforth/Fleming, Architects)*

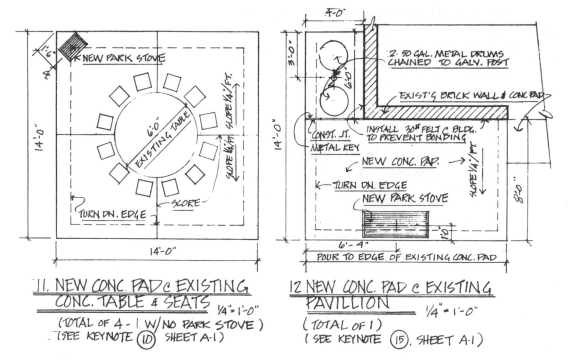

NEW PARK STOVE
6'-0"
EXISTING TABLE
SLOPE 1/4"/FT.
SCORE
TURN DN. EDGE
14'-0"
14'-0"
11. NEW CONC. PAD @ EXISTING CONC. TABLE & SEATS 1/4"=1'-0"
(TOTAL OF 4 - 1 W/NO PARK STOVE)
(SEE KEYNOTE 10 SHEET A-1)
4'-0"
3'-0"
6'-0"
2 - 50 GAL. METAL DRUMS CHAINED TO GALV. POST
EXIST'G BRICK WALL & CONC PAD
CONST. JT.
METAL KEY
INSTALL 30# FELT @ BLDG. TO PREVENT BONDING
NEW CONC. PAD.
TURN DN. EDGE
NEW PARK STOVE
SLOPE 1/4"/FT.
8'-0"
1'-0"
6'-4"
POUR TO EDGE OF EXISTING CONC. PAD
12 NEW CONC. PAD @ EXISTING PAVILLION 1/4"=1'-0"
(TOTAL OF 1)
(SEE KEYNOTE 15, SHEET A-1)

Fig. 14-15 *Drawings for Park Benches in Fig. 14-11. (Courtesy of MMH/Hall, Architects, Planners)*

15 ALTERNATE ENERGY CONSIDERATIONS

Consumer demand for alternate energy sources and energy conservation designs is creating new architectural challenges and problems. For the first time, drafters are drawing plans for commercial and residential buildings that include these concepts, designs, and specifications. With the projected future scarcity of traditional fossil-fuel energy resources, architectural firms will use new design concepts and material applications or find their buildings outdated and impractical before construction begins. Even today, it is almost impossible to find a project without some form of alternate energy source or energy-conservation consideration. This can be as simple as planning how a building is placed on a lot or as sophisticated as making use of technologically complex energy-saving designs.

At present there are various forms of alternate energy systems. These include geothermic, nuclear, coal-gasification, synthetic-fuel, wind, and solar energy. Of all these, only one has had—and in the near future will continue to have—a profound effect upon the architectural field: solar energy. Solar energy is available now; it does not have to be manufactured; it is not limited to narrowly defined geographic areas. With modifications in traditional designs and material usage, solar energy can be used *now*. It is anticipated that, by the year 2000, approximately five percent of the energy used in this country will come from solar-energy systems. For this reason, the architectural drafter should know of the various solar-energy systems, components, and details that will soon become commonplace.

GLOSSARY

Active system a solar-energy system that uses mechanical devices, such as fans and heat pumps, to circulate air in a structure

Passive system a solar-energy system that employs no mechanical devices to circulate air in a structure

R-value a measure of effectiveness of insulation

Solar gain the amount of heat a material absorbs from the sun's rays

Solarium a room or area separate from the main activity parts of a structure, used to collect and store solar energy

Thermal details drawings that show the special characteristics and features of elements and structural components, such as insulation and shading, that influence the temperature of the building

Thermosiphon a solar-gain system that moves warm and cool air in a structure, by siphoning action

TYPES OF SOLAR-ENERGY SYSTEMS

Before starting to lay out and draw details, the drafter should realize the basic differences and similarities of the various systems of solar-energy collection, storage, distribution, and control. Generally speaking, there are two broad categories: *passive* and *active* solar-energy systems.

PASSIVE SOLAR-ENERGY SYSTEMS

Passive solar-energy systems use the natural flow of hot and cool air, without the aid of mechanical devices, to circulate the air within a building. As shown in Fig. 15-1, a building can be heated by letting air warmed by solar energy rise into the building; it can be cooled by letting cooler air settle downwards in the building as the warm air escapes through upper ventilators. Passive solar-energy systems depend on the fact that *hot air rises and cool air falls.* Energy in the form of heat is transmitted through *conduction, convection,* and *radiation.*

ACTIVE SOLAR-ENERGY SYSTEMS

Active solar-energy systems use mechanical devices, such as heat exchangers, pumps, and fans, to circulate warm and cool air throughout a building. Active systems are used in buildings that are not designed to take full advantage of the sun. Passive solar-energy systems are usually poor choices for such buildings because of poor topographical layout, site location, types of vegetation around the building, or the building design itself. Fig. 15-2 shows a building similar to that in Fig. 15-1, but requiring an active solar-energy system. Note that active and passive solar-energy systems are not incompatible. In fact, the addition of mechanical devices to a passive solar-energy building can improve the efficiency of the heating and cooling system.

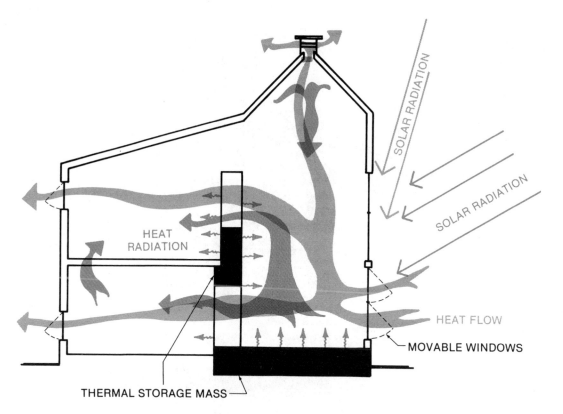

HEAT RADIATION

SOLAR RADIATION

SOLAR RADIATION

HEAT FLOW

MOVABLE WINDOWS

THERMAL STORAGE MASS

TYPES OF SOLAR GAIN

Collection and storage of solar energy is specified in terms of *gain*. Solar gain is the amount of heat a material absorbs from the sun's rays. More precisely, it is the amount of solar radiation, in BTUs (British Thermal Units), collected on a surface. There are three basic methods of solar gain: *direct, indirect,* and *isolated.* Both passive and active solar-energy systems use these, either separately or in combination.

DIRECT SOLAR GAIN

Direct solar-gain designs are the simpliest in concept and construction. In a direct solar-gain building, solar radiation enters an activity area and is stored as heat in the floors, walls, and furniture. See Fig. 15-3.

Fig. 15-1 *Passive Solar System. A. Solar radiation can be blocked during summer months by use of overhangs, shades, and deciduous trees. Cross-ventilation and use of louvers remove heat from the building. B. Solar radiation enters glazing at lower angles during winter months and is stored in and given off from the thermal-storage mass. Floor louvers control the natural rise of hot air for good circulation.*

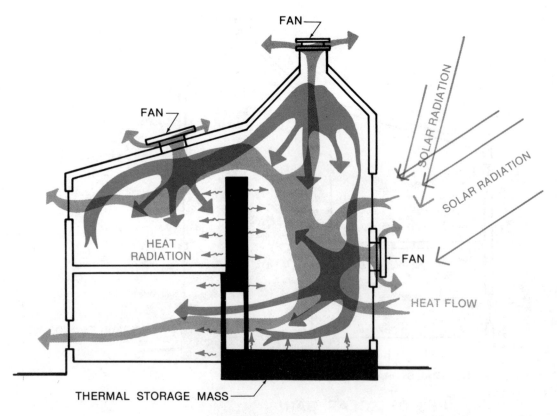

FAN

FAN

SOLAR RADIATION

SOLAR RADIATION

HEAT
RADIATION

FAN

HEAT FLOW

THERMAL STORAGE MASS

Fig. 15-2 *Active Solar System. A. Heat can be minimized with fans to remove heated air and facilitate cross-ventialation. B. Solar heat is distributed throughout building: the reversal of heat-removal flow forces heated air downward.*

The components that allow the sun's rays to enter the building, that is, the windows, are called *collectors;* the components that store solar energy are called *thermal-storage masses.*

Fig. 15-4 illustrates how a direct solar-gain design works. There are two areas of concern: system *requirements* and system *controls.* In an efficient direct solar-gain building, there is a collector area with a southern exposure (in the northern hemisphere), sufficient thermal-storage mass, and an effective method of separating the thermal-storage mass from the outside environment.

System Requirements The first requirement for a direct solar-gain design is a large collector, preferably one with a southern exposure, since this lets in more sunlight than other exposures. The collectors in

commercial and residential structures are usually glazed; that is, they are windows. *Double glazing* usually proves more efficient in preventing heat loss; in very severe climates, *triple* glazing may be specified. See Fig. 15-5.

The thermal-storage mass's function is to store the heat collected during the day and release it for use on overcast days and during the night. Storage masses may be part of the walls, ceilings, and floors; they can also be in independent containers, such as black barrels containing some type of heat-storing medium. Regardless of the type, the thermal-storage mass normally takes on heat *beyond* normal requirements. Without this quality, it would be ineffective. See Fig. 15-6 for varieties of storage masses.

Since the storage mass is used when more or, in some cases, less heat is required, it must be effectively protected from the outside environment. Proper insulation between the storage mass and the outside keeps down unnecessary heat loss. On the other hand, proper placement of the storage mass in relation to the activity area prevents the building from overheating during the sunny hours of the day.

Controls To assure maximum efficiency of a direct solar-gain design in raising or lowering the temperature of the building, several controls must be considered. Depending on building location and climate, the amount of heating and cooling needed is determined by personal reference. In the northern part of the country, heating is much more important than cooling; in the southern regions, the opposite is true. Regardless of location, heat storage is more important during the winter, and solar gain should be kept at a minimum during the summer. Controls determine the amount of heat gain and loss.

During the summer, sunshade and curtain systems can be used effectively for large south-facing collectors. Collectors on the east and west sides of the building are best controlled by shading. An important control technique is the use of overhangs that shade the collectors during the summer, because of the

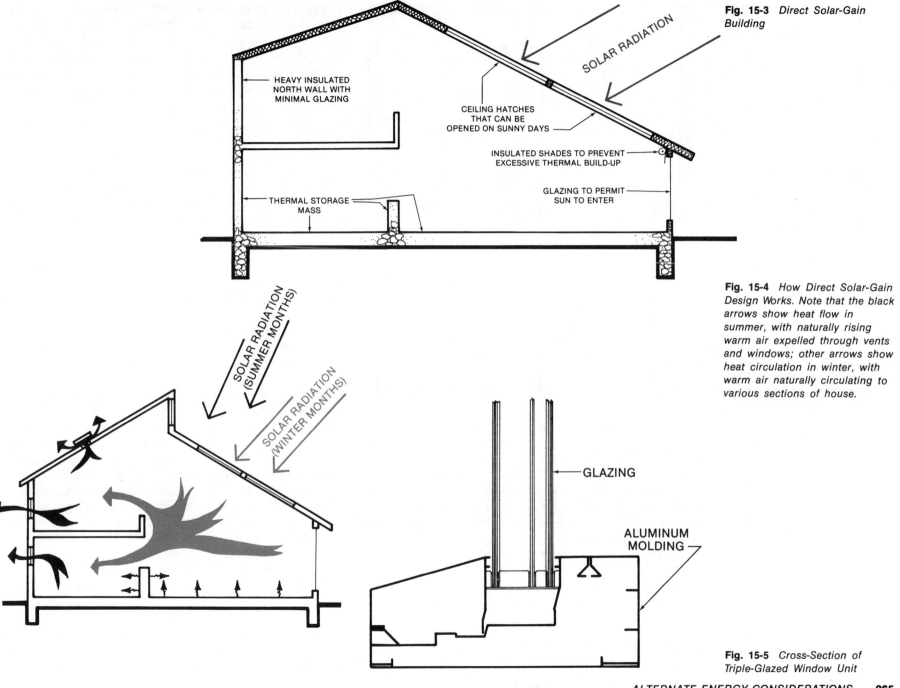

Fig. 15-3 *Direct Solar-Gain Building*

HEAVY INSULATED NORTH WALL WITH MINIMAL GLAZING

SOLAR RADIATION

CEILING HATCHES THAT CAN BE OPENED ON SUNNY DAYS

INSULATED SHADES TO PREVENT EXCESSIVE THERMAL BUILD-UP

GLAZING TO PERMIT SUN TO ENTER

THERMAL STORAGE MASS

Fig. 15-4 *How Direct Solar-Gain Design Works. Note that the black arrows show heat flow in summer, with naturally rising warm air expelled through vents and windows; other arrows show heat circulation in winter, with warm air naturally circulating to various sections of house.*

SOLAR RADIATION (SUMMER MONTHS)

SOLAR RADIATION (WINTER MONTHS)

GLAZING

ALUMINUM MOLDING

Fig. 15-5 *Cross-Section of Triple-Glazed Window Unit*

ALTERNATE ENERGY CONSIDERATIONS   265

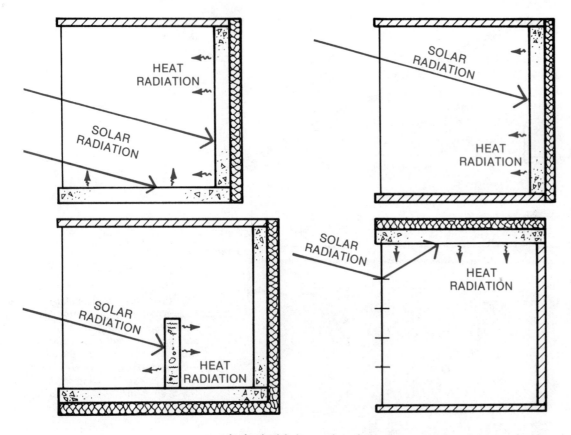

storage mass is receiving solar heat. When the sun sets, the insulation is replaced to keep heat to a minimum. In a passive solar system, with direct solar gain, the activity areas are in direct contact with and exposed to the collectors and the thermal-storage mass. Heat distribution is essentially instantaneous.

INDIRECT SOLAR GAIN

The concept of indirect solar gain is newer than that of direct gain. The basic difference is in the use of the thermal-storage mass. Indirect solar gain allows the sun's rays to enter through collectors and be absorbed by the storage mass, but the storage mass is *not* located in the activity area itself. The thermal-storage mass stores heat, which is then transferred to the desired area. See Fig. 15-8. The major advantage is that the mass can store heat at higher temperatures without overheating the activity area.

Several systems are used for indirect solar gain. These are the *mass Trombe system, the liquid-storage system,* and *the roof-storage system.* These may be used separately or in combination.

Mass Trombe System The mass Trombe system, developed by Dr. Felix Trombé, incorporates a thermal-storage mass. This system is relatively easy to implement. It requires two components: a large glazed collector and a massive, solid thermal-storage mass. See Fig. 15-9. The storage mass, ideally located on the south side of the building, is placed *directly* behind the collector. The mass, commonly called a *Trombe wall,* has its own window, which does not expose the interior of the building. Trombe walls are usually at least 12″ (30.48 mm) thick; they can be made of concrete, adobe, stone, composites of brick and block, or any other material that can store heat efficiently.

Once heat is stored in the Trombe wall, it can easily be distributed to the desired activity area for up to twelve hours. This period depends upon such factors as wall thickness, construction materials, and insula-

Fig. 15-6 *Four Variations of Direct Solar Gain Design. Note the additional insulation behind each thermal-storage mass and the use of concrete as the thermal-mass material. Remember that concrete is a thermal-gain not a cooling material.*

relatively high angle of the sun, yet let the sun in during the winter, when sunlight enters at a lower angle. See Fig. 15-7. Overhangs are more effective for southerly exposures than for east and west, which receive the full rays of the sun as it rises and sets. Other controls commonly used are vents, fans, and exhaust systems. Since hot air rises, it can be drawn out through ceiling and roof vents.

To keep heat winter heat loss at a minimum, the thermal-storage mass should be well insulated. Insulation should be *increased* as the mass's distance from the collector is *decreased.* This is because the low R-value of glazed collectors lets heat escape easily. Insulation of the storage mass, however, is not required at all times. Insulation panels or curtains can be set aside during the daytime, when the thermal-

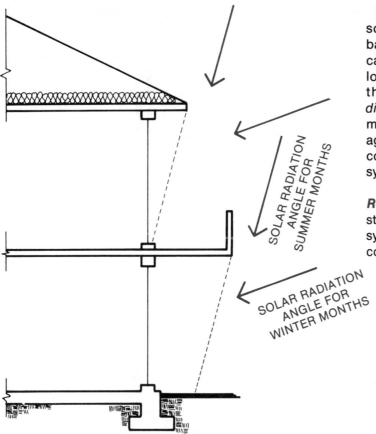

SOLAR RADIATION ANGLE FOR SUMMER MONTHS

SOLAR RADIATION ANGLE FOR WINTER MONTHS

The liquid-storage wall that serves as the thermal-solar mass can be made of bottles, tubes, bins, barrels, drums, bags, tin cans, or anything else that can contain liquid. The *larger* the storage mass, the longer the heat can be *stored*. However, the *smaller* the storage mass, the faster the heat can be *distributed*. The engineering of a liquid-storage wall must consider the trade-offs between length of storage and rate of distribution. Distribution of heat and control techniques are the same for the liquid storage system as for the Trombe wall.

Roof-Storage Systems The third system is the roof-storage system. Unlike the other two, the roof-storage system does not require a southern exposure. This collector, on the roof of the building, heats the stor-

Fig. 15-7 *Use of Overhangs for Thermal Control. The overhangs shade the glazed areas in summer to keep down thermal build-up, yet permit solar radiation to enter in winter.*

Fig. 15-8 *Indirect Solar-Gain Building*

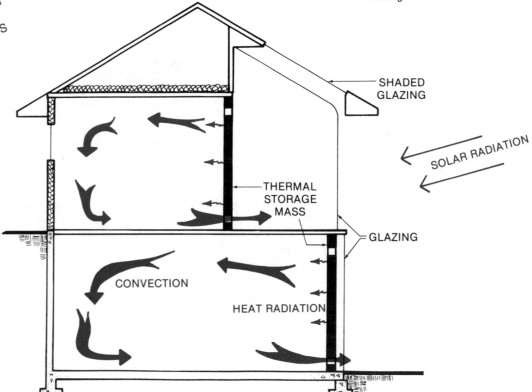

SHADED GLAZING

SOLAR RADIATION

THERMAL STORAGE MASS

GLAZING

CONVECTION

HEAT RADIATION

tion. In a passive solar system, the wall is an integral part of the activity area. In an active system, the heat is mechanically transferred from the Trombe wall to the desired activity area. A number of techniques are used to control and distribute the heat. See Fig. 15-10.

Liquid-Storage System The second type of indirect solar-gain system is the liquid-storage system. There are two requirements: a large glazed collector and a wall to hold water or some other liquid that stores the heat. See Fig. 15-11. The storage has the same function as the Trombe wall, the difference being the medium used to store heat.

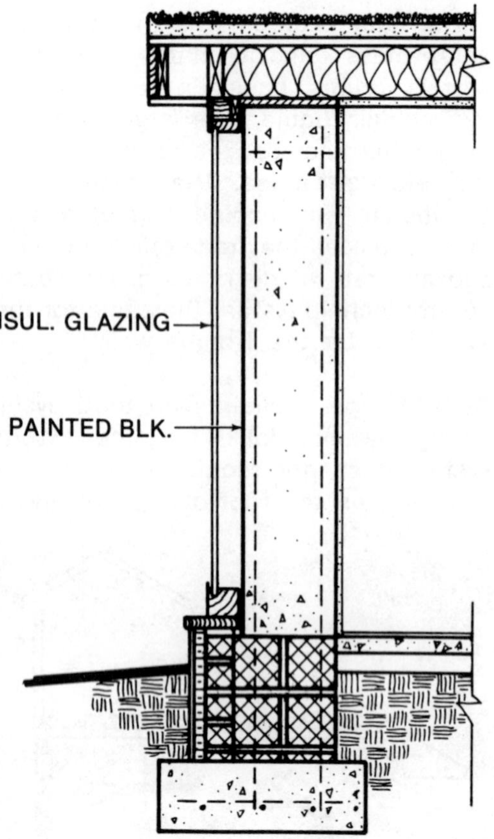

Fig. 15-9 *Trombe Wall System*

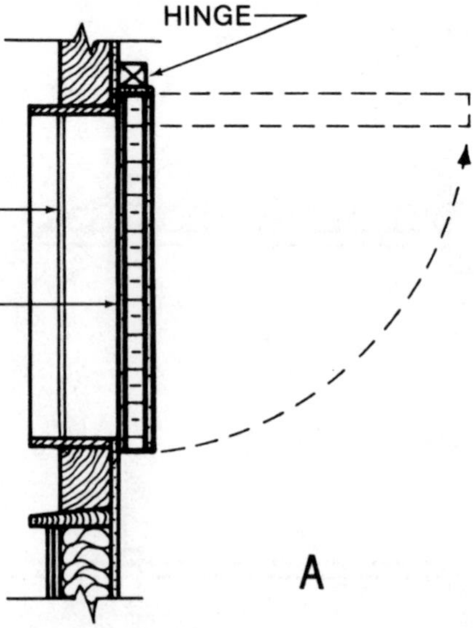

HINGE

DBL. GLAZING

HINGE PANEL W/
RIGID INSUL.

DBL. INSUL. GLAZING

18″ CONC. T.S.U. PAINTED BLK.

A

Fig. 15-10A *Casement Window
with Shutter System*

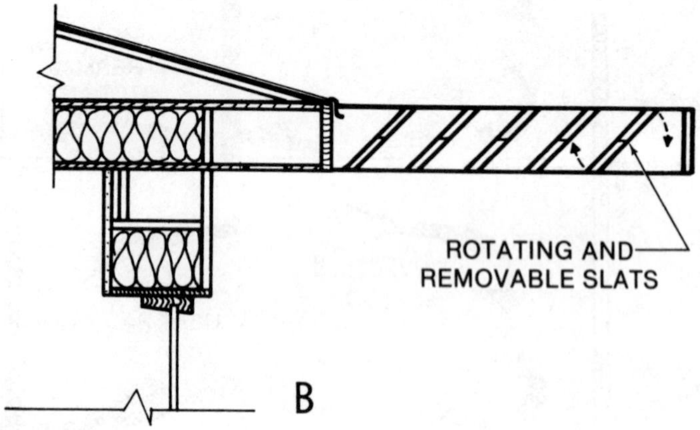

Fig. 15-10B *Dismountable and
Movable Louver System*

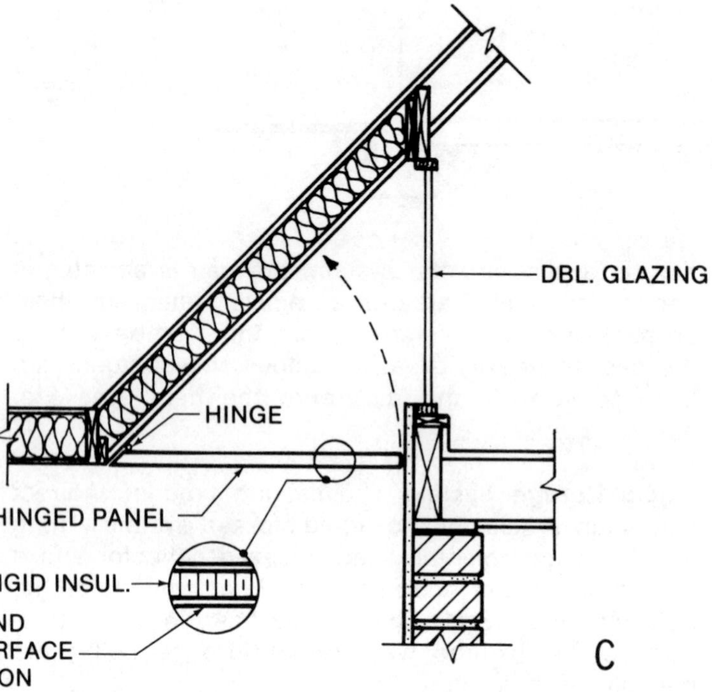

ROTATING AND
REMOVABLE SLATS

DBL. GLAZING

HINGE

B

HINGED PANEL

RIGID INSUL.

EXPOSED AND
REFLECTIVE SURFACE
OF INSULATION

C

Fig. 15-10C *Clerestory Window
with Shutter System*

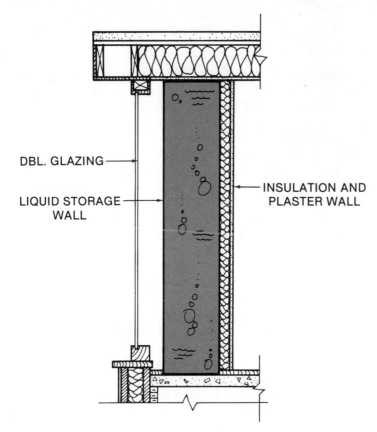

DBL. GLAZING

LIQUID STORAGE WALL

INSULATION AND PLASTER WALL

ISOLATED SOLAR GAIN

The isolated solar-gain technique is similar in some ways to direct and indirect techniques, but differs from them in one basic consideration. It incorporates an appendage of the main building. See Fig. 15-13. That is, an addition or separate built-on area collects and stores solar heat. Once stored, the heat can be distributed to the main part of the building by conventional methods, such as windows, doors, and vents.

Isolated solar-gain methods are used in *solarium* and *thermosiphon* designs. Like the other designs and systems discussed here, solaria and thermosiphons can be used alone or with one another, as well as with other systems.

Fig. 15-11 *Wall Liquid-Storage System*

Fig. 15-12 *Two Types of Roof Liquid-Storage Systems*

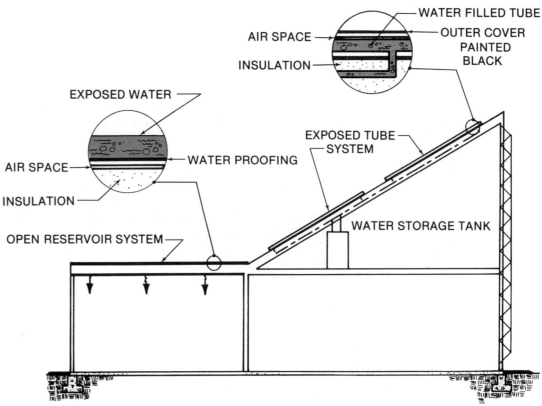

WATER FILLED TUBE

AIR SPACE

OUTER COVER PAINTED BLACK

INSULATION

EXPOSED WATER

EXPOSED TUBE SYSTEM

AIR SPACE

WATER PROOFING

INSULATION

WATER STORAGE TANK

OPEN RESERVOIR SYSTEM

age mass, usually water. See Fig. 15-12. The water may be in tubes, bins, and barrels, or even an open reservoir. This may be part of a passive system, with the heat transferred directly through the roof and ceiling into the activity area. It can also be part of an active system, with the heat distributed through pipes or other mechanical devices.

The amount of heat stored by the system can be controlled by a variety of methods. The most common are by shading and by movable insulation panels. At the end of a sunny winter day, the insulation covers the storage mass, so that as little heat as possible is lost. During the summer, the collectors are exposed to cool air at night and insulated from the sun in the daytime.

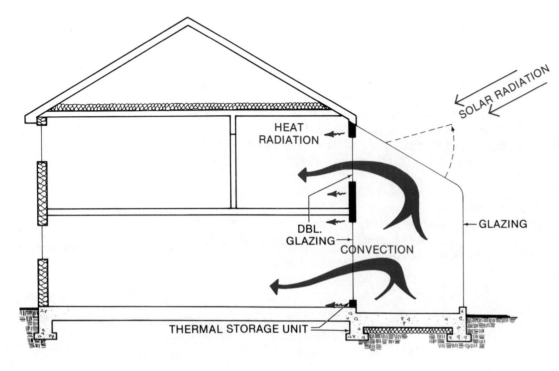

HEAT
RADIATION

SOLAR RADIATION

GLAZING

DBL.
GLAZING
CONVECTION

THERMAL STORAGE UNIT

Fig. 15-13 *Isolated Solar-Gain Building*

Solaria A solarium (plural *solaria*) is a room or area separate from the main activity areas of a building. It collects solar energy and stores it for later distribution. Solaria are common in the form of atria, sun porches, greenhouses, and sunrooms. The major advantage of a solarium is that it isolates both the collectors and the thermal-storage mass from the major activity areas. This makes it possible to store heat above minimum requirements for later distribution, without raising the daytime temperature of the building beyond the level of comfort.

Though solaria are not part of the main activity areas, they are integral parts of the total building. Solaria are usually constructed on the south side for efficient use of the sun's rays. An important part of all solaria is the type of construction that joins them and thereby transfers energy to the main building. The wall between the solarium and the rest of the building

is perhaps the most critical feature. Fig. 15-14 presents some ways to connect solaria to the main activity areas.

Thermosiphons The second type of isolated solar-gain design is the thermosiphon. As the name implies, it siphons warm and cool air. Because fluids, such as air and water, are denser when cold than when warm, heat can be transferred by the natural rise of warm and fall of cool air or some other fluid. When the thermosiphon is properly designed, the rising and falling currents keep the air circulating through the building.

A thermosiphon includes a collector and a thermal-storage mass that is an appendage of the main structure. The most common thermosiphon design has the collector and thermal-storage mass below the activity area. See Fig. 15-15 for several types of thermosiphon.

The collector is usually covered with a dark surface that absorbs solar radiation and heats the air or liquid. The heated medium rises, and the cooler medium falls into the collector area. Thermal-storage masses can be below the windows, under the floor, or within sections of the wall. Most designs do not use any mechanical devices to provide circulation; that is, they are suited for passive-gain systems. However, it is possible to supply larger areas with mechanical circulation devices.

ASSESSING SOLAR-GAIN SYSTEMS

To select the most efficient and appropriate solar-gain system, the U.S. Department of Housing and Urban Development, in cooperation with the U.S. Department of Energy, has developed a sample checklist for assessing the cost of both direct and indirect solar-gain systems. In each checklist in Tables 15-1 and 15-2, there are two primary considerations. These are the *minimum cost* and *maximum effectiveness* of the system. Components, functions, and recommended specifications are listed for each of the two considerations.

Table 15-1 Direct-Gain Solar-System Checklist[1]

Objective	Function	Requirements	Recommended Specifications
Minimum Cost	Collection Roof Wall	Single glazing Fixed windows	0.125″ glass; 0.040″ fiberglass; 0.040″ plastic
	Storage Roof Wall Floor	Water roof ponds Mass wall Mass floor	60 BTU/sq. ft. collector area min. 12″ concrete; 10″ brick; 8″ adobe; 6″ water 6″ concrete; 4″ brick
	Distribution Radiant		
	Controls for Heat Gain	Vegetation	Deciduous trees planted for summer shading

Maximum Value	Collection
	Roof
	
	Wall
		Double glazing
		Operable windows
		
		Diffusion devices
		Conduction devices
		Exterior reflectors
			0.250″ glass; 0.050″ fiberglass; 0.050″ plastic
			Diffusion fabric screens; vertical glazing slats;
			  reflective venetian blinds; special irregular glass
			  over plastic;
			Dark venetian blinds
			Reflective surface on insulation panel; light-colored
			  gravel or patio surface; snow

	Storage Roof Wall Floor Freestanding	Water roof pond Mass wall Mass floor Additional remote storage	 18″ concrete; 14″ brick; 12″ adobe; 12″ water 8″ concrete; 6″ brick 55-gallon water drums; 8″ CMU
	Distribution Radiant Convective	 Fan to storage Exterior vents	 Roof exhaust (hot); floor supply (cool)
	Controls Heat loss Heat gain	 Movable exterior insulation Movable interior insulation Vegetation Roof eave Shading devices	 Solid hinged/sliding panels; blown-in Beadwall® Roll-down curtains; bifold/sliding doors Deciduous trees planted for summer shading Project designed for summer shading Fixed/operable louvers

[1] *Source: U.S. Department of Energy*

INSULATION

The Department of Energy estimates that over 75-million residential and commercial buildings are improperly insulated against climatic conditions. Proper insulation practices are essential to an effective alternate energy design.

The importance of proper insulation cannot be overemphasized. Proper insulation—and reinsulation—can reduce utility costs by twenty to thirty per-

Table 15-2 Indirect-Gain Solar-System Checklist[2]

Objective	Function	Requirements	Recommended Specification
Minimum Cost	Collection Wall	Single glazing	0.125'' glass; 0.040'' fiberglass; 0.040'' plastic
	Storage Wall	Mass wall	12'' concrete; 10'' brick; 8'' adobe; 6'' water
	Distribution Radiant		
	Controls Heat gain	Roof eave Vegetation	Project designed for summer shading Deciduous trees planted for summer shading

Maximum Value	Collection
	Wall
		Double glazing
		
		Exterior reflectors
			0.025'' (2 at 0.125'') glass; 0.050'' (2 at 0.025'')
			   fiberglass; 0.050'' (2 at 0.025'') plastic
			Reflective surface on insulation panel;
			   light-colored gravel or patio surface

	Storage Wall Floor	Mass wall Additional remote storage	18'' concrete; 14'' brick; 12'' adobe; 12'' water
	Distribution Radiant Convective	Interior vents Exterior vents Fan to interior or exterior	Ceiling supply (warm); floor return (cool) Roof exhaust (hot)
Maximum Value	Controls Heat loss Heat gain	Backdraft dampers Operable vents Movable exterior insulation Movable interior insulation Roof eave Shading devices Vegetation	0.006'' polyethylene Hinged panels Solid hinged/sliding panels; blown-in Beadwall™ Roll-down curtains; bifold/sliding doors Projection designed for summer shading Operable/fixed louvers Deciduous trees planted for summer shading
	Natural light	Windows in mass wall	

[2]Source: U.S. Department of Energy

cent for most buildings; the reduction can reach eighty percent for others. Effective insulation can also reduce the need for costly sophisticated HVAC systems. In only a very few cases, however, have proper design and adequate insulation eliminated the need for furnaces and air-conditioning systems altogether.

INSULATION RATINGS

The efficiency of various insulation materials is rated in *R-values*. The *R* in this rating stands for the material's *resistance* to winter heat loss and summer heat gain. The higher the R-value, the higher the insulation effectiveness. Specific information on the

R-values of various materials is provided by the American Society of Heating, Refrigeration, and Air-conditioning Engineers (ASHRAE).

To determine the effectiveness of various combinations of materials, such as insulation and exterior wall facing, a rating system based upon *U-factors* is calculated. The U-factor is the number of BTUs that will flow through one square foot of the building from one area to another in one hour's time as a result of a temperature difference of one degree Fahrenheit. U-factors are calculated with the formula $U = 1/R$. The higher the U-factor, the less effective the insulation is; the more effective the insulation, the lower the U-factor. Additional information on U-factors can be obtained from ASHRAE. An excellent report on the U-factors for common construction and insulation materials is the *Forest Laboratory Report R1740*.

DETERMINING APPROPRIATE INSULATION

Before specifying insulation materials, determine the most appropriate R-value for the geographic location. Fig. 15-16 is a heating-zone map, with recommended R-values for each zone. The R-values are specified for attic floors and for ceilings over unheated crawl spaces and basements. For further reference, Table 15-3 gives R-values for different amounts and thicknesses of batt, blanket, loose-fill, and plastic insulation.

INSULATION MATERIALS

Many insulation materials are available. The most common are plastic foams, mineral and organic fibers, and glass fibers. These are available in a variety of forms, such as blankets and batts, sheets, loose fill, foam, and reflective-foil packaging. Blankets and batts can be rolled out for installation, they are used primarily for insulation between framing members. Sheet insulation is rigid and comes in 4′ × 8′ sheets that can be cut to the size needed. It is used for roof decks and for floor and foundation perimeters. Loose-fill insulation is commonly used between ceil-

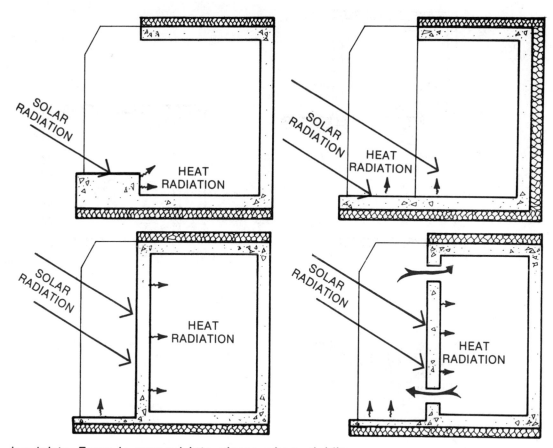

ing joists. Foam is sprayed into places where rigidity is advantageous. Insulation backed with reflective foils is usually placed in cavities of the building, with the reflective surface facing air spaces.

Each type insulates in different ways. Fibrous materials, such as that in blankets, batts, reflective foils, and some loose fill, provide a film of air around each individual fiber, reducing the transmission of heat. Foam materials, such as sheet and sprayed insulation, have small air pockets (cells or bubbles) trapped in the plastic.

An alternative insulation material is earth. There are over three thousand underground homes in the United States. Commercial and industrial projects are also being built underground. Among these are the

Fig. 15-14 *Four Techniques Used to Connect Solaria to Main Activity Areas. Additional insulation may be used to retain heat or to prevent heat build-up.*

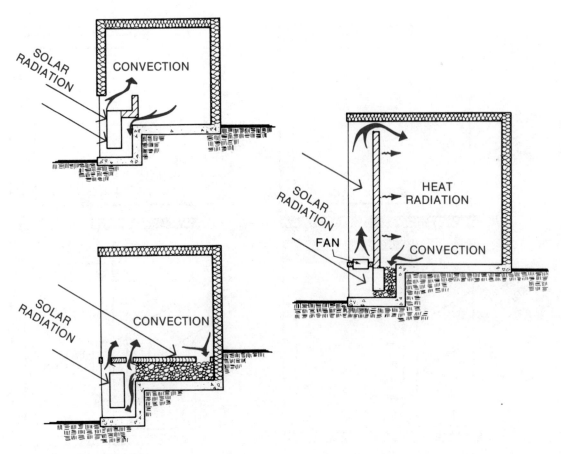

Safe City project in the Upper Hudson Valley region and the industrial-park complex beneath Kansas City, Missouri.

When used properly, earth, dirt, soil, the ground, or whatever we wish to call it provides an excellent insulation material. With surface temperatures of from 0° to 95°F, at a depth of approximately ten feet, temperatures vary only from 50° to 65°F. Note that this is a below-ground range of 15° compared to a surface range of 95°. Obviously, underground architecture has great potential for energy conservation. At the Under-

Fig. 15-15 *Three Types of Thermosiphons. Note how air is circulated: cool air falls, is reheated, and rises into activity area.*

Table 15-3A Recommended R-Values

Heating Zone	Attic Floors	Exterior Walls	Ceiling over Unheated Crawl Space or Basement
1	R-26	R-value of 3½''-thick	R-11
2	R-26	full wall insulation	R-13
3	R-30	depends on material	R-19
4	R-33	used:	R-22
5	R-38	R-11 to R-13	R-22

Table 15-3B R-Values for Urethane and Polystyrene Foam and Board

R-Values	Urethane	Polystyrene
R-5		1'' board
R-7.5		1½'' board
R-9.3	1½'' board	
R-25	4'' injected foam	

Table 15-3C R-Values for Batts and Loose Fill

R-Values	Batts or Blankets (Thickness)		Loose Fill (Depth)		
	Glass Fiber	Rock Wool	Glass Fiber	Rock Wool	Cellulose Fiber
R-11	3½''–4''	3''	5''	4''	3''
R-13	4''	4½''	6''	4½''	3½''
R-19	6''–6½''	5¼''	8''–9''	6''–7''	5''
R-22	6½''	6''	10''	7''–8''	6''
R-26	8''	8½''	12''	9''	7''–7½''
R-30	9½''–10½''	9''	13''–14''	10''–11''	8''
R-33	11''	10''	15''	11''–12''	9''
R-38	12''–13''	10½''	17''–18''	13''–14''	10''–11''

Fig. 15-16 *Heating Zones*

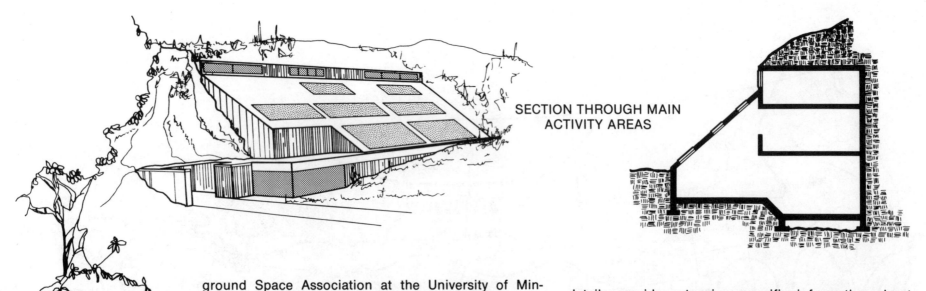

SECTION THROUGH MAIN
ACTIVITY AREAS

Fig. 15-17 *Example of Underground Architecture. The earth around the major sides of the building provides insulation.*

ground Space Association at the University of Minnesota, a number of underground buildings have been designed; an energy saving of 75% over conventional buildings is typical. Not only does the earth insulate well, underground architecture also reduces external vibration, provides privacy, uses "living" land for roofing material, saves water waste, and makes it possible to put buildings closer together without the feeling of crowding. See Fig. 15-17.

Alternate-energy architecture uses traditional materials and construction procedures. The difference is in the specific applications of these materials and in variations on common construction procedures. The insulation, shading, wall construction, window placement, and all other building components are integrated, with the major goal being energy conservation and efficiency. Similarly, architectural drawings for buildings with alternate-energy considerations employ the same practices as do those for traditional buildings, but the details and specifications are different in emphasis.

INSULATION DETAILS

The first type of thermal detail in alternate-energy working drawings is the insulation detail. Insulation

details provide extensive, specific information about the placement and type of insulation in the building. Figs. 15-18 and 15-19 illustrate insulation details for foundation and basement walls and for structural walls and ceilings.

In preparing insulation details, consider the type of insulating material and the techniques to be used for each aspect of the building. The first consideration is the insulation of the foundation and basement walls. It is common practice to use foam-plastic insulation on the exterior of the walls that take the load of the soil around the building. During the winter months, the temperature increases with depth, so more insulation is used near the top of the foundation and basement walls. As shown in Fig. 15-18, both loose and rigid insulation are used on interior surfaces.

Detail drawings explain the increased efficiency of wall insulation that can be obtained by specifying a higher R-value than the minimum required. Detail drawings also show other common practices that increase the efficiency of the insulation. Among these are filling all openings and cavities with foam insulation, adding foam or sheathing insulation to exterior walls, and increasing the width of the insulated cavity. The last technique usually requires the use of 2' × 8' instead of 2′ × 4′ exterior wall studding. See Fig. 15-19.

TROMBE WALL SECTIONS

The second type of thermal detail is the Trombe wall section. As mentioned, Trombe walls are massive walls, usually constructed with 12″ to 16″ block. When concrete blocks are used, they are preferably of heavy aggregate and filled with mortar, concrete grout, or pea gravel.

As Fig. 15-20 illustrates, vents are normally built into the Trombe wall, near the floor and ceiling. This permits heat convection into the activity area during the daylight hours, when the wall is storing heat. Trombe walls are often glazed on the exposed side with a double layer of glass or plastic, which decreases heat loss during the winter. Ventilation to avoid excessive heat build-up is important during the summer.

SHADING DETAILS

Shading details are the last type of special detail commonly found. These provide information about the devices that control the amount of solar energy entering the building. Shades are typically classified into two major categories: *fixed* and *movable*. See Fig. 15-21.

Fixed shades are commonly part of the structure itself. Examples are overhangs, decks, balconies, exterior stairs, floor cantilevers, and wall extensions. For shading purposes, the amount of overhang is determined by the angle of the sun in the sky during the summer. Though fixed shades are cost-effective and easily adopted to most buildings, they cannot adjust to the sun's movement.

Movable shades are generally the most efficient type of shading for adjusting to the position of the sun and to changes in the weather. Movable shades are frequently equipped with reflective panels, insulation, or both to increase energy efficiency. Common

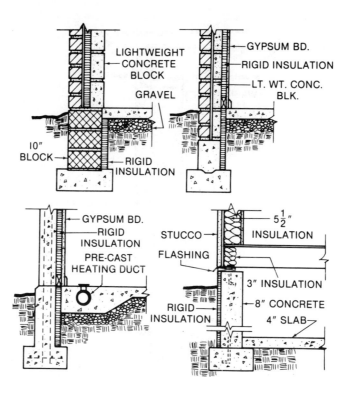

Fig. 15-18 *Use of Insulation in Various Foundation/Basement Wall Details*

Fig. 15-19 *Use of Insulation in Wall Details*

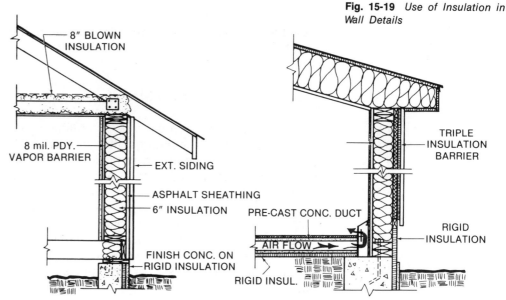

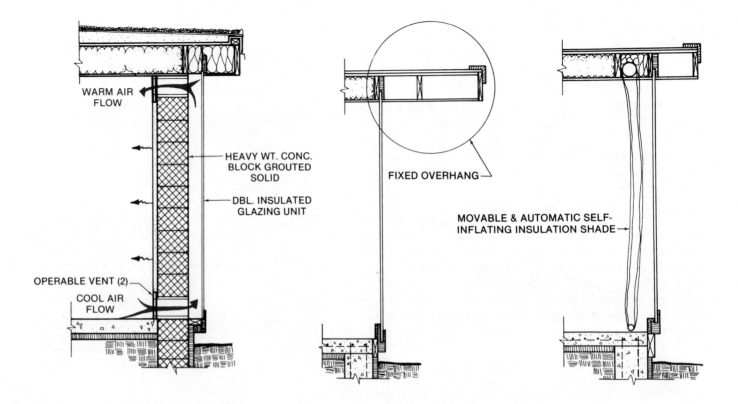

Fig. 15-20 *Vents Built into Trombe Wall*

WARM AIR FLOW

HEAVY WT. CONC. BLOCK GROUTED SOLID

DBL. INSULATED GLAZING UNIT

FIXED OVERHANG

MOVABLE & AUTOMATIC SELF-INFLATING INSULATION SHADE

OPERABLE VENT (2)

COOL AIR FLOW

Fig. 15-21 *Two Major Types of Shades*

movable shades are shutters, demountable louvers, and hinged panels.

SUMMARY

Architectural firms must meet problems of designing energy-efficient buildings that use alternate energy sources. Because drafters must prepare drawings that deviate from traditional construction methods, they must be familiar with the basic principles and techniques of alternate-energy design.

All solar-energy systems are either passive or active. Passive systems utilize conduction, convection, and radiation. Active systems employ mechanical devices for circulation, such as heat exchanges, pumps, and fans.

Three methods are used to collect and store energy. Direct solar gain allows sunlight to enter the building through windows, to heat floors, walls, and furniture. Indirect solar gain stores energy in a mass separate from the activity area. Isolated solar gain stores energy in a mass separate from the rest of the building.

Perhaps most important in efficient-energy design is insulation. Proper insulation can reduce energy loss and heating and cooling costs. Insulation is rated by R-value and by U-factor when used in combination with other building materials. It is available in different forms and materials, which are used for specialized purposes.

The drafter must be able to prepare common alternate-energy thermal details. These include insulation, Trombe wall sections, and shading details.

REVIEW QUESTIONS

1. Explain why the sun can be considered the most important alternate source of energy.
2. What is the difference between passive and active solar-energy systems?
3. Explain the meaning of the term *solar gain.*
4. What are the system requirements and controls for the following?

   a. Direct solar gain
   b. Indirect solar gain
   c. Isolated solar gain

5. Explain how a Trombe mass can be utilized effectively in existing and new commercial buildings.
6. What is the difference between solaria and thermosiphons?
7. What is meant by *R-values*? *U-factors*?
8. What are the minimum desirable insulation requirements for your geographic area?
9. Describe the different forms insulation comes in and the materials each form is made of. Where would each be appropriate? Inappropriate? Explain why.
10. Briefly describe the use and purpose of the following drawings:

    a. Insulation details
    b. Trombe wall sections
    c. Shading details

EXERCISES

1. Adapt an existing set of architectural plans, making the structure as energy-efficient as possible.
2. Using the same plans, change the requirements to include either a passive or an active solar energy system.
3. Work up a set of plans for a commercial building with the following systems as options:

   a. Mass Trombe
   b. Solarium
   c. Thermosiphon

4. Develop a set of drawings for an existing residential building with the following systems as options:

   a. Liquid storage
   b. Roof storage
   c. Mass Trombe

CHAPTER

ARCHITECTURAL DRAFTING STRUCTURE AND ENVIRONMENT

16 GRAPHIC PROCEDURES AND REPRODUCTION SYSTEMS

Cost is one of the most important aspects of any architectural project. Costs in architectural drafting are mainly board time and reproduction expenses. Therefore, architectural firms try to keep board time and reproduction expenses at a minimum, without sacrificing quality.

Part of the cost of paying experienced drafters more for their work than novices are paid is made up by the speed and quality that come from experience, practice, and confidence. Good drafters, even though they are more expensive per hour, save the firm money by accomplishing a given task in less time. Also, architectural drafters use a number of graphic procedures that reduce board time without sacrificing quality. In some cases, these techniques even add to the quality of the drawing.

A wide variety of systems can be used in reproducing architectural drawings. Unlike board time, reproduction costs must take into account one additional factor: the impact of presentation. This is both the impression and the information communicated to the users. Reproductions for contractors and tradespeople are very different from those for financial backers or buyers. The least expensive method is not always the best.

GRAPHIC PROCEDURES

A number of techniques can considerably reduce the amount of time spent reproducing drawings. Two

GLOSSARY

Intermediate prints (also called Van Dykes) prints that can be used to produce other prints

Overlay drafting the use of drawings that can be placed upon each other (overlaid) to produce a composite drawing

Scissors drafting cutting out standardized drawings and adhering them to a new drawing, eliminating the need to do the same illustrations and details many times over

other recently developed techniques are *overlay drafting* and *scissors drafting.*

In this book, *traditional* drafting techniques are those shortcuts, such as notations and abbreviations, that help architectural drafters eliminate repetitive, unnecessary drawings. Fig. 16-1 presents some of these. Overlay and scissors drafting can reduce the cost of drawing preparation even more significantly.

OVERLAY DRAFTING

Overlay drafting has proved to be an effective time-saver. It can make redrawing architectural floor plans unnecessary when preparing layouts for electrical, plumbing, and HVAC systems. By eliminating the need to draw floor plans, you have more time and energy to spend on more productive activities.

The procedure is simple, involving either expensive photographic equipment or existing reproduction and print equipment. Overlay drafting follows these steps:

1. Draw the architectural floor plan.
2. For each drawing to be reproduced that uses the floor-plan layout, get a sheet of tracing paper, polyester film, or clear acetate.
3. Register (align) these sheets over the floor plans, one by one. Either punch reference holes or draw reference marks to align the drawings for reproduction.
4. For each system, place the registered sheet over the floor plan and draw the appropriate system plan. See Fig. 16-2.
5. Reproduce each complete drawing, using the base plan and overlay.

Polyester film can be used if there are not more than six overlays for the drawing. Clear acetate can be used for four or more overlays. Photographs may be made from the overlays of intermediate prints (frequently called *sepias* or *Van Dykes*) produced for the production of standard prints.

Overlay drafting has a number of advantages. The most obvious is that the drafter prepares only one floor-plan layout. Also, any changes or revisions in building systems or the floor plan can be made on

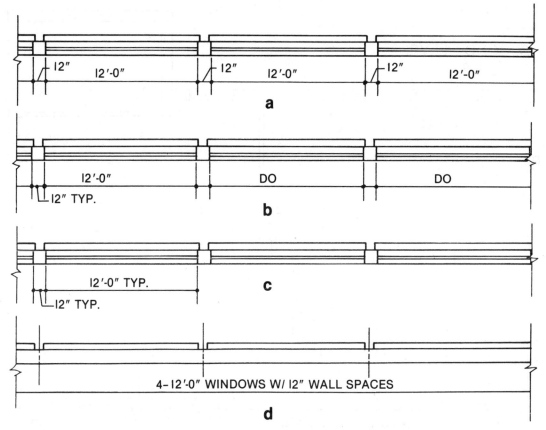

a

b

c

4–12'-0" WINDOWS W/ 12" WALL SPACES

d

the base plan or the appropriate overlay without redrawing the entire set of plans. Next, images from several separate sheets, including details, can be combined in one reproduced drawing. Finally, a relatively large number of overlays can be exposed at one time.

SCISSORS DRAFTING

In scissors drafting, drawings or details, sections, and other parts of drawings are cut out and pasted to a base or overlay drawing. This procedure is commonly used where typical details, sections, specifications, or schedules are prepared as part of the working drawing. The procedure not only cuts down on board time, it also can result in a higher quality drawing.

Fig. 16-1 *Shortcuts Used in Dimensioning. A. Dimensioning Without Shortcuts. B. Use of Notation.* TYP *means that this space is typical, i.e., all undimensioned spaces are 12";* DO *means a repetition of the 12'-0" dimension. C. Use of Notation.* TYP *is used to show that the undimensioned windows and spaces are 12'-0" and 12" respectively. D. Use of Notation and Semischematic. Providing specifications for the windows eliminates the need to draw in window and space details. Centerlines may be drawn to locate the centers of the individual windows.*

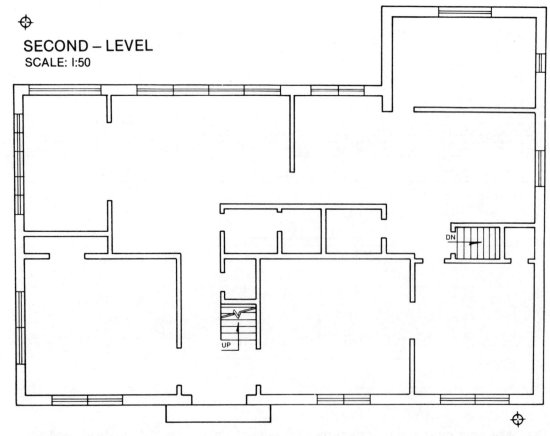

SECOND – LEVEL
SCALE: 1:50

DN

UP

Fig. 16-2A *Base Drawing Used in the Overlay Process*

The intermediate-print method involves cutting out the detailed drawing, specification, or schedule, and posting it to the master drawing. Intermediate prints are usually used if the plans have not been finalized or approved by the team leader. Drafters frequently find it more efficient to type notations, specifications, and schedules, then paste them to the master plan or intermediate. Obviously, typing extensive notations, specifications, and schedules cuts down on board time by eliminating detailed lettering.

Among the advantages of scissors drafting are

1. It eliminates the need for drawing and redrawing standard details and sections.
2. Several different details and sections can be combined on one master drawing.
3. Drawings with extensive notations, complex specifications, and detailed schedules can be photographically reduced.

REPRODUCTION SYSTEMS

Most people know one form of reproduction for architectural drawings: the blueprint. Actually, the blueprint, which has white lines on a deep blue background, is seldom used today. It was the first acceptable method of reproduction, but it has since been replaced by systems that give better quality and clearer reproductions, are dimensionally more stable, and are more cost-efficient. Though many reproduction techniques are used, most fall into one of four categories: *intermediate-print, ammonia-sensitized-print, Xerographic,* and *photographic* systems. See Table 16-1.

Before reviewing the various reproduction systems, it should be emphasized that the quality of the reproduction mainly depends on the quality of the master drawing prepared by the drafter. No matter how sophisticated a reproduction system is, *the reproduction can be no better than the drawing.*

Scissors drafting is quite simple. First, the master drawing is prepared to the final scale or a larger scale. It is then reproduced either by the photographic-offset or the intermediate-print method. With the photographic-offset method, the master drawing can be drawn to a larger scale and then photographically reduced to the final size. This eliminates or at least reduces minor drawing inconsistencies and improves quality. Offset prints are usually printed on polyester film, clear acetate, or tracing paper. With intermediate prints, the master drawing is prepared to the final scale, because there is no way to reduce the drawing.

INTERMEDIATE PRINTS

As already mentioned, intermediate prints are commonly referred to as sepias or Van Dyke prints. These serve either as masters for overlays or as second masters for other drawings. The major differences between the intermediate and the other print systems are *copy medium* and *line color.* The medium the intermediate print is made on is translucent paper, so that other copies can be reproduced from it; the lines on such a print are brown.

Intermediate prints are high-quality prints, with good dimensional stability over a long time. At first, intermediate prints may seem to be a waste of time and money; however, they serve a valuable function in many situations. Prints that are frequently used at the job site either will fade from continual exposure to the sun or will deteriorate from constant handling, and so additional prints are required. When modifications in the plans are necessary, it is simpler to make them on the intermediate print than to redo a complete set of overlays. Finally, intermediates save wear and tear on original drawings, which are better kept as permanent records of the project.

AMMONIA-SENSITIZED PRINTS

The most commonly used reproduction system is ammonia-sensitized prints, also referred to as the ozalid or diazode system. This process produces prints that are the opposite of blueprints—blue or black lines on a white background. Because these prints are easy to make and cost relatively little, most architectural firms have their own ammonia-print equipment. For very large jobs, however, many firms send out their drawings to other firms that specialize in reproducing drawings.

The process of producing an ammonia-sensitized print begins with placing the master or intermediate drawing on top of the sensitized paper. The two sheets are then sent together through a machine that exposes the drawing to ultraviolet light. Where there are no lines or markings on the translucent paper, the

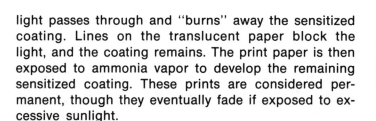

FLR. PLN

Fig. 16-2B *First Overlay Drawing. This identifies various rooms, doors, and cabinets. Note the use of the alignment keys in two corners.*

light passes through and "burns" away the sensitized coating. Lines on the translucent paper block the light, and the coating remains. The print paper is then exposed to ammonia vapor to develop the remaining sensitized coating. These prints are considered permanent, though they eventually fade if exposed to excessive sunlight.

XEROGRAPHIC SYSTEMS

Over the last few years, there have been many advancements in Xerography. Xerography is a form of photocopying that uses the principles of electrostatics and heat processing to produce images on paper, by either a dry powder or a liquid ink. In either case, copies can be produced as rapidly as one per second.

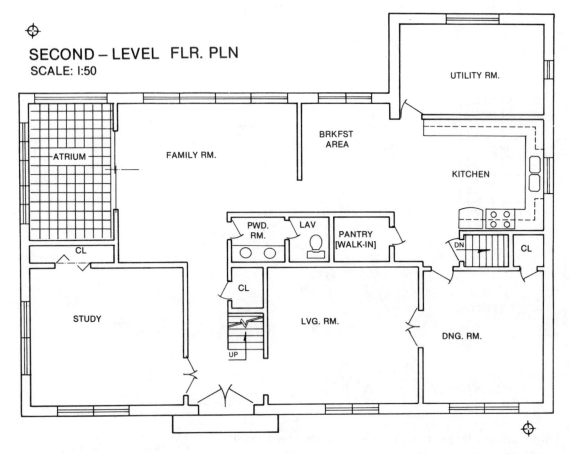

SECOND – LEVEL FLR. PLN
SCALE: 1:50

ATRIUM

FAMILY RM.

BRKFST
AREA

UTILITY RM.

KITCHEN

CL

STUDY

CL

PWD.
RM.

LAV

PANTRY
[WALK-IN]

CL

CL

LVG. RM.

UP

DN

CL

DNG. RM.

Fig. 16-2C *Completed Overlay Drawing*

The first system could produce only full-sized reproductions on 8½″ × 11″ or 8½″ × 14″ sheets. Today, copiers can produce prints the actual size of the master drawing. Some machines can reduce drawings and reproduce full-color prints and halftone pictures on papers and films. Because the changes in Xerographic technology have been so rapid, few architectural firms have realized the full potential of this form of reproduction. It is expected that within the next few years many more firms will include this system among their reproduction techniques.

PHOTOGRAPHIC SYSTEMS

Photographic processes have long been used to reproduce architectural drawings. Traditionally used for legal documentation, where precise duplication is also necessary, photographic techniques are well adapted for use by architectural firms. Frequent applications are storage and reproduction of large quantities of drawings.

The usual method of storing architectural plans was and is to roll them up and place them in storage tubes, to be filed in a vault or storage bin. Obviously, this requires lots of room and storage costs.

Today, drawings can be photographically reduced and stored in smaller file cabinets or even in card files. The process is quite simple. First, the drawing is mounted on the table of a horizontal or vertical camera. Second, the camera reduction is set to the desired reduction percentage (33⅓% for typical cameras; even smaller for microfilm cameras). The picture is taken and the negative developed. Finally, the negative is stored in a file cabinet, on cards, or on reels of film.

An extension of this is offset printing, used to reproduce large quantities of drawings at lower cost. Drawings are usually reduced to fit on an 8½″ × 11″ sheet of paper to be included in a pamphlet or brochure. However, this process is not limited to printing reduced drawings. It may be advantageous to reproduce drawings at full size or very close to full size, so as to include as much detail as needed to show the concepts of the design. It is not uncommon to find offset presses for this purpose that can handle sheets of paper up to 58″ × 77″.

The offset process begins with the negative. The negative is placed on top of a sensitized plate and exposed to an arc light. The plate is then mounted onto the press and readied for printing. In some instances, the negative is not needed. This involves a specially sensitized offset plate mounted on a "camera"; a picture of the drawing is shot directly onto the plate. The plate is then developed and mounted on the press.

Table 16-1 Reproduction Systems

Reproduction System	Copy Image	System Requirements Original Medium	Copy Medium	Remarks
Blueprint	Negative image	Translucent papers will reproduce all colors	Special copy paper	Wet process, via spray or immersion. Dimensionally unstable because of drying; copy becomes brittle after time. Rarely used today.
Ammonia-sensitized process, dry and wet	Positive image	Translucent papers will reproduce all colors	Special copy paper	Dry process develops by ammonia vapors; wet process develops with ammonia-salts solutions. Dry process most frequently used system in the field.
Xerography and electrostatic	Positive image	Translucent and opaque papers will reproduce all colors	Special and ordinary paper	Some units can reproduce multi-color prints on various types and weights of stock
Microfilm	Negative and positive images	Translucent and opaque papers will reproduce all colors	Special photographic film and paper	Typically displayed on screen for viewing. Will also reproduce prints to common size of 18″ × 24″.
Photograph	Negative and positive images	Translucent and opaque papers will reproduce all colors	Special photographic film and paper	Requires master copy or negative to provide photographic prints. Also has halftone and screening capability and can be combined with ammonia process.
Offset	Positive image	Translucent and opaque papers will reproduce all colors	Special photographic film and plate. Reproduction copies can be on almost any medium.	Typically used for high-volume copies. Can reproduce multi-color prints with one plate per color.

SUMMARY

A number of procedures have been used over the years to cut down the amount of board time. The most dramatic techniques, which are relatively new to the field, are overlay and scissors drafting. Overlay drafting consists of using a base drawing with translucent overlays, on which additional architectural features are drawn. In scissors drafting, details or portions of drawings are cut out and mounted onto the master drawing.

Many reproduction systems are available to the architectural drafter. However, the quality of reproduction depends on the quality of the original drawing. Some of the more common categories are intermediate prints, ammonia-sensitized prints, Xerography, and photography.

REVIEW QUESTIONS

1. What is meant by the term *board time*, and how can it raise costs on an architectural project?
2. Explain what overlay drafting is; briefly list the steps involved.
3. What is scissor drafting?
4. Can overlay drafting and scissors drafting be combined? Explain.
5. What factor ultimately determines the quality of a reproduced drawing?
6. Explain each of the following:

   a. blueprint
   b. sepia
   c. ozalide
   d. xerography

7. Explain how photographic processing can cut storage costs.

REFERENCES

There are hundreds of references available to those in architecture and related fields. Most firms have a library of books, periodicals, and catalogs for use by the staff. Architectural drafters will probably want to purchase their own copies of some references.

A number of important references are listed here; not all are required in any single firm's library. This list is intended as a broad review of materials that could be considered for both the firm's collection and the individual's library.

Because of technological change and frequent introduction of new materials and methods, references are revised and updated often. For this reason, the publication dates of the items listed here have been omitted. When ordering a reference, one should always request the most recent edition.

BOOKS

Architectural Graphics Standards, American Institute of Architects. New York: John Wiley and Sons. This is the basic encyclopedic reference for architectural drawing standards. It is used by architects, drafters, engineers, and contractors and is an esseential part of any reference library.

Building Construction Handbook, Fredrick S. Merritt. New York: McGraw-Hill Book Co. This reference gives information about accepted building practices and is especially valuable in explaining detailing drawings and building specifications.

Civil Engineering Handbook. New York: McGraw-Hill Book Co. People involved in structural design should seriously consider this basic reference if material and construction techniques for various types of structures are frequently researched.

Concrete Construction Handbook. New York: McGraw-Hill Book Co. This is an excellent reference for construction techniques and materials for concrete and related products.

Construction Materials: Types, Uses, and Applications. New York: John Wiley and Sons. This basic reference is useful in determining the appropriate type of construction for a particular project and for finding information about construction detailing.

Construction: Principles, Materials, and Methods, Harold B. Olin, et al. Chicago: The Institute of Financial Education and Danville, Illinois: Interstate Printers and Publishers, Inc. This excellent reference reviews the various types of construction techniques and materials, with their application to different situations. It is useful for determining construction techniques and detailing specifications.

Fire Protection Handbook. Boston: National Fire Protection Association. This practical guide for the design of safe buildings helps determine whether all precautions are taken to prevent fire and related hazards.

Foundation Design and Construction, M.J. Tomlinson. New York: Wiley-Interscience (A Division of John Wiley and Sons). This is a necessary reference for those involved with foundation design and drawings.

Handbook of Air Conditioning, Heating, and Ventilation. New York: The Industrial Press. This is a required reference for those who design, specify, and draw HVAC systems.

Handbook of Environmental Control, Volumes I and II.
Cleveland: The Chemical Rubber Co. This is an excellent resource for people designing industrial and commercial complexes; it is especially useful in dealing with gaseous, liquid, and solid wastes.

Handbook of Heavy Construction. New York: McGraw-Hill Book Co. This is a useful reference for anyone in commercial and industrial architecture and structural design.

Handbook of Noise Control. New York: McGraw-Hill Book Co. This is excellent for work in commercial and industrial design where excessive noise is a concern.

Handbook of Refrigeration Engineering, Volumes I and II. These are good sources for firms involved with specialized environmental control systems and commercial or industrial cooling and refrigeration.

Handbook of Structural Design, I.E. Morris. New York: Reinhold Publishing Corp. This reference gives basic information and specifications for the design and construction of structures ranging from buildings to bridges.

Handbook of Wiring, Cabling, and Interconnecting for Electronics. New York: McGraw-Hill Book Co. This is useful for those designing and organizing circuitry for specialized systems and for preparation of some power drawings.

How to Save Energy and Cut Costs in Existing Industrial and Commercial Buildings: An Energy Conservation Manual, Fred S. Dobin et al. Park Ridge, New Jersey: Noyes Data Corp. This is an excellent reference for recycling projects; it shows practical methods and techniques for making buildings more energy efficient.

Insulating Materials for Design and Engineering Practice, Frank M. Clark. New York: John Wiley and Sons. This provides useful information about insulation details and specifications.

Manual of Steel Construction. New York: American Institute of Steel Construction, Inc. This is a basic reference for the various types of steel construction practices in the industry and is recommended for those frequently involved with commercial and industrial buildings and structural drawings.

The National Building Code. New York: American Insurance Association. This is a necessary reference for any architectural firm; it sets down the minimum building standards and requirements.

NFPA Handbook of the National Electrical Code. New York: McGraw-Hill Book Co. Another necessary reference for architectural firms, this covers minimum requirements for electrical specifications as set down by the National Fire Prevention Association.

Piping Handbook, Reno C. King and Sabin Crocker. New York: McGraw-Hill Book Co. This gives basic information about piping procedures and recommended specifications. It is useful for those drawing plumbing and utility system designs.

Properties of Concrete, A.M. Neville. New York: John Wiley and Sons. This is useful in preparing specifications for concrete material use in any structure.

Refrigeration, Air Conditioning, and Cold Storage: Principles and Applications, Raymond C. Gunther. Philadelphia: Chilton Books. This basic reference is excellent for any person or firm involved in HVAC system design and construction.

Sweet's Catalog File: Products for General Building; Sweet's Catalog File: Products for Light Residential Construction; Sweet's Catalog File: Products for Industrial Construction and Renovation. New York: Sweet Division, McGraw-Hill Book Co. These three references are needed by all architectural firms. Each catalog file has information about the types of products on the market and where they can be bought. The catalogs are broken down into product categories by a reference coding system.

Timber Construction Manual, American Institute of Timber Construction. New York: John Wiley and Sons. This is a fine reference for projects using lumber and timber products.

Time Saver Standards for Architectural Design Data. New York: McGraw-Hill Book Co. This is a useful reference for those involved in the design and drawing phase of any architectural project. It is a valuable guide for the cost-effective firm.

PERIODICALS

The following periodicals are primarily concerned with innovative design techniques; they are also quite useful to drafters, who can benefit from seeing the techniques used by leading architectural firms in this and other countries. The articles and illustrations often present new applications for familiar building materials.

AIA Journal
American Institute of Architects
1735 New York Avenue N.W.
Washington DC 20006

Architect and Contractor
721 Santa Clara Avenue
Alameda CA 94501

Architectural Design
718 Holland Street
London W 8
England

Architectural Design, Cost and Data
1041 East Green Street
Pasadena CA

Architectural Record
McGraw-Hill Inc.
1220 Avenue of the Americas
New York NY 10020

Architectural Review
The Architectural Press, Ltd.
9 Queen Anne's Gate
London SW 1 H 9 BY
England

Building and Environment
Pergamon Press, Inc.
Maxwell House
Fairview Park
Elmsford NY 10523

Canadian Architect
Southam Business Pub., Ltd.
1450 Don Mills Road
Don Mills, Ontario
Canada

Guidelines Letters
Box 456
Orinda CA 94563

Home Plans
Davis Publications, Inc.
229 Park Avenue South
New York NY 10003

Plans and Specs
PPG Industries, Inc.
One Gateway Center
Pittsburgh PA 15222

Progressive Architecture
Reinhold Publishing Co., Inc.
600 Summer Street
Stamford CT 06904

Research and Design
AIA Research Corporation
1735 New York Avenue N.W.
Washington DC 20006

Review of Architecture and Landscape Architecture
University of Toronto
School of Architecture
Department of Landscape Architecture
230 College Street
Toronto, Ontario M5T 1R2
Canada

APPENDIX

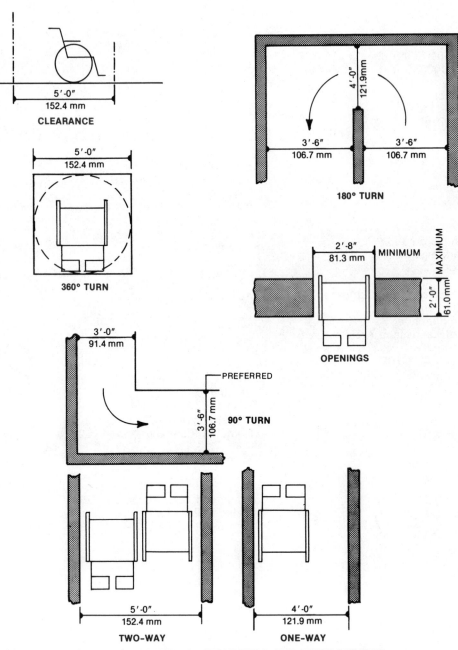

CLEARANCE
5'-0"
152.4 mm

360° TURN
5'-0"
152.4 mm

180° TURN
4'-0"
121.9mm
3'-6"
106.7 mm
3'-6"
106.7 mm

OPENINGS
2'-8"
81.3 mm MINIMUM
MAXIMUM
2'-0"
61.0 mm

90° TURN
3'-0"
91.4 mm
PREFERRED
3'-6"
106.7 mm

TWO-WAY
5'-0"
152.4 mm

ONE-WAY
4'-0"
121.9 mm

BARRIER-FREE ARCHITECTURAL CONSIDERATIONS

In 1968 the Architectural Barriers Act, Public Law 90-480, officially made certain federal facilities accessible to physically handicapped persons. Since then, all states and many local governments have passed laws and ordinances requiring public buildings to meet the standards set forth under P.L. 90-480.

The most widely used specifications available on barrier-free architecture are the *American National Standards Institute Specifications for Making Buildings Accessible to and Usable by the Physically Handicapped* (ANSI A117.1). These have been accepted by the federal government as the *minimum* standards for barrier-free design.

Because the many local, state, and federal codes are both complex and at times contradictory, this text cannot possibly cover them all in any detail. This appendix will deal with some of the *general* considerations involved in barrier-free design. For more in-depth information on the subject, write to:

Access America
United States Architectural and Transportation
 Barrier Compliance Board
Washington DC 20201

Considerations for the Physically Handicapped

Specification	Functions	Specifications
Wheelchair	Turning Radius	
	Fixed, Wheel-to-Wheel	18'' (45.7 cm)
	Fixed, Front to Rear	31.5'' (80.0 cm)
	Turning Space Required	60'' × 60'' (152.4 cm × 152.4 cm)
	Unilateral Vertical Reach	
	(Adult)	54'' to 78'' (137.2 cm to 193.0 cm)
	Horizontal Working Reach	
	(Adult)	28.5'' to 33.2'' (72.4 cm to 78.2 cm)
	Bilateral Horizontal Reach	
	(Adult)	54'' to 71'' (137.2 cm to 180.3 cm)
Crutches, Canes,	Normal Gate	
Braces, or Any	Persons 5'-6'' Tall	31'' (78.7 cm)
Combination	Persons 6'-0'' Tall	32.5'' (82.6 cm)

INDEX